Data Science Projects Using Python

Step-by-step guide for data science beginners with a practical approach

Dr. Pratiyush Guleria

www.bpbonline.com

First Edition 2026

ISBN: 978-93-65894-547

LIMITS OF LIABILITY AND DISCLAIMER OF WARRANTY

Distributors:

BPB PUBLICATIONS
20, Ansari Road, Darya Ganj
New Delhi-110002
Ph: 23254990/23254991

DECCAN AGENCIES
4-3-329, Bank Street,
Hyderabad-500195
Ph: 24756967/24756400

MICRO MEDIA
Shop No. 5, Mahendra Chambers,
150 DN Rd. Next to Capital Cinema,
V.T. (C.S.T.) Station, MUMBAI-400 001
Ph: 22078296/22078297

To View Complete BPB Publications Catalogue Scan the QR Code:

Published by Manish Jain for BPB Publications, 20 Ansari Road, Darya Ganj, New Delhi-110002 and Printed by him at Repro India Ltd., Rewari.

Dedicated to

Almighty God,

my parents,

and

my family

About the Author

Dr. Pratiyush Guleria has a Ph.D. in computer science. He has done M.Tech in computer science with a gold medal from Himachal Pradesh University, Shimla, India. He has a consistent track record in academics throughout his career. He has cleared the **State Level Eligibility Test** (**SLET**) as well. Pratiyush Guleria has more than 17 years of experience in the IT industry and academics. He has research papers published in peer-reviewed international journals and conferences. He has been a technical program committee member and reviewer for journals and international conferences. His research interests include data mining, machine learning, and web technologies.

About the Reviewers

- **Gouri Sankar Dash** is a seasoned technology leader and enterprise practitioner with over two decades of professional experience across enterprise platforms, large-scale system modernization, cloud architecture, data science, database engineering, cybersecurity, and applied AI. His expertise spans cloud assessment and migration, application modernization, enterprise governance, data protection, and AI-driven optimization in regulated and large-scale enterprise environments.

  He has led multi-million-dollar technology portfolios, architected and delivered mission-critical systems, and managed globally distributed engineering teams supporting complex enterprise systems, particularly in healthcare and financial domains. His work includes modernization of EHR platforms, enterprise database ecosystems, security and encryption frameworks, and cloud-native architectures.

  He is a multi-cloud certified professional and has authored and contributed to technical articles published in industry and academic journals. As a technical writer and reviewer, Gouri brings a strong practitioner's perspective, focusing on architectural soundness, scalability, security, and real-world applicability of solutions. He is currently working with Tata Consultancy Services, America, and is part of HealthCare business group.

- **Raja Chattopadhyay** is an accomplished technology leader and technical reviewer with deep expertise in fintech, large-scale distributed systems, cloud engineering, and data security. He brings extensive professional experience in API platforms, high-performance transaction systems, external data orchestration, and enterprise-grade encryption frameworks used by major credit bureaus and identity providers.

  His work spans cloud architecture, event-driven systems, and secure data exchange models that support millions of customers and mission-critical financial operations. Raja actively contributes to the technology community through mentoring, conference speaking, and peer review of research papers.

  He holds multiple industry certifications and has authored several patents in data privacy, encryption, and AI-driven financial data orchestration, demonstrating his commitment to advancing secure and scalable technology solutions.

Acknowledgement

I want to express my deepest gratitude to Almighty God, my family, and my friends for their unwavering support and encouragement throughout this book's writing, especially my family and my parents.

I am also grateful to BPB Publications for their guidance and expertise in bringing this book to fruition. It was a long journey of writing and conceptualizing this book, with the valuable participation and collaboration of reviewers, technical experts, and editors.

I would also like to acknowledge the valuable contributions of my colleagues and co-workers during many years working in academia, who have taught me so much and provided valuable feedback on my work.

Finally, I would like to thank all the readers who have taken an interest in my book and for their support in making it a reality. Your encouragement has been invaluable.

Preface

The author is optimistic that students who want to complete a thorough task will find relief in the current work. This book provides a range of real-world examples, conceptual challenges, and methodically worked-out solutions to help readers understand programming ideas through clear explanations and examples. Additionally, it covers every topic that is necessary for students to gain a thorough understanding of the fundamentals of Python. This book looks to be a great resource for anyone with programming knowledge, as well as a great place for newbies to start.

The abilities needed to understand the fundamentals of data science using Python at a beginner's level are taken into account when writing this book. The book presents real-world Python examples following a simple, illustrative approach that makes it easy for students to learn and comprehend. Each chapter of the book will introduce the candidate to programming principles, along with the fundamental basics, and will feature illustrative examples of Python, including coverage of data science topics such as NumPy, Pandas data structures, data preprocessing, and visualization using Matplotlib, and so on.

Although the book is written with honesty and sincerity, it is the author's hope that its flaws will be overlooked. Having said that, the author is receptive to any form of helpful critiques and recommendations for additional development. All insightful recommendations are welcome, and the author will do their utmost to include them in worthwhile additions to this work in future versions.

Chapter 1: Introduction to Data Science and Python - This chapter explores the field of data science and highlights why Python is a highly popular language for data science. In addition to that, learners will also learn about the various Python libraries and the distinct features of Python. The other subjects covered in this chapter include identifiers, reserved words, and indentation, etc. The fundamental concepts of variables, including their data types, type conversions, and various types of operators, are all covered with comprehensive examples.

Chapter 2: Conditions, Loops, Control Statements, and Functions - This chapter presents a program's flow that can be controlled and decisions made based on certain conditions using conditional and control statements. The statements like as if and if-elif-else enable the program to run a block of code only in the event that a certain condition is true or to check several conditions sequentially. The control statements modify the loop's or conditional structure's typical execution flow. Apart from it, functions are covered in this chapter. Functions are blocks of reusable code that perform specific tasks. Packages and modules are used in Python to organize and structure code for improved reuse and maintainability.

Chapter 3: Lists, Tuples, and Dictionary - This chapter covers the differences between lists, tuples, and dictionaries, which are fundamental data structures in Python. Learners will explore predefined methods associated with lists and how they can be used to manipulate data effectively. This chapter will help learners understand the relationship between lists and tuples, highlighting their similarities and key differences. They will also learn about various dictionary methods used for storing and accessing key-value pairs efficiently. The chapter also introduces iterators and generators, enabling learners to work with sequences of data efficiently and in a memory-friendly way. Additionally, learners will learn about sets, which store unique elements and support useful set operations.

Chapter 4: Exception Handling and File Handling - This chapter covers the subjects of file handling and exception handling. Python's exception handling mechanism lets programmers deal with errors or exceptions in an easy manner while the program is running. In addition to preventing unexpected program crashes, this guarantees that the software can recover from errors and display informative error messages. Apart from it, topics related to Python's file handling module allow you to read from and write to files.

Chapter 5: Object-oriented Programming and Regular Expressions - This chapter covers key OOP principles such as classes, objects, inheritance, method overriding, encapsulation, and polymorphism. In addition to OOP, this chapter also introduces **regular expressions (regex)** in Python, a powerful tool for pattern matching and string manipulation. Regular expressions allow searching, matching, and replacing text based on specific patterns, which is particularly useful in data validation, web scraping, and text processing tasks.

Chapter 6: Database Connectivity using MySQL and MongoDB - This chapter helps students understand the concept and significance of database connectivity using Python. Learners will first gain a brief overview of how Python interacts with relational databases like MySQL using the mysql.connector module to establish a connection and execute basic SQL queries. The focus then shifts to NoSQL databases, specifically MongoDB, where learners will explore its structure and how it differs from traditional relational databases.

Chapter 7: NumPy Library - This chapter introduces the fundamental concepts of NumPy, one of the core libraries in Python for numerical and scientific computing. It focuses on working with arrays (ndarrays) and performing vectorized computations efficiently. Learners will learn how to create and manipulate NumPy arrays, explore basic indexing and slicing techniques, and apply arithmetic operations on arrays. The chapter also explains the use of NumPy's universal functions (ufuncs), which provide fast element-wise operations, including mathematical, logical, and statistical functions. These tools form the foundation for high-performance computing in Python and are widely used in data analysis, machine learning, and scientific applications.

Chapter 8: Introduction to Pandas Data Structure - This chapter introduces the essential components of the Pandas library, a powerful and widely used tool for data manipulation and analysis in Python. It begins with an overview of Series and DataFrame, the fundamental data structures in Pandas, followed by practical techniques for accessing and modifying data. The chapter also delves into real-world data preparation tasks, such as data cleaning and filtering, applying functions with apply(), and exploring datasets using methods like unique() and count(). Additionally, learners will learn how to read data from external CSV files and write processed data back into files, making this chapter a practical foundation for data handling in Python.

Chapter 9: Data Cleaning and Preparation - This chapter covers foundational understanding of data preprocessing, which is essential for effective data analysis. Learners will learn to replace incorrect or inconsistent values and convert data types to ensure compatibility. In addition to it, they will explore how to rename columns for clarity, clean string data by trimming or modifying text, and filter rows based on specific conditions. Additionally, the chapter introduces indexing for accessing specific data, techniques for categorizing continuous data into bins, and methods to combine or merge columns. By the end of the chapter, learners will be able to handle missing values through imputation techniques or by removing null entries, thereby preparing clean and usable datasets. The chapter also focuses on identifying and eliminating duplicate and incorrect data entries to ensure data integrity.

Chapter 10: Data Visualization Using Matplotlib - This chapter focuses on data visualization using the Matplotlib library in conjunction with Pandas. While Pandas offers robust tools for managing and analyzing structured data, Matplotlib enables users to present that data visually through various types of charts, which is essential for interpreting results in real-world applications such as business analytics and research reporting. By utilizing Pandas' built-in integration with Matplotlib, users can generate plots directly from Series and DataFrames with minimal effort. The chapter introduces the fundamentals of creating common visualizations such as line plots, bar charts, pie charts, histograms, and scatter plots using matplotlib.pyplot alongside Pandas.

Chapter 11: Introduction to ML and Supervised Learning - This chapter provides learners with a practical and beginner-friendly introduction to the fundamental concepts of **machine learning** (**ML**). By the end of the chapter, learners will be able to differentiate between supervised, unsupervised, and reinforcement learning, explain how machines learn from data and make decisions without explicit programming, compare the approaches used in the three types of learning, illustrate real-world applications such as recommendation systems, customer segmentation, and autonomous agents, and identify commonly used machine learning algorithms along with their basic purposes.

Chapter 12: Introduction to Unsupervised and Reinforcement Learning - This chapter covers a clear understanding of the concepts of unsupervised learning and reinforcement learning. Learners will be able to differentiate these approaches from supervised learning and identify where each method is most applicable in real life. Learners will learn how clustering algorithms, such as K-means, can group unlabelled data into meaningful categories, and how reinforcement learning enables an agent to make decisions based on rewards and penalties. They will gain hands-on experience by implementing simple Python programs for clustering.

Appendix A: Simple Projects Using Pandas - This chapter presents a collection of small applications that demonstrate how to use the Pandas library in Python for analyzing data stored in CSV files. Each example is designed to be simple, clear, and practical so that readers can easily follow and apply the concepts. The applications include analyzing students' performance, summarizing sales records, and extracting insights from employee salary data. Examples also show how Python data structures such as lists, tuples, and dictionaries can be converted into DataFrames and then saved or used as CSV files for further analysis. Through these hands-on exercises, readers are introduced to essential analytical techniques that form the foundation of data-driven decision making, which is a key component of modern data science workflows.

Appendix B: Simple Projects Using Matplotlib - This chapter presents a collection of small applications that demonstrate how to use the Matplotlib library in Python for visualizing data stored in CSV files. Each example is designed to be simple, clear, and practical so that readers can easily follow and apply the concepts. The applications include plotting using a line chart, visualizing product sales through bar charts, and examining employee salary distribution with histograms. Additional case studies cover data visualization and analysis using illustrative examples that combine real-world scenarios with effective visual techniques, allowing readers to see how charts and plots can turn raw data into meaningful insights.

Code Bundle and Coloured Images

Please follow the link to download the
Code Bundle and the *Coloured Images* of the book:

https://rebrand.ly/1154w9p

The code bundle for the book is also hosted on GitHub at
https://github.com/bpbpublications/Data-Science-Projects-Using-Python.
In case there's an update to the code, it will be updated on the existing GitHub repository.

We have code bundles from our rich catalogue of books and videos available at https://github.com/bpbpublications. Check them out!

Errata

We take immense pride in our work at BPB Publications and follow best practices to ensure the accuracy of our content to provide an indulging reading experience to our subscribers. Our readers are our mirrors, and we use their inputs to reflect and improve upon human errors, if any, that may have occurred during the publishing processes involved. To let us maintain the quality and help us reach out to any readers who might be having difficulties due to any unforeseen errors, please write to us at: **errata@bpbonline.com**

Your support, suggestions and feedback are highly appreciated by the BPB Publications' Family.

Piracy

If you come across any illegal copies of our works in any form on the internet, we would be grateful if you would provide us with the location address or website name. Please contact us at **business@bpbonline.com** with a link to the material.

If you are interested in becoming an author

If there is a topic that you have expertise in, and you are interested in either writing or contributing to a book, please visit **www.bpbonline.com**. We have worked with thousands of developers and tech professionals, just like you, to help them share their insights with the global tech community. You can make a general application, apply for a specific hot topic that we are recruiting an author for, or submit your own idea.

Reviews

Please leave a review. Once you have read and used this book, why not leave a review on the site that you purchased it from? Potential readers can then see and use your unbiased opinion to make purchase decisions. We at BPB can understand what you think about our products, and our authors can see your feedback on their book. Thank you!

For more information about BPB, please visit **www.bpbonline.com**.

Join our Discord space

Join our Discord workspace for latest updates, offers, tech happenings around the world, new releases, and sessions with the authors:

https://discord.bpbonline.com

Table of Contents

CHAPTER 1
Introduction to Data Science and Python

Introduction

Data science is a multidisciplinary domain that employs various techniques, algorithms, and systems to derive insights and knowledge from structured and unstructured data. It integrates concepts from statistics, computer science, **machine learning** (**ML**), and big data analytics to interpret datasets and support data-driven decision-making. It begins with data collection from sources such as files, databases, or web services. This is followed by data cleaning, which involves handling missing values, removing duplicates, and correcting errors. Data exploration identifies patterns, trends, and anomalies using summaries and visual tools. Data analysis applies statistical techniques or algorithms to draw conclusions. Data visualization represents data in the form of charts or graphs. After analysis, machine learning techniques may be applied to build models. In the case of large datasets, big data technologies such as Hadoop or Spark are used. Finally, insights support decision-making, helping organizations solve problems, optimize processes, or automate tasks.

Data science finds applications in healthcare (disease prediction and patient monitoring), finance (fraud detection and risk analysis), education (personalized learning and student performance prediction), marketing (customer segmentation and targeted advertising), e-commerce (recommendation systems and sales forecasting), and social media (sentiment analysis and trend detection). Common tools and technologies include Python, R, and SQL. For data manipulation and numerical computations, Pandas and NumPy are widely used. Libraries like scikit-learn, TensorFlow, and PyTorch are common for ML, while Matplotlib, Seaborn, and Tableau are popular for visualization. Hadoop and Spark are used for handling massive datasets.

Despite its potential, data science faces challenges such as poor data quality, privacy and security concerns, the need for model interpretability, and scalability issues with large datasets.

Structure

The following topics are covered in this chapter:

- Artificial intelligence and machine learning with Python
- Choosing Python for data science

- Installing Python on Windows
- Python in online and offline environments
- Python libraries
- Features of Python
- Identifiers
- Indentation
- Comments
- Variables and data types
- Type conversion
- Operators in Python

Objectives

By the end of this chapter, learners will understand the significance of Python in the field of data science and recognize why it is widely used for data-related tasks. They will become familiar with Python's core features and advantages, which make it a powerful and flexible programming language. The chapter also provides a basic introduction to important libraries such as Pandas, NumPy, and Matplotlib to give learners an overview of their roles in data manipulation, numerical computing, and visualization. In addition, students will gain a solid understanding of Python fundamentals, including data types, variables, and operators. The chapter also introduces the basic concepts of **artificial intelligence** (**AI**) and machine learning, highlighting Python's relevance in these fields. Lastly, learners will be guided through the process of installing and setting up Python on a Windows platform to begin writing and running Python programs.

Artificial intelligence and machine learning with Python

The demand for AI and ML is rapidly increasing due to their ability to automate tasks, predict outcomes, and enhance user experiences. These fields rely heavily on the availability of clean, structured data and intelligent algorithms to train models. Python has emerged as the language of choice in this domain due to its simplicity, extensive libraries, and community support. Libraries such as Pandas and NumPy allow easy data manipulation, while scikit-learn simplifies the process of building and evaluating ML models. For data visualization, Matplotlib and Seaborn help create insightful charts and graphs. Python also supports advanced deep learning through frameworks like TensorFlow and PyTorch. With its versatility, Python empowers aspiring data scientists to work across the AI/ML pipeline, from data preparation to model deployment.

Choosing Python for data science

Python is a high-level, open-source programming language known for its simplicity, readability, and vast ecosystem of scientific libraries. First released in 1991 by *Guido van Rossum*, it is named in honor of *Monty Python*. Python supports multiple programming paradigms such as procedural, object-oriented, and functional programming.

Its ecosystem includes:

- Pandas for data manipulation and analysis
- NumPy for efficient numerical computation
- Matplotlib and Seaborn for data visualization
- Scikit-learn for machine learning
- Django and Flask for web development

Python's ease of learning makes it ideal for beginners, while its depth makes it powerful enough for professionals in scientific computing, automation, data science, and AI.

Installing Python on Windows

The following steps will guide the reader in installing Python on Windows:

1. To begin working with Python, visit the official website (**https://www.python.org**) as shown in the following figure:

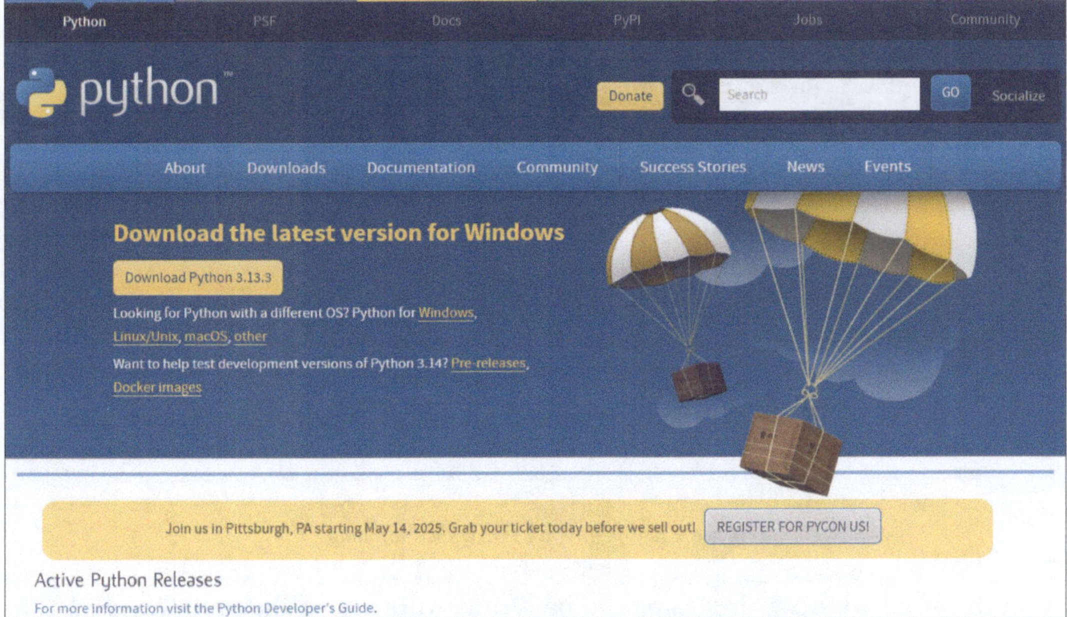

***Figure 1.1**: Downloading Python from the official website*

Download the latest version compatible with your operating system. The installer provides an option to add Python to the system path, which is recommended for easier access from the command line. Once installed, Python can be used through an interactive shell, terminal, or IDE such as Jupyter Notebook, VS Code, or PyCharm.

2. After installing the software, open the **integrated development and learning environment** (IDLE), as shown in the following figure:

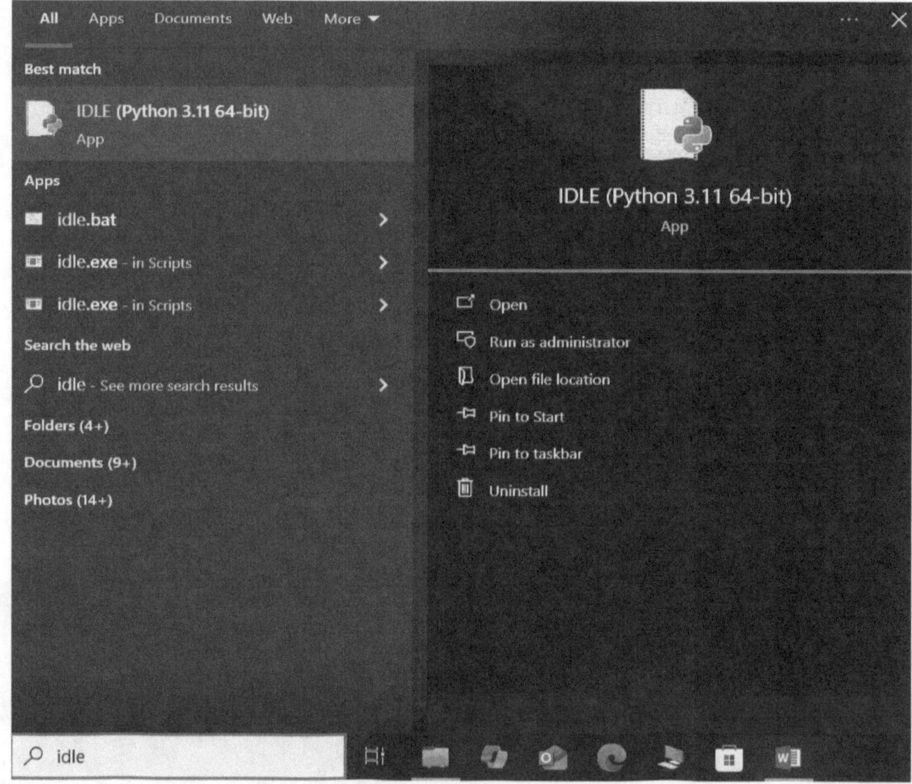

Figure 1.2: Opening an IDLE environment

After opening a screen as shown in *Figure 1.2*, an IDLE shell will be opened as shown in the following figure:

```
IDLE Shell 3.11.0
File Edit Shell Debug Options Window Help
    Python 3.11.0 (main, Oct 24 2022, 18:26:48) [MSC v.1933 64 bit (AMD64)] on win32
    Type "help", "copyright", "credits" or "license()" for more information.
>>>
```

Figure 1.3: Opening an IDLE shell window

In this shell window, programs can be written directly as shown in *Figure 1.4*. In the shell, the output of a program is also displayed.

```
IDLE Shell 3.11.0
File  Edit  Shell  Debug  Options  Window  Help
    Python 3.11.0 (main, Oct 24 2022, 18:26:48)
    Type "help", "copyright", "credits" or "lice
>>> a = 10
>>> b = "Hello Python"
>>> print (a)
    10
>>> print(b)
    Hello Python
```

Figure 1.4: *Running a program in the IDLE shell*

Note: Another way to execute a program is to save it as a Python file, i.e., to save a file with a .py extension, as shown in Figure 1.5:

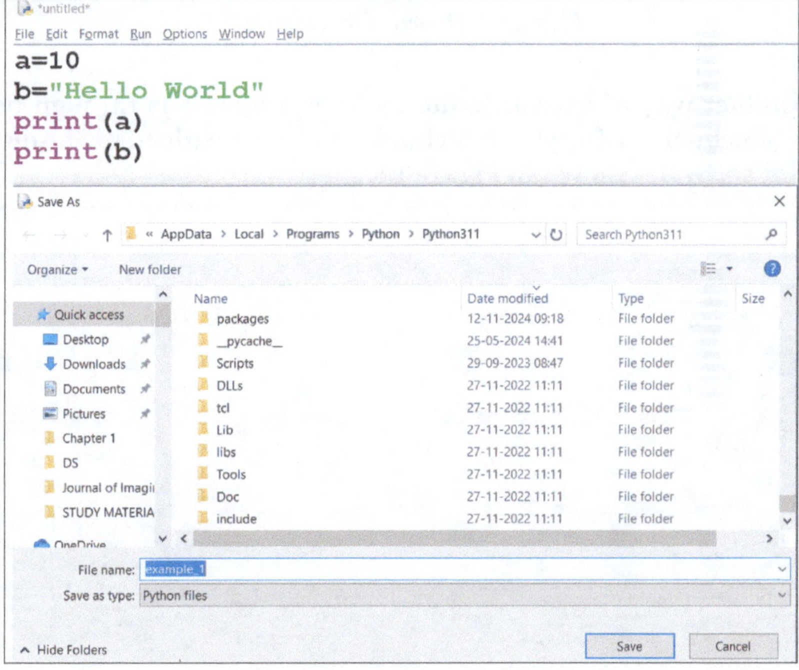

Figure 1.5: *Saving a Python program*

3. In order to execute the program, click on the **Run** tab and get the output as shown in *Figure 1.6*:

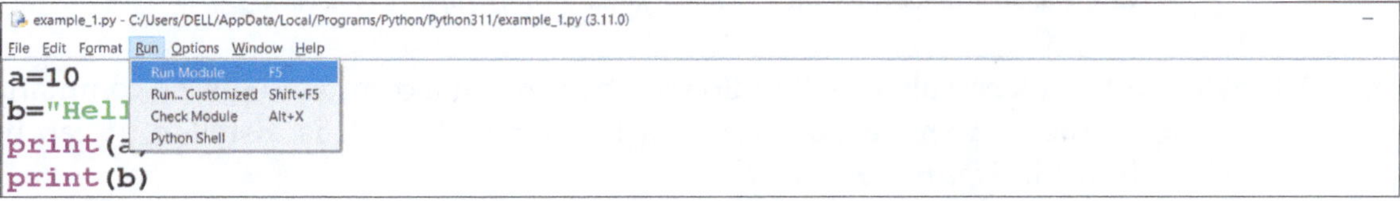

Figure 1.6: *Click on the Run tab*

The output of the program mentioned is shown in the following figure:

```
example_1.py - C:/Users/DELL/AppData/Local/Programs/Python/Python311/example_1.py (3.11.0)
File Edit Format Run Options Window Help
a=10
b="Hello World"
print(a)
print(b)
```

```
IDLE Shell 3.11.0
File Edit Shell Debug Options Window Help
Python 3.11.0 (main, Oct 24 202
Type "help", "copyright", "cred
>>>
== RESTART: C:/Users/DELL/AppDat
10
Hello World
```

***Figure 1.7**: Output of the example*

Note: Another way of executing the Python programs is through notebook, i.e., Jupyter Notebook. A Jupyter Notebook can be downloaded through Anaconda Navigator software, shown in Figure 1.8:

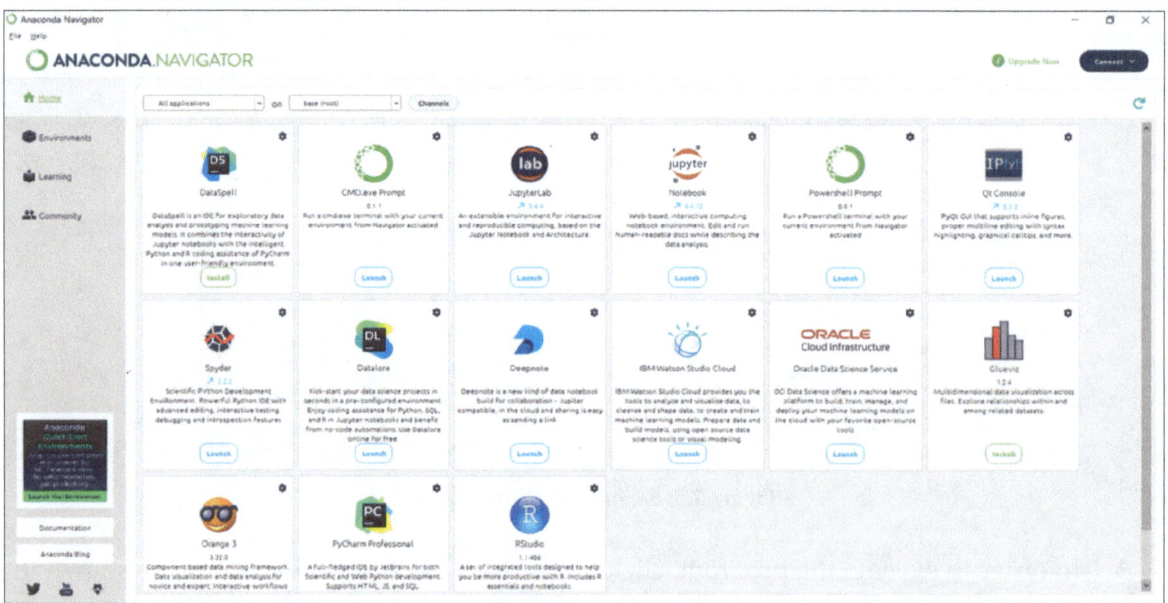

***Figure 1.8**: Anaconda Navigator Window for launching Jupyter Notebook*

4. A Jupyter Notebook can also be downloaded by writing a command on the command prompt: **`pip install notebook`**. When a Jupyter Notebook is installed, it can be opened as shown in *Figure 1.9*:

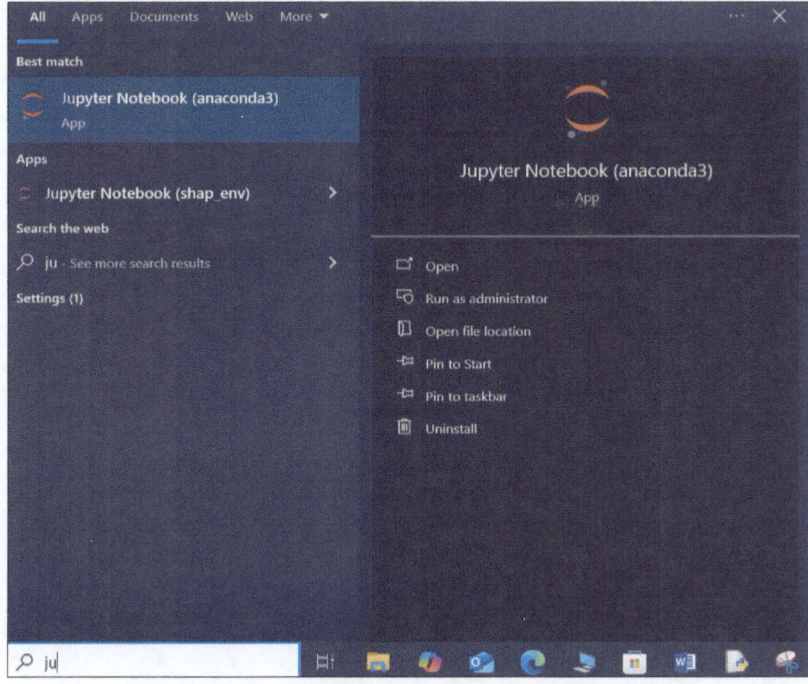

Figure 1.9: Opening a Jupyter Notebook

Jupyter Notebook is one of the most widely used tools in the data science ecosystem, allowing users to write and execute Python code interactively within a web browser.

5. After successfully launching Jupyter from your system (usually via the command prompt using **`jupyter notebook`**) or as shown in *Figure 1.9*, the browser interface opens, displaying a list of folders and files from your working directory.

6. As shown in *Figure 1.10*, to begin writing code, you can click on the **New** dropdown button on the right side of the screen. From the dropdown, selecting **Python 3 (ipykernel)** creates a new notebook where Python code can be written and executed line by line. This environment is ideal for learning, experimentation, data analysis, and creating data science projects.

Figure 1.10: Launching a new notebook in Jupyter interface

7. The same program as written in the IDLE environment can also be written in a Jupyter Notebook cell and the output obtained is shown in the following figure:

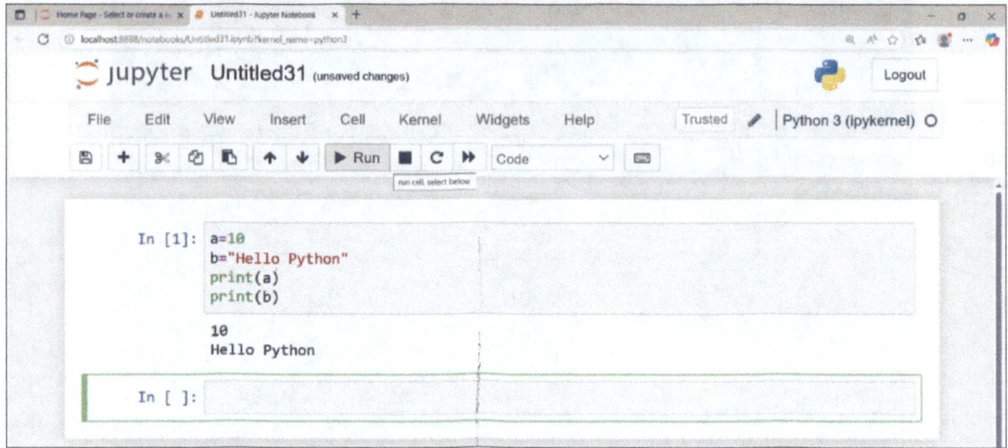

***Figure 1.11**: Writing a program in Jupyter Notebook and obtaining the output*

The detailed steps are supported by the following summary table, which provides a quick overview of installation methods and their outcomes:

Step	Action	Result
1	Go to **python.org/downloads** and download the latest version for Windows	Python installer downloaded
2	Run the installer and select **Add Python to PATH**, then click **Install Now**	Python successfully installed
3	Open command prompt and type **`python --version`**	Confirms Python installation
4	Open IDLE from the **Start** menu and write a simple program, e.g., **`print("Hello, Python!")`**	Program runs successfully in IDLE
5	Install Jupyter Notebook using **`pip install notebook`** (in command prompt)	Jupyter Notebook installed
6	Launch Jupyter Notebook using **`jupyter notebook`**	Opens Jupyter interface in browser
7	Create a new notebook and run **`print("Hello, Jupyter!")`**	Code executes and output appears
8	Install PyCharm (download from **jetbrains.com/pycharm**) and configure Python interpreter	Python projects can be created and run inside PyCharm
9	Install **Visual Studio Code** (**VS Code**) (download from **code.visualstudio.com**) and add the Python Extension	Python scripts can be written, debugged, and executed in VS Code

***Table 1.1**: Summary table for installing and running Python*

The table shows all popular ways beginners can use Python:

- IDLE (comes with Python)
- Jupyter Notebook (interactive coding and data science)
- PyCharm (IDE for larger projects)
- VS Code (lightweight editor with Python support)

Python in online and offline environments

Students can also practice Python programs through online environments like Google Colab. Google Colab fully supports Python programming, and there is no installation needed as it runs in your browser. In this, libraries like **`pandas`**, **`matplotlib`**, **`numpy`**, and even **`scikit-learn`** are pre-installed. The following steps serve as a guide:

1. In order to start, first go to the official website at **https://colab.research.google.com** as shown in *Figure 1.12* and open a new notebook to perform programs in the online environment of Google Colab and obtain the output as shown in *Figure 1.13*. It is to be noted that while opening the Google Colab website, sign in with your Gmail account.

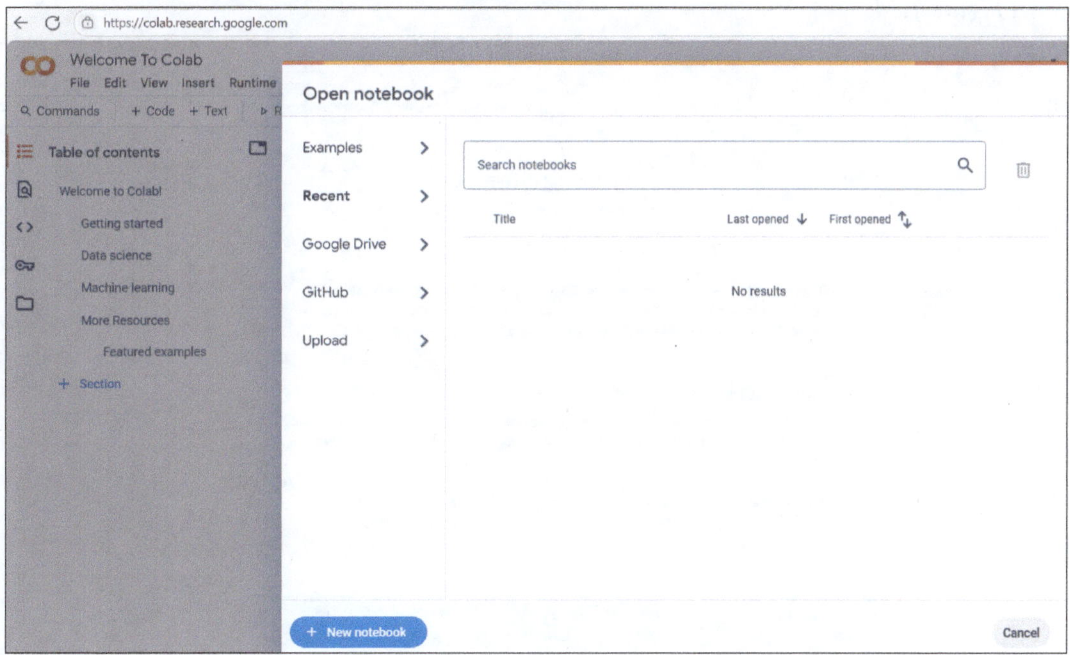

Figure 1.12: *Open a notebook in Google Colab*

Source: *https://colab.research.google.com*

2. On clicking a **New notebook** tab, a Jupyter file with extension **`.ipynb`** opens, and learners can start writing code in it and obtain the output as shown in *Figure 1.13*:

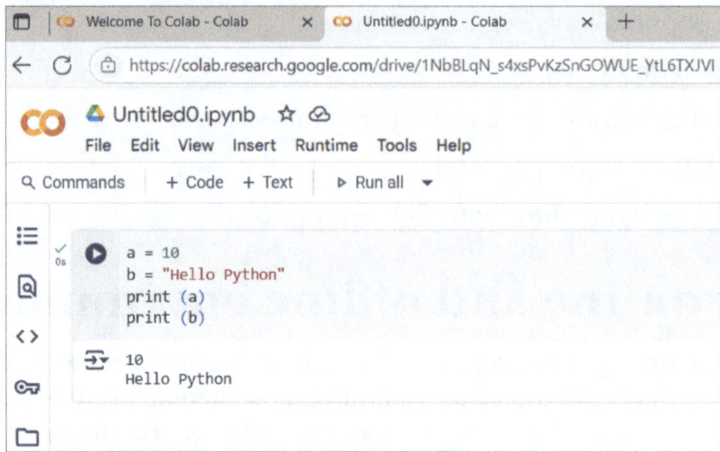

***Figure 1.13**: Running a Python program on the Google Colab online environment*

3. In a similar way, learners can run the Python programs through the JupyterLab official website or by installing Jupyter Notebook locally as discussed. In order to try Python programs online on it, go to **https://jupyter.org/try** and select **Try JupyterLab** as shown in *Figure 1.14*:

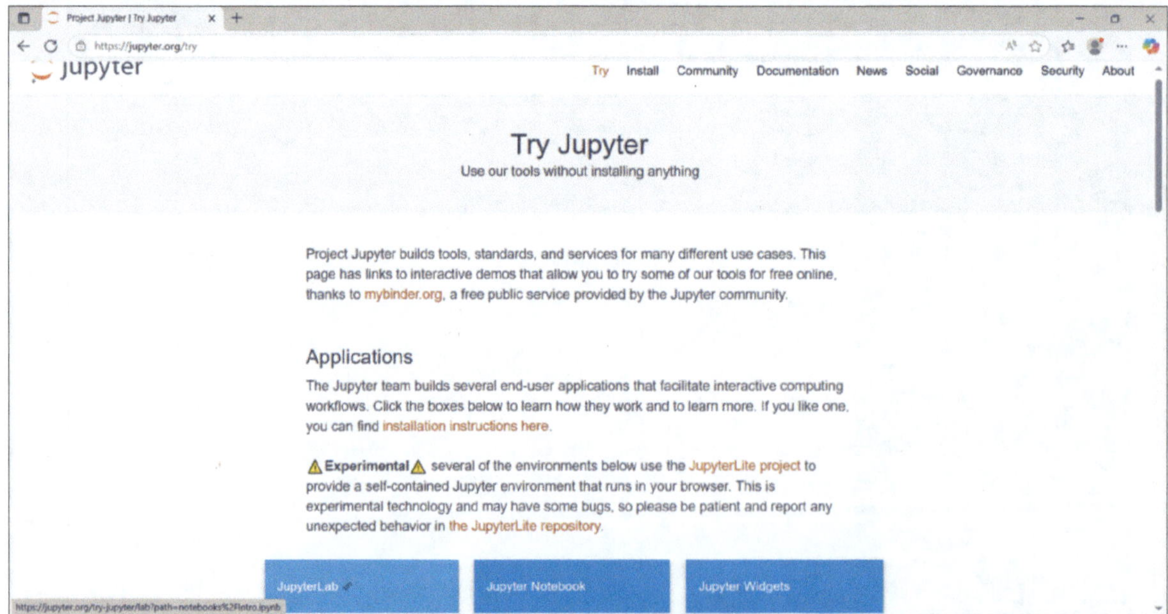

***Figure 1.14**: Try JupyterLab online*

4. After clicking on **JupyterLab**, open a new notebook as shown in the following figure to write and execute the Python program:

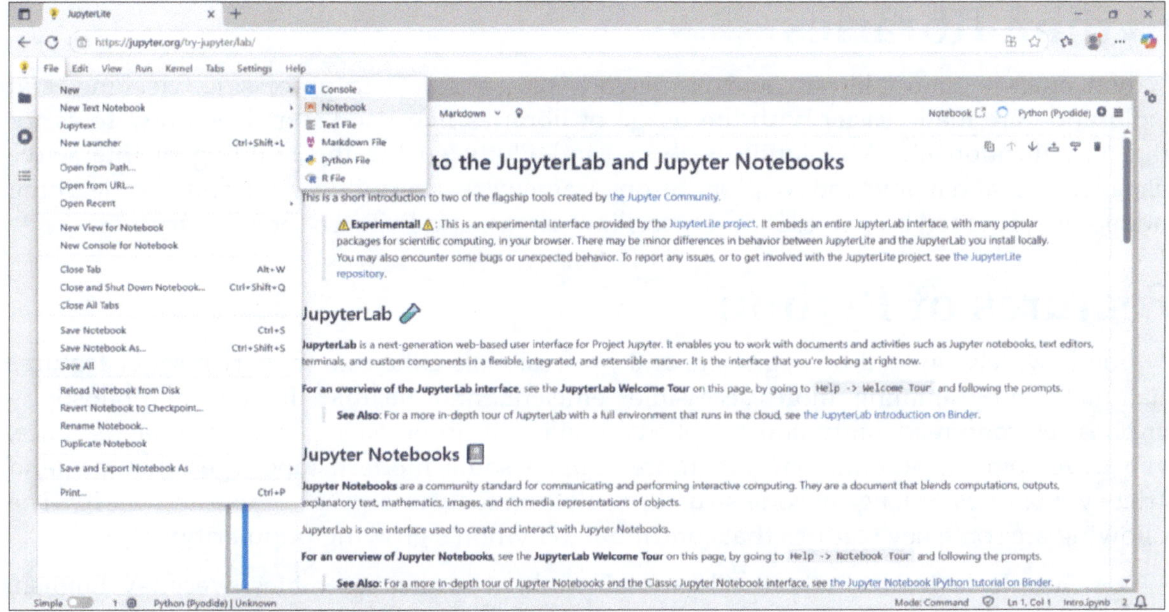

Figure 1.15: Opening a new notebook in online JupyterLab environment

5. In this notebook, write a program of Python in cell and run the program to get output as shown in *Figure 1.16*:

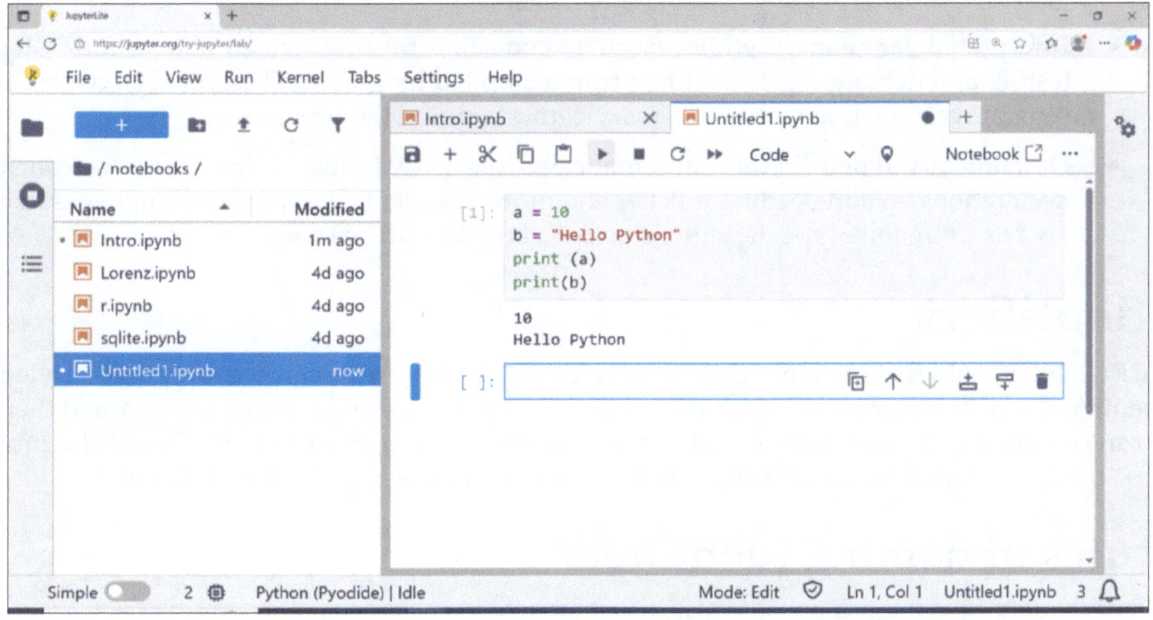

Figure 1.16: Writing a Python program in online JupyterLab environment and obtain output

Python libraries

Python offers a robust library and framework ecosystem. Data processing, cleaning, and exploration are made easier with the usage of libraries like Pandas and NumPy. Tools for data visualization like Matplotlib, Seaborn, and Plotly enable the building of interactive visualizations and many kinds of plots. Strong frameworks for building ML and deep learning models are provided by scikit-learn, TensorFlow, Keras, and PyTorch for ML purposes.

Features of Python

Python is widely favored by beginners and professionals alike due to its rich set of features that make programming more accessible, efficient, and flexible. Its design philosophy emphasizes code readability and simplicity, making it an excellent choice for data science, web development, automation, and more. Unlike some modern languages that demand strict syntax rules or lengthy code structures, Python focuses on ease of use and clarity. The following are some key features that contribute to Python's growing popularity:

- **Simple to learn**: Python's clean and minimal syntax resembles everyday English, making it easier for newcomers compared to languages like C++ or Java, which require more complex structures.
- **Readable code**: Python emphasizes simplicity and readability, allowing developers to write clear code with fewer lines. In contrast, languages such as Java often require additional boilerplate code for the same tasks.
- **Interpreted language**: Python executes code line by line, which allows for faster testing and debugging. This differs from compiled languages like C or C++, where a separate compilation step is necessary before running the program.
- **Dynamically typed**: Python automatically infers a variable's type without explicit declarations, making coding quicker and more flexible. In comparison, languages like Java or C# require type definitions before variables can be used.

Identifiers

In Python, variables, functions, classes, and other objects are identified by names called identifiers. An identifier must begin with a letter (a to z, A to Z) or an underscore (_), and then it can contain any combination of underscores, letters, and numerals (0 to 9). Due to the case sensitivity of identifiers, **`myVar`**, **`MyVar`**, and **`myvar`** would all be regarded as different.

Rules of naming identifiers

Naming identifiers follows certain rules, listed as follows:

- Identifiers can be a combination of letters in lowercase (a to z) or uppercase (A to Z), digits (0 to 9), or an underscore_.

- Variable names like **var1**, **var_1**, and **myVar** are all valid examples.
- An identifier cannot start with a digit. For example, **1Var** is invalid, but **var1** is a valid name.

Note: **Keywords cannot be used as identifiers. We cannot use special symbols like !,@,#,$,%, etc., in identifiers. An identifier can be of any length.**

Reserved words

Reserved words, which are preset words in Python with specific meanings and cannot be used as identifiers, are also referred to as **keywords**. Reserved terms include **def**, **class**, **try**, **except**, **with**, **if**, **otherwise**, **for**, **while**, and **return**. As of Python 3.x, there are 35 reserved keywords in the language.

Note: **You cannot use keywords as constants, variables, or any other type of identifier since they are reserved words. Every Python keyword is composed entirely of lowercase characters.**

Indentation

Python uses indentation to specify the code's structure, including the code blocks that are contained within loops, functions, and conditionals. Python indentation must be consistent in order for the code not cause an **IndentationError**. The example of indentation is shown as follows:

```
if True:
    print("This is inside the if block")  # Indented code
print("This is outside the if block")  # Not indented
```

Comments

The code is explained and documented using comments. They have no effect on how the code is executed and are ignored by the Python interpreter.

Comments are of the following types:

- **Single-line comment**: To add a comment that finishes at the end of the line, use the # symbol.
- **Multi-line comment**: For comments that cross many lines, use triple quotes (''' or """).

The example of a comment in code is shown as follows:

```
# This is a single-line comment
x = 5  # This comment is next to a code line

"""
This is a multi-line comment.
It can span several lines.
"""
print("Hello, World!")
```

Variables and data types

Variables are the locations in memory; they do not have to be defined with a specific type, and once they are set, they can change types. There is no command in Python for declaring variables. The data values are stored in case-sensitive variables. Variable names can begin with a letter or an underscore (_), or they can be made up of characters like a to z, A to Z, and digits (0 to 9).

In Python, a variable is a designated memory area used to hold a value. Data that can be changed and referred to throughout a program is stored in variables. As variable names are case-sensitive, there is a difference between variables named **`myVar`**, **`MyVar`**, and **`myvar`**.

Note: Do not name variables with reserved Python terms like `if`, `for`, or `while`. The example of variable declaration is shown as follows:

```
x = 5           # 'x' is a variable holding the value 5
name = "Ram"    # 'name' is a variable holding the string "Ram"
_var = 10       # '_var' is a variable holding the value 10
```

In this code, the value **`5`** is assigned to a variable **`x`** using the assignment operator. The variable values can be changed by assigning a new value. The value in variable **`x`** is changed by replacing it with another value, as shown in the following code:

```
x = 5
x = 25    # Now 'x' holds the value 25, not 5
```

The variables are used in functions, computations, and expressions. Python loads a variable's most recent value from memory when you use it, as shown in the following example:

```
x = 15
y = 10
result = x + y  # 'result' variable will hold the value 25 (15 + 10)
```

Python data types

In Python, data types define the kind of value a variable can hold. Understanding these types is essential, as they form the foundation of any Python program. Python provides several built-in data types, which can be grouped into the following categories:

- **Numeric types**: These are used to represent numbers. Python supports:
  - **int**: Used for whole numbers (e.g., `5`, `-10`, `200`, `age: int = 30`).
  - **float**: Used for decimal or floating-point numbers (e.g., `3.14`, `-0.001`, `2.0`, `pi: float = 3.14`).
- **Sequence types**: Sequences are ordered collections of items. Python includes:
  - **str**: Used for strings or sequences of characters (e.g., `"Hello"`, `"123"`, `greeting: str = "Hello World"`).
  - **list**: Used for mutable sequences of items, which can be of mixed data types (e.g., `[1, "apple", 3.14]`, `fruits: list = ["apple", "banana", 10]`).
- **Mapping type**:
  - **dict**: Short for dictionary, this type stores key-value pairs (e.g., `{"name": "Anil", "age": 25}`, `student: dict = {"name": "Anil", "age": 25}`).
- **Set types**: Sets are collections of unique items. Python provides:
  - **set**: An unordered collection of distinct elements (e.g., `{1, 2, 3}`, `numbers: set = {1, 2, 3, 3}` results in `{1, 2, 3}`).
  - **frozenset**: An immutable version of a set (e.g., `frozenset([1, 2, 3])`).
- **Boolean type**:
  - **bool**: Represents truth values, either True or False (e.g., `True`, `False`, `is_active: bool = True`).

Each of these types plays a specific role in Python programming and allows developers to work with different kinds of data efficiently and effectively.

Example 1.1: Write a program showing Python built-in data types

In this example, we explore several of Python's built-in data types through a variety of variable declarations. The `age` variable is an integer that represents a whole number, while `temperature` is a floating-point number that includes decimal values, showcasing Python's numeric types. The string `"Delhi"` is assigned to `city_name`, and the list `["red", "green", "blue"]` stored in `colors`, illustrates Python's sequence types, i.e., ordered collections of data. The `book` dictionary holds key-value pairs, mapping descriptive keys like `"title"` and `"pages"` to their respective values, which is characteristic of the mapping type. Sets, used for storing unique items, are represented by `rollnumbers`, while `regid` demonstrates a `frozenset`, which is a fixed, unchangeable version of a set. The Boolean value `False` stored in `has_passed` is useful for logical decisions and conditions in programming. Finally, the variable **response** is assigned **None**, signifying the absence of a value or a null state. The **type()** function is then used to confirm the data type of each variable, providing a clear and structured view of how Python categorizes and manages different types of data. The following is a program showing Python built-in data types:

```
# Numeric Types
age = 28                    # Integer (int)
temperature = -5.75         # Floating-point number (float)
# Sequence Types
city_name = "Delhi"      # String (str)
colors = ["red", "green", "blue"] # List
# Mapping Type
book = {"title": "Python Basics", "pages": 320} # Dictionary (dict)
# Set Types
rollnumbers = {4, 7, 15, 22}      # Set
regid = frozenset({101, 102})     # Frozenset
# Boolean Type
has_passed = False           # Boolean (bool)
# None Type
response = None              # NoneType (represents no value)
# Type Checking using type()
print(type(age))              # <class 'int'>
print(type(temperature))      # <class 'float'>
print(type(city_name))        # <class 'str'>
print(type(colors))           # <class 'list'>
print(type(book))             # <class 'dict'>
print(type(rollnumbers)) # <class 'set'>
print(type(regid))    # <class 'frozenset'>
print(type(has_passed))       # <class 'bool'>
print(type(response))         # <class 'NoneType'>
```

The output of this example is shown in *Figure 1.17*:

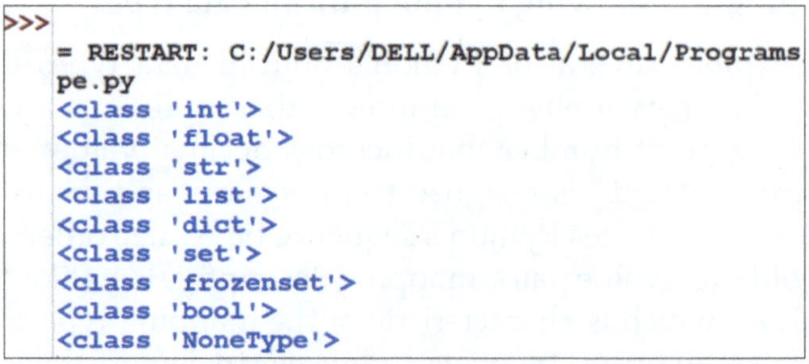

```
>>>
= RESTART: C:/Users/DELL/AppData/Local/Programs
pe.py
<class 'int'>
<class 'float'>
<class 'str'>
<class 'list'>
<class 'dict'>
<class 'set'>
<class 'frozenset'>
<class 'bool'>
<class 'NoneType'>
```

Figure 1.17: *Output of the Python built-in data types*

Type conversion

Transforming one data type into another is known as type conversion. Python comes with built-in functions to convert between various kinds. There are two different kinds of conversions, explicit and implicit.

Implicit type: Python performs implicit type conversion, which is the automated conversion of one data type to another as required, typically during operations. In *Example 1.2*, Python automatically converts the integer to a float when you add an integer and a float.

Why it matters: Type conversion is essential because in real-world programming, data often comes in as text, especially when reading from external sources such as files, user input, or databases. For example, **"100"** may be stored as a string, and to perform calculations, you would need to convert it into an integer using **int("100")**.

Note: **When working with comma-separated values (CSV) files, numbers are often stored as strings. For instance, a column with "250" must be converted to an integer (int("250")) before you can add or compare values.**

Example 1.2: Example of an implicit type

Take a look at this example:

```
x = 5      # int
y = 3.5      # float
result = x + y    # int + float = float
print(result)  # Output: 8.5, the result is a float
```

Explicit type: Using the built-in Python functions **int()**, **float()**, **str()**, **list()**, and so on, you can manually convert one data type to another. When a certain data type is required for operations, this is useful.

Example 1.3: Write a program for explicit data type conversion

In the following code, explicit data type conversion is done. In this example, a float value is converted to an integer, an integer to a float type, and similarly, a string value is converted to an integer and vice versa:

```
# Convert float to int
x = 2.8
y = int(x) #y will be 2(integer)
print(y)
# Convert int to float
a = 5
b = float(a)  #b will be 5.0(float)
print(b)
```

```
# Convert string to int
num_str = "100"
num = int(num_str) # num will be 100(integer)
print(num)
# Convert int to string
num_str2 = str(num)  # num_str2 will be "100"(string)
print(num_str2)
```

The output is shown in *Figure 1.18*:

```
>>>
    = RESTART: C:/Users/DELL/AppData/Local/Programs
    /typeconvert1.py
    2
    5.0
    100
    100
```

***Figure 1.18**: Explicit type conversion*

Operators in Python

In Python, operators are unique symbols used for working with variables and values. Python supports multiple kinds of operators, which include arithmetic, comparison, logical, assignment, bitwise, membership, and identity operators. Let us take a look at each of them.

Arithmetic operators

Arithmetic operators are detailed in *Table 1.2*:

Operator	Operation performed
+	Addition
-	Subtraction
*	Multiplication
/	Division (result is always a float)
%	Modulus(remainder after division)
**	Exponentiation (power)
//	Floor division (It discards the fractional part, i.e., the quotient after division)

***Table 1.2**: Arithmetic operators*

The arithmetic operators mentioned in *Table 1.2* are implemented in *Example 1.4*:

Example 1.4: Write a program for displaying arithmetic operators

In this example, arithmetic operators like **+**, **-**, *****, **/**, **%**, ******, and **//** are applied on the variables **a** and **b**:

```
a = 10
b = 4
print(a+b)  # Output:14(addition)
print(a-b)  # Output: 6(subtraction)
print(a*b)  # Output: 40(multiplication)
print(a/b)  # Output: 2.5(division)
print(a%b)  # Output: 2(modulus i.e. remainder)
print(a**b) # Output: 10000(exponentiation i.e.power,10^4)
print(a//b) # Output: 2(floor division)
```

The output of arithmetic operators is shown in *Figure 1.19*:

```
>>>
    = RESTART: C:/Users/DELL/AppData/Local/Programs
    /airthmetic.py
    14
    6
    40
    2.5
    2
    10000
    2
```

***Figure 1.19**: Output of arithmetic operators*

Comparison operators

Comparison operators are shown in the following table:

Operator	Operation performed
==	Equal to
!=	Not equal to
>	Greater than
<	Less than
>=	Greater than or equal to
<=	Less than or equal to

***Table 1.3**: Comparison operators*

The result is displayed in the form of a Boolean type, i.e., either true or false. The comparison operators mentioned in *Table 1.3* are implemented in *Example 1.5*.

Example 1.5: Write a program for comparison operators

In this example, comparison operators shown in *Table 1.3* are applied to the variables **a** and **b**:

```
a=10
b=5
print(a==b)  # Output: False (10 is not equal to 5)
print(a!= b)  # Output: True (10 is not equal to 5)
print(a>b)  # Output: True (10 is greater than 5)
print(a<b)   # Output: False (10 is not less than 5)
print(a>=b)  # Output: True (10 is greater than or equal to 5)
print(a<=b)  # Output: False (10 is not less than or equal to 5)
```

The output of comparison operators is shown in *Figure 1.20*:

```
>>>
    = RESTART: C:/Users/DELL/AppData/Local/Programs
    /comparison.py
    False
    True
    True
    False
    True
    False
```

***Figure 1.20**: Output of the comparison operators*

Logical operators

Logical operators implemented in Python are shown in the following table:

Operator	Operation performed
and	Returns true if both statements are true
or	Returns true if at least one statement is true
not	Returns true if the statement is false. It reverses the result

***Table 1.4**: Logical operators*

The logical operators mentioned in *Table 1.4* are shown in *Example 1.6*.

Example 1.6: Example of logical operators

In this example, logical operators are applied to the variables **x** and **y**:

```
x = True
y = False
print(x and y) # Output: False(both are not true)
print(x or y) # Output: True (one is true)
print(not x) # Output: False (reverses True to False and False to True)
```

The output of the logical operator is shown in *Figure 1.21*:

```
>>>
= RESTART: C:/Users/DELL/AppData/Local/Programs
.py
False
True
False
```

***Figure 1.21**: Output of logical operators*

Assignment operator

Assignment operators are shown in *Table 1.5*:

Operator	Operation performed
=	Assigns a value to a variable
+=	Adds and assigns the result to the variable
-=	Subtracts and assigns the result to the variable
*=	Multiplies and assigns the result to the variable
/=	Divides and assigns the result to the variable
%=	Performs modulus and assigns the result to the variable
**=	Performs exponentiation and assigns the result to the variable
//=	Performs floor division and assigns the result to the variable

***Table 1.5**: Assignment operators*

Example 1.7: Example of assignment operator

In this example, the assignment operators shown in *Table 1.5* are applied to a variable **x**:

```
x=4
print(x)
x+=4  # x = x + 4, now x is 8
print(x)
x*=3  # x = x * 3, now x is 24 as the variable x is updated
print(x)
x/=6  # x = x / 6, now x is 4.0, the variable x is updated
print(x)
```

The output of the code is shown in the following figure:

```
>>>
= RESTART: C:/Users/DELL/AppData/Local/Programs
ent.py
4
8
24
4.0
```

Figure 1.22: Output of the assignment operator

Bitwise operators

The bitwise operators like bitwise AND, OR, XOR, NOT, left shift, and right shift operators are shown in *Table 1.6*:

Operator	Operation performed
&	Bitwise AND
|	Bitwise OR
^	Bitwise XOR
~	Bitwise NOT
<<	Left shift
>>	Right shift

Table 1.6: Bitwise operators

Example 1.8: Example of bitwise operators

The bitwise, left shift, and right shift operators shown in *Table 1.6* are applied to variables **a** and **b**:

```
a = 10  # Binary:1010
b = 4   # Binary: 0100
print(a & b)  # Output: 0 (0000)
print(a | b)  # Output: 14 (1110)
print(a ^ b)  # Output: 14 (1110)
print(~a)     # Output: -11 (inverse of 1010)
print(a << 1) # Output: 20 (10100)
print(a >> 1) # Output: 5 (0101)
```

Using the bitwise **&** operator, if one condition is true (i.e., 1), and the other is false (i.e., 0), then the output is false (i.e., 0). While using bitwise **&**, both conditions should be true to get the output to be true. Using the bitwise **|** operator, if one condition is true (i.e., 1), and the other is false (i.e., 0), then the output is true (i.e., 1). Here, at least one condition must be true to get the output as true. Using the bitwise ^ operator, if one condition is true (i.e., 1), and another condition is true (i.e., 1), then the output will be false (i.e., 0). Here, both conditions should change to get the output as true. Using the bitwise ~ operator, the complement, i.e., the inverse of the value, is obtained. Here, 1 will be changed to 0, and 0 will be changed to 1. In the left shift operator, the bit will be shifted towards the left. If the left shift is of one bit, then the bit will be shifted one bit towards the left. In the right shift >> operator, the bit will be shifted towards the right side.

Membership operators

There are two membership operators, which are shown in *Table 1.7:*

Operator	Operation performed
in	Returns the status true if a value is found in the sequence
not in	Returns the status true if a value is not found in the sequence

Table 1.7: *Membership operators*

The concept of the membership operator is shown in *Example 1.9.*

Example 1.9: Write a program demonstrating membership operators

Take a look at the following code:

```
courses=["C","Java","Python"]
print("Java" in courses) #Output:True
print("C++" not in courses) #Output:True
```

The output of the membership operator is shown in the following figure:

```
>>>
    = RESTART: C:/Users/DELL/AppData/Local/Programs
    hip.py
    True
    True
```

Figure 1.23: *Membership operators*

Identity operators

The identity operators used in Python are shown in *Table 1.8*:

Operator	Operation performed
is	Returns the status true if a value is found in the sequence
is not	Returns the status true if a value is not found in the sequence

Table 1.8: *Identity operators*

Example 1.10: Example of identity operator

In this example, the identity operator **is** is applied to the variables **var1** and **var2**:

```
var1=["python","java"]
var2=["python","java"]
var3=var1
print(var1 is var3) # Output:True(var3 is the same object as var1)
print(var1 is var2) # Output:False(var1 and var2 are different objects)
print(var1==var2)   # Output:True(var1 and var2 have the same content)
```

In statement **print(var1 is var3)**, the output is coming as **True** because both are pointing to the same memory address . In statement **print(var1 is var2)**, even though **var1** is **var2** have the same values, but they are created as two different lists (objects). Their location (identity) in memory is different. Therefore, output is **False**. In statement **print(var1==var2)**, **==** operator only checks the value (content) of the variables.

The output of the identity operator is shown in *Figure 1.24*:

```
>>>
    = RESTART: C:\Users\DELL\AppData\Local\Programs\Python
    y.py
    True
    False
    True
```

Figure 1.24: Output of identity operator

Conclusion

In this chapter, we have explored the field of data science and highlighted why Python is a highly popular language for data science. In addition to that, students will also learn about the various Python libraries and the distinct features of Python. The other subjects covered in this chapter include identifiers, reserved words, and indentation, etc. The fundamental concepts of variables, including their data types, type conversions, and various types of operators, are all covered with comprehensive examples. In these examples, we discussed the fundamental concepts of variables, including different data types, how to perform type conversions, and the role of various operators such as arithmetic, relational, logical, and assignment. These basic building blocks help students write effective and error-free Python code. By the end of this chapter, learners should be comfortable with installing Python, writing simple scripts, and understanding how Python's syntax supports clear and readable code. This foundation will enable them to progress smoothly into more complex topics in the upcoming chapters, such as control flow, functions, modules, and working with packages.

Points to remember

The following points are to be kept in mind:

- The field of data science incorporates multiple disciplines, and it entails extracting valuable insights from both organized and unorganized data through the use of tools such as Python, R, SQL, and libraries including Pandas, NumPy, Matplotlib, among others.
- Python is one of the most popular programming languages used in data science due to its simplicity, readability, open-source nature, and rich set of libraries.
- Python libraries such as Pandas, NumPy, scikit-learn, TensorFlow, Matplotlib, and Seaborn play a crucial role in data manipulation, analysis, ML, and visualization.
- Variables in Python are used to store data values in memory. They do not need an explicit declaration of data type.
- Identifiers are names used for variables, functions, classes, etc., and must follow naming rules (e.g., cannot start with a digit, no special characters except _, etc.).
- Comments in Python are written using # for single-line comments and triple quotes ''' or """ for multi-line comments. They help in code readability and documentation.
- Data types in Python include:
    - **Numeric types**: int, float
    - **Sequence types**: str, list, tuple
    - **Mapping type**: dict
    - **Set types**: set, frozenset
    - **Boolean type**: bool
    - **Special type**: NoneType
- Python programs can be executed using platforms like:
    - Command prompt/Terminal
    - Jupyter Notebook
    - Google Colab
    - JupyterLab (web-based IDE)
- Operators in Python are used to perform operations on variables and values, including arithmetic, comparison, logical, assignment, and bitwise operators.
- Python supports different programming paradigms such as procedural, object-oriented, and functional programming.

Key terms

- **Data science**: A field that involves extracting meaningful insights from structured and unstructured data using analytical and computational techniques.
- **Python**: A popular, high-level, and open-source programming language known for its simplicity, readability, and large ecosystem of libraries.
- **Interpreter**: A program that executes Python code line by line.
- **Jupyter Notebook**: A browser-based interactive environment used for writing and executing Python code, especially in data science.
- **Google Colab**: A cloud-based platform by Google that allows users to write and run Python code using free GPU resources.
- **Variable**: A named reference to a value stored in memory, used to hold data for processing.
- **Identifier**: The name used to identify variables, functions, classes, etc., in Python. Must follow naming rules.
- **Data type**: Specifies the type of data a variable can hold, such as integers (int), floating-point numbers (float), strings (str), lists (list), and more.
- **Comment**: Non-executable lines in Python used to explain code, marked using #.
- **Keywords (reserved words)**: Words that have special meaning in Python, such as if, else, def, return, etc., and cannot be used as identifiers.
- **Operators**: Symbols that perform operations on variables and values.
    - o Arithmetic operators (+, -, *, /, %, //, **)
    - o Relational/comparison operators (==, !=, >, <, >=, <=)
    - o Logical operators (and, or, not)
    - o Assignment operators (=, +=, -=, *=, /=, etc.)
- **Expression**: A combination of variables, values, and operators that produces a result.
- **Script**: A file containing Python code meant to be executed all at once.
- **Interactive mode**: Running Python commands directly in the Python shell.
- **Integrated development environment (IDE)**: A software application like Jupyter Notebook, or Google Colab, that helps in writing and running code.

Multiple choice questions

1. **Which of the following is the main reason Python is popular for data science?**
   a. It is only used in web development
   b. It has complex syntax
   c. It has many useful libraries
   d. It cannot be used with data

2. **What is the correct way to write a comment in Python?**
   a. // This is a comment
   b. /* This is a comment */
   c. # This is a comment
   d. This is a comment

3. **Which of these is a valid Python variable name?**
   a. 2value
   b. value_2
   c. my-value
   d. class

4. **What type of operator is >= in Python?**
   a. Arithmetic operator
   b. Logical operator
   c. Assignment operator
   d. Comparison operator

5. **What does the int data type represent in Python?**
   a. Decimal values
   b. Whole numbers
   c. Text
   d. Boolean values

6. **Which of the following tools can be used to write and run Python code online?**
   a. MS Paint
   b. Notepad
   c. Google Colab
   d. VLC Media Player

7. **What is the purpose of = in Python?**
   a. It adds two numbers
   b. It compares values
   c. It assigns a value to a variable
   d. It prints the result

8. **Which of the following is true about Jupyter Notebook?**
   a. It is used only for creating presentations
   b. It cannot run Python code
   c. It allows you to write and run Python code in small cells
   d. It is not useful for data science tasks

9. **Which statement is true about identifiers in Python?**
   a. They can start with a number
   b. They can include spaces
   c. They are case-sensitive
   d. They can use symbols like @ and #

10. **Which of the following is a correct example of using a string data type in Python?**
    a. name = 123
    b. name = "Jubin"
    c. name = [1, 2, 3]
    d. name = True

Answers

1	c
2	c
3	b
4	d
5	b
6	c
7	c
8	c
9	c
10	b

Questions

1. Define the term data science.
2. Why is Python a suitable language for the data science field? Justify.
3. What are the features of Python?
4. What are identifiers?
5. What do you mean by indentation?
6. What do you mean by a variable?
7. What is a data type?
8. Explain the different types of operators along with suitable examples.

CHAPTER 2

Conditions, Loops, Control Statements, and Functions

Introduction

A program's flow can be controlled and decisions made based on certain conditions using conditional and control statements. The statements like as if and if-elif-else enable the program to run a block of code only in the event that a certain condition is true or to check several conditions sequentially. The control statements modify the loop's or conditional structure's typical execution flow. Apart from it, functions are covered in this chapter. Functions are blocks of reusable code that perform specific tasks. Packages and modules are used in Python to organize and structure code for improved reuse and maintainability.

Structure

The following topics are covered in this chapter:

- Conditional statements
- Loop control statements
- Functions
- Lambda function
- Modules
- Packages

Objectives

The main goal of this chapter is to provide students with the basic Python programming constructs they need to create effective, modular, and reusable code. These frameworks serve as the foundation for methodically resolving challenging problems. This chapter equips students with fundamental Python programming constructs that are essential for writing logical, efficient, and modular code. Through conditional statements and loop control structures, students learn how to manage the flow of execution in their programs. The chapter also introduces the concept of functions, including lambda functions for building reusable code blocks, which enhance readability and maintainability. Additionally, students gain exposure to the use of modules and packages, laying the groundwork for organizing larger Python projects effectively.

Conditional statements

If statements are used in Python for conditional execution, which enables your code to execute distinct code blocks in response to specific situations. In the case of the **if** keyword, a condition and a block of code that runs if the condition is **True** make up the fundamental building blocks of an **if** statement. **Elif** (else if) and **else** can also be used to handle various situations and give different code blocks, as shown in *Example 2.1*.

Example 2.1: Example using the if-else condition

In this example, the **input()** function is used to take the user's age from the keyboard. Since **input()** returns a string, **int()** is used to convert it into an integer. The **if** statement checks whether the age is less than or equal to 10. If true, it prints **You are a child**. If the first condition is false, **elif** checks whether the age is between 11 and 18. If true, it prints **You are eligible for voting**. If the age is between 19 and 65, the program prints **You are an adult**. If none of these conditions are true, the **else** block is executed, printing **You are a senior citizen**.

```
age = int(input('Enter your age'))
if age<=10:
    print("You are a child.")
elif 11<=age<=18:
    print("You are eligible for voting.")
elif 19<=age<65:
    print("You are an adult.")
else:
    print("You are a senior citizen.")
```

Figure 2.1 shows the output of *Example 2.1*:

```
Enter your age18
You are eligible for voting.

================================
Enter your age25
You are an adult.

================================
Enter your age60
You are an adult.

================================
Enter your age66
You are a senior citizen.
```

***Figure 2.1**: Output of the if-else condition*

Example 2.2 is another example of the **if** condition.

Example 2.2: Finding whether the number is even or odd using the if condition

In this example, a **number** is entered, and if the **number** is greater than 10, then the condition will be checked again, and if the **number** is divided by 2, and the remainder is zero, then the **number** is even; otherwise, it is odd. This is shown in the following code:

```
number = int(input("Enter a number:"))
if number > 10:
    if number%2 == 0:
        print("The number is greater than 10 and is even.")
    else:
        print("The number is greater than 10 and is odd.")
else:
    print("The number is 10 or less.")
```

The output obtained is shown in the following figure:

```
Enter a number:14
The number is greater than 10 and is even.

============================= RESTART: H:/DS/If_1.py
Enter a number:15
The number is greater than 10 and is odd.
```

Figure 2.2: Output of finding whether the number is even or odd using if condition

Loop control statements

Python loop control statements are used to change the way loops execute. They allow you to manage how loops are carried out, letting you skip iterations, break out of them, or go on to the next one. In Python, loop control statements are used to modify the behavior of loops. These include the **break** and **continue** statements.

Break statement

In some cases, it may be necessary to stop a loop early when a certain condition is met, rather than allowing it to complete all its iterations. Python provides the **break** statement for this purpose. To end the loop before it has iterated over every item, use the **break** statement as shown in *Example* 2.3.

Example 2.3: Example of break statement

In this example, a **for** loop is used, and an in-built **range()** function is used that generates a sequence of numbers. It is used with the **for** loop to repeat a block of code a specified number of times. The syntax of the **range()** function is **range(start,stop,step)**. Here, **start** is the starting number of the sequence. The default value is 0. **stop** is the ending number, which means that the sequence moves up to this, but does not include this number. **step** is the difference between each number in the sequence. The default value is **1**.

Take a look at the following:

```
for i in range(6):
    if i == 4:
        break  # Exit loop when i equals 4
    print(i)
```

Loop iterates from 0 to 5. Here, the **if** condition is used, and when the value of **i** becomes equal to **4**, the **break** statement will immediately terminate the loop. The output of this example is shown in the following figure:

```
= RESTART: C:/Users/LENOVO/AppData
0
1
2
3
```

Figure 2.3: Output of the break statement

Note: A common real-world example of using the break statement in Python is when searching for a specific item within a collection and wanting to stop the search as soon as the item is found. This prevents unnecessary iterations and improves efficiency.

Continue statement

In the **continue** statement, on encountering some condition, the current iteration of the loop is skipped, and it moves to the next iteration, as shown in *Example 2.4*.

Example 2.4: Example of the continue statement

In this example, on encountering the condition equal to **4**, the current iteration of the loop is skipped, and it moves to the next iteration:

```
for i in range(6):
    if i == 4:
        continue  # Skip printing 4
    print(i)
```

The output of the example is shown in *Figure 2.4*:

```
= RESTART: C:/Users/LENOVO/AppData/Local
.py
0
1
2
3
5
```

Figure 2.4: Output of the continue statement

For loop

Loops are used in Python to repeat a block of code multiple times, which is especially useful when working with sequences of data. One of the most commonly used looping structures is the **for** loop, which allows you to iterate over items in a sequence efficiently. A **for** loop iterates over a sequence like a list or a range, as shown in *Example 2.5*.

Example 2.5: Print numbers from 1 to 5 using a for loop

In this example, the **for** loop iterates over numbers from 1 to 5 and the **range()** function:

```
# Print numbers from 1 to 5 using a for loop
for i in range(1, 6):#range(1, 6) generates numbers from 1 to 5
    print(i)
```

The output of this example is shown in *Figure 2.5*:

```
>>>
    = RESTART: C:/Users/LENOVO/AppData/
    5.py
    1
    2
    3
    4
    5
```

Figure 2.5: Output of the for loop

While loop

A **while** loop repeats as long as a condition is True and it checks the condition at the beginning, allowing to execute the code, only if the condition is True. The working of the **while** loop is shown in *Example 2.6*.

Example 2.6: Print numbers from 1 to 5 using a while loop

In this example, a variable **i** is initialized to 1, and the **while** loop will check the condition in the beginning, and the loop will run as long as **i** is less than or equal to 5. In between the loop, the value of **i** will increment by **1**:

```
# Print numbers from 1 to 5 using a while loop
i = 1
while i <= 5:
    print(i)
    i += 1  # Increment i by 1 in each iteration
```

The output of this example is shown in *Figure 2.6*:

```
>>>
    ===================== RESTART:
    1
    2
    3
    4
    5
```

Figure 2.6: Output of the while loop

Example 2.7: Write a program for validating a password using the while loop and a break statement

In this example, a **break** statement in Python is used to exit a loop prematurely when a specific condition is met. This is especially useful when you do not want the loop to continue running through all its iterations. Here, a **while** loop will continue to iterate until the condition is **True**. A variable name is **'pwd'**, and if the password matches, then a message will be displayed that says **Password Correct. Access Granted**, and the **break** statement will execute to exit from a loop. Here, a **break** statement is used to exit the loop to stop further attempts:

```
while True:
    pwd = input("Enter password: ")
    if pwd == "python":
        print("Password Correct. Access Granted")
        break
    else:
        print("Incorrect! Try again.")
```

It is important to note that the statement **while True:** creates what is known as an infinite loop, meaning the loop would continue endlessly unless a stopping condition like **break** is provided. In this program, the infinite loop is intentional because the password check should keep asking until the correct password is entered.

The output window of this program is shown in *Figure 2.7 (a)*:

```
>>>
    ==================== RESTART: G:/DS/
    Enter password: python
    Password Correct. Access Granted
>>>
    ==================== RESTART: G:/DS/
    Enter password: PYTHON
    Incorrect! Try again.
    Enter password: Python
    Incorrect! Try again.
    Enter password: python
    Password Correct. Access Granted
```

Figure 2.7 (a): Output of the while loop and the break statement to check the password

The code can be improved by limiting the number of attempts to prevent the loop from running indefinitely in case of repeated incorrect inputs. The updated code is shown as follows:

```
# Password check with maximum 3 attempts
attempts = 0
max_attempts = 3
while attempts < max_attempts:
    pwd = input("Enter password: ")
    if pwd == "python":
        print("Password Correct. Access Granted")
        break
    else:
        attempts = attempts + 1
        print(f"Incorrect! Attempt {attempts} of {max_attempts}.")
else:
    print("Maximum attempts reached. Access Denied.")
```

The output of the code with a limit of maximum attempts is shown in *Figure 2.7 (b)*:

```
    Enter password: python
    Password Correct. Access Granted
>>>
    ========================== RESTART: G:/passwordcheck.py
    Enter password: Pyton
    Incorrect! Attempt 1 of 3.
    Enter password: Pythn
    Incorrect! Attempt 2 of 3.
    Enter password: Pythne
    Incorrect! Attempt 3 of 3.
    Maximum attempts reached. Access Denied.
```

Figure 2.7 (b): Limiting the number of attempts

Nested loop

A nested loop is a loop that runs inside another loop. In Python, it means placing one **`for`** loop (or **`while`** loop) inside another. The inner loop runs completely for each iteration of the outer loop.

Nested loops are useful when you need to repeat actions in two dimensions, such as printing patterns, working with rows and columns in a matrix, or generating combinations.

Example 2.8: Write a program demonstrating a simple nested loop

In this example, the outer loop runs two times (the third element is the upper bound, so the loop will iterate up to two). For each value of **`i`**, the inner loop runs three times, printing a pair of values. In total, it prints six lines. This is how nested loops help in performing repeated operations within another loop, especially useful in patterns and multi-level iterations:

```
for i in range(1, 3):# Outer Loop
    for j in range(1, 4):# Inner Loop
        print(i, j)
```

The output is shown in *Figure 2.8*:

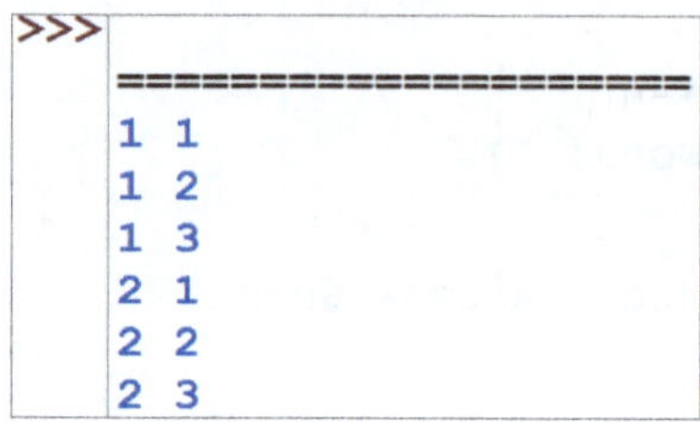

***Figure 2.8**: Output of the nested loop*

Example 2.9: Write a program to print a pattern using nested for loops

In this example, nested **`for`** loops are used to create a pyramid pattern with stars (**`*`**). The outer loop runs from the first to the number of rows (three in this case), controlling the number of lines in the pyramid. Inside it, the first inner loop prints spaces to align the stars in the center, while the second inner loop prints an increasing number of stars to form each level of the pyramid. The expression **`2 * i - 1`** ensures that the number of stars on each line is odd and increases by two with each row, creating the pyramid shape. The **`print()`** function at the end of each outer loop iteration moves the cursor to the next line:

```
n = 3
for i in range(1,n+1):
    for j in range(n-i):
        print(" ", end="")#Print spaces
    for y in range(2*i-1):
        print("*", end="")# Print stars
    print()# Move to the next Line
```

The following figure displays the output of a pyramid using a nested for loop:

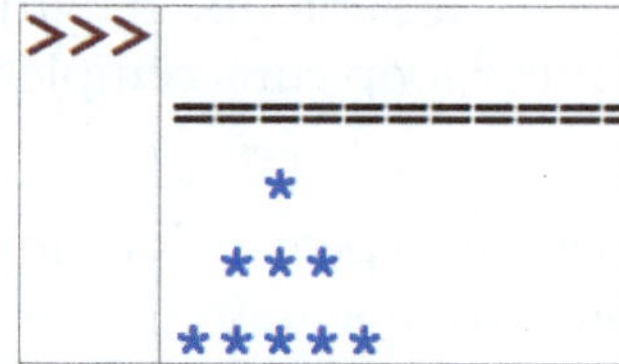

***Figure 2.9**: Output of pyramid using nested for loop*

Functions

In Python, functions are blocks of reusable code that perform specific tasks. Functions help organize and manage code more efficiently, especially when tasks need to be repeated. Functions allow you to:

- Break large problems into smaller, manageable parts.
- Avoid repeating code (reusability).
- Increase code readability and modularity.

User-defined and pre-defined functions

Functions can be broadly categorized into two types, which are pre-defined (built-in) functions and user-defined functions. While built-in functions come with Python and are ready to use, user-defined functions are written by programmers to perform specific tasks based on their requirements. Understanding the difference between these two types of functions is essential for writing clean, modular, and efficient code.

Basic structure of a Python user-defined function

A function in Python is defined using the **`def`** keyword, followed by the function name, parentheses `()`, and a colon `:`. The code inside the function is indented, just like any other block in Python.

To define and use functions effectively in Python, it is important to understand the essential components that make up a function. Each part plays a specific role in how the function is defined and executed. The following are the key components of a Python function:

- **Function name**: The name used to call the function. In *Example 2.8*, the function name is **`welcome()`**.
- **Parameters**: The values you pass to the function to work with. In this example, **`name`** is the parameter.
- **Docstring**: Triple-spaced quotes represent the optional explanation of the function's capabilities (`""" """`).
- **Code block**: The set of statements that make up the function. This block will execute when the function is called.
- **Return statement**: Functions can return a value using **`return`**. This is optional if the function does not need to return anything.

A simple example of defining a function in Python is shown in *Example 2.10*.

Example 2.10: Defining a function with a single parameter

In this example, a function is defined using the **def** keyword, and the name of a user-defined function is **welcome**. A function is called, and a parameter is passed into it, and the values **Sunil** and **Ajay** are passed as parameters to the function **welcome**:

```
# Defining a function
def welcome(name):
#This function greets the person whose name is passed as an argument."""
    print(f"Hello, {name}!")

# Calling the function
welcome("Sunil")  # Output: Hello, Sunil!
welcome("Ajay")    # Output: Hello, Ajay!
```

The output of *Example 2.10* is shown in *Figure 2.10*:

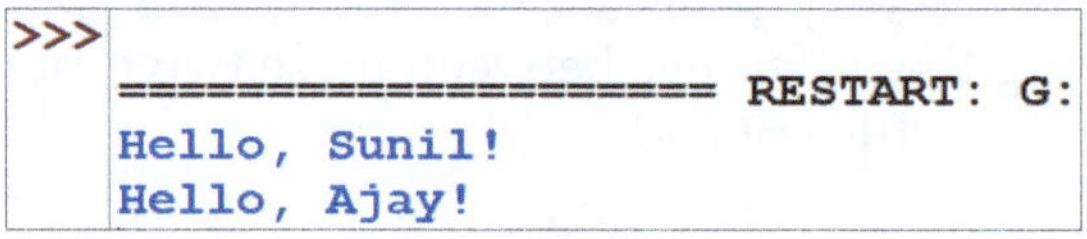

```
>>>
    ===================== RESTART: G:
    Hello, Sunil!
    Hello, Ajay!
```

***Figure 2.10**: Output of functions with parameters*

Example 2.11: Example of functions with multiple parameters

In this example, we can pass multiple parameters to a function. Here, a function **subtract()** is defined, and two parameters are passed into a function:

```
def subtract(a, b):
    return a-b

print(subtract(8, 4))  # Output: 4
```

The output window of *Example 2.11* is shown in *Figure 2.11*:

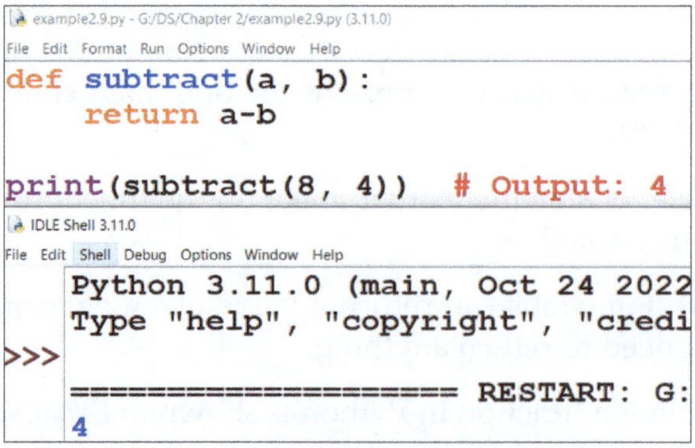

```
example2.9.py - G:/DS/Chapter 2/example2.9.py (3.11.0)
File  Edit  Format  Run  Options  Window  Help
def subtract(a, b):
    return a-b

print(subtract(8, 4))   # Output: 4

IDLE Shell 3.11.0
File  Edit  Shell  Debug  Options  Window  Help
    Python 3.11.0 (main, Oct 24 2022
    Type "help", "copyright", "credi
>>>
    ===================== RESTART: G:
    4
```

***Figure 2.11**: Functions with multiple parameters*

Example 2.12: Write a program for performing addition, subtraction, multiplication, and division using functions

In this example, a function can take multiple arguments and handle different operations like addition, subtraction, multiplication, and division. Here, a function name is **`calc()`** with parameters **`a, b, operation`**. The values are passed as arguments into a function **`calc()`**. The operations are checked using **`if-elif`** condition, and values are returned after the specific operations are performed:

```
def calc(a, b, operation):
    if operation == "add":
        return a + b
    elif operation == "subtract":
        return a - b
    elif operation == "division":
        return a/b
    elif operation == "multiply":
        return a*b
    else:
        return "Invalid operation"
print("Result after addition is:",calc(10, 5, "add"))
print("Result after subtraction is:",calc(10, 5, "subtract"))
print("Result after division is:",calc(10, 5, "division"))
print("Result after multiplication is:",calc(10, 5, "multiply"))
```

The output window is shown in *Figure 2.12*:

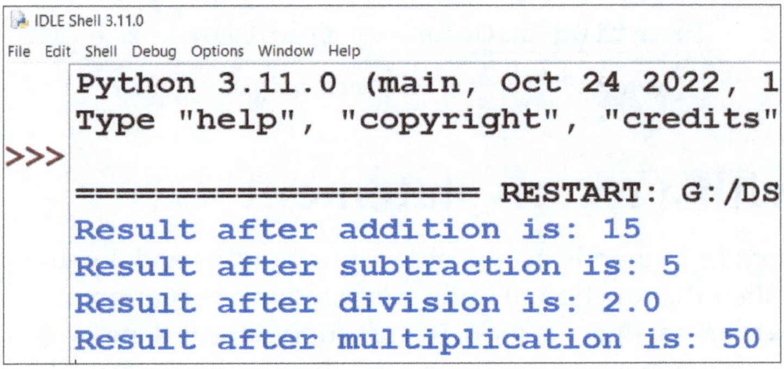

```
IDLE Shell 3.11.0
File Edit Shell Debug Options Window Help
    Python 3.11.0 (main, Oct 24 2022, 1
    Type "help", "copyright", "credits"
>>>
    ===================== RESTART: G:/DS
    Result after addition is: 15
    Result after subtraction is: 5
    Result after division is: 2.0
    Result after multiplication is: 50
```

Figure 2.12: Output of addition, subtraction, multiplication, and division using functions

Function scope

Function scope refers to the area in a program where a variable is accessible. In Python, variables defined inside a function are said to have **local scope**, meaning they can only be accessed within that function. On the other hand, variables defined outside any function have **global scope** and can be accessed anywhere in the program unless shadowed by a local variable of the same name.

Example 2.13: Write a program demonstrating the local and global scope of a variable

In the following code, **x** is a global variable and is accessible both inside and outside the function **display()**. However, **y** is a local variable defined inside the function and can only be accessed there.

Note: **Attempting to print y outside the function would result in an error because it falls outside its scope.**

```
x = 12  # Global variable
def display():
    y = 3  # Local variable
    print("Value of x Inside function: x =",x)
    print("Value of y Inside function: y =",y)
display()
print("Printing x Outside function: x =", x)
# This would cause an error, variable 'y' falls outside its scope
# print("Printing y Outside function: y =", y)
```

The output of this code is shown in *Figure 2.13*:

```
>>>
===================== RESTART: H:/DS/
Value of x Inside function: x = 12
Value of y Inside function: y = 3
Printing x Outside function: x = 12
```

Figure 2.13: Output of using local and global variable

Function with a return statement

The **return** statement in Python is used inside a function to send a value back to the part of the program that called the function. It ends the function's execution and provides the result to the caller. If no **return** statement is used, the function returns **None** by default. Using **return** makes a function more flexible because the returned value can be stored in a variable or used in another expression.

Example 2.14: Demonstrating a return statement in a function

In this example, the function **addition()** takes two parameters **x** and **y**, adds them, and returns the result using the **return** statement. When the function is called with the values **6** and **4**, it returns **10** in the local variable **add**, which is then stored in the variable **result_value**. The final result is printed using the **print()** function. Without the **return** statement, the function would not provide a value that can be used later in the program:

```
def addition(x,y):
    add = x + y
    return add

result_value = addition(6,4)
print("The sum is:", result_value)
```

The output of this example is shown in *Figure 2.14*:

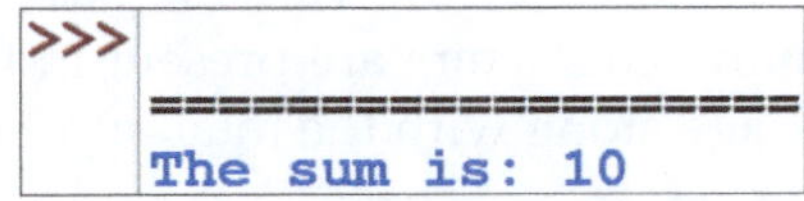

***Figure 2.14**: Output of the addition of two variables using a return statement*

Example 2.15: Write a program of finding a square of a number using the return statement

In this example, the function **square()** takes a single argument called number. It calculates the square of the given number by multiplying it by itself and returns the result using the **return** statement. When the function is called with the value **7**, it returns **49**, which is then stored in the variable **result** and printed. This shows how the **return** statement can be used to pass the output of a function back to the **main** program, where it can be used further if needed:

```
def square(number):
    return number * number

result = square(7)
print("The square of the number is:", result)
```

The output of this example is shown in *Figure 2.15*:

```
>>>
==================== RESTART: H:
The square of the number is: 49
```

***Figure 2.15**: Output of finding the square of a number using the return statement*

Pre-defined functions

Python offers a wide range of pre-defined (built-in) functions that are readily available for use without the need for any additional coding. These functions perform common tasks such as calculating values, manipulating data, or displaying output. They save time and effort by allowing programmers to carry out frequent operations with simple function calls.

String functions

String functions are pre-defined functions in Python that help you perform common operations on strings quickly and efficiently. For example, you can find the length of a string, convert its case, or check for certain characters without writing complex code. Using these built-in functions simplifies your programs and reduces errors.

Example 2.16: Write a program for finding the length of a sequence using a pre-defined function (len())

In this example, the program first uses the **`input()`** function to ask the user to enter their name. Whatever the user types is stored in the variable **`name`** as a string. Then, the **`len()`** function is used to count how many characters are present in the entered name. Finally, the **`print()`** function displays a message along with the total number of characters in the name:

```
name = input("Enter Your name:")
print("Hello,total characters in your name are:",len(name))
```

The output of this example is shown in *Figure 2.16*:

```
>>>
    ==================== RESTART: H:/DS/Chapter
    Enter Your name:Anil
    Hello,total characters in your name are: 4
```

Figure 2.16: Output of finding the length of a sequence using a pre-defined function

Numeric functions

Numeric functions are built-in Python functions that make working with numbers easier and more efficient. They allow you to perform operations like converting between data types, finding the maximum or minimum values, or calculating the sum of a set of numbers without writing long custom code. These functions help simplify calculations and reduce programming errors.

Example 2.17: Write a program for data type conversion using a pre-defined function

The program first prompts the user to enter their name using the **`input()`** function and stores it in the variable **`name`**. It then calculates the number of characters in the **`name`** using the **`len()`** function and displays the result with a greeting message. Next, the user is asked to input their age. Since **`input()`** always returns a string, the **`int()`** function is used to convert the entered age into an integer and store it in the variable **`age`**. The program then prints the **`age`** using the **`print()`** function. Finally, to demonstrate data types, the **`type()`** function is used to show that the **`name`** variable is of type **`str(string)`**, while **`age`** is of type **`int(integer)`**:

```
name = input("Enter Your name:")
print("Hello,total characters in your name are:",len(name))
# Convert age from string to integer
```

```
age = int(input("Enter Your Age:"))
print("Hello,Your Age is:",age)
# Display the type of variable
print("Data type of name variable is:", type(name))
print("Data type of age variable is:", type(age))
```

The output of this example is shown in *Figure 2.17*:

```
>>>
    ==================== RESTART: H:/DS/Chapter 2
    Enter Your name:Anil
    Hello,total characters in your name are: 4
    Enter Your Age:23
    Hello,Your Age is: 23
    Data type of name variable is: <class 'str'>
    Data type of age variable is: <class 'int'>
```

***Figure 2.17**: Output of data type conversion using a pre-defined function*

List or sequence functions

List and sequence functions are built-in Python functions designed to work with ordered collections, such as lists, tuples, or other sequences. These functions help you quickly find the length of a list, sum numeric elements, or perform other common operations without writing lengthy code.

Example 2.18: Write a program to analyze a list of marks using pre-defined functions

This example works with a list of marks and uses Python's built-in functions to analyze the data. The list **marks** contain five numerical values representing scores. The **max()** function finds the highest mark, while the **min()** function gives the lowest mark. The **sum()** function adds all the marks together to calculate the total score. Additionally, the **len()** function is used to determine the total number of students in the list:

```
# A list of marks (sequence of numbers)
marks = [23, 89, 63, 91, 85]
# Using numeric functions: min, max, sum
print("Highest mark is:", max(marks)) # Maximum value in the list
print("Lowest mark is:", min(marks))   # Minimum value in the list
print("Total sum of marks obtained:", sum(marks))  # Sum of all values
# Using list/sequence function: len()
# Length of the list (number of elements)
print("Total number of students:", len(marks))
```

After executing the code, the program applies built-in numeric and sequence functions to the list of marks to compute the highest score, the lowest score, the total marks, and the total number of students. The resulting output is shown in *Figure 2.18*:

```
>>>
==================== RESTART: H:/DS/Chapter 2
Highest mark is: 91
Lowest mark is: 23
Total sum of marks obtained: 351
```

Figure 2.18: Output of finding maximum, minimum, and sum using a pre-defined function

Note: A list in Python is a versatile and widely used data structure that allows storing multiple items in a single variable. It can hold different data types such as numbers, strings, or even other lists. Lists are ordered, mutable (changeable), and allow duplicate values. Although only a brief use of lists has been made here to support examples, a more detailed explanation of lists, along with related data structures like tuples, dictionaries, and sets, will be discussed in the upcoming chapter to help learners work more effectively with collections of data.

Math functions in Python

The **math** module in Python offers a range of mathematical functions for purposes like **sqrt** functions and power computation. In *Example 2.19*, some of the commonly used in-built functions of the math module are discussed, like **sqrt()**, **pow()**, **log()**, etc.

Example 2.19: Write a program demonstrating built-in math functions

In this example, the **math** library is imported using an **import** keyword. The in-built math functions like **pow()**, **sqrt()** and **log()** are used in the example:

```
import math
# Power
print(math.pow(3, 2))# 3 raised to the power 2
# Square root
print(math.sqrt(64))# Square root of 64
# Logarithms
print(math.log(10))# Natural log of 10
```

In order to use these built-in functions of the **math** module, the **import math** statement is to be used at the start of the program. The output of this example is shown in *Figure 2.19*:

```
>>>
= RESTART: C:/Users/DELL/AppData/Local
/mathfunctions.py
9.0
8.0
2.302585092994046
```

Figure 2.19: Output of math built-in functions

Random number functions

To create random integers, utilize the random package in Python. *Example 2.20* discusses a few of the common random functions. **randint()** is used to generate random integers between 20 and 30. In order to get a random choice from a list, the **choice()** function is used. To shuffle the numbers in a list, the **shuffle()** function of the random module is used in the example.

Example 2.20: Write a program demonstrating random number functions

This program demonstrates how to use the **random** module in Python to perform various operations related to randomness. First, the **random** module is imported, which provides built-in functions to generate random numbers. The program then shows how to generate a **random** integer within a specific range using **random.randint(20, 30)**. This function returns a random whole number between 20 and 30, including both endpoints.

Next, **random.random()** is used to generate a random floating-point number between 0 and 1. This is useful when working with probabilities or when a decimal value is needed. The example also shows how to randomly select an item from a list using **random.choice()**. In this case, a number is picked randomly from a predefined list of numbers. Finally, the program uses **random.shuffle()** to rearrange the elements of the list in a random order. This is done in place, meaning the original list is changed and then printed to display the new shuffled order:

```
import random
# Random integer between two numbers
print(random.randint(20, 30)) # Random integer between 20 and 30
# Random floating-point number between 0 and 1
print(random.random())  # Random float between 0 and 1
# Random choice from a list
numbers = [12, 23, 34, 45, 56]
print(random.choice(numbers)) # Randomly selects a number from the list
# Shuffle a list
random.shuffle(numbers)  # Shuffle the list in place
print(numbers)
```

The output of this example is shown in *Figure 2.20*:

```
>>>
    = RESTART: C:/Users/DELL/AppData/Local/Programs
    /randomfunctions.py
    30
    0.22087894357642168
    12
    [34, 12, 23, 45, 56]
>>>
    = RESTART: C:/Users/DELL/AppData/Local/Programs
    /randomfunctions.py
    28
    0.8366939929279815
    34
    [34, 56, 45, 12, 23]
```

***Figure 2.20:** Output of using random number functions*

Lambda function

A lambda function in Python is a short, unnamed function that can be created in a single line of code. This method is typically used for simple operations because creating a complete function with the **def** keyword would be overly complicated.

Lambda function versus def keyword for functions

The fundamental **lambda** function is employed to generate quick, simple functions without a standard **def** block. In *Example 2.21,* the program demonstrates how to add a value to a variable **x**, first by defining a function using the **def** keyword and then performing the same by using a **lambda** function.

Example 2.21: Write a program using the lambda function and using def

In this example, a value of **10** is added to a variable by using the standard method of function definition. In a similar manner, a **lambda** function is implemented for performing the same operation of adding the value **10** to a variable **x**. The **lambda** function is better to use as it performs the operation in a single line instead of a complex method of defining a function. The code is as follows:

```
# Normal function
def addition(x):
    return x + 10
print(addition(10))  # Output: 20
# Equivalent lambda function
lambda1 = lambda x: x + 10
print(lambda1(10))  # Output: 20
```

The output window is shown in *Figure 2.21*:

Figure 2.21: *Output of the program using normal function and equivalent lambda function*

map() function

In Python, the **map()** function is a built-in function used to apply another function to every item in a sequence, like a list or tuple, without using a loop. It returns a **map** object, which can be converted to a list, tuple, etc. The syntax of the **map()** function is **map(function, iterable)**. Here, a function can be built-in or user-defined that you want to apply, and a sequence means a list whose items the function will be applied to.

Example 2.22: Write a program demonstrating the functionality using the map() function

The **map()** function is useful when you want to perform the same operation on every element of a collection, such as squaring each number in a list. Instead of writing a loop, you can pass the function and the list to **map()**, which applies the function to each element and returns the results. In the example, the **square()** function is applied to each number in the list **[2,3,4,5,6]**, and the resulting squares are returned as a new list:

```
def square(n):
    return n * n


list1 = [2,3,4,5,6]
square_value = list(map(square,list1))
print(square_value)
```

The output of this code is shown in *Figure 2.22*:

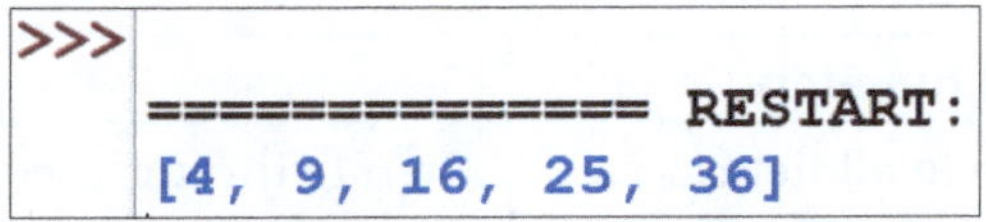

Figure 2.22: Output using map() function

Example 2.23: Write a program converting a list of strings to uppercase

In this example, a list has names in lowercase letters. We use the built-in **str.upper** method along with the **map()** function to convert each name to uppercase. The **map()** function applies **str.upper** to each element of the list names, and the result is then converted into a list using **list()**. This is a quick and clean way to perform the same transformation on each element of a list without writing a loop. Take a look at the following code:

```
list_names = ['ajay','chetan','dinesh']
# Using map to convert each name to uppercase
convert_upper = list(map(str.upper,list_names))
print("Letters in Uppercase are:",convert_upper)
```

The output of this code is shown in *Figure 2.23*:

```
>>>
============== RESTART: H:/DS/Chapter 2/codebundle/Exa
Letters in Uppercase are: ['AJAY', 'CHETAN', 'DINESH']
```

***Figure 2.23**: Output of converting a list of strings to uppercase using a map() function*

While **`lambda`** functions and the **`map()`** function are very useful for concise, one-line operations, beginners may wonder when to use them instead of normal functions (**`def`**) or traditional loops. To clarify this, *Table 2.1* provides a side-by-side comparison, showing the differences in syntax, use cases, and examples. This comparison helps you quickly decide which approach is most suitable for a given problem.

Feature	Lambda function	Normal function (def)
Definition	Anonymous, single-line function	Named function, can have multiple lines
Syntax	`lambda x: x*2`	`def double(x): return x*2`
Use case	Quick, short operations	Complex logic, multiple statements
Return	Always returns the expression result	Uses return statement explicitly
Example	`square = lambda x: x**2`	`def square(x): return x**2`

***Table 2.1**: Comparison of the lambda function and the normal function*

Tables 2.2 provides a side-by-side comparison of the **`map()`** function and **`for`** loop:

Feature	map() function	For loop
Purpose	Apply a function to all items in a sequence	Iterate through sequence with custom logic
Syntax	`map(function, iterable)`	`for item in iterable: ...`
Use case	Quick transformations of sequences	Complex operations, multiple steps per item

Example	`numbers = [1, 2, 3, 4, 5]`
	`doubles = list(map(lambda n: n*2, numbers))`
		`numbers = [1, 2, 3, 4, 5]`
		`doubles = []`
		`for n in numbers:`
		`    doubles.append(n*2)`

***Table 2.2**: Comparison of map() function and for loop*

Modules

A Python file (**`.py`**) that contains code (variables, classes, or functions) that you want to reuse in other areas of your program is called a module. It facilitates the logical organization of code and allows for its reuse across several files and projects. You need to follow two steps to run a module.

Creating a module

The following steps help with the process of creating a module:

1. To begin with, write a Python code that you want to reuse in a file.
2. Save the file with a **.py** extension **modulewelcome.py**:

```
# file: modulewelcome.py
# Save this file 'modulewelcome.py' in a folder

def welcome(name):
    return f"Hello, {name}!"
```

3. To use the functions or variables defined in the module, you **import** the module into another Python file:

```
# filename: main.py
# Save this file in the same folder
import modulewelcome

# Using the welcome function from welcomemodule
print(modulewelcome.welcome("Python"))
```

The output after running the **main.py** is shown in *Figure 2.24*:

```
>>>
= RESTART: C:/Users/DELL/AppData/Local/Programs
/module/main.py
Hello, Python!
```

Figure 2.24: Output of running a module

Packages

A package is a group of related modules that have been bundled together and stored in a directory that has the **__init__.py** file to identify it as such. This enables you to arrange your code more hierarchically. The following are the steps needed to be followed for packages:

1. Create a directory, i.e., a folder for the package.
2. Add a file named **__init__.py** in the directory (it can be empty or contain initialization code).
3. Include your modules (Python files) inside this directory:

```
mypackage/
    __init__.py
```

```
    arithmeticoperations.py
    stringoperations.py
```

stringoperations.py and **arithmeticoperations.py** are the Python modules used to organize related functions such as string operations and arithmetic operations into separate files, making the code more modular, reusable, and easier to maintain:

Filename: stringoperations.py

```
def upper(data):
    return data.upper()

def lower(data):
    return data.lower()
```

Filename: arithmeticoperations.py

```
def addition(a,b):
    return a + b

def subtract(a,b):
    return a - b
```

Filename: main.py

```
from packages import arithmeticoperations, stringoperations

# Using functions from the package modules
module1 = arithmeticoperations.addition(15,13)
module2 = stringoperations.upper("string")
print(module1)
print(module2)
```

The output of this code is shown in *Figure 2.25*:

```
= RESTART: C:/Users/DELL/AppData/Local/Programs/Python
y
28
STRING
```

Figure 2.25: Output using packages

In this code, both modules **arithmeticoperations** and **stringoperations** are imported from the **packages** directory. The **addition** function defined in the **arithmeticoperations** module is called here. In a similar manner, the **upper** function defined in the **stringoperations** module is called to convert the lower string passed to uppercase.

Note: To put it simply, a package is a group of related modules arranged in a directory with a __init__.py file, while a module is a single Python file with reusable code.

Conclusion

By the end of this chapter, students will be able to write reusable and well-structured code using functions, organize programs into modules and packages for better maintainability, and use iterative constructs to handle repetitive tasks efficiently. Python functions facilitate the writing of reusable and modular code, which simplifies the administration of complex projects. They add flexibility and functionality to your programs by accepting arguments, carrying out operations, and returning outcomes. The concepts learned in this chapter will also help students develop solutions for real-world problems that call for a combination of these topics. In the upcoming chapter, learners will go through the commonly used data structures in Python, like tuples, dictionaries, and sets, which help them to work more effectively with collections of data.

Points to remember

The following points are to be kept in mind:

- Conditional statements like if, elif, and else help us make decisions in a program based on different conditions.
- Loops like for and while are used to repeat a block of code multiple times.
- The break statement is used to stop a loop early when a specific condition is met.
- The continue statement skips the current loop cycle and moves to the next one.
- Functions are reusable blocks of code that help avoid repetition and keep programs organized.
- Built-in functions are functions that come with Python and are ready to use, whereas user-defined functions are written by programmers to perform specific tasks based on their requirements.
- You can define your own functions using the def keyword.
- Lambda functions are small anonymous functions used for simple one-line tasks.
- A map() function is a built-in function used to apply another function to every item in a sequence, like a list or tuple, without using a loop. It returns a map object, which can be converted to a list, tuple, etc.
- A module is a Python file with reusable code (functions, variables, etc.) that you can import into other programs.
- A package is a folder containing one or more modules, often used to group related functionalities.
- Using functions, modules, and packages helps in writing clean, structured, and manageable Python programs.

Key terms

- **Conditional statement**: A way to execute different code blocks based on certain conditions using if, elif, and else.
- **if statement**: Checks a condition and runs a block of code only if the condition is true.
- **elif statement**: Used after if to check multiple conditions one by one.
- **else statement**: Runs a block of code if none of the previous conditions are true.
- **Loop**: A way to repeat a block of code multiple times using for or while.
- **break statement**: Used to exit a loop early when a certain condition is met.
- **continue statement**: Skips the current iteration of the loop and moves to the next one.
- **Function**: A reusable block of code that performs a specific task when called.
- **Lambda function**: A small anonymous function defined using the lambda keyword, often used for short operations.
- **Module**: A Python file containing functions, variables, or classes that can be reused in other programs using import.
- **Package**: A collection of Python modules organized in directories, used to group related code together.

Multiple choice questions

1. **What will be the output of the following code?**

```
x = 7
if x > 5:
    print("Condition is True")
else:
    print("Condition not True")
```

   a. Condition is True b. Condition not True
   c. Error d. Nothing

2. **Which keyword is used to create a function in Python?**

   a. function b. def
   c. define d. fun

3. **What is the purpose of the break statement in a loop?**
   a. Skips the current iteration
   b. Ends the program
   c. Stops the loop immediately
   d. Repeats the loop again

4. **What will be the output of this code?**

```
for i in range(3):
    if i == 1:
        continue
    print(i)
```

   a. 0 1 2
   b. 0 2
   c. 1 2
   d. 0 1

5. **Which of the following is a valid lambda function?**
   a. lambda x, y: x + y
   b. def lambda(x, y): return x + y
   c. lambda(x, y) return x + y
   d. function lambda(x, y): x + y

6. **Which of the following is true about modules in Python?**
   a. They cannot be reused
   b. They are only for storing variables
   c. They allow code reuse across programs
   d. They slow down the program

7. **Which loop is used when we do not know how many times to repeat?**
   a. for loop
   b. while loop
   c. repeat loop
   d. do loop

8. **How do you import a module named math in your Python code?**
   a. include math
   b. using math
   c. import math
   d. use math

9. **Which of the following best describes a function in Python?**
    a. A list of numbers
    b. A tool to repeat code
    c. A named block of code that performs a task when called
    d. A loop used to filter values

10. **Which of the following is the correct use of an if-elif-else statement?**
    a. It checks all conditions even if one is true
    b. It is used to handle multiple conditions one by one
    c. It replaces the need for comparison operators
    d. It can only be used inside loops

Answers

1	a
2	b
3	c
4	b
5	a
6	c
7	b
8	c
9	c
10	b

Questions

1. What are conditional statements? Give suitable example.
2. Differentiate between break and continue statement.
3. What are loop control statements?
4. What is random number function?
5. What is the difference between functions and modules? Give a suitable example.
6. Discuss packages with the help of a suitable example.

CHAPTER 3
Lists, Tuples, and Dictionary

Introduction

Python provides flexible data structures for efficiently storing and manipulating collections of data, such as dictionaries, tuples, and lists. These structures help manage collections of data efficiently and allow easy access, modification, and organization. Since each data structure has a distinct function, Python is adaptable to a variety of programming tasks. A List is an ordered and changeable collection that can hold multiple values. It supports different data types and allows duplicate entries. Lists are useful when you want to store a group of related items and modify them later. A tuple is similar to a list, but it is immutable, meaning once it is created, its values cannot be changed. Tuples are preferred when you need to protect the data from unforeseen changes. A dictionary stores data in key-value pairs. Unlike lists and tuples, dictionaries are unordered and allow for fast access to data based on unique keys rather than numeric indexes. They are especially useful for representing structured data, such as a person's name, age, email, etc. This chapter introduces these data structures in detail, with examples to show how they are created, accessed, and used in real-world programming tasks.

Structure

The following topics are covered in this chapter:

- Brief introduction to chapter flow
- Lists
- Tuples
- Dictionary
- Iterators
- Python generators
- Sets

Objectives

After going through this chapter, you will be able to understand the differences between lists, tuples, and dictionaries, which are fundamental data structures in Python. You will explore predefined methods associated with lists and how they can be used to manipulate data effectively. Additionally, the chapter will help you understand the relationship between lists and tuples, highlighting their similarities and key differences. You will also learn about various dictionary methods used for storing and accessing key-value pairs efficiently. The chapter also introduces iterators and generators, enabling you to work with sequences of data efficiently and in a memory-friendly way. Additionally, you will learn about sets, which store unique elements and support useful set operations. By the end of this chapter, you will be equipped with a strong understanding of how to use these data structures and tools effectively in Python programs.

Brief introduction to chapter flow

The topics listed in the *Structure* form the foundation of Python programming. We start with lists and tuples to understand different types of collections, followed by dictionaries for key-value data storage. Next, we explore iterators and generators, which allow efficient traversal of sequences. Finally, sets are introduced to handle unique, unordered collections. By covering these topics sequentially, you will gain a solid understanding of Python's core data structures and iteration mechanisms. Before getting into the details, it is helpful to have an overview of the main topics covered in this chapter. The following table summarizes these topics along with a short description of each:

Topic	Description
Lists	Ordered, mutable collections of items.
Tuples	Ordered, immutable collections of items.
Dictionaries	Key-value pairs for efficient data lookup.
Iterators	Objects used to iterate over sequences.
Python Generators	Special iterators that generate values on the fly.
Sets	Unordered collections of unique items.

Table 3.1: *Overview of topics in this chapter*

Lists

In Python, a list is an ordered collection of elements that can store items of different data types, such as integers, strings, floats, or even other lists. Lists are mutable, meaning their contents can be changed; you can add, remove, or modify items after the list is created. Elements in a list are accessed using indexing, where the first element has index 0. Lists allow duplicate values, and their flexible nature makes them useful for tasks such as storing user inputs, grouping related data, and performing operations on sequences. Python provides many built-in methods like **`append()`**, **`remove()`**, **`sort()`**, and **`reverse()`** to easily manipulate lists.

Example 3.1: Write a program for a list

In Python, a list is a collection that can hold multiple values. These values can be of the same type (like all strings or all integers), or different types (a mix of string, number, Boolean, etc.). Lists are ordered, and we can access their elements using indexing. In this example, the **courses** list contains only strings, the **marks** list contains only integers, and the **dtype** list has mixed types: a string, an integer, a Boolean, and a float. Python uses zero-based indexing, which means the first element is at position 0, the second at 1, and so on:

```
courses = ['Python','Java','DotNet'] #string type
marks = [87,52,53,34,75]    #integer type
dtype = ['python',67,True,12.5] #mixed type
print(courses[0])  # Output: Python
print(courses[2])  # Output: DotNet
print(marks[3]) #Output:34
print(dtype[3]) #Output:12.5
```

In this example, the list **courses** consists of a string type, whereas the list **marks** is of integer type, **dtype** of mixed type. In these lists, the items are accessed from the 0th index.

The output of the example is shown in the following figure:

```
Python
DotNet
34
12.5
```

Figure 3.1: Displaying a list

These lists can be modified as shown in *Example 3.2*.

Example 3.2: Write a program for modifying a list

In this code, three different lists are defined and then modified to show that lists in Python are mutable, meaning their elements can be changed after the list is created. The first list, **courses**, initially contains three programming languages. The second element (**Java**) is replaced with **C++**, and the updated list is printed. Next, the **marks** list contains integer values, and the value at index 2 (**53**) is changed to **45**. Similarly, the **dtype** list is a mixed-type list containing a string, an integer, a Boolean, and a float. The last value (**12.5**) is modified to **10.5**. In each case, the original list is updated in place, demonstrating that lists are mutable and allow direct access and modification of their elements using index positions:

```
courses = ['Python','Java','DotNet'] #string type
courses[1] = 'C++'
print(courses)
marks = [87,52,53,34,75]    #integer type
marks[2]= 45
print(marks)
dtype = ['python',67,True,12.5] #mixed type
dtype[3]=10.5
print(dtype)
```

The output window of this example is shown in *Figure 3.2*:

```
['Python', 'C++', 'DotNet']
[87, 52, 45, 34, 75]
['python', 67, True, 10.5]
```

***Figure 3.2**: Output after modifying a list*

Example 3.3: Write a program using in-built methods of list

In lists, items can be added using the in-built methods **append()** and **insert()**. In a similar way, items can be removed from the list using the in-built methods **remove()**, **pop()**. The functionality of these in-built methods on lists is shown in this example. In this example, the operations performed using pre-defined methods **append()**, **remove()**, and **pop()** show how lists in Python are mutable, meaning their content can be changed after creation, items can be added, removed, or updated. The **append()** method is used to add a new item to the end of the list. In this case, **C++** is added to an already existing list. The **remove()** method is then used to delete a specific item by value. Here, **Java** is removed from the list. Finally, the **pop(0)** method is called to remove the item at index 0:

```
courses = ['Python','Java','DotNet']
courses.append('C++') #Added one more item.
print(courses)  # Output: 'Python','Java','DotNet','C++'
courses.remove('Java') #remove the item.
print(courses)  #Output: 'Python','DotNet','C++'
courses.pop(0)  #remove item at 0th position.
print(courses)  #Output:'DotNet','C++'
```

The output of this example is shown in the following figure:

```
>>>
= RESTART: I:/DS/List3.py
['Python', 'Java', 'DotNet', 'C++']
['Python', 'DotNet', 'C++']
['DotNet', 'C++']
```

***Figure 3.3**: Output using in-built methods of list*

Example 3.4: Write a program for finding the average of marks using a list

In this example, we have a list called **marks** that stores the scores of a student. The **sum()** function adds all the numbers, and **len()** gives the total number of **marks**. By dividing the total by the count, we calculate the **average** marks, shown as follows:

```
marks = [80, 91, 79, 93, 84]
average = sum(marks)/len(marks)
print("Average Marks:", average)
```

The output of this program is shown in *Figure 3.4*:

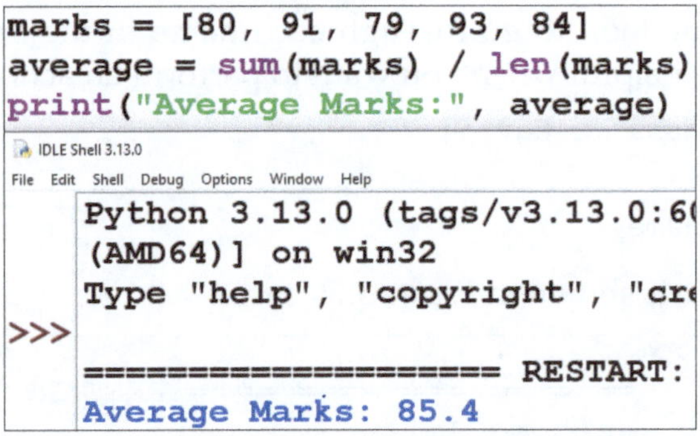

```
marks = [80, 91, 79, 93, 84]
average = sum(marks) / len(marks)
print("Average Marks:", average)
```

```
IDLE Shell 3.13.0
File Edit Shell Debug Options Window Help
    Python 3.13.0 (tags/v3.13.0:6(
    (AMD64)] on win32
    Type "help", "copyright", "cre
>>>
    ===================== RESTART:
    Average Marks: 85.4
```

***Figure 3.4**: Output window of finding an average*

Example 3.5: Write a program for reversing elements in a list

In this example, the **`reverse()`** method is used to change the order of elements in the list. This is helpful when you want to see the items from the last to the first:

```
courses = ['Python', 'Java', 'C++', 'C']
courses.reverse()
print("Reversed List:", courses)
```

The output window is shown in *Figure 3.5*:

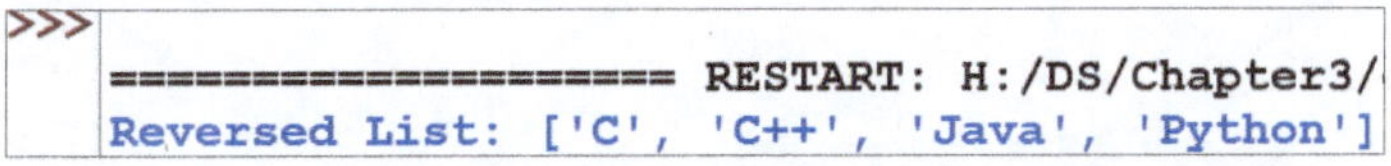

```
>>>
    ==================== RESTART: H:/DS/Chapter3/
    Reversed List: ['C', 'C++', 'Java', 'Python']
```

***Figure 3.5**: Reversing elements in a list using the reverse() method*

Example 3.6: Write a program for checking if an item exists in a list

This example uses the **`in`** keyword to check if a specific value exists in the list. It prints a message if **`Python`** is found. This is useful for searching in a list without writing complex code, shown as follows:

```
courses = ['Python', 'HTML', 'C', 'Java']
if 'HTML' in courses:
    print("HTML is available in the list.")
else:
    print("HTML is not found.")
```

The output window is shown in *Figure 3.6*:

```
>>>
    ===================== RESTART:
    HTML is available in the list.
```

***Figure 3.6**: Output of checking if an item exists in a list*

Example 3.7: Write a program using a for loop to print all items in a list

This example uses the **for** loop to go through each name in the **students** list and print a welcome message. This is helpful when you want to perform an action on every item in a list.

```
students = ['Amit', 'Neha', 'Ravi']
for name in students:
    print("Welcome", name)
```

The output of the example is shown in *Figure 3.7*:

```
>>>
    ======================== RESTART:
    Welcome Amit
    Welcome Neha
    Welcome Ravi
```

***Figure 3.7**: Printing all items in a list using a for loop*

Example 3.8: Write a program displaying a nested list or 2D list

A nested list, also called a two-dimensional list, is used to store both the **course** name and **marks** for each course. Each sublist contains two values: the **course** and its **marks**. The loop prints both values in a formatted sentence:

```
marks = [
    ['Python', 85],
    ['Java', 78],
    ['C++', 92]
]
for course in marks:
    print(f"Course: {course[0]}, Marks: {course[1]}")
```

The output of the example is shown in *Figure 3.8*:

```
>>>
    ====================== RESTART:
    Course: Python, Marks: 85
    Course: Java, Marks: 78
    Course: C++, Marks: 92
```

***Figure 3.8**: Displaying elements from a nested list*

Slicing in lists

Slicing in Python refers to accessing a subset of elements from a list using index ranges. It allows you to extract specific parts of a list without modifying the original list. The syntax of list slicing is: **list[start:stop: step]**. Slicing is helpful for tasks like getting part of a list, reversing a list (**list[::-1]**), skipping elements, and working with sublists without loops.

Example 3.9: Write a program to demonstrate basic slicing

In this example, a list **course** is created, and from list, using slicing, we extract elements from index 1 to 3 (index 4 is excluded):

```
# Original list
course = ['java', 'php', 'python', 'html']
# List with indices for understanding slicing
# Index:   0       1       2       3
# List:   'java'  'php'  'python' 'html'
# Slice:          [——————>——————>——————>]  course[1:4]
# Extract elements from index 1 to 3 (index 4 is excluded)
print(course[1:4])  # Output: ['php', 'python', 'html']
```

The output of the example is shown in *Figure 3.9*:

```
>>>
    ==================== RESTART:
    ['php', 'python', 'html']
```

Figure 3.9: Output using basic slicing

Example 3.10: Write a program to demonstrate slicing using step

In this example, the statement **course[0:5:2]** means to extract elements from the list starting at index 0 up to, but not including, index 5, taking every second element (i.e., with a step of 2):

```
course = ['java','php','python','html','IoT']
#Starts from index 0 to 4,skipping one element each time with step of 2.
print(course[0:5:2])
```

The output of the code is shown in *Figure 3.10*:

```
>>>
    =================== RESTAR
    ['java', 'python', 'IoT']
```

Figure 3.10: Output of slicing using step

Example 3.11: Demonstrate slicing operations by omitting start or end elements

In this program, the list named **course** contains five subjects: **['java', 'php', 'python', 'html', 'IoT']**. **print(course[:3])** line prints the elements from the beginning of the list up to index 2 (i.e., index 3 is excluded). The line **print(course[2:])** prints the elements starting from index 2 to the end of the list. The line **course[:3]** can also be written as **course[0:3]**. Take a look at the following code:

```
course = ['java','php','python','html','IoT']
# From beginning to index 2
print(course[:3])
# From index 2 to the end
print(course[2:])
```

The output of the example is shown in *Figure 3.11*:

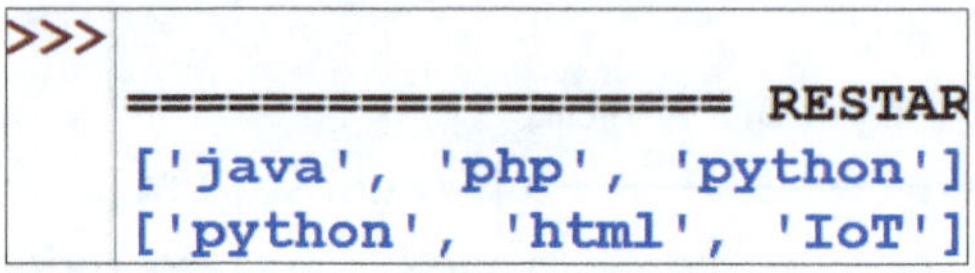

```
>>>
    ==================== RESTAR
    ['java', 'php', 'python']
    ['python', 'html', 'IoT']
```

***Figure 3.11**: Output of slicing by omitting start or end elements*

Example 3.12: Write a program for reversing a list using slicing

In this code, the slice **`[::-1]`** means start from the end and move backwards one step at a time. It is a quick way to reverse a list without using loops or functions. The code is as follows:

```
course = ['java','php','python','html','IoT']
print(course[::-1])
```

The output of the example is shown in *Figure 3.12*:

```
>>>
    =================== RESTART: H:/DS/Chapte
    ['IoT', 'html', 'python', 'php', 'java']
```

***Figure 3.12**: Output of reversing a list*

Example 3.13: Write a program extracting the middle part of list using slicing

In this example, elements will be extracted from index 1 to 3 (index 4 is not included):

```
course = ['java','php','python','html','IoT']
print(course[1:4])
```

The output is shown in the following figure:

```
>>>
    =================== RESTAR
    ['php', 'python', 'html']
```

***Figure 3.13**: Output of extracting the middle part of list using slicing*

Example 3.14: Write a program demonstrating start to stop and skipping elements with step in slicing

In this program, a list named **`marks`** is defined with five integer values. Here, we apply list slicing to extract specific elements from this list. The statement **`print(marks[2:])`** will start from index 2 and go up to the end of the list. The statement **print(marks[:3])** starts from the beginning of the list, i.e., 0th index, and stops just before index 3 (index 3 is not included). The statement **print(marks[::2])** starts from the beginning, i.e., 0th index, and goes till the end by picking up every second element (step=2). This is shown in the following code:

```
marks = [82,74,91,82,92]
print(marks[2:])#start from index 2 and go to the end
print(marks[:3])#start from the beginning and stop just before index 3.
print(marks[::2])#prints every second element starting from index 0
```

The output of the code is shown in *Figure 3.14*:

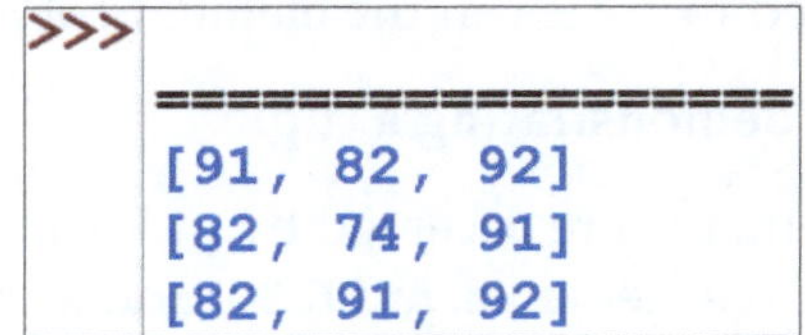

***Figure 3.14**: Output of using start:stop:step syntax in list slicing*

Example 3.15: Write a program for slicing with a negative step

This code prints the elements from the list **marks** in reverse order, starting from index 4 and stopping before index 1. It is a backward slice. In this example, a list slicing is done with a negative step, which means moving backward through the list. Here, we start at index 4, which is 92, then we have to go up to index 1, but not including index 1, and step -1 move in reverse, i.e., from right to left. In this code, we stop before reaching index 1. The statement **print(marks[4:0:-1])** will start at index 4 up to index 0 but not include index 0, and step -1 will move in reverse order:

```
marks = [82,74,91,82,92]
#start at index 4,go up to index 1 but not including index 1
#Step -1  move in reverse
print(marks[4])#Output:92
print(marks[4:1:-1])#Output:[92, 82, 91]
print(marks[4:0:-1])#Output:[92, 82, 91, 74]
```

The output of the code is shown in *Figure 3.15*:

```
>>>
==================
92
[92, 82, 91]
[92, 82, 91, 74]
```

***Figure 3.15**: Output of slicing with a negative step*

Note: A list in this format `list[start:stop]`, i.e., single colon `:` slices the list from the start index up to but not including the stop index. If start is omitted, it starts from the beginning. If stop is omitted, it goes to the end. The double colon `::` includes a step value. A list in this format `list[start:stop:step]` works like the single colon, but with an added step. Here, `step` controls how many elements to skip. It can also be negative for reversing the list.

Tuples

A tuple is similar to a list, but it is immutable, and once it is created, it cannot be modified. A tuple is created in *Example 3.16*. In this example, a tuple is created, and the value at the 0th index is accessed. Looping is performed to access all the elements of a tuple using the **`for`** loop.

Example 3.16: Write a program demonstrating a tuple

This code demonstrates that elements are accessed by index and iterates over all items using a loop. A tuple is created with three elements: **`Anil`**, **`34`**, and **`Python`**. Tuples are similar to lists but are immutable, meaning their contents cannot be changed after creation. Here, **`student_tuple[0]`** accesses the first item in the tuple using indexing and prints **`Anil`**. A **`for`** loop is used to iterate through all elements in the tuple. On each iteration, the variable **`student`** takes one value from the tuple and prints it:

```
student_tuple = ('Anil', '34', 'Python')
print(student_tuple[0])        # Output: Anil
for student in student_tuple:
    print(student)
```

The output of *Example 3.16* is shown in *Figure 3.16*:

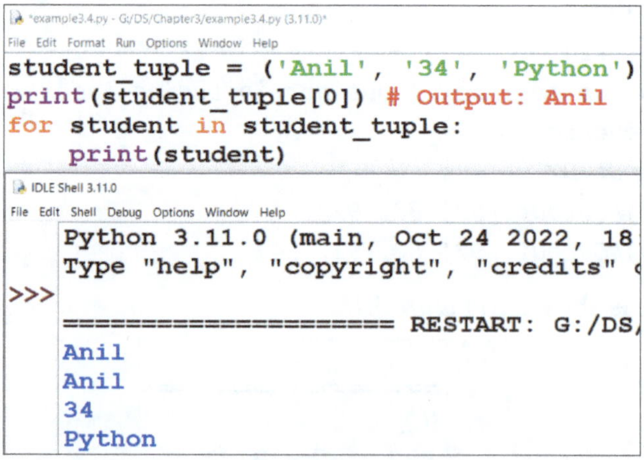

```
*example3.4.py - G:/DS/Chapter3/example3.4.py (3.11.0)*
File Edit Format Run Options Window Help
student_tuple = ('Anil', '34', 'Python')
print(student_tuple[0]) # Output: Anil
for student in student_tuple:
    print(student)

IDLE Shell 3.11.0
File Edit Shell Debug Options Window Help
Python 3.11.0 (main, Oct 24 2022, 18
Type "help", "copyright", "credits"
>>>
===================== RESTART: G:/DS/
Anil
Anil
34
Python
```

Figure 3.16: Output window of a tuple

In the example, if you try to add or remove an item in the tuple created, it will result in an error, as shown in *Figure 3.17*. The code is as follows:

```
student_tuple = ('Anil', '34', 'Python')
print(student_tuple[0])        # Output: Anil
student_tuple[1]='Vijay' # This result into error
for student in student_tuple:
    print(student)
```

The output with error is displayed in the following figure:

```
Anil
Traceback (most recent call last):
  File "H:/DS/Tuple1.py", line 3, in <module>
    student_tuple[1]='Vijay' # This result into error
TypeError: 'tuple' object does not support item assignment
```

***Figure 3.17**: Error window on removing some item in a tuple*

Example 3.17: Write a program for creating and accessing a tuple

In this example, a tuple is created, and its elements are accessed using index values. Tuples store fixed collections of items:

```
student = ('Akshay', 22, 'Python')
print("Name:", student[0])
print("Age:", student[1])
print("Course:", student[2])
```

The output of the program is shown in *Figure 3.18*:

```
>>>
    ==================== RESTART: H:
    Name: Akshay
    Age: 22
    Course: Python
```

***Figure 3.18**: Output of creating and accessing a tuple*

Example 3.18: Write a program for tuples with mixed data types

Tuples can store different data types like strings, numbers, and Boolean values:

```
details = ('Python', 3.13, True)
print(details)
```

The output of the program is shown in *Figure 3.19*:

```
>>>
    ==================== RESTART: H:
    ('Python', 3.13, True)
```

***Figure 3.19**: Output of mixed data type in tuples*

Example 3.19: Write a program for looping through a tuple

In this example, a **`for`** loop can be used to access each item in a tuple one by one, just like with lists:

```
courses = ('c++', 'c', 'php')
for n in courses:
    print(n)
```

The output of the example is shown in *Figure 3.20*:

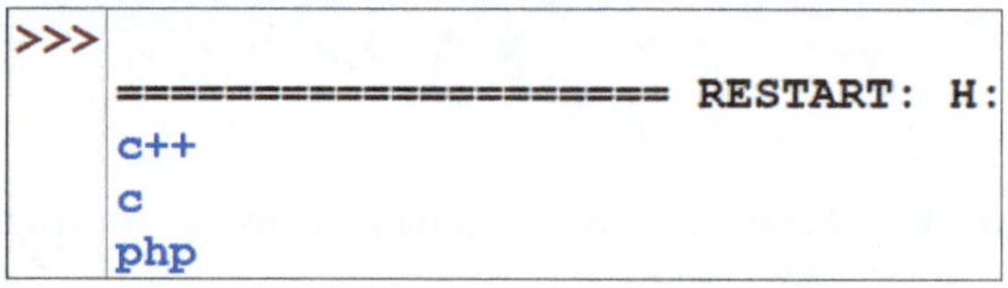

```
>>>
    ==================== RESTART: H:
    c++
    c
    php
```

***Figure 3.20**: Output window of looping through a tuple*

Example 3.20: Example of checking membership in a tuple using the in keyword

The **`in`** keyword checks whether an item exists in the tuple. This is useful for searching:

```
courses = ('c', 'c++', 'php')
if 'php' in courses:
    print("This course is available.")
```

The output of the example is shown in *Figure 3.21*:

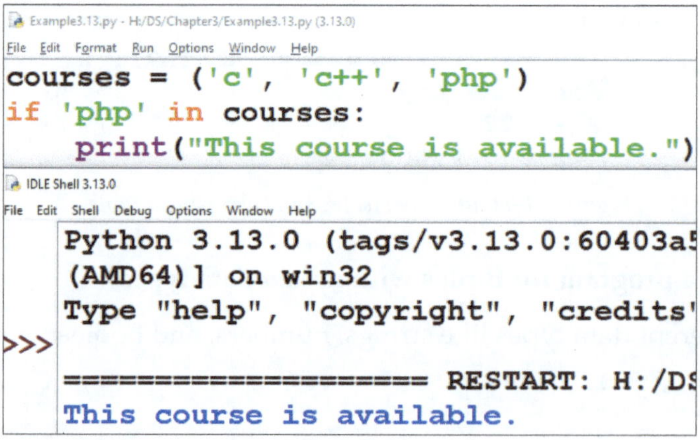

```
Example3.13.py - H:/DS/Chapter3/Example3.13.py (3.13.0)
File Edit Format Run Options Window Help
courses = ('c', 'c++', 'php')
if 'php' in courses:
    print("This course is available.")

IDLE Shell 3.13.0
File Edit Shell Debug Options Window Help
    Python 3.13.0 (tags/v3.13.0:60403a5
    (AMD64)] on win32
    Type "help", "copyright", "credits'
>>>
    ==================== RESTART: H:/DS
    This course is available.
```

***Figure 3.21**: Output of checking membership in a tuple using in keyword*

Example 3.21: Write a program for tuple unpacking

This example shows tuple unpacking, where each value from the tuple is assigned to its own variable in one step. In this example, all three values in a **`course`** variable will be passed into respective variables:

```
course = ('Java', 'Beginner', 120)
name, level, duration = course
print(f"Course Name: {name}")
print(f"Level: {level}")
print(f"Duration: {duration} hours")
```

The output window is shown in *Figure 3.22*:

```
>>>
    ===================== RESTART:
    Course Name: Java
    Level: Beginner
    Duration: 120 hours
```

Figure 3.22: Output window of tuple unpacking

Note: Beyond demonstrating immutability and iteration, tuples are useful in several practical situations:

- **Returning multiple values from a function**
- **As dictionary keys**
- **Grouping related data**

Let us look at these situations in more detail:

- **Returning multiple values from a function**: For example, a function can return a student's **name** and **grade** together as a tuple, as shown in the following example:

```
def get_student_info():
    return ("Anil", 85)

name, grade = get_student_info()
print(name)   # Output: Anil
print(grade)  # Output: 85
```

- **As dictionary keys**: Tuples can be used as keys to store combinations of items. For example, storing scores for a pair of subjects:

```
scores = {("Math", "English"): 95}
print(scores[("Math", "English")])  # Output: 95
```

- **Grouping related data**: Tuples can group items that should stay together and not change. For example, storing a product name and its price:

```
product = ("Laptop", 50000)
print(product)  # Output: ('Laptop', 50000)
```

Dictionary

In Python, a dictionary is an unordered set of key-value pairs. Every key is distinct and is used as a means of accessing the associated value. A dictionary is created using the symbols **{ ..... }**.

Example 3.22: An example of dictionary

In this example, a dictionary is created, and the items are accessed by their key:

```
student = {
    'name': 'Anil',
    'age': 34,
    'courses': ['Python', 'AI']
 }
print(student['name'])# Output: Anil
print(student['age'])# Output: 34
print(student['courses'])#Output:['Python','AI']
```

The output window is shown in *Figure 3.23*:

```
>>>
    ==================== RESTART: H:
    Anil
    34
    ['Python', 'AI']
```

Figure 3.23: Output window of a dictionary

Example 3.23: Write a program for modifying an existing dictionary

In dictionary, we can add a new key-value pair or modify an existing one. The code is shown as follows:

```
student = {
     'name': 'Anil',
     'age': 34,
     'courses': ['Python', 'AI']
}
print(student['name'])  # Output: Anil
print(student['age'])   # Output: 34

student['age']=35
student['semester']='Fifth'
print(student['semester'])# Output: Fifth
print(student['age'])     # Output: 35
```

The output is shown in *Figure 3.24*:

```
= RESTART: H:/DS/Dict1.py
Anil
34
Fifth
35
```

***Figure 3.24**: Output of modifying a dictionary*

Example 3.24: Removing items from a dictionary using pop() method

In a dictionary, in order to remove items, **`pop()`** is used to remove an item by key. In a dictionary, **`del`** is the keyword to remove an item or the entire dictionary, as shown in the following code:

```
student = {
    'name': 'Anil',
    'age': 34,
    'courses': ['Python', 'AI']
}
print(student['name'])  # Output: Anil
print(student['age'])   # Output: 34

student['age']=35
student['semester']='Fifth'
print(student['semester'])# Output: Fifth
print(student['age'])     # Output: 35
student.pop('age') #Removes an item by key
del student['courses'] #Removes an item or the entire dictionary

for key, value in student.items():
    print(key, value)  # Only prints name and semester
```

The output of the example is shown in *Figure 3.25*:

```
>>>
= RESTART: H:/DS/Dict1.py
Anil
34
Fifth
35
name Anil
semester Fifth
```

***Figure 3.25**: Output of a dictionary using in-built functions*

Example 3.25: Write a program of looping through a dictionary

The **.items()** method allows you to loop through both keys and values in the dictionary. It is useful for displaying all data:

```
student = {'name': 'Sunil', 'age': 20, 'course': 'Java'}
for key, value in student.items():
    print(key, ":", value)
```

The output is shown in *Figure 3.26*:

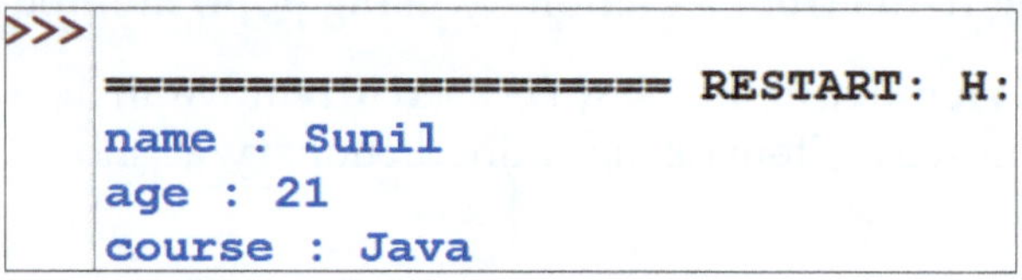

```
>>>
==================== RESTART: H:
name : Sunil
age : 21
course : Java
```

Figure 3.26*: Output of looping through a dictionary*

Iterators

An iterator in Python is a special type of object that allows sequential access to elements in a collection, such as a list or tuple. Instead of manually handling each element, iterators simplify repetition using loops. Python provides two essential methods to support iteration:

- **__iter__()**
- **__next__()**

These two methods form the basis of the iterator protocol. When an iterable object is passed to a loop (like a **for** loop), Python first calls the **__iter__()** method to get the iterator. Then, each time through the loop, the **__next__()** method is called to retrieve the next item in the sequence.

Example 3.26: Write a program iterating through a list using an iterator

Here, we convert the **courses** list into an iterator using the **iter()** function. Then we use the **next()** function to access elements one by one. Each call to **next()** gives the next item in the list.

```
courses = ['C','C++','Python']
n_iter = iter(courses)
print(next(n_iter))# Output:C
print(next(n_iter))# Output:C++
print(next(n_iter))# Output:Python
```

The output window of the program is shown in *Figure 3.27*:

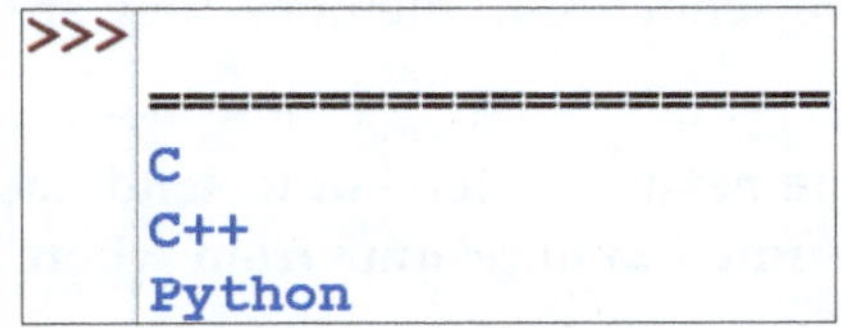

Figure 3.27: Output of iterating through a list using an iterator

Example 3.27: Write a program of iterating on a string

In this example, a string **"PYTHON"** is passed to the **iter()** function, which creates an iterator called **n_iter**. Using **next()**, we access each character of the string one by one. Strings are iterable in Python, and iterators can help fetch their characters in sequence.

The code is as follows:

```
txt = "PYTHON"
n_iter = iter(txt)
print(next(n_iter))  #Output: P
print(next(n_iter))  # Output:Y
print(next(n_iter))  #Output: T
print(next(n_iter))  # Output: H
print(next(n_iter))  # Output: O
print(next(n_iter))  # Output: N
```

The output of the code is shown in *Figure 3.28*:

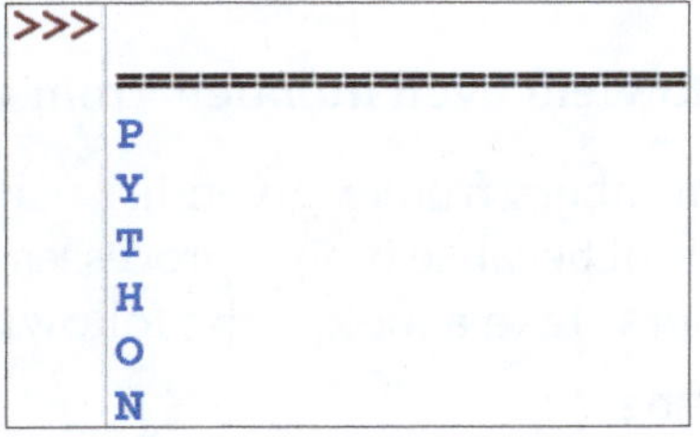

Figure 3.28: Output of iterating on a string

Python generators

Generators provide an easy and efficient way to create iterators in Python. Unlike traditional functions that use **return**, generators use the **yield** keyword to produce values one at a time as they are needed. They are defined using the **def** keyword, just like regular functions, but instead of returning a single value, they pause and resume with each call to **next()**. One of the key benefits of generators is that they simplify the code while being highly memory-efficient. Unlike custom iterator classes that require defining both **__iter__()** and **__next__**

`()` methods, generators allow for a more concise approach. Since they yield values on the fly rather than storing the entire sequence in memory, they are ideal for working with large datasets or infinite sequences.

Note: Generators do not use the `return` statement to send back values instead, they make use of yield, which allows the function to resume from where it left off.

Example 3.28: Write a program for a simple generator to yield numbers

This generator function **`display_numbers()`** uses **`yield`** to produce values one at a time. When used in a for loop, it returns 1, then 2, and then 3. After that, the loop ends automatically. This shows how a generator works, just like a loop, but yields values step by step:

```
def display_numbers():
    yield 1
    yield 2
    yield 3
for num in display_numbers():
    print(num)
```

The output of this example is shown in *Figure 3.29*:

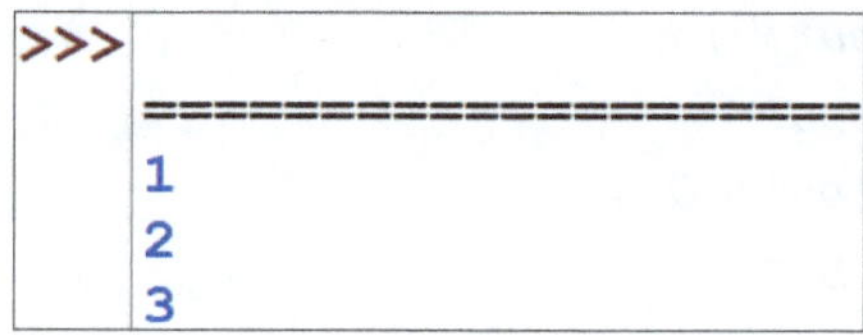

***Figure 3.29**: Output of simple generator to yield numbers*

Example 3.29: Write a program to yield even numbers from a list using generators

This generator filters out even numbers from a given list using the modulus operator `%` and yields them one by one. It is efficient because it only processes one number at a time instead of creating a new list of even numbers. Take a look at the following code:

```
def display_even_numbers(number):
    for n in number:
        if n % 2 == 0:
            yield n
nums = [8, 15, 32, 37, 50]
for even in display_even_numbers(nums):
    print(even,"is even number")
```

The output of the program is shown in *Figure 3.30*:

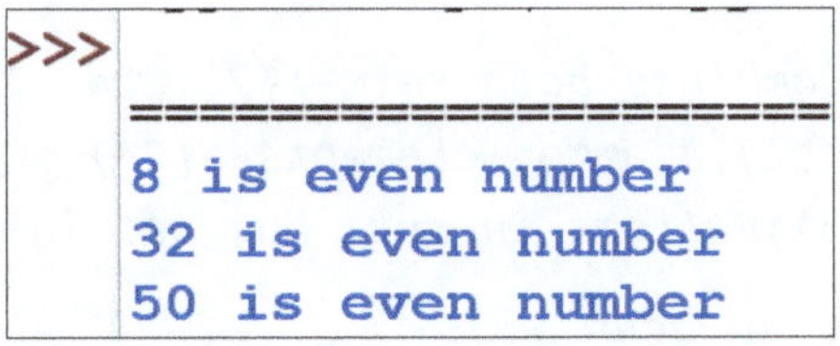

```
>>>
    =====================
    8 is even number
    32 is even number
    50 is even number
```

Figure 3.30: *Yield even numbers from a list using generators*

Sets

In Python, a **`set`** is a built-in data structure used to store multiple unique values in an unordered way. Sets are similar to lists and tuples, but they do not allow duplicate items and do not maintain the order of elements.

Sets are useful when you need to remove duplicates from a collection, perform mathematical operations like union, intersection, and difference. Sets quickly check if an item exists in a group of unique values or not.

Example 3.30: Write a program demonstrating sets in Python

In this example, even though **`'PHP'`** appears twice in the set definition, Python only keeps one copy because sets automatically remove duplicates:

```
courses = {'PHP', 'C', 'JAVA', 'PHP'}
print(courses)
```

The output of the program is shown in *Figure 3.31*:

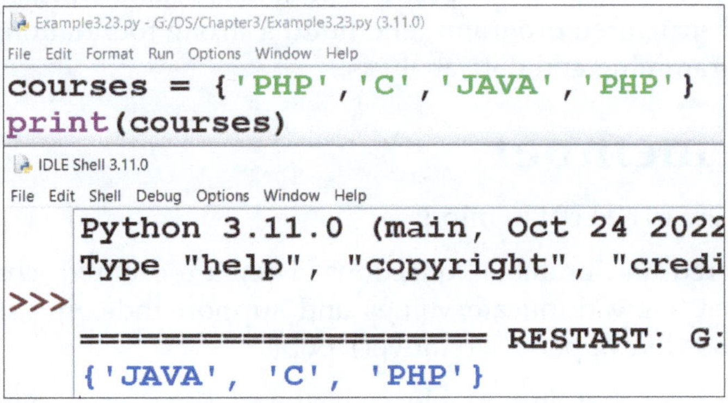

```
Example3.23.py - G:/DS/Chapter3/Example3.23.py (3.11.0)
File Edit Format Run Options Window Help
courses = {'PHP','C','JAVA','PHP'}
print(courses)

IDLE Shell 3.11.0
File Edit Shell Debug Options Window Help
    Python 3.11.0 (main, Oct 24 2022
    Type "help", "copyright", "credi
>>>
    ==================== RESTART: G:
    {'JAVA', 'C', 'PHP'}
```

Figure 3.31: *Output of sets*

Example 3.31: Write a program in Python demonstrating set operations

In this example, Python set operations **`union`**, **`intersection`**, and **`difference`** are demonstrated with the help of suitable code:

```
set1 = {12,24,13}
set2 = {23,24,25}
print(set1.union(set2))# Combines both sets->{23, 24, 25, 12, 13}
print(set1.intersection(set2))#Common elements->{24}
print(set1.difference(set2))# Items in set1 but not in set2->{12,13}
```

The output of the code is shown in *Figure 3.32*:

```
>>>
===================== RESTART: G:
{23, 24, 25, 12, 13}
{24}
{12, 13}
```

Figure 3.32: *Output of the Python set operations*

Conclusion

By the end of this chapter, students will be able to work confidently with Python's built-in data structures, such as lists, tuples, dictionaries, and sets, to organize and manage data effectively. They will understand how to store ordered or unordered collections, retrieve elements using indexing or keys, and apply common operations like updating, deleting, or iterating through values.

Students will also gain insight into iterators and generators, learning how to process sequences efficiently using Python's iterator and generator functions. These concepts equip learners with tools to write memory-efficient code that handles large or infinite data streams one item at a time.

The skills developed in this chapter will prepare students to handle practical data processing tasks, write clean and structured programs, and build a strong foundation for more advanced topics in Python programming and data analysis.

Points to remember

The following points are to be kept in mind:

- Lists are ordered and mutable collections. They are ordered, changeable (mutable) collections that allow duplicate values and support indexing, slicing, and various built-in methods like append(), remove(), pop(), etc.
- Tuples are ordered but immutable collections. They are ordered but immutable collections, meaning their values cannot be changed once created. They are used to store fixed data
- Dictionaries are unordered, mutable collections of key-value pairs. They store data as key-value pairs. Keys must be unique, and values are accessed using their corresponding keys. Useful methods include .get(), .items(), .update(), and .pop().

- Sets are unordered collections that do not allow duplicate values. Common set operations include union(), intersection(), and difference().
- Iterators are objects that allow you to access items one at a time using __iter__() and __next__() methods. Lists, tuples, strings, and sets are all iterable.
- Generators are a special type of iterator defined using the yield keyword. They produce values on the fly, making them memory-efficient and suitable for large datasets.
- The in keyword is commonly used to check whether a value exists in lists, tuples, dictionaries (keys), and sets.
- For loops can be used to iterate over all of these data structures.
- Use tuples when data should not change, and use lists when data needs to be updated or modified.
- Generators help reduce memory usage by yielding items one at a time instead of storing the entire sequence in memory.

Key terms

- **List**: An ordered and mutable collection of items that can include duplicates.
- **Tuple**: An ordered and immutable collection used for storing fixed sequences of values.
- **Dictionary**: A collection of key-value pairs where keys must be unique.
- **Set**: An unordered collection of unique elements, used to remove duplicates and perform set operations.
- **Indexing**: Accessing elements in sequences like lists and tuples using their position.
- **Mutable**: Objects that can be changed after creation, like lists, dictionaries, and sets.
- **Immutable**: Objects that cannot be changed after creation (e.g., tuples, strings).
- **Iterator**: An object that allows one-by-one traversal over a sequence using __iter__() and __next__() methods.
- **Iterable**: Any object that can be looped over (e.g., list, tuple, set, string).
- **Generator**: A function that produces a sequence of values using the yield keyword, allowing memory-efficient iteration.
- **Yield**: A keyword used in generators to return values without exiting the function.
- **pop()**: A method used to remove and return an item from a list or dictionary.
- **append()**: A method used to add an item to the end of a list.

- **add()**: A method used to add elements to a set.
- **get()**: A safe way to retrieve a value from a dictionary using a key.

Multiple choice questions

1. **Which of the following data structures in Python is immutable?**
   a. List
   b. Dictionary
   c. Tuple
   d. Set
2. **What will be the output of the following code?**
   ```
   my_list = [10, 20, 30]
   print(my_list[1])
   ```
   a. 10
   b. 20
   c. 30
   d. IndexError
3. **Which of the following is not true about dictionaries?**
   a. Keys must be unique
   b. Values can be duplicated
   c. Keys can be of any data type
   d. Duplicate keys are allowed
4. **Which keyword is used in generator functions to return values one at a time?**
   a. return
   b. yield
   c. pass
   d. def
5. **Which method is used to add an element to a set?**
   a. append()
   b. insert()
   c. add()
   d. push()
6. **Which method is used to safely access a value in a dictionary?**
   a. access()
   b. retrieve()
   c. get()
   d. fetch()

7. **Which of the following statements is true about tuples?**
   a. Tuples are mutable
   b. Tuples can be changed after creation
   c. Tuples are unordered
   d. Tuples can be accessed using a loop

8. **What is true about Python generators?**
   a. They store all values in memory
   b. They return values using the return keyword
   c. They generate values only when needed using yield
   d. They are slower than regular functions

9. **Which of the following best describes a Python dictionary?**
   a. A collection of unique items in order
   b. A group of key-value pairs
   c. An immutable group of values
   d. A random set of characters

10. **Which method is used to remove and return the last element from a list?**
    a. delete()
    b. pop()
    c. remove()
    d. cut()

Answers

1	c
2	b
3	d
4	b
5	c
6	c
7	d
8	c
9	b
10	b

Questions

1. What do you mean by lists?
2. How tuples are different to lists?
3. Discuss dictionary with the help of a suitable example.
4. What do you mean by sets? Give example.
5. Explain the concept of iterators and generators with the help of suitable example.
6. What is the purpose of the __iter__() and __next__() methods in Python? Explain with an example of an iterator.
7. Define a generator in Python. How is it different from a normal function? Write a generator that yields even numbers from 1 to 10.
8. What do you understand by slicing in lists? Illustrate slicing with three different examples using a list.
9. How can you reverse a list using slicing? Explain with an appropriate example.
10. Explain any four common set operations in Python with examples (e.g., union, intersection, difference, adding/removing elements).

Chapter 4
Exception Handling and File Handling

Introduction

This chapter covers the subjects of file handling and exception handling. Python's exception handling mechanism lets programmers deal with errors or exceptions in an easy manner while the program is running. In addition to preventing unexpected program crashes, this guarantees that the software can recover from errors and display informative error messages. An exception is a program execution event that breaks the program's regular flow. Apart from it, topics related to Python's file handling module allow you to read from and write to files. An exception is an event that disrupts the normal flow of a program, such as dividing by zero or accessing an invalid index. By using constructs like try, except, finally, and raise, developers can manage such events and provide informative messages to users.

In addition to exception handling, this chapter also covers file handling, which enables reading from and writing to files stored on disk. Python provides simple and powerful functions for working with files through its built-in file handling module. Students will learn how to open files, read content, write data, and close files securely using functions like open(), read(), write(), and close().

Structure

The following topics are covered in this chapter:

- Exception handling
- File handling

Objectives

The objective of this chapter is to equip students with the essential skills to write reliable, efficient, and user-friendly Python programs. A significant focus is placed on understanding and implementing Python's exception handling mechanisms, which are crucial for managing runtime errors in a structured and graceful manner. By learning how to use **`try`**, **`except`**, **`finally`**, and other related constructs, students will be able to build applications that do not crash unexpectedly but instead provide meaningful feedback to users when errors occur. This greatly improves the robustness and usability of their programs. Furthermore, the chapter emphasizes the importance of file handling, which allows programs to read data from and write data to external files. Through the use of Python's built-in functions like **open()**, **read()**, **write()**, and file modes, students gain practical knowledge on storing and retrieving information persistently. This skill is vital in real-world applications such as data logging, user input storage, and configuration management. By the end of this chapter, students will be confident in managing exceptions and handling files effectively, forming a strong foundation for more advanced programming tasks.

Exception handling

Python's exception handling feature allows you to deal with errors that arise while a program is running without halting it. It ensures that the software can continue running other code segments and handle unforeseen events gracefully. The following list gives a brief insight:

- **try** and **except** blocks are the statements that monitor the code.
- **try** block is a block of code that has the potential to raise an exception.
- **except** block is the code block that deals with the exception.
- **else** is the optional block that runs if no exceptions are raised.
- **finally** is an optional block that runs no matter what, often used for cleanup actions.
- **raise** is used to manually trigger an exception.

Example 4.1: Write a program for DivisionByZero and ValueError exception

The statements are monitored inside a **try** block, which attempts to execute the code. If the user enters 0, a **ZeroDivisionError** is caught in the **except ZeroDivisionError** block. If the user enters a non-integer value, a **ValueError** is caught in the **except ValueError** block. The **else** block runs only if no exceptions occur. The **finally** block executes regardless of whether an exception occurred or not:

```
try:
    num = int(input("Enter a number: "))
    result = 10/num
    print("Result is:", result)
except ZeroDivisionError:
    print("Error: You are dividing a number by zero.")
except ValueError:
    print("Error: Please enter a valid number.")
else:
    print("The input provided is Ok.")
finally:
    print("Thank you!")
```

The output of the example is shown in *Figure 4.1*:

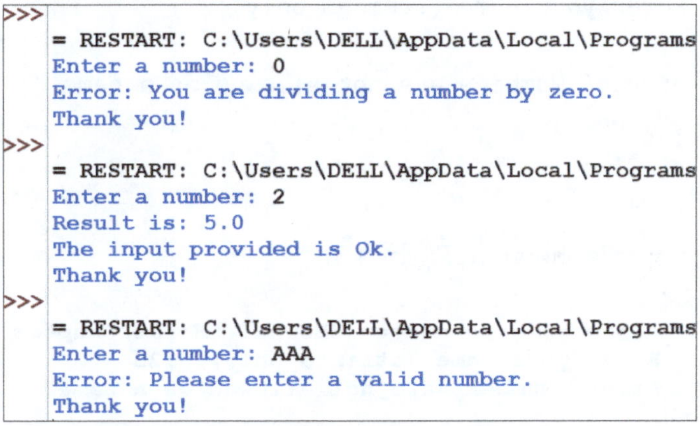

```
>>>
    = RESTART: C:\Users\DELL\AppData\Local\Programs
    Enter a number: 0
    Error: You are dividing a number by zero.
    Thank you!
>>>
    = RESTART: C:\Users\DELL\AppData\Local\Programs
    Enter a number: 2
    Result is: 5.0
    The input provided is Ok.
    Thank you!
>>>
    = RESTART: C:\Users\DELL\AppData\Local\Programs
    Enter a number: AAA
    Error: Please enter a valid number.
    Thank you!
```

Figure 4.1*: Output of DivisionByZero exception*

Example 4.2: Write a program for handling invalid input values using ValueError exception

In this example, if the user enters a text instead of a number, Python raises a **`ValueError`**, the program catches it, and displays a user-friendly message:

```
try:
    mob_no = int(input("Enter your mobile number: "))
    print("You entered mobile number:", mob_no)
except ValueError:
    print("Error: Please enter a valid number.")
```

The output of the program is shown in *Figure 4.2*:

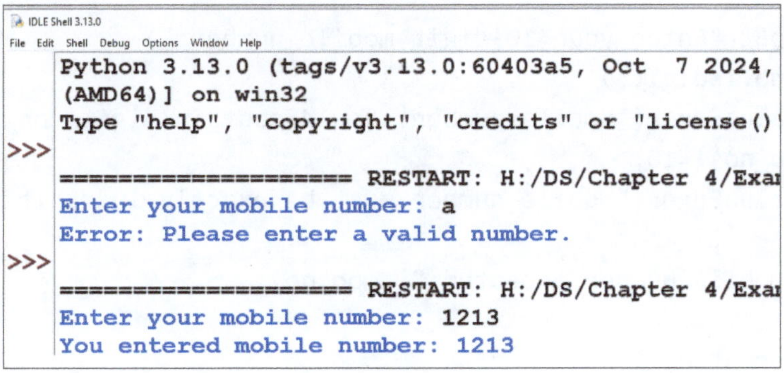

```
IDLE Shell 3.13.0
File Edit Shell Debug Options Window Help
    Python 3.13.0 (tags/v3.13.0:60403a5, Oct  7 2024,
    (AMD64)] on win32
    Type "help", "copyright", "credits" or "license()
>>>
    ==================== RESTART: H:/DS/Chapter 4/Exa
    Enter your mobile number: a
    Error: Please enter a valid number.
>>>
    ==================== RESTART: H:/DS/Chapter 4/Exa
    Enter your mobile number: 1213
    You entered mobile number: 1213
```

Figure 4.2*: Output of handling invalid input values using exception handling*

Example 4.3: Write a program for validating only string value

In this example, if the user enters only digits, it raises a **`ValueError`** with a custom message. The digit values are checked with the help of the prebuilt **`isdigit()`** function:

```
try:
    name = input("Enter your name (strings only): ")
    if name.isdigit():
        raise ValueError("Numbers are not allowed as a name.")
    print("Welcome,", name)
except ValueError as e:
    print("Error:", e)
```

The output of this example is shown in *Figure 4.3*:

```
>>>
    ==================== RESTART: H:/DS/Chapter
    Enter your name (strings only): 123
    Error: Numbers are not allowed as a name.
>>>
    ==================== RESTART: H:/DS/Chapter
    Enter your name (strings only): Anil
    Welcome, Anil
```

***Figure 4.3**: Output of validating only string values*

Example 4.4: Write a program for validating a 10-digit mobile number

This program takes the mobile number as a string and checks if the input contains only digits using **`.isdigit()`** function. It then checks if the length is exactly 10 characters using **`len()`** function, and if either condition fails, a **`ValueError`** is raised and handled with a user-friendly message. The **`exceptValueError`** statement checks that if a **`ValueError`** happens in the **`try`** block above, then it can be handled, and **`e`** is the object that captures the actual error message in a variable called **`e`**:

```
try:
    mob_no = input("Enter your 10-digit mobile number:")
    if not mob_no.isdigit():
        raise ValueError("Mobile number should contain digits only.")
    elif len(mob_no)!=10:
        raise ValueError("Mobile number must be exactly 10 digits.")
    else:
        print("Mobile number accepted:", mob_no)

except ValueError as e:
    print("Invalid input:", e)
```

The output of the above is shown in *Figure 4.4*:

```
>>>
    ==================== RESTART: H:/DS/Chapter 4
    Enter your 10-digit mobile number:12
    Invalid input: Mobile number must be exactly
>>>
    ==================== RESTART: H:/DS/Chapter 4
    Enter your 10-digit mobile number:1235678909
    Mobile number accepted: 1235678909
```

***Figure 4.4**: Output of validating a 10-digit mobile number*

Example 4.5: Write a program for file not found exception

In this example, a file named **test1.txt** is read from the **c:** drive, but if the file is not found in the current location, then file not found exception error will occur; otherwise, if the file is found, then the contents of the file will be displayed. Take a look at the following code:

```
try:
    f = open("c:\\test1.txt", "r")
    data = f.read()
    print(data)
except FileNotFoundError:
    print("Error: The file does not exist.")
finally:
    print("Closing the file.")
    try:
        f.close()
    except NameError:
        pass
```

The output of the program, considering two cases, i.e., when the file is present in the location given, and another case is when the file is not available in the current location, is shown in *Figure 4.5*:

```
>>>
    == RESTART: C:/Users/DELL/AppData/Local/Programs/
    Python is one of the popular language

    Closing the file.
>>>
    == RESTART: C:/Users/DELL/AppData/Local/Programs/
    Error: The file does not exist.
    Closing the file.
```

***Figure 4.5**: Output of the program for file not found exception*

Example 4.6: Write a program for TypeError exception

When a Python action or function is applied to an object of the wrong type, a **`TypeError`** is raised. For instance, attempting to combine an integer and a string will result in a **`TypeError`**:

```
try:
    # Adding a string and an integer
    result = "Python" + 3
except TypeError as e:
    print("Error of wrong type error:", e)
```

In this example, adding a string and an integer value results into **`TypeError`**, as shown in *Figure 4.6*:

```
>>>
== RESTART: C:/Users/DELL/AppData/Local/Programs/Python/Python311/typeerror.py
Error of wrong type error: can only concatenate str (not "int") to str
```

***Figure 4.6:** Output screen of TypeError*

Example 4.7: Write a program using else and raise in exception handling

In this example, the program asks the user to enter their **`age`**. If the input is not a valid integer or is less than or equal to zero, a **`ValueError`** is raised. The **`except`** block catches and displays a meaningful error message. If no exception occurs, the **`else`** block runs and confirms the valid age input entered.

Note: `raise` in exception handling is being used to manually trigger an exception when input is logically invalid, whereas `else` is executed only when no exception occurs.

Take a look at the following code:

```
try:
    age = int(input("Enter your age: "))
    if age <= 0:
        raise ValueError("Age must be greater than zero.")
except ValueError as e:
    print("Invalid input:", e)
else:
    print("Entered age value is correct:", age)
```

The output of is shown in *Figure 4.7*:

```
>>>
==================== RESTART: H:/DS/Chapter 4
Enter your age: 12
Entered age value is correct: 12
```

***Figure 4.7:** Output of checking an input value using else and raise in exception handling*

File handling

In Python, there are built-in functions which help to read, write, and modify the data in a file. In file handling, to open a file, Python provides the **`open()`** function, in which we pass two arguments, i.e., filename and access mode. The commonly used modes in file handling are:

- **`r`** is the read mode, which is the default mode for opening the file for read-only.
- **`w`** is the mode for writing. Using this mode, we can create a new file, truncate the existing file, or allow for writing.
- **`a`** is the mode for appending. This mode opens the file and writes at the end without truncating.
- **`r+`** is the mode for read and write both. It allows reading and writing to a file.

Example 4.8: Write a program for reading data from a file

In this example, first of all, manually create a new file named **`test.txt`** and enter some content into it. Data is read from **`test.txt`** using the **`read()`** function, and stored in a variable **`data`**:

```
# Open the file "test.txt" in read ("r") mode
with open ("c:\\test.txt","r") as file:
# Read the entire content of the file
    data = file.read()
  # Print the content on the screen
    print (data)
```

To read data from a file in Python, we use several built-in functions depending on how much content we want to read at once:

- **`read()`** is a function to read the entire file.
- **`readline()`** reads one line at a time.
- **`readlines()`** reads all lines and returns them as a list.

The output of the program after reading data from a file is shown in *Figure 4.8*:

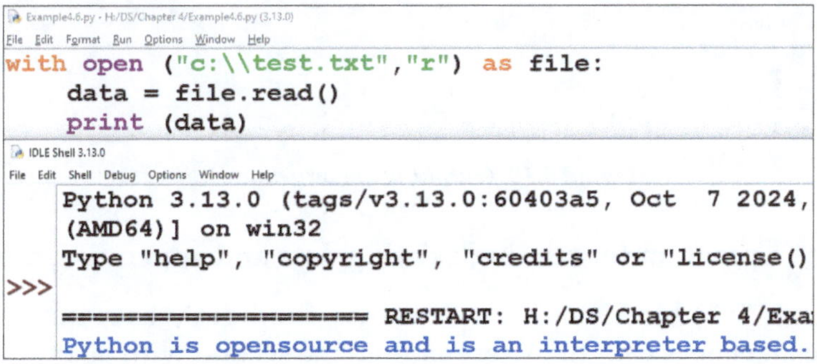

```
Example4.8.py - H:/DS/Chapter 4/Example4.8.py (3.13.0)
File Edit Format Run Options Window Help
with open ("c:\\test.txt","r") as file:
    data = file.read()
    print (data)
```

```
IDLE Shell 3.13.0
File Edit Shell Debug Options Window Help
Python 3.13.0 (tags/v3.13.0:60403a5, Oct  7 2024,
(AMD64)] on win32
Type "help", "copyright", "credits" or "license()
>>>
==================== RESTART: H:/DS/Chapter 4/Exa
Python is opensource and is an interpreter based.
```

Figure 4.8: Output window of data read from a file

Example 4.9: Write a program to write and append data into a file

In order to write data into a file, a pre-defined function **write()** will be used for writing to a file. If the file does not exist, it will be created:

```
with open("c:\\test.txt","w") as file:
     file.write("It is a sample data")
     file.write("Sample data to write into a file")
with open("c:\\test.txt", "a") as file:
    file.write("Adding a new line at the end.\n")
```

The output of the program is shown in *Figure 4.9*:

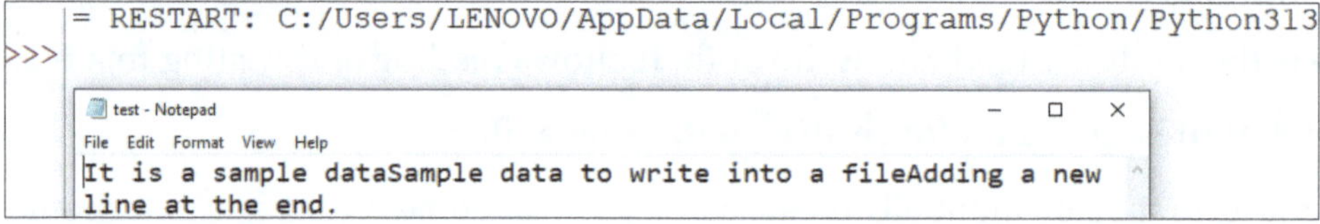

***Figure 4.9**: Output screen of writing and appending data into a file*

The data will be written into a file named **c:\\test.txt**. The file **test.txt** will be saved in the location where the Python code mentioned in *Example 4.9* is saved. In this program, it will append data to the existing file as well.

Example 4.10: Write a program demonstrating the use of the writelines() function

For writing multiple lines, we use **writelines()**, as shown in the following code:

```
lines = ["Line 1\n", "Line 2\n", "Line 3\n"]
with open("c:\\test.txt", "w") as file:
    file.writelines(lines)
```

In the output as shown in *Figure 4.10*, the string values **Line1**, **Line2**, and **Line3** will be displayed when writing this data into a file:

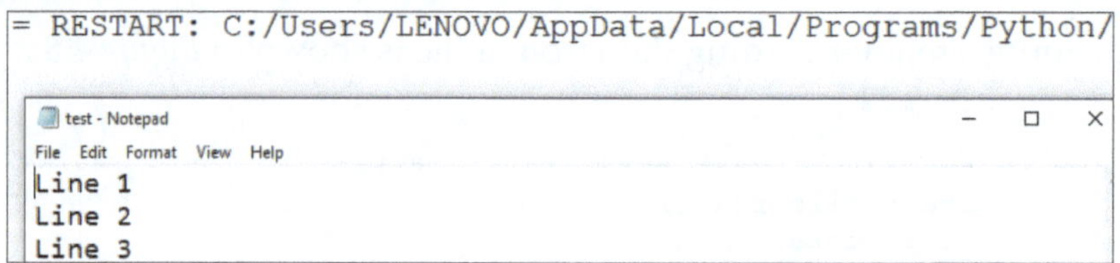

***Figure 4.10**: Output using writelines()*

Example 4.11: Write a program for reading existing data and appending new data to it

The with **open (..., "r")** block reads the file safely from **c:\\test.txt**. If the file does not exist, a **FileNotFoundError** is caught. After reading, the second with **open(..., "a")** block is used to **append** new content into a file **c:\\test.txt**:

```
# Read existing content from the file
try:
    with open("c:\\test.txt", "r") as file:
        content = file.read()
        print("Original Content in file:\n", content)
except FileNotFoundError:
    print("File not found. Creating a new one.")
# Append new content to the file using append mode 'a'
with open("c:\\test.txt", "a") as file:
    file.write("\nThis is new content added after reading.")
    print("New content has been added.")
```

In *Figure 4.11*, the already existing content of a file is displayed:

```
>>>
    ===================== RESTART:
    Original Content in file:
     Line 1
    Line 2
    Line 3

    New content has been added.
```

***Figure 4.11**: Output of reading data from a file showing already existing data*

On opening a file **`test.txt`** in the **`c:\`** drive, *Figure 4.12* shows the data that is being appended into this already existing file using the append **a** mode:

```
test - Notepad
File Edit Format View Help
Line 1
Line 2
Line 3

This is new content added after reading.
```

***Figure 4.12**: Data added into an already existing file using append a mode*

Conclusion

In this chapter, we explored two essential aspects of Python programming, which are exception handling and file handling. Exception handling enables programs to respond to unexpected situations, such as invalid input or division by zero, without crashing. By using constructs like try, except, else, finally, and raise, developers can make their programs more robust, readable, and user-friendly. We also learned how Python provides a simple and effective way to interact with files. Through file handling, we can read data from files, write data into files, or update existing content. Whether we use open() with different modes (r, w, a) or the safer with statement, file operations are a fundamental part of many real-world applications. By the completion of this chapter, students will be able to use exception handling techniques to write programs that are resistant to errors. It facilitates the development of apps that can store and retrieve data by interacting with binary files and text. Additionally, it aids in managing real-world situations where file operations and exceptions are essential.

Points to remember

The following points are to be kept in mind:

- An error usually refers to serious problems in the program (like syntax mistakes or running out of memory) that cannot be easily handled.
- An exception refers to unexpected events during program execution (like dividing by zero or opening a missing file) that can be handled using try-except. These are errors that occur during program execution and can interrupt the normal flow of a program.
- Python uses try-except blocks to catch and handle exceptions without crashing the program.
- The try block contains the code that may raise an exception.
- The except block handles the error, allowing the program to continue or exit gracefully.
- The else block(optional) runs if no exceptions occur in the try block.
- The finally block (optional) runs regardless of whether an exception occurred or not, typically used for cleanup actions.
- The raise keyword is used to trigger a custom exception manually.
- Common exceptions include ValueError, ZeroDivisionError, TypeError, FileNotFoundError, etc.
- Python provides built-in functions like open(), read(), write(), and close() to work with files.
- Files can be opened in various modes: r (read), w (write), a (append), b (binary), and x (create).
- Always close a file after use using file.close() or preferably use a with statement for automatic closing.
- The read(), readline(), and readlines() methods help read file content.
- The write() and writelines() methods are used to write content to files.
- File handling combined with exception handling is useful to manage cases like file not found or read and write errors smoothly.

Key terms

- **Exception**: An error that occurs during program execution.
- **try block**: The block of code where exceptions are anticipated.
- **except block**: The block that catches and handles exceptions.
- **else block**: Executes if no exception occurs in the try block.
- **finally block**: Executes regardless of whether an exception occurred or not.
- **Raise**: Used to manually trigger an exception.
- **ValueError**: Raised when a function receives an argument of the correct type but inappropriate value.
- **ZeroDivisionError**: Raised when division by zero occurs.
- **File Handling**: The process of creating, opening, reading, writing, and closing files.
- **open()**: A function used to open a file.
- **read(), readline(), readlines()**: Methods to read content from a file.
- **write(), writelines()**: Methods to write content to a file.
- **file.close()**: Closes the open file and frees system resources.
- **with statement**: Used for automatically managing file opening and closing.
- **FileNotFoundError**: Raised when trying to access a file that does not exist.

Multiple choice questions

1. **What is the purpose of the try block in Python?**
   a. To define a function
   b. To catch and handle errors
   c. To import a module
   d. To monitor error

2. **Which keyword is used to raise an exception manually in Python?**
   a. raise
   b. error
   c. exception
   d. throw

3. **What will happen if an exception occurs in a try block and there is no matching except block?**
   a. The program will stop immediately
   b. The error will be ignored
   c. The finally block will execute
   d. The program will fix the error automatically

4. **What is the purpose of the finally block?**
   a. It is only used for debugging
   b. It runs only if an error occurs
   c. It always runs, whether there is an exception or not
   d. It is optional and never used

5. **Which of the following exceptions occurs when dividing a number by zero?**
   a. NameError
   b. TypeError
   c. ZeroDivisionError
   d. FileNotFoundError

6. **What does the open('testfile.txt', 'r') command do?**
   a. Creates a new file
   b. Opens the file for writing
   c. Opens the file for reading
   d. Deletes the file

7. **Which of the following modes opens a file for writing and overwrites it if the file already exists?**
   a. a
   b. w
   c. r+
   d. x

8. **Which method is used to read the entire contents of a file as a string?**
   a. read()
   b. readline()
   c. readlines()
   d. write()

9. **What will file.close() do in Python?**
   a. Delete the file
   b. Save the file to the desktop
   c. Close the file and free up system resources
   d. Rename the file

10. **What type of error is raised when trying to open a file that does not exist?**
    a. IOError
    b. FileNotFoundError
    c. NameError
    d. SyntaxError

Answers

1	b
2	a
3	a
4	c
5	c
6	c
7	b
8	a
9	c
10	b

Questions

1. What do you mean by exception?
2. What are exception handling methods?
3. What do you mean by file handling?
4. What are the file handling modes? Give example.
5. What is the purpose of using try and except blocks in Python?
6. What is the difference between finally and else blocks in exception handling?
7. How can you open a file and write data into it in Python?
8. Write a short program that reads a file and handles the exception if the file is not found.

Join our Discord space

Join our Discord workspace for latest updates, offers, tech happenings around the world, new releases, and sessions with the authors:

https://discord.bpbonline.com

CHAPTER 5
Object-oriented Programming and Regular Expressions

Introduction

The principles of **object-oriented programming** (**OOP**) are discussed in this chapter. Python's support for OOP concepts, such as classes and objects, abstraction, and inheritance, is highlighted. Python supports OOP concepts. This chapter will cover key OOP principles such as classes, objects, inheritance, method overriding, encapsulation, and polymorphism. A class is a template for creating objects and consists of data members and methods. An object is an instance of a class. In classes, methods are defined to operate on object data using dot notation, enabling organized and reusable code structures.

In addition to OOP, this chapter also introduces **regular expressions** (**regex**) in Python, a powerful tool for pattern matching and string manipulation. Regular expressions allow searching, matching, and replacing text based on specific patterns, which is particularly useful in data validation, web scraping, and text processing tasks.

By the end of this chapter, students will not only be able to design modular, object-oriented programs, but also apply regular expressions to solve practical problems involving string data.

Structure

The following topics are covered in this chapter:

- Class and object
- Constructor
- Inheritance
- Polymorphism
- Abstraction
- Encapsulation
- Regular expressions and pattern matching

Objectives

This chapter aims to introduce students to the core principles of Python's OOP paradigm. It helps learners understand how classes serve as blueprints for creating objects, and how constructors are used to initialize those objects. The concept of inheritance is explored to demonstrate the parent-child relationship between classes and how it encourages code reuse and organization. The chapter also covers abstraction, enabling students to focus on essential features while hiding complex implementation details. Additionally, students will be introduced to regular expressions in Python, which are powerful tools for searching, matching, and manipulating text using specific patterns, an essential skill for working with real-world data and inputs.

Class and object

A class serves as a template for the creation of objects, specifying the methods and properties that the objects derived from the class will possess. An object is an instance or small entity of a class. When a class is created, it provides a structure. Using this structure, we create objects. In simple terms, a class is a blueprint or template that defines the properties (attributes) and behaviors (methods) that its objects will have. An object is a concrete instance created from a class, representing a specific entity that follows the structure defined by the class. A class describes how something should look and behave, while objects are the actual realizations of that description.

Example 5.1: Example of creating a simple class and object

This program defines a class called **`Student`**. Inside it, we use a *constructor* method **`__init__()`** to automatically set the student's **`name`** when a new object is created. When we create an object **`'s1'`** with the name **`Ajay`**, it stores that name, and **`print(s1.studentname)`** displays it. Take a look at the following code:

```
class Student:
    def __init__(self, name):
        self.studentname = name


# Creating an object of the class
s1 = Student("Ajay") #s1 is the object
print("Your name is:",s1.studentname)
```

The output of this is shown in *Figure 5.1*:

```
>>>
    =====================
    Your name is: Ajay
```

***Figure 5.1**: Output window of creating a simple class and an object*

Example 5.2: Write a program for creating objects using a class with a constructor and a method in Python

In this example, a class named **Student** is defined with two attributes **cname** and **cduration**. **cname** represents the course name, and **cduration** represents the course duration. A method named **display()** is defined using **def** keyword. Here, **student1** and **student2** are the objects of a class **Student**. On creating an object of a class, values will be passed into the constructor previously created. The method is also known as a function and is defined inside a class to describe the behavior or functionality of objects. The first parameter is **self**, which refers to the current object. In this example, **__init__** represents the constructor, which is a special method or function called when an object is created. It is used to initialize the attributes. The code example is as follows:

```
# Defining a class
class Student:
    # Constructor to initialize attributes
    def __init__(self, cname, cduration):
        self.cname = cname          # Attribute
        self.cduration = cduration # Attribute

    # Method to display details
    def display(self):
        print(f"CourseName: {self.cname}, CourseDuration: {self.cduration}")
# Creating objects (instances of the class)
student1 = Student("Java", "One Month")  # Object1
student2 = Student("Python", "One Month") # Object2
# Accessing attributes and methods
student1.display() #Output: CourseName: Java,CourseDuration:One Month
student2.display() #Output: CourseName: Python,CourseDuration:One Month
```

The output of this program is shown in *Figure 5.2*:

```
>>>
= RESTART: C:\Users\DELL\AppData\Local\Programs\Python
6.1_class.py
CourseName: Java, CourseDuration: One Month
CourseName: Python, CourseDuration: One Month
```

***Figure 5.2**: Output of class and object*

Note: The self parameter is used as the first parameter in methods defined within a class. It acts as a reference to the current instance of the class and is used to access variables and methods that belong to that specific object. It ensures that each object maintains its own data and behavior.

Example 5.3: Write a program demonstrating functions, i.e., methods in a class

In this example, a class **`Calc`** is defined with three functions: **`addition()`**, **`subtraction()`**, and **`multiply()`**. These are called methods when they are defined inside a class. The keyword **`self`** refers to the current object of the class. An object **`calc1`** of the **`Calc`** class is created to call its methods. The methods perform addition, subtraction, and multiplication on two given numbers, shown as follows:

```
# Define a class named Calculator
class Calc:
    # A method to add two numbers
    def addition(self,a,b):
        return a + b
    # A method to subtract two numbers
    def subtraction(self,a,b):
       return a - b
    # A method to multiply two numbers
    def multiply(self,a,b):
        return a*b

# Create an object of the Calculator class
calc1 = Calc()
# Call the add method
result1 = calc1.addition(25,20)
print("Addition of two numbers:",result1) # Output:45
# Call the subtract method
result2 = calc1.subtraction(25,20)
print("Subtraction:", result2) # Output:5
result3=calc1.multiply(2,3)
print("Multiplication:",result3)#Output:6
```

The output of this code is shown in *Figure 5.3*:

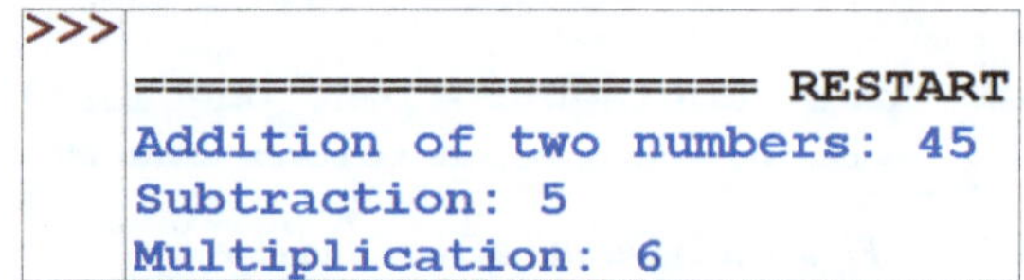

Figure 5.3: Output of performing operations using methods in a class

Constructor

A constructor is a special method or function in a class used to initialize the object's attributes when an object is created. In Python, the constructor is named as **__init__**. **init** means to *initialize*. The constructor is automatically called when an object of the class is created.

Example 5.4: Write a program demonstrating the concept of a constructor

In this example, a class with a constructor is defined. A class named **Student** is defined, and a constructor named **__init__** is defined, and three parameters are given. In these three parameters, **self** refers to the current object, **name**, **rollno** are the other parameters. The values will be passed to these parameters, the moment an object of a class is created. Here, **student1** is the name of an object, and the values **ABC** and **101** will be passed automatically into a constructor. A function **display** is called with the help of an object **student1**. The code example is as follows:

```
# Defining a class with a constructor
class Student:
    def __init__(self, name, rollno):
        self.name = name  # Initializing the 'name' attribute
        self.rollno = rollno # Initializing the 'rollno' attribute
    def display(self):
        print(f"Student Name: {self.name}, RollNo: {self.rollno}")
# Creating objects
student1 = Student("ABC", 101)
# Accessing attributes and methods
student1.display() #Output: Student Name: ABC, RollNo: 101
```

The output of this example is shown in *Figure 5.4*:

```
>>>
    = RESTART: C:/Users/DELL/AppData/Local/Programs/Python/
    6.2_constructor.py
    Student Name: ABC, RollNo: 101
>>>
```

Figure 5.4: Output of a constructor

Example 5.5: Write a program for defining a class with a constructor

The class **Course** uses a constructor (**__init__**) to initialize two attributes, i.e., **course_name** and **course_duration**. The method **display_details()** displays the course information. An object **course1** is created and initialized using the constructor. This helps demonstrate how constructors are used to assign values to class attributes when an object is created:

```
# Defining a class with a constructor
class Course:
    def __init__(self,course_name,course_duration):
        self.course_name = course_name #Initializing the 'course_
name' attribute
        self.course_duration =course_duration #Initializing the 'course_
duration' #attribute
    def display_details(self):
        print(f"Course Name: {self.course_name}, Duration: {self.course_
duration}")
# Creating an object of the Course class
course1 = Course("Python","1 Month")
# Accessing method to display details
course1.display_details()
```

The output of this code is shown in *Figure 5.5*:

```
>>>
    ===================== RESTART: G:/DS/Ch
    Course Name: Python, Duration: 1 Month
```

***Figure 5.5**: Output of defining a class with a constructor*

Inheritance

Inheritance is a fundamental concept in OOP that allows a derived class, also called a subclass, to inherit the properties and methods of a base class or superclass. This promotes code reuse, reduces redundancy, and supports the creation of a well-structured class hierarchy. It is a key principle of OOP that enables a class (called the subclass or derived class) to acquire the attributes and behaviors (methods) of another class (called the superclass or base class). This mechanism encourages code reusability, minimizes duplication, and helps build a clear and organized class hierarchy, where common functionality is defined once in the base class and extended or customized in the subclasses.

Example 5.6: Write a program demonstrating the concept of simple inheritance using constructors

In this example, **Student1** is the name of a parent class which contains a constructor to initialize **name** and **age** attributes. The child class name is **Student2**, which inherits from the class **Student1** and adds a new attribute, **regid**. It calls the parent class constructor using **super()** to initialize **name** and **age**. The **display_details()** method calls the **display()** method from the parent class to show the **name** and **age**, and then it prints the **regid**. The code example is as follows:

```
# Base class (Parent class)
class Student1:
    def __init__(self, name, age):
        self.name = name # Initializing the 'name' attribute
        self.age = age    # Initializing the 'age' attribute

    def display(self):
        print(f"Name: {self.name}, Age: {self.age}")
# Derived class(Child class) inherits from Student1 class
class Student2(Student1):
    def __init__(self, name, age, regid):
        # Calling the constructor of the parent class (Student1)
        super().__init__(name, age)
# Initializing the 'regid' attribute specific to Student2 class
        self.regid = regid

    def display_details(self):
        self.display()  # Calling the display method of the parent class
        print(f"RegId: {self.regid}")
# Creating an object of the derived class (child class)
s2 = Student2("Sunil", 20, 101)
# Accessing the methods and attributes
s2.display_details()
# Output: Name: Sunil, Age: 20, RegId: 101
```

The output of this code is shown in *Figure 5.6*:

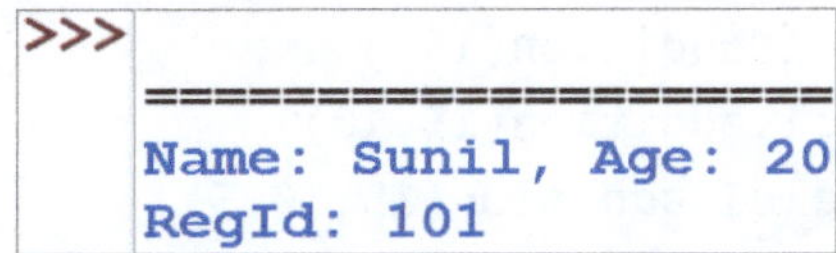

Figure 5.6: Output using a concept of simple inheritance using constructors

Note: `super()` is a built-in function in Python which is used in inheritance to call a method (usually the constructor) from the parent class. When a child class inherits from a parent class, and we want to reuse the code from the parent, especially the `__init__()` constructor, we use `super()`. Always prefer using `super().__init__()` in inheritance when calling the parent class constructor. `super()` is the preferred and cleaner way to inherit and initialize attributes from the parent class. In the absence of `super()`, we will need to manually initialize the attributes from the parent class (`Student1`) inside the child class (`Student2`). `super()` lets you reuse code from the parent class and it helps in avoiding repetition. It is especially useful when working with inheritance.

Polymorphism

Polymorphism means taking more than one form. It allows the same method or function to behave differently based on the object it is acting upon. Polymorphism in Python generally refers to method overriding and method overloading. Method overriding means using the same method name in both the parent and child classes, but with different behavior. Although method overloading is not natively supported in Python like in some other languages, similar functionality can be achieved using default arguments.

Method overloading

Method overloading refers to multiple methods with the same name but different parameters, as shown in *Example 5.7*. This example shows how default parameter values in Python functions can allow a method to behave differently depending on the number of arguments, which is a form of polymorphism.

Example 5.7: Write a program that demonstrates behavior similar to method overloading

A class named **`Calc`** is defined, and inside the class, there is a method **`addition()`** which takes one required parameter **`a`**, and two optional parameters **`b`** and **`c`**. These optional parameters have default values of 0. Here, the **`addition()`** method is to be called with one, two, or three arguments. In this code, a method named **`addition()`** is the same but has different parameters, as shown in the following code:

```
class Calc:
    def addition(self,a,b=0,c=0):
        return a+b+c

calc1 = Calc() #calc1 is object of class Calc
print("One Parameter:",calc1.addition(15))
print("Two Parameter:",calc1.addition(15,10))
print("Three Parameter:",calc1.addition(15,10,5))
```

The output of this code is shown in *Figure 5.7*:

```
>>>
    =====================
    One Parameter: 15
    Two Parameter: 25
    Three Parameter: 30
```

Figure 5.7: Output using a concept of method overloading

Method overriding

Method overriding means using the same method name in both the parent and child classes, but with different behavior. It occurs when a subclass provides its own implementation of a method that is already defined in its parent class. While the method name and parameters remain the same, the behavior is redefined in the subclass to suit its specific requirements.

Example 5.8: Write a program demonstrating the concept of method overriding

In this example, a **`CourseDetail`** is the base class with a method **`display_detail()`** that prints **`duration`** and **`fees`**. **`CourseName`** is a subclass of **`CourseDetail`** that overrides the **`display_detail()`** method to print only the course name. Even though both classes have a method with the same name, the output differs depending on which class's object is calling it. This is **polymorphism** in action and is an example of runtime polymorphism, where the method call is resolved at runtime depending on the object type. The code example is as follows:

```
# Parent class
class CourseDetail:
    def __init__(self,duration,fees):
        self.duration = duration
        self.fees = fees

    def display_detail(self):
        print(self.duration,"is the duration and",self.fees,"is the fees of
the course.")

# Child class(Subclass)
class CourseName(CourseDetail):
    def __init__(self, name):
        self.name = name

    def display_detail(self):
        print(self.name,"is the name of the course.")

# Creating objects
C1 = CourseName("Php") # 'C1' is the object of CourseName class
C2 = CourseDetail("4 weeks", 4000) # 'C2' is the object of # CourseDetail
class

# Method overriding in action
C1.display_detail()
C2.display_detail()
```

The output of the given code is shown in *Figure 5.8*:

```
Php is the name of the course.
4 weeks is the duration and 4000 is the fees of the course.
```

***Figure 5.8**: Output showing method overriding behavior*

Example 5.9: Another example of using method overriding

In this example, all classes **Animal**, **Dog**, and **Lion** have a method named **make_sound()**, but each gives a different output. Even though we call the same method **make_sound()**, the behavior changes based on the object type, like **animal1, animal2**, and **animal3**. On calling a method **make_sound()** from object **animal1**, the output is **Animals make sound**, and on calling a method **make_sound()** using object **animal2**, the output is **Dog barks**, whereas on using object **animal3**, the output will be **Lion roars**. Here, we have achieved polymorphism through method overriding, which shows that the method name is the same, i.e., **make_sound()**, but with different behaviors. The code example is as follows:

```
class Animal:
    def make_sound(self):
        print("Animals make sound")
class Dog(Animal):
    def make_sound(self):
        print("Dog barks")
class Lion(Animal):
    def make_sound(self):
        print("Lion roars")

# Using polymorphism
animal1 = Animal() #animal1 is the object of Animal class
animal1.make_sound()
animal2=Dog() #animal2 is the object of Dog class
animal2.make_sound()
animal3=Lion() #animal3 is the object of Cat class
animal3.make_sound()
```

The output of this code is shown in *Figure 5.9*:

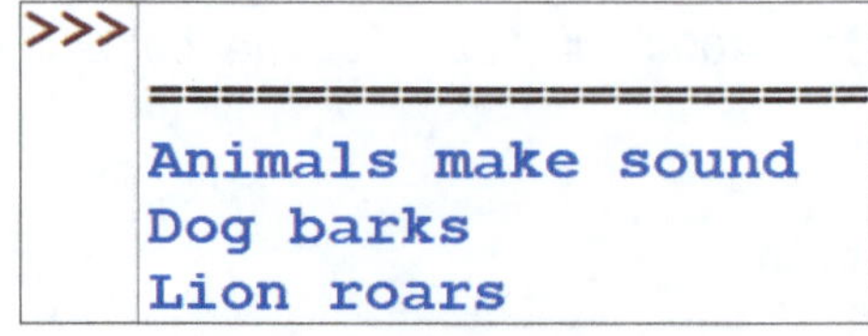

***Figure 5.9**: Output of using similar method make_sound() but with different behaviors*

Abstraction

The concept of abstraction involves the definition of a base class that contains a method that is then overridden by child classes in order to carry out the actions that are specified. Abstract classes act as blueprints for other classes and cannot be instantiated directly. The base class contains abstract methods, which are implemented in the child classes.

Example 5.10: Write a program demonstrating the concept of Abstraction

In this example, a base class **`Calculator`** is defined, and a **`compute()`** method is declared with a default parameter as **`self`**, but these methods are overridden in the child class with their implementations. The code example is as follows:

```
# Base Class
class Calculator:
    def compute(self):
        pass # Placeholder for specific operations
# Derived Class for Add
class Add(Calculator):
    def compute(self, a, b):
        return a + b
# Derived Class for Subtraction
class Subtract(Calculator):
    def compute(self, a, b):
        return a - b
# Using the classes
add = Add()
subtract = Subtract()
print("Addition:", add.compute(15, 10))       # Output: 25
print("Subtraction:", subtract.compute(20, 15)) # Output: 5
```

The output of the given program is shown in *Figure 5.10*:

```
>>>
= RESTART: C:/Users/DELL/AppData/Local/Programs/Python/
6.3_abstract.py
Addition: 25
Subtraction: 5
```

***Figure 5.10**: Output using abstraction*

Encapsulation

Encapsulation is one of the fundamental concepts of OOP. It means wrapping up data, i.e., variables and the code consisting of methods that operate on the data into a single unit called a class. It helps in protecting data from accidental changes, controlling access to internal variables using access modifiers like:

- Public (default in Python) modifier is accessible from anywhere.
- Private (using __ double underscores) modifiers are accessible only within the class.
- Protected (using _ single underscore) modifier is intended for internal use but still accessible.

Example 5.11: Write a program demonstrating the concept of encapsulation

In this code, the variables **`__name`** and **`__marks`** are private and cannot be accessed directly from outside. The **`display_details()`** method helps to see the data, and **`updatename()`** method is to update the name. The code example is as follows:

```
class Student:
    def __init__(self,name,marks):
        self.__name = name   # private attribute
        self.__marks = marks # private attribute

    # Method to display the data
    def display_details(self):
        print("Student Name is:", self.__name)
        print("Student Marks is:", self.__marks)
    # Method to change marks
    def updatename(self, update_name):
        self.__name = update_name
# Create object of Student
s1=Student("Anil",76)
# Accessing data using method 'display_details()'
s1.display_details()
# Changing marks using method 'updatename()'
s1.updatename("Anil Kumar")
# Display updated data
s1.display_details()
```

Note: Encapsulation helps to keep the data safe inside the class.

The output of the given code is shown in *Figure 5.11*:

```
>>>
===================== RESTART
Student Name is: Anil
Student Marks is: 76
Student Name is: Anil Kumar
Student Marks is: 76
```

***Figure 5.11**: Output of encapsulation*

Regular expressions and pattern matching

Regex in Python includes special patterns used to search, match, or replace specific sets of characters in strings. They help in identifying patterns like email addresses, phone numbers, dates, and specific words or characters. Regex is commonly applied in input validation tasks such as verifying email addresses, phone numbers, or passwords. Regex is also useful for data cleaning by removing unwanted characters, spaces, or HTML tags. In search and replace operations, regex helps modify or reformat text efficiently. It is often used to extract specific information like emails, dates, or URLs from large texts or web pages. Developers also use it in text editors and IDEs for syntax highlighting and code parsing. Other applications include web scraping, security filtering of malicious inputs, and preprocessing text in natural language processing tasks.

Note: **Python provides the `re` module to work with regular expressions.**

Regular expressions help in the following ways:

- Finding if a string contains a particular pattern.
- Replacing part of a string that matches a pattern.
- Splitting strings based on a pattern.
- Validating inputs like email or mobile number format.

Escape characters are special characters used inside strings, starting with a backslash (\). They allow us to add characters that are otherwise hard to type directly. The common escape characters are:

- `\n` for new line
- `\t` for tab space
- \ for backslash
- `\"` for double quote inside a string
- `\'` for single quote inside a string

Regular expressions are patterns used to match text like emails, phone numbers, or dates. The escape characters and regex cheat sheet are shown in *Table 5.1*:

Type	Pattern/code	Example
Escape characters	\n	**New line**: `Hello\nWorld` will prints on 2 lines
	\t	**Tab space**: `Name:\tAnil` will adds a tab
	\\	**Backslash**: `C:\\test.txt`
	\"	**Double quote inside string**: `She said \"Hello\"`
	\'	**Single quote inside string**: `It\'s fine`
Regex basics	\d	Any digit (0–9)
	\w	Any word character (a–z, A–Z, 0–9, _)
	\s	Any whitespace (space, tab, newline)
	^abc	String starting with **abc**
	abc$	String ending with **abc**
Common validations	Email	`\b[A-Za-z0-9._%+-]+@[A-Za-z0-9.-]+\.[A-Z|a-z]{2,}\b`
	Name (First letter capital)	`^[A-Z][a-z]+$` (Only alphabets, first letter must be capital)
	Phone number	`^\d{10}$` (10-digit phone number)
	Date (DD/MM/YYYY or DD-MM-YYYY)	`^(0[1-9]|[12][0-9]|3[01])[-/](0[1-9]|1[0-2])[-/](\d{4})$`
	Time (HH:MM in 24-hr format)	`^([01]\d|2[0-3]):([0-5]\d)$`
	Date-time (YYYY-MM-DD HH:MM:SS)	`^\d{4}-\d{2}-\d{2}\s\d{2}:\d{2}:\d{2}$`

Table 5.1: Escape characters and regex cheat sheet

Example 5.12: Write a program for email validation using regular expressions

In this example, the regex package is imported using the import keyword. The **\w+** matches letters, digits, or underscore, **@** is the at-symbol, and **\.** matches the **dot(.)**, since a plain dot means any character in regex. The statement **email_match.group()** shows the exact match, as the following code shows:

```
import re
email = input("Enter your email id")
# Search for an email pattern
email_check = r'\w+@\w+\.\w+'
email_match = re.search(email_check, email)
```

```
if email_match:
    print("Entered Email is correct:", email_match.group())
else:
    print("Entered Email is not correct")
```

The output of the given example is shown in *Figure 5.12*:

```
    Enter your email idabc@gmail
    Entered Email is not correct
>>>
    ==================== RESTART: G:/DS/Cha]
    Enter your email idabc@gmail.
    Entered Email is not correct
>>>
    ==================== RESTART: G:/DS/Cha]
    Enter your email idabc@gmail.com
    Entered Email is correct: abc@gmail.com
```

***Figure 5.12**: Output of email validation using regular expression*

Example 5.13: Write a program to search for a word in the given input string

In this code, **`re.search()`** checks if the word **`language`** exists in the string or not. In Python, the **`r`** before a string (like **`r"^\d+$"`**) stands for a raw string. It tells Python not to treat backslashes (\) as escape characters. The code example is as follows:

```
import re
input_text = "Python is a language for Data Science."
string_pattern = r"language"
if re.search(string_pattern, input_text):
    print("Yes, 'language' is in the given text.")
else:
    print("No, word is not found.")
```

Note: Here, Python tries to interpret `\d` as a special escape character (like `\n` for newline, `\t` for tab), which may not work correctly without `r`.

The output of the given example is shown in *Figure 5.13*:

```
>>>
    ==================== RESTART: G:/DS/C
    Yes, 'language' is in the given text.
```

***Figure 5.13**: Searching for a word in the given input string*

Example 5.14: Example to check only the digits in the entered mobile number

In this example, the entered mobile number is validated to ensure that only digits are allowed. Here, **`\d`** means a digit, **`+`** means one or more times, and **`^`** and **`$`** represent the start and end of the string, respectively. This ensures that the entire string consists of digits. The code example is as follows:

```
import re
mobile_number = input("Enter your mobile number: ")
# Pattern to match exactly 10 digits only
pattern = r"^\d{10}$"
if not re.match(r"^\d+$", mobile_number):
    print("Error: Mobile number must contain only digits.")
elif not re.match(pattern, mobile_number):
    print("Error: Mobile number must be exactly 10 digits long.")
else:
    print("Entered number is correct")
```

Note: `^\d+$` expression will check if the entire string contains only digits, and `^\d{10}$` expression will ensure that the string contains exactly 10 digits.

The output of this example is shown in *Figure 5.14*:

```
>>>
==================== RESTART: H:/DS/Chapter 5/Example
Enter your mobile number: abc
Error: Mobile number must contain only digits.
>>>
==================== RESTART: H:/DS/Chapter 5/Example
Enter your mobile number: 1234
Error: Mobile number must be exactly 10 digits long.
>>>
==================== RESTART: H:/DS/Chapter 5/Example
Enter your mobile number: 1234567891
Entered number is correct
```

***Figure 5.14**: Output of checking only the digits in the entered mobile number*

Example 5.15: Write a program to validate only the string values using regular expressions

In this example, to validate only string values, the expression **`^[A-Za-z]+$`** is used. Here, **^** and **$** denote the start and end of the string, ensuring that the entire input is matched. The expression **`A-Za-z`** allows both uppercase and lowercase letters only, and **+** means at least one character is required. The code example is as follows:

```
import re
input_name = input("Enter your name: ")
# Pattern to match only alphabets(uppercase and lowercase),minimum 1 character
pattern = r"^[A-Za-z]+$"
if re.match(pattern,input_name):
    print("Welcome.",input_name)
```

```
else:
    print("Invalid input:Only alphabetic characters are allowed")
```

The output of this code for validating only the input strings is shown in *Figure 5.15*:

```
>>>
    =================== RESTART: H:/DS/Chapter 5/Example
    Enter your name: 123
    Invalid input:Only alphabetic characters are allowed
>>>
    =================== RESTART: H:/DS/Chapter 5/Example
    Enter your name: Anil
    Welcome. Anil
```

***Figure 5.15**: Output window of validating only the string values*

Conclusion

In this chapter, students explored the foundational principles of OOP in Python, including how to define and use classes and objects. The concept of constructors is introduced to demonstrate how objects can be initialized with specific data. The important OOP concepts, such as inheritance and polymorphism, are discussed to show how code can be reused and extended for flexible program design. The chapter also emphasized abstraction and encapsulation, which help in hiding unnecessary details and protecting data within objects.

Additionally, students are introduced to regular expressions in Python, a powerful tool for working with text patterns. They learned how to use the re module to perform pattern matching and how regular expressions can be applied in real-world scenarios like input validation and searching specific patterns in strings.

Points to remember

The following points are to be kept in mind:

- Class is a blueprint for creating objects. It defines variables and methods that its objects will have.
- Object is an instance of a class. It allows access to class methods and variables using the dot . operator.
- The __init__() constructor is a special method used to initialize object attributes automatically when the object is created.
- Inheritance allows a class (child) to acquire properties and methods of another class (parent), promoting code reuse.
- Polymorphism means the same method or function can behave differently based on the object calling it. It includes method overriding in the child class and method overloading in Python using default arguments.

- Abstraction hides complex internal details and only shows the essential features to the user.
- Encapsulation protects data by bundling it with methods and restricting direct access using private members (e.g., __varname).
- Regex are patterns used to match and manipulate text efficiently in Python.
- Python's re module provides functions like match(), search(), findall(), and sub() for working with regular expressions.
- Common regex symbols are:
  - \d for any digit
  - \w for any word character (letter, digit, or underscore)
  - ^ for start of the string
  - $ for end of the string
  - + for one or more occurrences
  - [A-Za-z] for letters only

Key terms

- **Class**: A blueprint for creating objects in Python.
- **Object**: An instance of a class that holds data and behavior.
- **Constructor (__init__)**: A special method used to initialize object attributes.
- **Self**: A reference to the current instance of the class.
- **Method**: A function defined inside a class.
- **Inheritance**: A mechanism where a class can inherit properties and methods from another class.
- **Super()**: A function used to call methods of the parent class.
- **Polymorphism**: The ability to use the same function name with different implementations.
- **Overriding**: Redefining a method in the child class that exists in the parent class.
- **Abstraction**: Hiding unnecessary implementation details from the user.
- **Encapsulation**: Wrapping data and code together and restricting direct access to some components.

- **Private members:** Class variables/methods that are accessed using a double underscore prefix (e.g., __name).
- **Regular expression (Regex):** A sequence of characters used for pattern matching in strings.
- **re module**: A Python module used to work with regular expressions.
- **Pattern matching**: The process of checking a string against a regex pattern.
- **match()**: Checks for a match at the beginning of a string.
- **search()**: Searches for the first occurrence of the pattern.
- **findall()**: Returns all matches of the pattern.
- **sub()**: Replaces occurrences of a pattern with a specified string.
- **Special characters in regex**: Symbols like ^, $, \d, \w, [], +, * used for pattern rules.

Multiple choice questions

1. **What is a class in Python?**

   a. A function that stores data
   b. A blueprint to create objects
   c. A list of numbers
   d. A special variable in Python

2. **Which keyword is used to define a constructor in Python?**

   a. constructor()
   b. __start__()
   c. __init__()
   d. new()

3. **What does the self keyword refer to in a class method?**

   a. The main function
   b. The parent class
   c. The current object
   d. None of the above

4. **What is the purpose of inheritance in Python?**

   a. To delete methods from a class
   b. To store extra memory
   c. To reuse code from another class
   d. To convert classes into modules

5. **Which function is used to access the parent class from a child class?**

   a. inherit()
   b. super()
   c. base()
   d. parent()

6. **Which of these is an example of encapsulation?**
   a. Using a loop in a function
   b. Creating a tuple
   c. Using private variables and accessing them via methods
   d. Using global variables everywhere

7. **Which of the following best describes polymorphism?**
   a. Using two different class names
   b. Writing functions inside lists
   c. Same method name behaving differently in different classes
   d. Looping over a string

8. **What does the re.match() function do?**
   a. Searches for a number
   b. Finds all matching characters
   c. Matches pattern at the beginning of the string
   d. Prints the entire string

9. **Which regex pattern matches a 10-digit mobile number correctly?**
   a. ^\d{10}$
   b. [0-9]+
   c. ^[A-Za-z]+$
   d. ^\d$

10. **Which of these shows abstraction in Python?**
   a. Showing all methods to users
   b. Hiding internal details using simple interfaces
   c. Printing class variables
   d. Accessing private data directly

Answers

1	b
2	c
3	c

4	c
5	b
6	c
7	c
8	c
9	a
10	b

Questions

1. What do you understand by a class and object in Python? Give an example.
2. What is a constructor? How is it defined and used in Python classes?
3. Define inheritance with an example. How is polymorphism achieved in Python?
4. Explain the concept of abstraction. How does it help in hiding implementation details?
5. What is encapsulation? How is data hidden within a class?
6. What are regular expressions in Python? Why are they used?
7. Explain how to perform pattern matching in Python using the re module.
8. Write a short program to validate a 10-digit mobile number using regular expressions.
9. How do regular expressions help in checking string patterns like email?

Chapter 6
Database Connectivity using MySQL and MongoDB

Introduction

In modern data-driven applications, databases play a crucial role in storing, managing, and retrieving information. Python, being a versatile language, offers simple yet powerful tools to connect with various databases. This chapter introduces how Python connects with relational databases like MySQL and NoSQL databases like MongoDB.

We will begin with a brief overview of MySQL-Python connectivity using the mysql.connector library and executing basic SQL commands. The primary focus will then shift to MongoDB, where you will learn how to perform operations like inserting, updating, deleting, and querying documents using Python and the pymongo module.

By the end of this chapter, students will understand the differences between relational and NoSQL databases and how to integrate them into Python-based applications.

Structure

The following topics are covered in this chapter:

- Introduction to database
- Difference between MySQL and MongoDB
- DDL, DML, DQL, DCL, and TCL commands
- Steps for Python database connectivity using MySQL
- Alternative method to connect Python to MySQL connector
- Installing MongoDB software
- Importing JSON into MongoDB Compass

Objectives

The objective of this chapter is to help students understand the concept and significance of database connectivity using Python. Students will first gain a brief overview of how Python interacts with relational databases like MySQL using the mysql.connector module to establish a connection and execute basic SQL queries. The focus then shifts to NoSQL databases, specifically MongoDB, where learners will explore its structure and how it differs from traditional relational databases. Through the use of the pymongo library, students will learn how to perform essential database operations such as inserting, retrieving, updating, and deleting documents in MongoDB. By the end of this chapter, students will be equipped to integrate both relational and NoSQL databases into their Python applications, making them capable of building data-driven solutions efficiently.

Introduction to database

A database is a structured collection of data that is organized, maintained, and stored to enable efficient retrieval, modification, and management of information. In most databases, data is arranged in the form of tables, where each table consists of rows (records) and columns (fields). Each column is defined with a specific data type, which helps ensure data integrity and efficient storage. There are different types of databases. **Relational database management systems** (**RDBMS**), such as MySQL, PostgreSQL, Oracle Database, and Microsoft SQL Server, organize data into related tables with well-defined relationships. On the other hand, NoSQL databases are designed to handle unstructured, semi-structured, or rapidly changing data. A popular example of a NoSQL database is MongoDB. *Figure 6.1* illustrates the conceptual flow of communication between a Python application, the database connector such as `mysql.connector` or `pymongo`, and the database server:

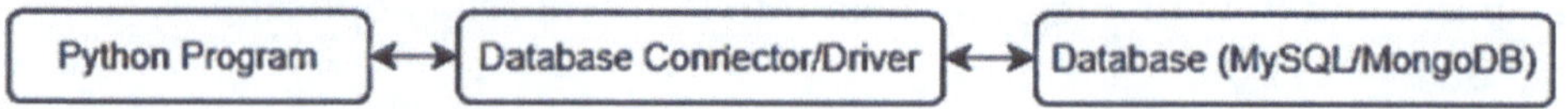

***Figure 6.1**: Conceptual flow of database connectivity using Python, connector, and database*

Difference between MySQL and MongoDB

MySQL and MongoDB are two widely used database systems, but they function in different ways. MySQL is a relational database, which means it stores data in tables with rows and columns and follows a fixed structure or schema. It uses **structured query language** (**SQL**) to manage and retrieve data, making it suitable for applications that require well-organized and consistent data, such as financial systems or school records. On the other hand, MongoDB is a NoSQL database that stores data in collections made up of documents, which are similar to **JavaScript Object Notation** (**JSON**) objects. It allows flexible data structures, meaning each document can have a different format. MongoDB is ideal for handling large volumes of unstructured or semi-structured data, such as data from social media platforms or IoT devices. While MySQL works best for data with strong relationships, MongoDB offers better performance for fast and dynamic data operations. In summary, MySQL is used where structure and reliability are important, while MongoDB is preferred when flexibility and scalability are needed. Both MySQL and MongoDB are popular database management systems, but they differ in structure, query language, and scalability. MySQL is widely used in traditional web applications where data is structured and relationships are well defined, such as banking systems, ERP applications, and e-commerce platforms.

MongoDB, on the other hand, is preferred for applications requiring flexibility and scalability, such as content management systems, real-time analytics, IoT platforms, and social media applications. *Table 6.1* summarizes the major differences:

Features	MySQL (relational)	MongoDB (NoSQL, document-based)
Data model	Table-based with rows and columns	Document-based (JSON-like documents)
Schema	Fixed schema; each table has a predefined structure	Schema-less; documents in the same collection can have different fields
Query language	SQL	MongoDB query language (MQL, JSON-style queries)
Storage format	Relational tables stored in rows and columns	Collections of key–value pairs stored as documents
Transactions	Supports multi-row **atomicity, consistency, isolation, durability** (**ACID**) transactions	Supports multi-document ACID transactions
Scalability	Vertically scalable (add more power to one server)	Horizontally scalable (add more servers)
Joins	Supports complex joins between tables	Limited joins; uses embedding or referencing instead
Performance	Slower for unstructured or variable data	Faster for large volumes of unstructured data
Use case type	Suitable for structured, relational data	Suitable for unstructured, flexible data models

***Table 6.1**: Comparison between MySQL and MongoDB*

Note: JSON is a lightweight format used to exchange data. It is easy for humans to read and write, and simple for machines to parse and generate. It is often used to transmit data between servers and web applications.

A simple JSON representation of a document (record) in the context of a MongoDB database is shown ahead. The same fields or attributes are used throughout this chapter in examples related to database operations using MySQL and MongoDB connectivity in Python. The file extension for a JSON file is .json. In MongoDB, data is stored in a format similar to JSON, which makes it easy to read, write, and manipulate. Each document in a collection can be considered a JSON object. This JSON object represents a single record in the **`student_tbl`** collection. The field names are enclosed in double quotes, and the values can be numbers (such as **`101`**) or strings (such as **`"Anuj"`**). This format aligns with the structure used for inserting and retrieving data using the **`PyMongo`** library, as demonstrated in the chapter:

```
{
  "studentid": 101,
  "first_name": "Anuj",
  "last_name": "Kumar",
  "course": "Python"
}
```

In the further sections, we will explore how Python can connect and interact with databases, focusing first on MySQL connectivity. The examples demonstrate the use of various SQL commands, including **data definition language** (**DDL**), **data query language** (**DQL**), **data manipulation language** (**DML**), **data control language** (**DCL**), and **transaction control language** (**TCL**), to perform essential database operations through Python programs. Additionally, the chapter also introduces MongoDB, highlighting how Python can interact with it using a flexible document-based approach, suitable for handling large-scale and dynamic datasets.

DDL, DML, DQL, DCL, and TCL commands

In relational databases, SQL commands are organized into distinct categories that define their role in managing and interacting with data. DDL commands deal with the structure of the database, such as creating or modifying tables. DML focuses on inserting, updating, and deleting records within those structures. DQL, primarily through the **`SELECT`** statement, retrieves and filters data for analysis. Meanwhile, DCL ensures proper access rights and security through commands like **`GRANT`** and **`REVOKE`**. Finally, TCL manages the logical units of work, ensuring data consistency with commands like **`COMMIT`** and **`ROLLBACK`**. Together, these categories form the backbone of SQL operations, offering a structured way to define, manipulate, secure, and preserve data integrity. *Figure 6.2* shows the classification of SQL commands into five main categories: DDL, DML, DQL, DCL, and TCL:

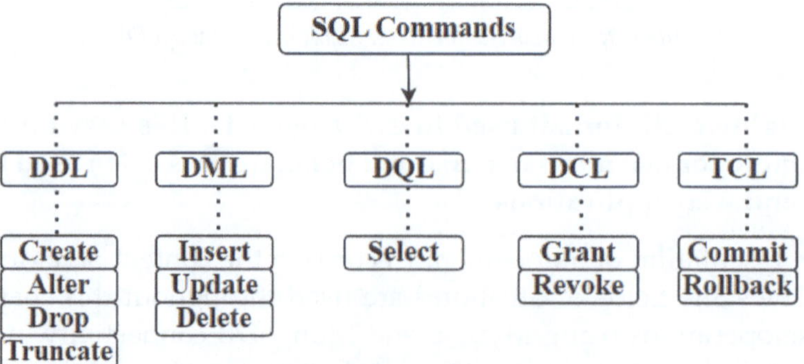

***Figure 6.2**: Classification of SQL commands*

Data definition language

DDL commands are used to define and modify the structure of a database. Common DDL commands include **CREATE**, **DROP**, and **ALTER**.

CREATE DATABASE and **USE** are DDL commands used in SQL, specifically in MySQL and similar relational databases. Let us understand a few commands:

- CREATE DATABASE: This command is used to create a new database. The syntax is **CREATE DATABASE databasename**. In the following command, the database name is **python**:

  ```
  create database python;
  ```

- USE: This command selects a specific database to work with. The syntax is **USE databasename;**

  ```
  use python;
  ```

- CREATE TABLE: Used to create a new table. The syntax is as follows:

  ```
  CREATE TABLE student (id INT, name VARCHAR(20), address VARCHAR(20));
  ```

  In this command, the table name is **student**, and it has three fields, namely **id**, **name**, and **address**. The **id** field is of type **INT**, and both name and address are of type **VARCHAR** with a size of **20** characters.

- DROP TABLE: Used to delete an existing table from the database. The syntax is as follows:

  ```
  DROP TABLE student;
  ```

- ALTER TABLE: Used to modify the structure of an existing table. For example, to add a new column **mobno** of type **INT**:

  ```
  ALTER TABLE student ADD mobno INT;
  ```

- DROP DATABASE: In order to permanently delete an existing database along with all its tables, data, and structure, the **DROP DATABASE** command is executed. The syntax is as follows:

  ```
  DROP DATABASE databasename;
  ```

Data manipulation language

DML commands are used to manipulate the data stored in the database. These include **INSERT**, **UPDATE**, and **DELETE**:

- INSERT: Adds a new record to a table:

  ```
  INSERT INTO student VALUES(1, 'Anil', 'Delhi');
  ```

- UPDATE: Modifies existing records:

  ```
  UPDATE student SET name = 'Anil Kumar' WHERE id = 1;
  ```

The `WHERE` clause ensures that only the record with `id = 1` is updated.

- **DELETE**: Removes specific records from a table. The syntax is as mentioned below:

```
DELETE FROM student WHERE id = 1;
```

Data query language

DQL is used to retrieve data from the database using the `SELECT` command. To fetch all records, the query is mentioned as follows:

```
SELECT * FROM student;
```

To fetch specific records using a condition:

```
SELECT * FROM student WHERE id = 1;
```

The `WHERE` clause is used to filter records based on a specific condition.

Data control language

DCL commands manage permissions and access controls. Common commands include:

- **GRANT**: Provides specific privileges to users.
- **REVOKE**: Removes the privileges granted to users.

Transaction control language

TCL commands manage transactions in a database. Common commands include:

- **COMMIT**: Saves all the changes made during the transaction permanently.
- **ROLLBACK**: Undoes changes if an error occurs during the transaction.

Transactions in SQL

A transaction is a group of one or more SQL statements that are executed as a single unit of work. It ensures that either all operations succeed or none of them take effect, maintaining the consistency of the database. For example, suppose a customer transfers ₹500 from Account A to Account B. The database must perform two operations:

1. Deduct ₹500 from Account A
2. Add ₹500 to Account B

Both steps must succeed together; if one fails, the other should not be saved.

COMMIT: Confirms all the changes permanently in the database. The SQL transaction shown represents a money transfer between two accounts. The command `START TRANSACTION;` begins the transaction, meaning the following statements will be treated as a single unit of work. The first `UPDATE` deducts ₹500 from account `101`, and the second UPDATE adds ₹500 to account **202**. These changes remain temporary until confirmed. When **COMMIT;** is executed, all changes made within the transaction are saved permanently in the database. If any error occurs before committing, the **ROLLBACK;** command can be used to cancel all pending changes, ensuring that either both updates happen together or none at all, thereby maintaining data consistency. Let us take a look:

```
START TRANSACTION;
UPDATE accounts SET balance = balance - 500 WHERE acc_number = '101';
UPDATE accounts SET balance = balance + 500 WHERE acc_number = '202';
COMMIT;
```

If any error occurs before **COMMIT**, you can use:

```
ROLLBACK;
```

ROLLBACK: Cancels all the changes since the last **COMMIT** and reverts both updates, keeping the data consistent.

Note: COMMIT makes the changes permanent, while ROLLBACK restores the database to its previous state before the transaction began.

The following steps help implement these commands on the MySQL command line environment:

1. First, open the MySQL command line interface, as shown in *Figure 6.3*:

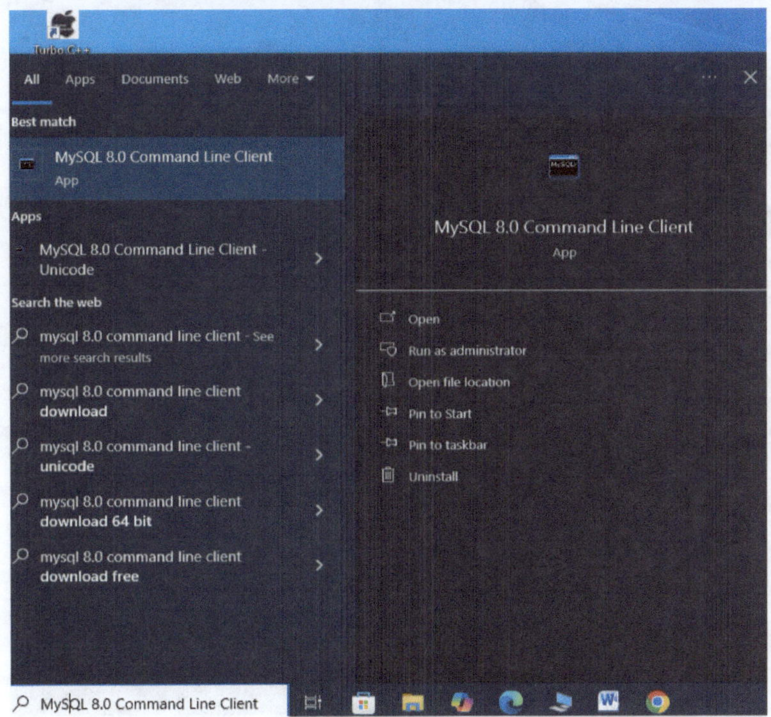

***Figure 6.3:** Open a MySQL command line environment*

2. Once opened, the screen will appear as shown in *Figure 6.4*. MySQL will prompt for a password; enter it if one is set; otherwise, press *Enter* to proceed if no password is required.

```
MySQL 8.0 Command Line Client
Enter password: *****
Welcome to the MySQL monitor.  Commands end with ; or \g.
Your MySQL connection id is 4
Server version: 11.7.2-MariaDB mariadb.org binary distribution

Copyright (c) 2000, 2023, Oracle and/or its affiliates.

Oracle is a registered trademark of Oracle Corporation and/or its
affiliates. Other names may be trademarks of their respective
owners.

Type 'help;' or '\h' for help. Type '\c' to clear the current input statement.

mysql>
```

***Figure 6.4**: MySQL terminal for executing DDL, DML, DCL commands*

In *Figure 6.5*, various DDL, DML, and DQL commands are demonstrated and executed using the MySQL command line environment:

```
mysql> create database python;
Query OK, 1 row affected (0.00 sec)

mysql> use python;
Database changed
mysql> CREATE TABLE student (id INT, name VARCHAR(20), address VARCHAR(20));
Query OK, 0 rows affected (0.17 sec)

mysql> INSERT INTO student VALUES(1, 'Anil', 'Delhi');
Query OK, 1 row affected (0.09 sec)

mysql> SELECT * FROM student;
+------+------+---------+
| id   | name | address |
+------+------+---------+
|    1 | Anil | Delhi   |
+------+------+---------+
1 row in set (0.00 sec)

mysql> UPDATE student SET name = 'Anil Kumar' WHERE id = 1;
Query OK, 1 row affected (0.05 sec)
Rows matched: 1  Changed: 1  Warnings: 0

mysql> SELECT * FROM student;
+------+------------+---------+
| id   | name       | address |
+------+------------+---------+
|    1 | Anil Kumar | Delhi   |
+------+------------+---------+
1 row in set (0.00 sec)

mysql> DELETE FROM student WHERE id = 1;
Query OK, 1 row affected (0.03 sec)

mysql> SELECT * FROM student;
Empty set (0.00 sec)

mysql>
```

***Figure 6.5**: Execution of DDL, DML, and DQL commands in MySQL command line interface*

Steps for Python database connectivity using MySQL

The steps for Python database connectivity using MySQL are as follows:

1. In Python, the **`mysql-connector-python`** package is commonly used to establish a connection with a MySQL database server. Among open-source databases, MySQL is widely used for storing data in Python-based applications. MySQL is popular for its speed and ease of use.

   Note: To establish a database connection in Python, you must first install the MySQL Server and the MySQL Connector for Python.

   These components can be installed using the **MySQL Installer**, as shown in *Figure 6.6*:

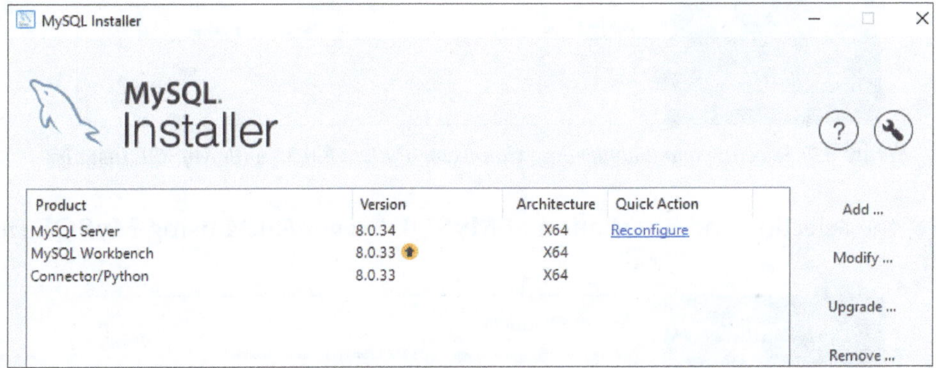

***Figure 6.6:** MySQL Installer dashboard showing installed components*

2. After the connector is successfully installed, you must also install and configure the MySQL Server, setting a username typically root and a secure password.

   In the examples discussed later, we assume username as **`root`**, password as **`sasml`**.

   Figure 6.7 displays selecting the **Connector/Python** module and downloading **Connector/Python 8.0.33** during installation using the **MySQL Installer**:

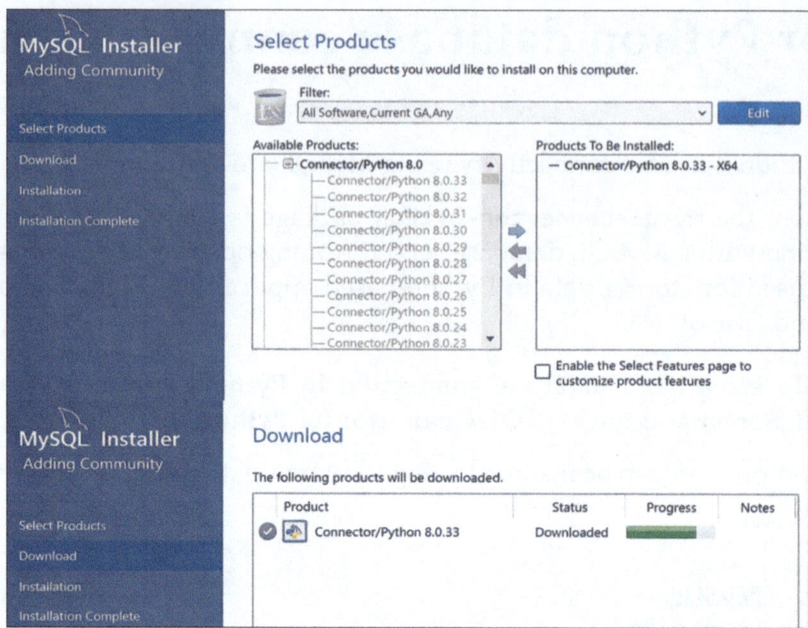

Figure 6.7: Selecting and downloading Connector/Python 8.0.33 with MySQL Installer

In *Figure 6.8*, the selection and installation of **MySQL Server 8.0.34** using **MySQL Installer** is performed:

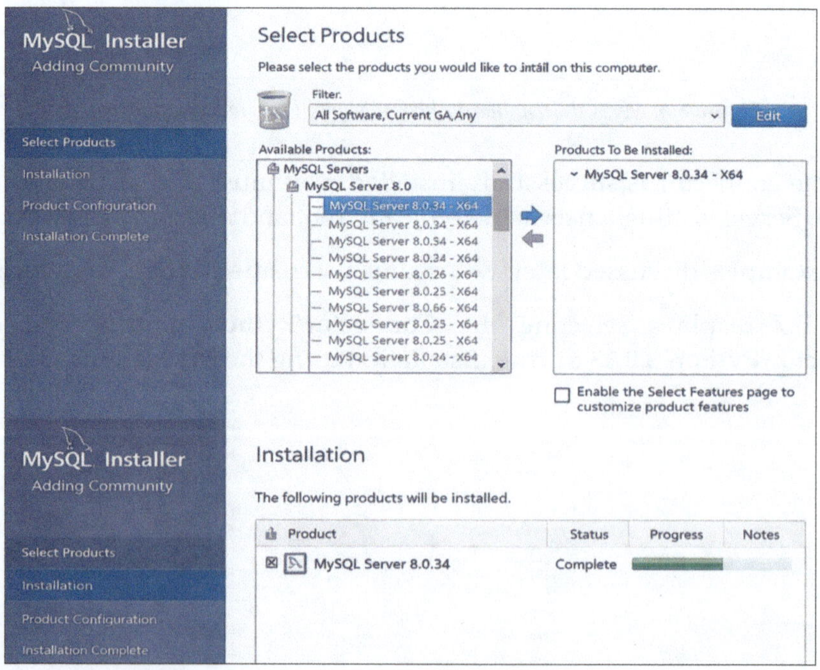

Figure 6.8: Selection and installation of MySQL Server 8.0.34 using MySQL Installer

Note: It is recommended to install the MySQL Server via the MySQL Installer along with the Connector/Python for full control and hands-on practice. If you want to run and manage your own local MySQL database server using Python, this setup allows you to:

- **Create databases and tables**
- **Run DDL, DML, and DQL commands**
- **Practice Python-MySQL connectivity locally**
- **Avoid reliance on cloud-based databases or external setups**

Alternative method to connect Python to MySQL connector

To simply connect Python to MySQL using the connector, you can run the following command in the command prompt by selecting the path browser as shown in *Figure 6.9*:

```
C:\Users\DELL>cd C:\Users\DELL\AppData\Local\Programs\Python\Python311

C:\Users\DELL\AppData\Local\Programs\Python\Python311>python -m pip install mysql-connector-python
Requirement already satisfied: mysql-connector-python in c:\users\dell\appdata\local\programs\python\python311\lib\site-
packages (8.0.33)
Collecting protobuf<=3.20.3,>=3.11.0
  Downloading protobuf-3.20.3-py2.py3-none-any.whl (162 kB)
     ---------------------------------------- 162.1/162.1 kB 649.1 kB/s eta 0:00:00
Installing collected packages: protobuf
Successfully installed protobuf-3.20.3

[notice] A new release of pip available: 22.3 -> 25.1.1
[notice] To update, run: python.exe -m pip install --upgrade pip

C:\Users\DELL\AppData\Local\Programs\Python\Python311>
```

Figure 6.9: Downloading MySQL connector for Python using pip command

Note: When to use `pip install mysql-connector-python`:

- **If MySQL Server is already installed on the system.**
- **If you are working in cloud, hosting, or lab environments where the server is preconfigured.**
- **When you want to avoid the longer MySQL Installer setup steps.**

`pip` stands for **Pip Installs Packages**. **`pip`** is the package manager for Python and is used to install, upgrade, and manage third-party Python packages and libraries from the **Python Package Index** (**PyPI**).

Example 6.1: Write a program for creating a database and table using MySQL

This Python program uses the **`mysql.connector`** library to establish a connection to a MySQL server running on the local machine (localhost) using the username **`root`** and the password

sasml. Once connected, it prepares a SQL query to create a database named **student**, but only if it does not already exist. A cursor object is then used to execute this SQL command. After the database is created or confirmed to exist, the program switches to using this database. Next, it defines and executes a SQL command to create a table named **student_tbl** within the database. The table includes four fields: **studentid** as an auto-incremented primary key, **first_name** and **last_name** as required text fields, and **course** as an optional text field. Once the table creation command is executed, the changes are committed to the database using **conn.commit()**, and the connection is then closed properly using **conn.close()**. Finally, a confirmation message is printed to indicate that the database and table were created successfully. The following code illustrates the use of SQL commands in MySQL to create a new database and define a table within it:

```
import mysql.connector
# Connect to the MySQL server
conn=mysql.connector.connect(
     host="localhost",
     user="root",
     password="sasml"
 )
 # Create a database
db_name = "student"
sql_query = f"CREATE DATABASE IF NOT EXISTS {db_name};"
cursor=conn.cursor()
cursor.execute(sql_query)
# Switch to the new database
conn.database=db_name
# Define a SQL command to create a table
cursor.execute("""CREATE TABLE IF NOT EXISTS student_tbl(studentid INT AUTO_
INCREMENT PRIMARY KEY,first_name VARCHAR(255) NOT NULL,last_
name VARCHAR(255) NOT NULL,course VARCHAR(255))""")
conn.commit()
conn.close()
print("Database and table created successfully")
```

The output of the code is shown in *Figure 6.10*, where a database and a table are created successfully:

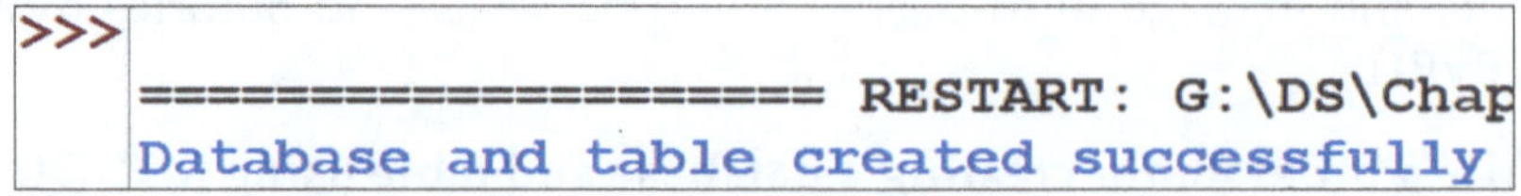

***Figure 6.10**: Database and table created successfully*

Example 6.2: Write a program for inserting a record into a database, taking input from a user

The program demonstrates how to insert a record into a MySQL database table using user input. First, the **mysql.connector** module is imported to establish a connection between Python and MySQL. The program connects to the local MySQL server using the **connect()** method with parameters like host, username, password, and the database name (**student**). Once connected, a cursor object is created to execute SQL commands. The program then prompts the user to input their **studentid**, **first_name**, **last_name**, and **course**. These values are captured using the **input()** function and stored in respective variables. An SQL **INSERT** query is constructed using **placeholders (%s)** in the SQL query, which is the safe practice to prevent SQL injection. The cursor executes this query to insert the data into the **student_tbl** table. After executing the query, the **commit()** function is called to save the changes permanently in the database. Finally, the cursor and connection are closed, and a success message is displayed on the screen confirming that the record has been inserted successfully. The following program demonstrates how to insert a new record into a database table by taking input from the user:

```
import mysql.connector
# MySQL Database Connection Configuration
conn = mysql.connector.connect(
    host="localhost",
    user="root",
    password="sasml",
    database="student"
)
# Cursor object and Connection interaction
cursor = conn.cursor()
# Taking input from user
studentid = int(input("Enter Student ID: "))
first_name = input("Enter First Name: ")
last_name = input("Enter Last Name: ")
course = input("Enter Course Name: ")
# Executing SQL Query with placeholders to insert a record
query = """INSERT INTO student_tbl(studentid,first_name,last_name,course)
           VALUES (%s, %s, %s, %s)"""
values = (studentid,first_name,last_name,course)
cursor.execute(query, values)
# Committing the changes
conn.commit()
# Closing the cursor and connection
cursor.close()
conn.close()
print("Record inserted successfully.")
```

Note: When inserting user input into SQL queries, always use placeholders like %s instead of directly inserting the values into the query string. This helps prevent SQL injection attacks, which can harm your database. Placeholders ensure that user inputs are treated as data, not as part of the SQL command.

The output of inserting a record into a table is shown in *Figure 6.11*:

```
>>>
    ===================== RESTART:
    Enter Student ID: 101
    Enter First Name: Anil
    Enter Last Name: Kumar
    Enter Course Name: C++
    Record inserted successfully.
```

Figure 6.11: *Inserting a record into a database by taking input*

Example 6.3: Write a program to fetch the records from a database

In this example, records are fetched from the table after establishing a database connection. The **SELECT** SQL query is used to retrieve data from the table. To fetch all records, the **fetchall()** method is used. A **for** loop iterates through the result set, accessing each row using indexing. The **\n** newline character is used to display records on separate lines. A cursor object is responsible for traversing the rows in the result set, allowing the program to read and display each record. The following program retrieves and displays records from a database table using a SQL **SELECT** query:

```
import mysql.connector
# MySQL Database Connection Configuration
conn=mysql.connector.connect(
     host="localhost",
     user="root",
     password="sasml",
     database="student"
)
# Cursor object and Connection interaction
cursor = conn.cursor()
# Executing SQL Query to insert a record into table 'studenttbl'
cursor.execute("""SELECT * from student_tbl""")
# fetch all the records in a table using fetchall()
display_record = cursor.fetchall()
# fetch the records using loops and display using '\n'
for x in display_record:
    print(x,'\n')
```

```
# Changes are commit to the database
conn.commit()
# Close the cursor and connection
cursor.close()
conn.close()
```

The program output using the IDLE environment is shown in *Figure 6.12*:

```
>>>
    ====================== RESTART:
    (101, 'Anil', 'Kumar', 'C++')
```

***Figure 6.12**: Output window displaying the records from a database*

Example 6.4: Write a program for updating a record in the database

In this program, the `UPDATE` query is used to modify a record using the `WHERE` clause. The attributes being updated are **studentid**, **first_name**, **last_name**, and **course**. The table name is **student_tbl**, and the database name is **student**. The following program shows how to update an existing record in a database table using an SQL `UPDATE` command:

```
import mysql.connector
# MySQL Database Connection Configuration
conn=mysql.connector.connect(
    host="localhost",
    user="root",
    password="sasml",
    database="student"
 )
# Cursor object and Connection interaction
cursor = conn.cursor()
# Executing SQL Query to update a record into table 'student_tbl'
cursor.execute("""UPDATE student_tbl SET first_name = 'Ajay',
                 last_name='Singh',course='Java'
                where studentid = 101""")
# fetch all the records in a table using fetchall()
display = cursor.fetchall()
conn.commit()
cursor.execute("""SELECT * FROM student_tbl
                 where studentid = 101""")
display_record = cursor.fetchall()
# fetch the records using loops and display using '\n'
for x in display_record:
```

```
    print(x,'\n')
# Changes are commit to the database
conn.commit()
# Close the cursor and connection
cursor.close()
conn.close()
```

The output of updating a record is shown in *Figure 6.13*:

```
>>>
    ====================== RESTART:
    (101, 'Ajay', 'Singh', 'Java')
```

Figure 6.13*: Output of updating a record*

Example 6.5: Write a program for deleting a record into database

In this example, a record is deleted from the table using the SQL **DELETE** query with the **WHERE** clause, and the remaining records are displayed using the **SELECT** SQL query:

```
import mysql.connector
# MySQL Database Connection Configuration
conn = mysql.connector.connect(
    host="localhost",
    user="root",
    password="sasml",
    database="student"
)
# Cursor object and Connection interaction
cursor = conn.cursor()
# Executing SQL Query to delete a record from table 'student_tbl'
cursor.execute("""DELETE FROM student_tbl WHERE studentid = 101""")
print("Record deleted successfully.\n")
# Commit the deletion to the database
conn.commit()
# Display the remaining records
cursor.execute("""SELECT * FROM student_tbl""")
display_record = cursor.fetchall()
# Fetch and print records
for x in display_record:
    print(x, '\n')
# Close the cursor and connection
cursor.close()
conn.close()
```

The output of deleting a record using MySQL is shown in *Figure 6.14*:

```
>>>
    ===================== RESTART:
    Record deleted successfully.
```

Figure 6.14: *Output window of deleting a record*

Installing MongoDB software

To work with MongoDB, the software must first be installed and properly configured on the system. The installation process involves downloading the MongoDB package, running the installer, and completing the necessary setup to ensure the database server is ready for use.

MongoDB can be installed locally, and the MongoDB Compass tool provides a user-friendly interface to view and manage databases. In addition to local installation, MongoDB Atlas offers a cloud-based platform for hosting databases online. It simplifies deployment and management while supporting secure access through Compass or code-based connectors. MongoDB Atlas is a cloud-based alternative to installing MongoDB locally. It allows users to create and manage databases on cloud servers through a web interface, without manual setup. Atlas provides built-in scalability, automated backups, and security features, making it ideal for applications that need remote access and easy deployment. Users can connect MongoDB Compass directly to their Atlas cluster by using the connection string provided in the Atlas dashboard.

Figure 6.15 illustrates how MongoDB Compass serves as a graphical interface for connecting to MongoDB databases, either locally installed on a computer or hosted on the cloud through MongoDB Atlas. Both connections allow users to explore databases and manage collections visually.

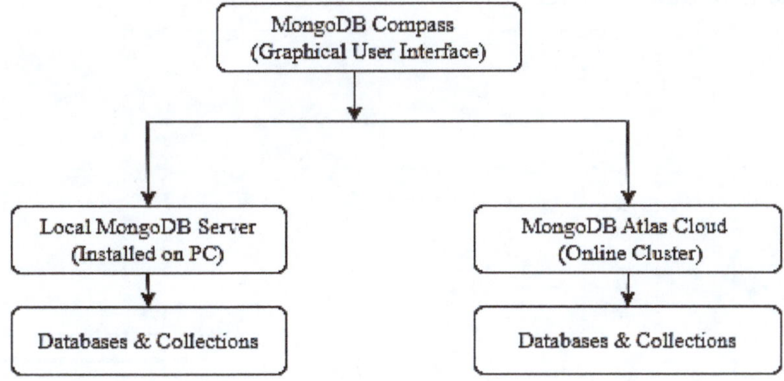

Figure 6.15: *Interaction of MongoDB Compass with local MongoDB server and cloud-based MongoDB Atlas*

The following steps outline the procedure for installing the MongoDB software:

1. To install MongoDB, first download the MongoDB Community Edition for Windows from the official website: **https://www.mongodb.com/try/download/community**.

2. After downloading, run the installer to complete the setup. Once installed, the **MongoDB Compass** icon will appear on your desktop. Open **MongoDB Compass** and click on the **Add new connection** button in the window that appears, as shown in *Figure 6.16*:

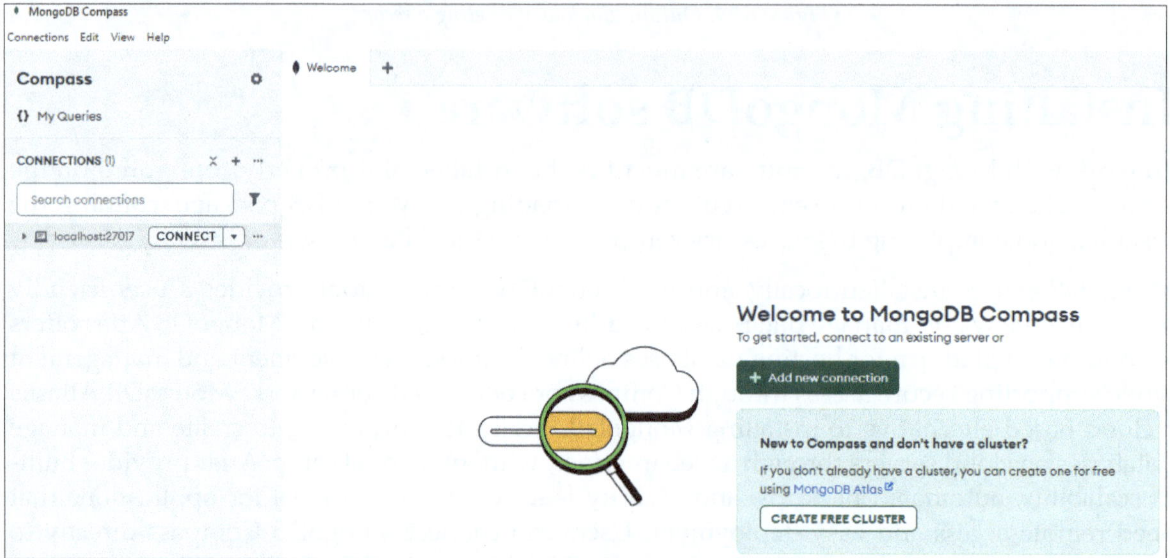

***Figure 6.16**: Installing MongoDB Compass*

3. Then click on the **CONNECT** tab to establish a connection.

   By default, MongoDB connects to localhost on port 27017, and you will be able to view the available databases listed under it, shown in *Figure 6.17*:

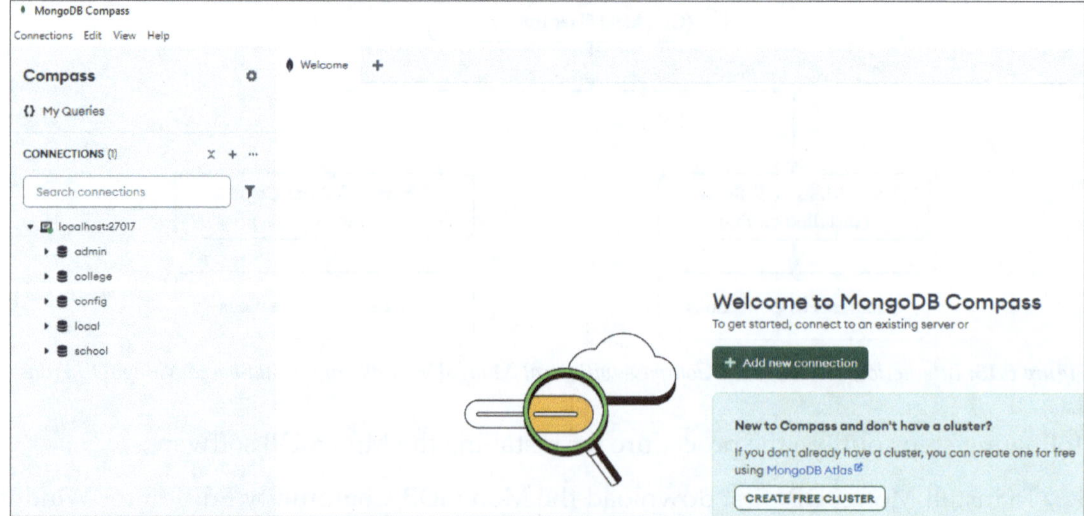

***Figure 6.17**: Installing MongoDB Compass*

Note: The default port of MongoDB Compass is 27017.

4. After installing MongoDB and ensuring the server is running via Compass or terminal, the next step to connect MongoDB with Python is to install the **pymongo** library, which acts as a driver to interact with MongoDB databases from Python. To connect Python to MongoDB, the **pymongo** library must be installed. This library allows Python programs to communicate with MongoDB databases easily.

Note: If you are having issues with `pip` not being recognized in the command prompt (a common situation on Windows if the PATH is not set properly), you can install it using the following command in your command prompt or terminal by selecting the path browser: `python -m pip install pymongo`

5. This command tells Python explicitly to run its **pip** module, and it works even when **pip** alone is not recognized as a command. If the library is already installed, then a message will be shown, as is visible in *Figure 6.18*:

```
C:\Users\LENOVO>cd C:\Users\LENOVO\AppData\Local\Programs\Python\Python313

C:\Users\LENOVO\AppData\Local\Programs\Python\Python313>python -m pip install pymongo
Requirement already satisfied: pymongo in c:\users\lenovo\appdata\local\programs\python\python313\lib\site-packages (4.1
3.0)
Requirement already satisfied: dnspython<3.0.0,>=1.16.0 in c:\users\lenovo\appdata\local\programs\python\python313\lib\s
ite-packages (from pymongo) (2.7.0)

[notice] A new release of pip is available: 24.3.1 -> 25.1.1
[notice] To update, run: python.exe -m pip install --upgrade pip
```

Figure 6.18: Installing pymongo using pip command

Note: Make sure Python and pip are correctly installed and configured in your system's PATH before running this command.

Once installed, you can start writing Python code to insert documents into MongoDB collections as well as query, update, or delete records. You can also perform aggregation and other database operations.

Note: Before importing data into MongoDB, make sure the JSON file is valid. If the JSON structure is incorrect (for example, missing commas, brackets, or quotes), MongoDB will not import it. Sometimes errors occur while inserting data, such as a duplicate _id or a missing field. These can be handled using try–except in Python, discussed in Chapter 4, Exception Handling and File Handling.

Example 6.6: Write a program for database and table creation using MongoDB in Python

In this example, **`MongoClient`** connects your Python program to the MongoDB server. The **`student`** database is created if it is not already, and inside it, a collection (like a table) called **`student_tbl`** is also created or connected. MongoDB automatically creates both when data is inserted, but defining them this way prepares the structure. The following program demonstrates how to connect to MongoDB using Python and create a new database along with a collection (table equivalent):

```
# Import MongoClient
from pymongo import MongoClient
# Connect to MongoDB server
client = MongoClient("mongodb://localhost:27017/")
print("Connected to MongoDB")
# Create or connect to a database named 'student'
db = client["student"]
print("Database 'student' created or connected")
# Create or connect to a collection (table) named 'student_tbl'
collection = db["student_tbl"]
print("Collection 'student_tbl' created or connected")
```

Key MongoDB terms are:

- **Database**: A logical container that holds collections. In this example, the student database is created or connected automatically when referenced.
- **Collection**: A group of related documents, similar to a table in SQL. Here, **student_tbl** acts as a collection inside the student database.
- **Document**: The actual data record stored inside a collection, represented as key–value pairs (similar to a JSON object). Although not inserted yet in this code, each document is stored with a unique identifier called **ObjectId**, which MongoDB generates automatically.

The output of the code is shown in *Figure 6.19*:

```
>>>
===================== RESTART: H:/DS/Chapter 6
Connected to MongoDB
Database 'student' created or connected
Collection 'student_tbl' created or connected
```

***Figure 6.19**: Output of creating a database and table using MongoDB*

Example 6.7: Write a program for inserting a record into a database using MongoDB

In this example, a record is inserted into a MongoDB database. The **student_record** is a Python dictionary that holds the data, and the **insert_one()** function is used to insert this document into the **student_tbl** collection. MongoDB automatically creates the database and collection if they do not already exist. The **inserted_id** confirms that the data has been successfully saved. The following program illustrates how to insert a record into a MongoDB collection using Python:

```
from pymongo import MongoClient
# Connect to MongoDB
client=MongoClient("mongodb://localhost:27017/")
```

```
db = client["student"]  # Database name
collection = db["student_tbl"] # Collection name(like a table)
# Create the record (document)
student_record = {
    "studentid": 101,
    "first_name": "Anil",
    "last_name": "Kumar",
    "course": "Python"
}
# Insert the record into the collection
result = collection.insert_one(student_record)
print("Record inserted successfully. ID:", result.inserted_id)
```

The output of inserting a record into a MongoDB is shown in *Figure 6.20*:

```
>>>
==================== RESTART: H:/DS/Chapter 6/Example6.7.py
Record inserted successfully. ID: 6872250840baf6d8f88019d5
```

***Figure 6.20**: Output of inserting a record into a MongoDB*

The inserted record can also be viewed in the MongoDB Compass window, as shown in *Figure 6.21*:

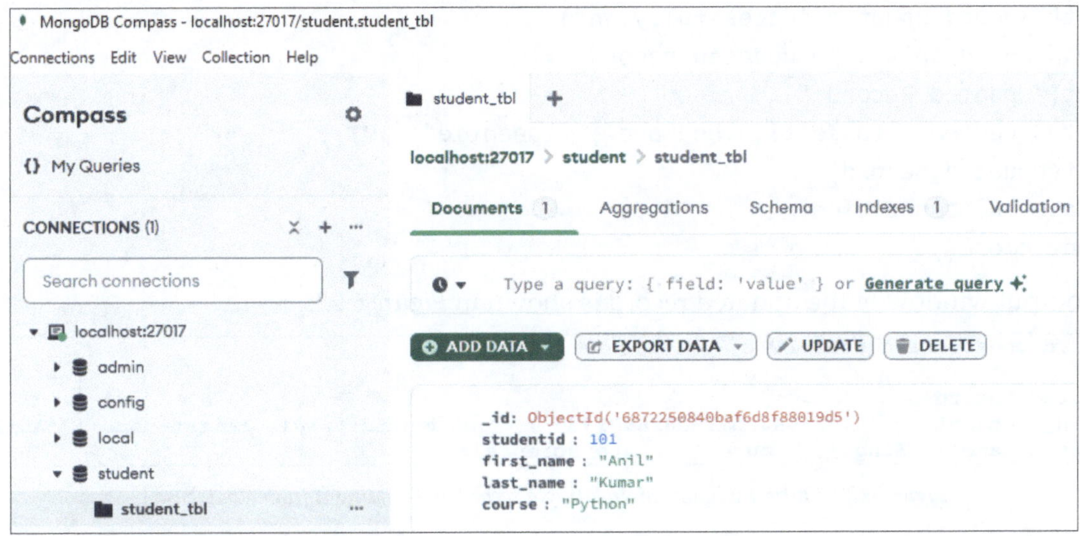

***Figure 6.21**: Output window of the inserted record in the MongoDB Compass window*

Example 6.8: Write a program for updating a record in a database and reading it from a database using MongoDB

In this example, a record is updated in a MongoDB database, and the same record is then fetched. The **update_one()** method is used to modify the document where **studentid** is **101**. The **$set** operator specifies the fields to be updated, while the **find_one()** method retrieves the updated record to verify the changes. Ensure that a record with **studentid: 101** already exists in the collection; if not, insert it first. The following program demonstrates how to update an existing record in a MongoDB collection and then retrieve it using Python:

```
from pymongo import MongoClient
# Connect to MongoDB
client = MongoClient("mongodb://localhost:27017/")
db = client["student"] # Database name
collection = db["student_tbl"]  # Collection (table) name
# Update the record where studentid is 1001
collection.update_one(
    {"studentid": 101},    # Filter condition
    {"$set": {"first_name": "Anil",
              "last_name": "Singh",# Field to update
              "course": "Data Science"}}# Field to update
)
print("Record updated successfully.\n")
# Read and display the updated record
print("Updated Record:")
updated_record = collection.find_one({"studentid": 101})
print(updated_record)
# Close the connection
client.close()
```

The output window of the updated record is shown in *Figure 6.22*:

```
Record updated successfully.

Updated Record:
{'_id': ObjectId('6872250840baf6d8f88019d5'), 'studentid': 101, 'first_name': 'Anil'
, 'last_name': 'Singh', 'course': 'Data Science'}
```

***Figure 6.22**: Output window of updating a record and reading it from a database*

The updated record can also be viewed in the MongoDB Compass window, as shown in *Figure 6.23*:

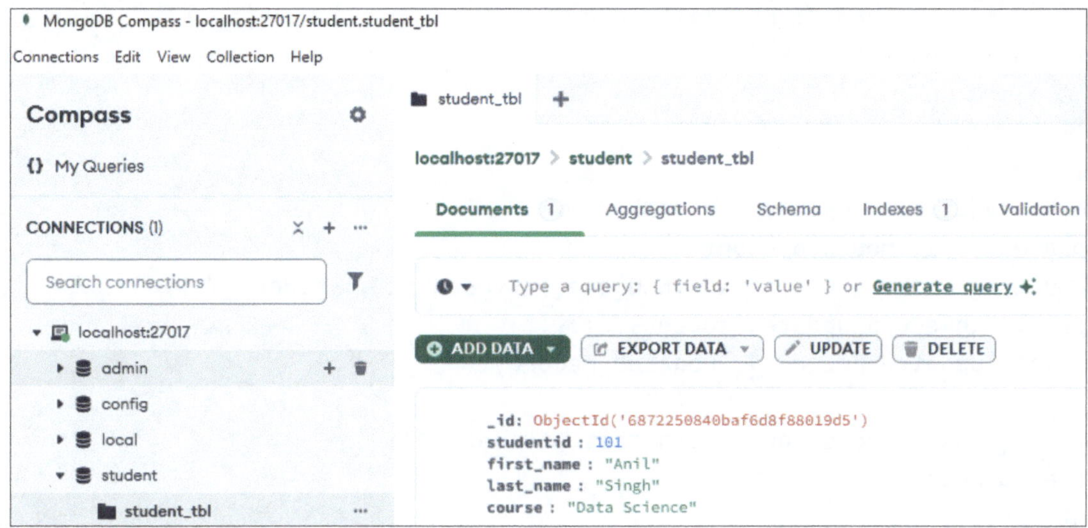

Figure 6.23: Updated record on the MongoDB Compass window

Example 6.9: Write a Python program for updating a record in MongoDB, taking user input

In this example, the previous program is enhanced to update a record by taking input from the user instead of hardcoding the values. The program connects to the student database and the **student_tbl** collection. It prompts the user to enter the student ID and new details for updating. The **update_one()** method, along with the **$set** operator, is used to modify specific fields. After the update, the **find_one()** method retrieves and displays the updated document. Finally, the database connection is closed.

```
from pymongo import MongoClient
# Connect to MongoDB
client = MongoClient("mongodb://localhost:27017/")
db = client["student"]#Database name
collection = db["student_tbl"]#Collection name
# Take input from user for updating a record
student_id = int(input("Enter Student ID to update: "))
new_first_name = input("Enter new First Name: ")
new_last_name = input("Enter new Last Name: ")
new_course = input("Enter new Course Name: ")
# Update the record
update_result = collection.update_one(
    {"studentid": student_id},
    {
        "$set": {
            "first_name": new_first_name,
```

```
            "last_name": new_last_name,
            "course": new_course
        }
    }
)
# Check and display updated record
if update_result.modified_count > 0:
    updated_record = collection.find_one({"studentid": student_id})
    print("\nRecord updated successfully!")
    print("Updated Record:", updated_record)
else:
    print("\nNo record found with that Student ID")
# Close connection
client.close()
```

The output of the code for updating a record in a database, taking input from a user, is shown in *Figure 6.24*:

```
>>>
====================== RESTART: H:/DS/Chapter 6/Example6.9.py ======================
Enter Student ID to update: 101
Enter new First Name: Amit
Enter new Last Name: Kumar
Enter new Course Name: Web Designing

Record updated successfully!
Updated Record: {'_id': ObjectId('6872250840baf6d8f88019d5'), 'studentid': 101, 'first_name': 'Am
it', 'last_name': 'Kumar', 'course': 'Web Designing'}
```

Figure 6.24*: Updating a record in a database, taking input from a user*

The updated record in the MongoDB Compass window can be viewed in *Figure 6.25*:

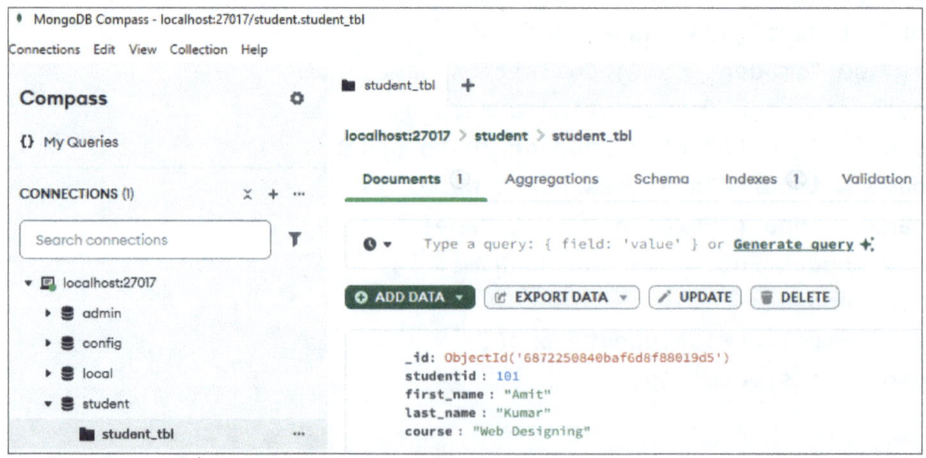

Figure 6.25*: Updated record viewed in MongoDB Compass window*

Example 6.10: Write a Python program for deleting a record, taking input from a user

In this example, a record is deleted from a MongoDB database based on input taken from the user. A connection is established to MongoDB using **MongoClient("mongodb://localhost:27017/")**. The program then accesses the collection using **db["student_tbl"]**. The **delete_one({"studentid": student_id})** method deletes a single document where the **studentid** matches the user input. The **deleted_count** attribute is used to check whether any record was actually deleted. Take a look at the code:

```
from pymongo import MongoClient
# Connect to MongoDB
client = MongoClient("mongodb://localhost:27017/")
db = client["student"]  # Database name
collection = db["student_tbl"] # Collection name
#  Take input from the user for studentid to delete
student_id = int(input("Enter the student ID to delete: "))
# Delete the record with the matching studentid
delete_result = collection.delete_one({"studentid": student_id})
# Check if a record was deleted
if delete_result.deleted_count > 0:
    print(f"Record with student ID {student_id} deleted successfully.")
else:
    print(f"No record found with student ID {student_id}.")
# Close the connection
client.close()
```

The output of the code for deleting a record from the database, taking **studentid** as input from a user, is shown in *Figure 6.26*:

```
>>>
    ===================== RESTART: H:/DS/Chapter 6/Ex
    Enter the student ID to delete: 101
    Record with student ID 101 deleted successfully.
```

***Figure 6.26**: Deleting a student ID 101 from the database*

This result can also be verified in the MongoDB Compass window, as shown in *Figure 6.27*:

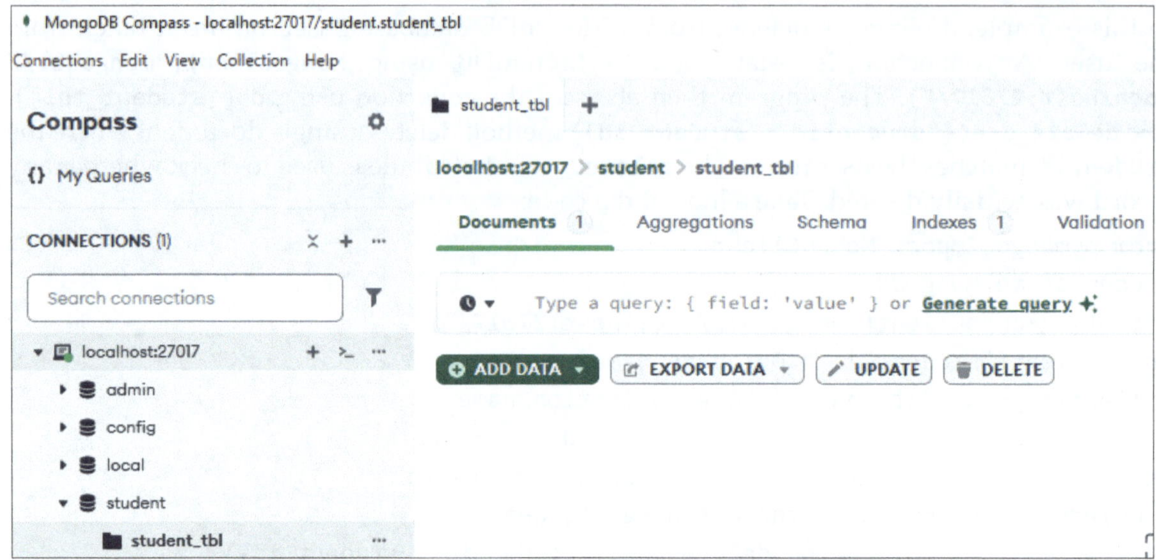

Figure 6.27: Deleted record in MongoDB Compass window

Example 6.11: Write a program for fetching records, taking studentid as input from the user

In this example, a record is fetched based on the **studentid** entered by the user. The program connects to MongoDB using the **pymongo** library, takes **studentid** as input, and searches for the matching record using the **find_one()** method. If a record is found, it prints the student's details; otherwise, it displays a message indicating that no record was found. The following program retrieves records from a MongoDB collection based on a student ID entered by the user:

```
from pymongo import MongoClient

# Step 1: Connect to MongoDB
client = MongoClient("mongodb://localhost:27017/")
db = client["student"]#Database name
collection = db["student_tbl"] #Collection (table) name
#Take studentid as input from the user
try:
    student_id = int(input("Enter the student ID to search: "))
except ValueError:
    print("Please enter a valid integer student ID.")
    exit()
#Find the record with given studentid
record = collection.find_one({"studentid": student_id})
```

```
# Display the result
if record:
    print("\nStudent Record Found:")
    print("Student ID:", record.get("studentid"))
    print("First Name:", record.get("first_name"))
    print("Last Name:", record.get("last_name"))
    print("Course:", record.get("course"))
else:
    print("\nNo record found with student ID:", student_id)
# Close the connection
client.close()
```

The output of the code is shown in *Figure 6.28*:

```
>>>
    ==================== RESTART: H:\DS\
    Enter the student ID to search: 102

    Student Record Found:
    Student ID: 102
    First Name: Sunil
    Last Name: Kumar
    Course: Java
```

***Figure 6.28**: Output of fetching records from a database, taking studentid as input*

Example 6.12: Write a menu-driven student record management system using Python and MongoDB

This program is a menu-driven application that manages student records using Python and MongoDB. It performs basic **create, read, update, and delete** (**CRUD**) operations. Each task, such as inserting, updating, deleting, or reading records, is defined as a separate function to improve modularity, readability, and code reusability. The use of functions allows the program to be better organized and makes it easier to maintain or extend in the future. The user interacts with the system through a simple menu interface, and based on the selected option, the corresponding function is called to perform the required database operation. There are five functions defined using the **def** keyword: **insert_record()**, **view_all_records()**, **search_by_id()**, **update_record()**, and **delete_record()**. The following program presents a menu-driven student record management system using Python and MongoDB, allowing users to perform operations such as inserting, updating, fetching, and deleting student records:

```
from pymongo import MongoClient
# Connect to MongoDB
client = MongoClient("mongodb://localhost:27017/")
db = client["student"]#Database name
collection = db["student_tbl"] # Table name (Collections)
```

```
def insert_record():
    sid = int(input("Enter Student ID: "))
    fname = input("Enter First Name: ")
    lname = input("Enter Last Name: ")
    course = input("Enter Course: ")
    collection.insert_one({
        "studentid": sid,
        "first_name": fname,
        "last_name": lname,
        "course": course
    })
    print("Record inserted successfully!\n")
def view_all_records():
    print("\nAll Student Records:")
    for record in collection.find():
        print(record)
    print()
def search_by_id():
    sid = int(input("Enter Student ID to Search: "))
    record = collection.find_one({"studentid": sid})
    if record:
        print(record)
    else:
        print("Record not found.\n")
def update_record():
    sid = int(input("Enter Student ID to Update: "))
    fname = input("Enter New First Name: ")
    lname = input("Enter New Last Name: ")
    course = input("Enter New Course: ")
    result = collection.update_one(
        {"studentid": sid},
        {"$set": {
            "first_name": fname,
            "last_name": lname,
            "course": course
        }}
    )
    if result.modified_count:
        print("Record updated.\n")
```

```
    else:
        print("No matching record found.\n")
def delete_record():
    sid = int(input("Enter Student ID to Delete: "))
    result = collection.delete_one({"studentid": sid})
    if result.deleted_count:
        print("Record deleted.\n")
    else:
        print("No record found with that ID.\n")
# Menu-driven interface
while True:
    print("1. Add Record\n2. View All Records\n3. Search by ID\
n4. Update Record\n5. Delete Record\n6. Exit")
    choice = input("Enter your choice: ")
    if choice == '1':
        insert_record()
    elif choice == '2':
        view_all_records()
    elif choice == '3':
        search_by_id()
    elif choice == '4':
        update_record()
    elif choice == '5':
        delete_record()
    elif choice == '6':
        print("Exiting...")
        break
    else:
        print("Invalid Choice. Try again.\n")
```

The output of the example is shown in *Figure 6.29*:

```
>>>
==================== RESTART: H:/DS/Chapter 6/Example6.12.py ===================
1. Add Record
2. View All Records
3. Search by ID
4. Update Record
5. Delete Record
6. Exit
Enter your choice: 1
Enter Student ID: 103
Enter First Name: Sumit
Enter Last Name: Kumar
Enter Course: Python
Record inserted successfully!

1. Add Record
2. View All Records
3. Search by ID
4. Update Record
5. Delete Record
6. Exit
Enter your choice: 2

All Student Records:
{'_id': ObjectId('68733d93778a64fd94978d8c'), 'studentid': 102, 'first_name': 'Sunil', 'last_name': 'Kumar', 'course': 'Java'}
{'_id': ObjectId('68734936dcfa6d0730f7ba73'), 'studentid': 103, 'first_name': 'Sumit', 'last_name': 'Kumar', 'course': 'Python'}

1. Add Record
2. View All Records
3. Search by ID
4. Update Record
5. Delete Record
6. Exit
Enter your choice: 3
Enter Student ID to Search: 103
{'_id': ObjectId('68734936dcfa6d0730f7ba73'), 'studentid': 103, 'first_name': 'Sumit', 'last_name': 'Kumar', 'course': 'Python'}
1. Add Record
2. View All Records
```

***Figure 6.29**: Output window of the menu-driven student record management system using Python and MongoDB*

Note: In this chapter, the database connection and configuration steps are shown in multiple examples for clarity and easy understanding. However, in real-world applications, these steps can be encapsulated inside a user-defined function to avoid repetition and make the code more modular. This approach helps in reusing the same connection logic throughout the program. For instance, the code shown in Example 6.7 demonstrates how the database configuration can be stored inside a function:

After executing the following code, a connection to the MongoDB database is established using a user-defined function. A student record is then inserted into the specified collection, and the program displays a confirmation message along with the unique ID generated for the inserted document.

```
from pymongo import MongoClient
# Function to connect and return a collection
def database_connection(db_name, collection_name):
    client = MongoClient("mongodb://localhost:27017/")
    db = client[db_name]
    return db[collection_name]


# Using the function
```

```
collection = database_connection("student", "student_tbl")

# Insert a record
student_record = {
    "studentid": 101,
    "first_name": "Anil",
    "last_name": "Kumar",
    "course": "Python"
}
result = collection.insert_one(student_record)
print("Record inserted successfully. ID:", result.inserted_id)
```

Importing JSON into MongoDB Compass

A JSON file with the .json extension can be directly dragged and dropped into the MongoDB Compass window. The same data can later be accessed from the database using the Python PyMongo library. The following steps demonstrate how to import a JSON file into MongoDB Compass by using the drag-and-drop feature:

1. Copy the following content and paste it into a text editor like Notepad. Then, save the file as **`sample.json`** (with **`.json`** extension):

```
[
 {
   "studentid": 104,
   "first_name": "Dinesh",
   "last_name": "Singh",
   "course": "Data Science"
 },
 {
   "studentid": 105,
   "first_name": "Riya",
   "last_name": "Sharma",
   "course": "Java"
 },
 {
   "studentid": 106,
   "first_name": "Sujata",
   "last_name": "Singh",
   "course": "IoT"
 }
]
```

2. Open MongoDB Compass.
3. Select your student database, and choose (or create) the **student_tbl** collection.
4. Use the **ADD DATA**, and then **Import JSON** or drag and drop the **sample.json** file directly into the collection window.
5. Now, the records will appear in your MongoDB Compass as shown in *Figure 6.30* and can also be accessed through your Python PyMongo scripts:

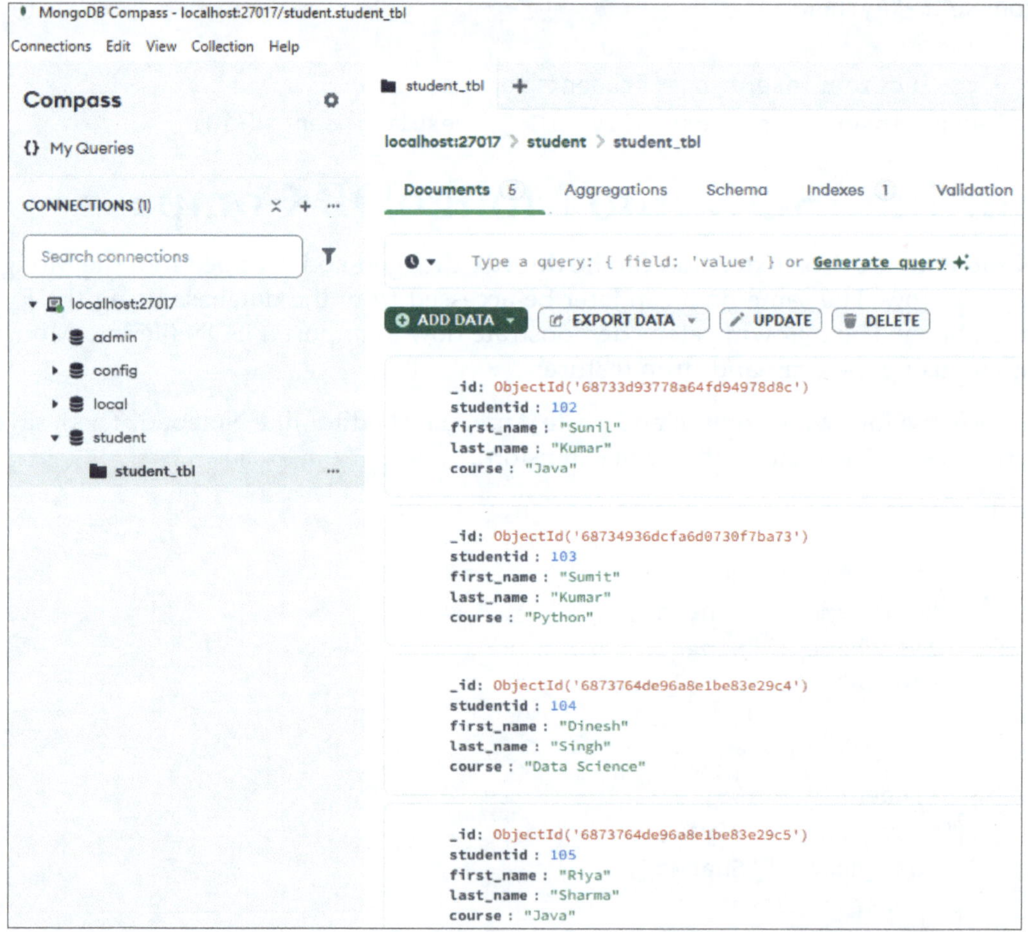

***Figure 6.30**: Importing a data (collections) from sample.json file to MongoDB Compass*

Example 6.13: Write a program to fetch and display JSON data import using sample.json file from MongoDB

In this code, the data imported using the **sample.json** file in the previous example is fetched and displayed from the MongoDB database. The following program demonstrates how to fetch and display data stored in MongoDB after importing it from a JSON file:

```
from pymongo import MongoClient
# Step 1: Connect to MongoDB
client = MongoClient("mongodb://localhost:27017/")
db = client["student"] # Access the 'student' database
collection = db["student_tbl"]# Access the 'student_tbl' collection
# Step 2: Fetch all records
records = collection.find()
# Step 3: Display records
print("Student Records from MongoDB:\n")
for record in records:
    print(f"Student ID: {record['studentid']}")
    print(f"First Name: {record['first_name']}")
    print(f"Last Name: {record['last_name']}")
    print(f"Course: {record['course']}")
    # Print 30 dashes(-) in a row after each record
    print("-" * 30)
# Step 4: Close the connection
client.close()
```

The output of the code is shown in *Figure 6.31*:

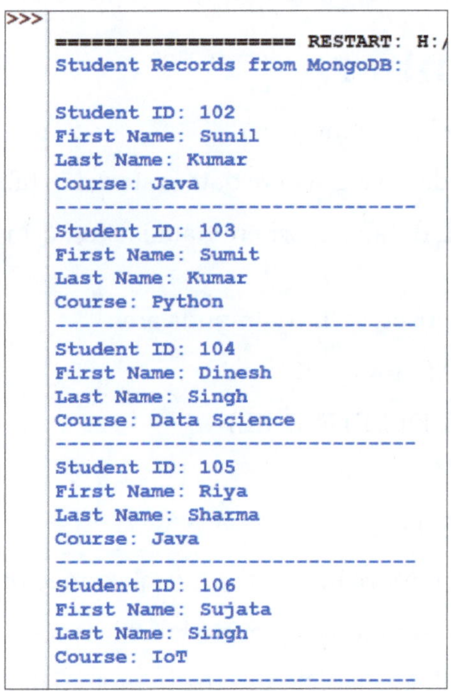

***Figure 6.31**: Fetched data of sample.json file from MongoDB*

Conclusion

This chapter introduces students to the concept of database connectivity in Python using both relational (MySQL) and non-relational (MongoDB) databases. It begins with a brief overview of databases, including DDL, DML, DQL, DCL, and TCL commands in MySQL, and how these operations are executed using Python code through the mysql.connector library. Students learn how to create databases and tables, insert, update, delete, and retrieve records using SQL queries.

The chapter also covers the step-by-step process of installing MySQL Server, MySQL Connector, and establishing a connection from Python. It emphasizes best practices, such as using placeholders (%s) in queries to avoid SQL injection.

The second part introduces MongoDB, a NoSQL database that stores data in JSON-like documents. Students learn how to install MongoDB and pymongo, connect Python to MongoDB, and perform basic CRUD operations. The examples demonstrate inserting, updating, deleting, and reading documents using Python. The concept of importing JSON files into MongoDB Compass is also discussed, along with a sample mini-application for managing student records.

By the end of this chapter, students will have understood the core differences between MySQL and MongoDB, the use of structured versus unstructured data, and how to apply Python code to interact with both types of databases effectively for real-world data management tasks.

Points to remember

The following points are to be kept in mind:

- MySQL is a relational database, where data is stored in tables using rows and columns.
- MongoDB is a NoSQL database, where data is stored in documents similar to JSON format.
- In MySQL, commonly used SQL commands are:
    - CREATE, DROP, ALTER (DDL)
    - INSERT, UPDATE, DELETE (DML)
    - SELECT (DQL)
    - GRANT, REVOKE (DCL)
- To connect Python with MySQL, use the mysql.connector module.
- SQL queries in Python should use placeholders like %s to prevent SQL injection.
- To connect Python with MongoDB, use the pymongo library.
- MongoDB uses collections instead of tables and documents instead of rows.

- The insert_one(), find(), update_one(), and delete_one() methods are used in MongoDB for CRUD operations.
- A JSON file can be directly dragged and dropped into MongoDB Compass to import data easily.
- File extension of JSON file is .json.
- Always close the database connection after performing database operations to free up resources.

Key terms

- **Database**: It is a structured collection of data for easy access and management.
- **Table**: Table in MySQL is defined as a set of rows and columns used to store related data in a relational database.
- **Collection**: Collection in MongoDB is a group of MongoDB documents, equivalent to a table in MySQL.
- **Document**: Document in MongoDB is a single record in MongoDB, stored in a JSON-like format.
- **Record**: Record is a single row of data in a table (MySQL) or a document (MongoDB).
- **SQL**: SQL is a language used to perform operations like create, insert, update, and query in relational databases.
- **DDL**: DDL are the SQL commands like CREATE, ALTER, DROP used to define or change the structure of the database.
- **DML**: DML are commands like INSERT, UPDATE, DELETE to manipulate data.
- **DQL**: DQL used to retrieve data from databases using SELECT.
- **PyMySQL/mysql.connector**: These are Python libraries used to connect and interact with MySQL databases.
- **PyMongo**: PyMongo is a Python library used to connect and work with MongoDB.
- **JSON**: JSON is a lightweight data format used in MongoDB to store documents.
- **Query**: It is defined as a request to access or modify data from the database.
- **Placeholder (%s)**: It is used in SQL statements in Python to safely insert values and prevent SQL injection.
- **Cursor**: Cursor is a control structure used in Python to interact with the database and execute SQL queries.

- **commit()**: It is prebuilt method or function saves changes permanently to the database after insert, update, or delete operations. It is important in MySQL to ensure data is not lost.
- **fetchall() or fetchone()**: It is used to Retrieve all or one row from the result set of a query. It is used to read data from MySQL queries.
- **MongoClient()**: MongoClient() from pymongo establishes a connection to the MongoDB server.Example: MongoClient("mongodb://localhost:27017/")
- **insert_one() or insert_many()**: These methods are used in MongoDB to insert one or multiple documents into a collection. Example: collection.insert_one(data)
- **find() or find_one()**: It is used to retrieve documents from a MongoDB collection.
- **update_one() and delete_one()**: These are MongoDB methods to update or delete a document using conditions.
- **input()**: It is a Python function to take user input, often used for dynamic record insertion or updates.
- **print()**: It displays output messages or records on the screen.
- **String Formatting (f-strings):** It is used for building dynamic SQL or output strings. Example: print(f"Student Name: {name}, ID: {regid}")

Multiple choice questions

1. **Which method is used to establish a connection to a MySQL database in Python?**
   a. connect_db() b. mysql()
   c. connect() d. open()
2. **Which object is created to execute SQL queries in MySQL from Python?**
   a. command b. cursor
   c. session d. executor
3. **What is the use of commit() method in MySQL connectivity?**
   a. To delete a database
   b. To close the connection
   c. To permanently save changes
   d. To create a table

4. **Which method is used in PyMongo to insert one document into a MongoDB collection?**
   a. insert_doc()
   b. insert_one()
   c. add()
   d. insert()

5. **Which of the following is used to retrieve all records from a MySQL table?**
   a. getall()
   b. select_all()
   c. fetchall()
   d. read()

6. **Which library in Python is used to connect with MongoDB?**
   a. mysql.connector
   b. sqlalchemy
   c. pymongo
   d. mongosql

7. **Which method in PyMongo is used to find a specific document?**
   a. finddata()
   b. get()
   c. search_one()
   d. find_one()

8. **What does the close() method do in MySQL and MongoDB code?**
   a. Deletes the database
   b. Closes the connection to the database
   c. Hides records
   d. Commits changes

9. **Which Python function is used to take user input for database operations?**
   a. raw_input()
   b. get()
   c. input()
   d. readline()

10. **Which of the following best describes cursor.execute() in MySQL?**
    a. It defines a function
    b. It runs SQL queries from Python
    c. It saves data
    d. It exits the program

Answers

1	c
2	b
3	c
4	b
5	c
6	c
7	d
8	b
9	c
10	b

Questions

1. What is a database? Explain the difference between MySQL and MongoDB with examples.
2. How can we create a database and a table in MySQL using Python? Write a short program to demonstrate.
3. What are DDL, DML, and DQL commands? Explain each with suitable MySQL command examples.
4. What is the purpose of the cursor() and commit() methods in Python-MySQL connectivity?
5. Write a Python program to insert a record into a MySQL table named student_tbl having fields: studentid, first_name, last_name, and course.
6. How can you fetch and display all records from a MySQL table using Python? Write a simple program and explain.
7. How do you connect Python with MongoDB using the PyMongo library? Explain the steps briefly.
8. Write a Python program to insert a document into a MongoDB collection student_tbl with fields: studentid, first_name, last_name, and course.
9. How can you update and delete a record in MongoDB using Python? Write separate examples and explain.
10. What is a JSON document in MongoDB? Give an example of how the same data is represented in JSON format.

CHAPTER 7
NumPy Library

Introduction

This chapter introduces the fundamental concepts of NumPy, one of the core libraries in Python for numerical and scientific computing. It focuses on working with arrays (ndarrays) and performing vectorized computations efficiently. Students will learn how to create and manipulate NumPy arrays, explore basic indexing and slicing techniques, and apply arithmetic operations on arrays. The chapter also explains the use of NumPy's **universal functions** (**ufuncs**), which provide fast element-wise operations, including mathematical, logical, and statistical functions. These tools form the foundation for high-performance computing in Python and are widely used in data analysis, machine learning, and scientific applications.

Structure

The following topics are covered in this chapter:

- NumPy
- Creating ndarrays
- Basic indexing and slicing
- Arithmetic with NumPy arrays
- Boolean indexing
- Universal functions in NumPy
- Broadcasting in NumPy
- Reshaping arrays
- NumPy for data preprocessing and statistical analysis

Objectives

The objective of this chapter is to introduce students to the core concepts of the NumPy library in Python, which is essential for numerical and scientific computing. Students will gain an understanding of how to work with arrays and perform vectorized computations efficiently. The chapter focuses on creating and manipulating ndarrays, performing arithmetic operations on NumPy arrays, and applying universal functions for mathematical and statistical tasks.

Additionally, students will learn basic indexing and slicing techniques, all explained through simple and illustrative examples to build a solid foundation in NumPy programming.

NumPy

NumPy, the abbreviation for **Numerical Python**, is a well-known Python package for carrying out mathematical operations on sizable, multi-dimensional arrays and matrices. The NumPy library provides support for arrays, which helps in storing and manipulating huge datasets effectively. The mathematical functions provide support for complex mathematical operations such as statistics, linear algebra, and trigonometry. Similar to Python lists, arrays are designed for numerical operations. The size and data type of arrays are fixed.

Note: **Before executing NumPy programs, ensure the NumPy library is installed. You can install it using the command prompt by running the command:**

```
pip install numpy
```

This can be done from any directory, provided Python and **`pip`** are correctly set up in your system's PATH. It is not mandatory to run the installation from the Python installation directory if Python is properly added to the system PATH variable. To install the NumPy library, this can be done by opening the command prompt and running the installation command in the directory where Python is installed, as shown in *Figure 7.1*:

```
Command Prompt
Microsoft Windows [Version 10.0.19045.5247]
(c) Microsoft Corporation. All rights reserved.

C:\Users\LENOVO>cd C:\Users\LENOVO\AppData\Local\Programs\Python\Python313
```

***Figure 7.1**: Command prompt for installing NumPy library in the Python directory*

Now type the command **`python -m pip install numpy`** on the command prompt as shown in *Figure 7.2* for installing the NumPy library:

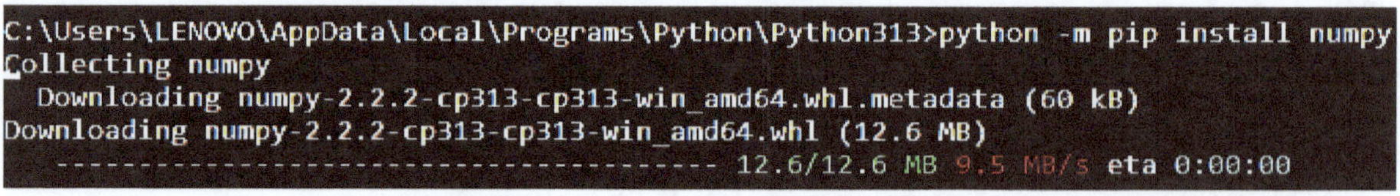

```
C:\Users\LENOVO\AppData\Local\Programs\Python\Python313>python -m pip install numpy
Collecting numpy
  Downloading numpy-2.2.2-cp313-cp313-win_amd64.whl.metadata (60 kB)
Downloading numpy-2.2.2-cp313-cp313-win_amd64.whl (12.6 MB)
   ---------------------------------------- 12.6/12.6 MB 9.5 MB/s eta 0:00:00
```

***Figure 7.2**: Command for installing numpy library*

Creating ndarrays

In NumPy, the core data structure is the **N-dimensional array** (**ndarray**). An ndarray is a powerful, flexible container that can hold large amounts of data in one or more dimensions.

Unlike Python lists, which can store mixed data types, an ndarray is homogeneous, meaning all elements share the same data type (e.g., all integers or all floats). This consistency allows NumPy to store data more efficiently and perform operations much faster than built-in Python sequences. Arrays can be **one-dimensional (1D)**, similar to a list, **two-dimensional (2D)**, like a table or matrix, or even multi-dimensional for more complex data such as images or scientific datasets. Since ndarrays provide a foundation for mathematical and statistical operations, they are considered the building blocks of numerical computing in Python.

Example 7.1: Using NumPy, write a program for one and 2D arrays

Here, we import the NumPy library. NumPy works with arrays, and the array object in NumPy is known as ndarray. A NumPy ndarray object is created using the **`array()`** function. The variables **`student_marks`** and **`subject_marks`** are used for creating a 1D array and a 2D array. Take a look at the following code:

```
import numpy as np
# 1D Array representing marks of students
student_marks = np.array([12, 22, 31, 42, 52])

# 2D Array representing marks of students in two subjects
subject_marks = np.array([[12, 22], [32, 42]])
# Printing the arrays
print("1-Dimensional Array (Student Marks):", student_marks)
print("2-Dimensional Array (Subject-wise Marks):\n", subject_marks)
```

The output of the code is shown in *Figure 7.3*:

```
>>>
    = RESTART: C:\Users\LENOVO\AppData\Local\Programs
    y
    1-Dimensional Array: [12 22 31 42 52]
    2-Dimensional Array:
     [[12 22]
     [32 42]]
```

Figure 7.3: Output of one and 2D arrays using the numpy library

Example 7.2: Write a program for finding array attributes using NumPy

In this example, the attributes of an array are utilized using the NumPy library. Here, the properties of an array are defined using attributes such as **`shape`**, **`ndim`**, **`dtype`**, and **`size`**. Take a look at the following code:

```
import numpy as np
# 1D Array
var1 = np.array([12, 22, 31, 42, 52])
# 2D Array
```

```
var2 = np.array([[12, 22], [32, 42]])
print("Displaying rows and columns of an array:", var2.
shape)# Rows and columns
print("Number of dimensions:", var2.ndim) # Number of dimensions
print("Data type of elements:", var2.dtype)  # Type of elements
print("Total number of elements:", var2.size)    # Total elements
```

The output is shown in *Figure 7.4*:

```
>>>
= RESTART: C:/Users/LENOVO/AppData/Local/Programs/Python/
y
Displaying rows and columns of an array: (2, 2)
Number of dimensions: 2
Data type of elements: int64
Total number of elements: 4
```

Figure 7.4: Output of a program for finding array attributes using NumPy

Note: Make note of the following:

- **NumPy arrays are preferred over Python lists because they store elements of the same data type, making them more memory-efficient and faster for numerical operations. Unlike lists, arrays allow vectorization, which means applying operations on the entire array at once without writing explicit loops. This approach not only makes the code shorter and easier to read but also provides a significant speed advantage. They support vectorized operations, so you can perform mathematical calculations on entire arrays without writing loops.**
- **Vectorization means applying operations to entire arrays or large chunks of data at once, rather than processing each element individually with loops. Example: Squaring all elements in an array using `arr**2` is vectorized, while using a `for` loop is not.**

Basic indexing and slicing

NumPy indexing and slicing are used to fetch some specific data or elements from NumPy arrays. Indexing starts from 0, and slicing is performed using indexing.

Basic indexing and slicing allow us to access specific elements or portions of a NumPy array using their positions. Indexing refers to selecting a single element by its index, while slicing extracts a range of elements by specifying a start, end, and optional step value. In multi-dimensional arrays, indexing and slicing can be applied across rows and columns to select subarrays. This provides a simple and efficient way to work with different parts of an array without creating new data structures.

It works like Python lists and accesses elements using integer indices (**arr[0]**, **arr[-1]**). Suppose, in a code statement **arr = np.array([10,15,20,25,30])**, if we **print(arr[0])**, the value will be displayed as **10**, and if we write a statement, **print(arr[-1])**, the value will be displayed as **30**.

Example 7.3: Write a program that utilizes the NumPy library for array indexing and slicing operations

This example demonstrates an array being initialized with specified values. The element at the first position is displayed using the indexing method. The elements in positions 1 through 3 are displayed via slicing. In the slicing operation, **var1 [0:4]**, the elements will be printed from the 0th position to the 3rd position. Here, the fourth position element will not be considered as the slice ends just before index 4. Take a look at the following code:

```
import numpy as np
var1 = np.array([11, 21, 32, 43, 51])
# Indexing
print("Print first element at index 0:", var1[0])
# Slicing
print("Print elements from index 0 to 3:", var1[0:4])
# Modify elements
var1[2] = 101
print("Print modified array:", var1)
```

The output is shown in *Figure 7.5*:

```
>>>
= RESTART: C:/Users/LENOVO/AppData/Local/Programs
y
Print first element at index 0: 11
Print elements from index 0 to 3: [11 21 32 43]
Print modified array: [ 11  21 101  43  51]
```

Figure 7.5: Output of the array indexing and slicing operations

Arithmetic with NumPy arrays

Arithmetic with NumPy arrays allows us to perform mathematical operations directly on arrays, element by element, without writing explicit loops. Operations such as addition, subtraction, multiplication, division, and exponentiation can be applied between arrays of the same shape, or between an array and a scalar value.

Example 7.4: Write a program for performing element-wise computations on arrays

Using the NumPy library, element-wise calculations can also be carried out on arrays, as shown in the following program:

```
import numpy as np
var1 = np.array([2, 3, 4])
var2 = np.array([5, 6, 7])
# Addition
print("Addition of array:", var1 + var2)
# Multiplication
print("Multiplying array:", var1 * var2)
# Scalar operations
print("Multiplying Array * 2:", var1 * 2)
```

The output of the code is shown in *Figure 7.6*:

```
>>>
= RESTART: C:/Users/LENOVO/AppData/Local/Programs/Python/
y
Addition of array: [ 7  9 11]
Multiplying array: [10 18 28]
Multiplying Array * 2: [4 6 8]
```

Figure 7.6: Output of the element-wise operations on arrays

Example 7.5: Write a program for matrix operations

Matrix operations, including addition, subtraction, multiplication, and transposition, can be carried out using the NumPy library. Take a look at the following code:

```
import numpy as np
# Define two matrices
matrix1 = np.array([[2, 3], [4, 5]])
matrix2 = np.array([[1, 2], [2, 2]])
# Matrix Addition
addition = matrix1 + matrix2
print("Matrix Addition:\n", addition)
# Matrix Subtraction
subtraction = matrix1 - matrix2
print("Matrix Subtraction:\n",subtraction)
# Matrix Multiplication (Dot Product)
matrix_multiply = np.dot(matrix1, matrix2)
print("Matrix Multiplication:\n", matrix_multiply)
# Transpose of a Matrix
transpose = matrix1.T
print("Transpose of matrix1:\n", transpose)
```

The output is shown in *Figure 7.7*:

```
>>>
= RESTART: C:/Users/LENOVO/AppData/Local/Programs/Python/Python313/
y
Matrix Addition:
 [[3 5]
 [6 7]]
Matrix Subtraction:
 [[1 1]
 [2 3]]
Matrix Multiplication:
 [[ 8 10]
 [14 18]]
Transpose of matrix1:
 [[2 4]
 [3 5]]
Transpose of matrix2:
 [[1 2]
 [2 2]]
```

***Figure 7.7**: Output of the matrix operations on arrays*

Example 7.6: Create a NumPy array using arrange() function

In this example, a **numpy** array is created using a predefined **arange()** function. The elements of an array are accessed using indexing. The program is mentioned as follows:

```
import numpy as np
var1 = np.arange(1,10,1)
print("Elements of array:",var1)
var2 = var1[np.array([3,1,2,-1,-2])]
print("Fetching the elements using indexing",var2)
```

The output of the program is shown in the following figure:

```
>>>
=== RESTART: C:/Users/DELL/AppData/Local/Programs/Python/
Elements of array: [1 2 3 4 5 6 7 8 9]
Fetching the elements using indexing [4 2 3 9 8]
```

***Figure 7.8**: Output of indexing using NumPy arange() function*

Boolean indexing

Boolean indexing enables the filtering of array elements according to specific criteria. In *Example 7.7*, an array is initialized using the **array()** function, and the elements greater than or equal to 25 are filtered using Boolean indexing.

Example 7.7: Write a program for filtering arrays using Boolean conditions

This NumPy example demonstrates how to use Boolean indexing to filter values from an array based on a condition. First, a NumPy array **arr** is created containing the elements **[20,**

25, 30, 45, 55]. A condition **arr >= 25** is then applied, which checks each element and returns a Boolean array: **[False, True, True, True, True]**. This indicates which values in the original array meet the condition of being greater than or equal to 25. Using this Boolean array to index the original array, a new array **arr1** is created, containing only the values that satisfy the condition: **[25, 30, 45, 55]**. Finally, the original array, the Boolean result of the condition, and the filtered array are printed. Take a look at the following figure:

```
import numpy as np
# Create a NumPy array
arr = np.array([20, 25, 30, 45, 55])
# Boolean condition: Find elements greater than or equal to 25
check = arr >= 25
# Use the condition to index the array
arr1 = arr[check]
print("Original Array:", arr)
print("Conditional array (array >= 25):", check)
print("Filtered Array:", arr1)
```

The output of the code is shown in *Figure 7.9*:

```
>>>
    === RESTART: C:/Users/DELL/AppData/Local/Programs/Python/Python311
    Original Array: [20 25 30 45 55]
    Conditional array (array >= 25): [False  True  True  True  True]
    Filtered Array: [25 30 45 55]
```

Figure 7.9: Output of the Boolean indexing

Universal functions in NumPy

NumPy contains several universal functions. The universal functions are built-in functions from NumPy that carry out operations on arrays, element-wise. These functions have been designed for speed, resulting in them being significantly quicker than their loop counterparts in Python.

Example 7.8: Write a program demonstrating NumPy universal functions

In this example, scenario element-wise operations are carried out via NumPy's universal functions. The array is manipulated using the **square()** function to calculate the square of each element, the **sqrt()** function to find the square root of each element, and the **exp()** function to compute the exponential of each element. Take a look at the following code:

```
import numpy as np
# Create an array
var1 = np.array([12, 22, 23, 34, 45])
# Element-wise operations
```

```
square1 = np.square(var1)  # Squares each element
sqrt1 = np.sqrt(var1)      # Square root of each element
exp1 = np.exp(var1)        # Exponential of each element
print("Original array displayed:", var1)
print("Square of each element:", square1)
print("Square root of each element:", sqrt1)
print("Exponential of each element:", exp1)
```

The output of *Example 7.8* is shown in *Figure 7.10*:

```
>>>
= RESTART: C:/Users/LENOVO/AppData/Local/Programs/Python/Python313/ch7_numpy6.p
y
Original array displayed: [12 22 23 34 45]
Square of each element: [ 144  484  529 1156 2025]
Square root of each element: [3.46410162 4.69041576 4.79583152 5.83095189 6.708
20393]
Exponential of each element: [1.62754791e+05 3.58491285e+09 9.74480345e+09 5.83
461743e+14
 3.49342711e+19]
```

***Figure 7.10**: Element-wise operations using NumPy universal functions*

Example 7.9: Write a program to sort the elements using the sort() function

Using the NumPy **sort()** function in *Example 7.9*, elements are arranged in ascending order. This Python example demonstrates how to sort a NumPy array using the **np.sort()** function. First, an array **var1** is created with the elements [25, 2, 18, 11, 9]. The **np.sort(var1)** function is then used to return a new array containing the same elements in ascending order without modifying the original array. The sorted array is stored in the variable sort, which becomes **[2, 9, 11, 18, 25]**. Finally, both the original array and the sorted array are printed to show the difference. This example highlights how NumPy simplifies sorting operations and preserves the original data unless explicitly modified. Take a look at the following code:

```
import numpy as np
var1 = np.array([25, 2, 18, 11, 9])
sort = np.sort(var1)
print("Original Array:", var1)
print("Array after sorting:", sort)
```

The output is shown in *Figure 7.11*:

```
>>>
= RESTART: C:/Users/LENOVO/AppData/Local/Progra
y
Original Array: [25  2 18 11  9]
Array after sorting: [ 2  9 11 18 25]
```

***Figure 7.11**: Output of the sorted array using sort () function*

A 2D array can also be sorted row-wise by utilizing the **sort()** function, as shown in *Example 7.10.*

Example 7.10: Write a program for sorting 2D array

This example demonstrates how to sort a 2D NumPy array row-wise using the **np.sort()** function. The array **var2** contains two rows: **[[32, 21, 15], [11, 4, 64]]**. By specifying **axis=1**, the **np.sort()** function sorts the elements within each row individually in ascending order. As a result, the sorted array becomes **[[15, 21, 32], [4, 11, 64]]**. This is useful when you want to organize data across each row without altering the structure of the array. Take a look at the following code:

```
import numpy as np
var2 = np.array([[32, 21, 15], [11, 4, 64]])
sort = np.sort(var2, axis=1)  # Sort row-wise
print("Sorted row-wise elements in 2-D array",sort)
```

The output of the code is shown in *Figure 7.12*:

```
>>>
= RESTART: C:/Users/LENOVO/AppData/Local/Programs/Python
y
Sorted row-wise elements in 2-D array [[15 21 32]
 [ 4 11 64]]
```

***Figure 7.12**: Sorting of 2D array using sort() function*

Broadcasting in NumPy

NumPy features powerful broadcasting operations that enable arithmetic operations between arrays of varying dimensions. When performing operations, such as addition and multiplication, between a NumPy array and a scalar, NumPy automatically adjusts the scalar to match the array's shape without duplicating the data.

Example 7.11: Write a program for broadcasting scalar to array

In this example, even though **scalar = 5** is a single number, NumPy broadcasts it to behave like an array of the same shape as **arr1.** Broadcasting allows operations between different-sized arrays, i.e., array and scalar. It avoids memory wastage by not copying values. NumPy just pretends the smaller array is expanded. In this program, a NumPy array **arr1** is created with values **[12, 25, 35]**, and a scalar value **5** is defined. When you perform **arr1 + scalar**, NumPy automatically applies broadcasting, which means the scalar 5 is added to each element of the array. Take a look at the following code:

```
import numpy as np
arr1 = np.array([12, 25, 35])
scalar = 5
```

```
result = arr1 + scalar  # Broadcasting scalar to array
print("Original array:", arr1)
print("Result after adding scalar (broadcasting):", result)
```

The operation is done element-wise, and the result is stored in result. The output of *Example 7.11* is shown in *Figure 7.13*:

```
>>>
==================== RESTART: G:/DS/Chapter 7/Example
Original array: [12 25 35]
Result after adding scalar (broadcasting): [17 30 40]
```

***Figure 7.13**: Output of broadcasting scalar to array*

Note: Broadcasting is a method that NumPy uses to allow arithmetic between arrays of different shapes. In this case, a scalar (single value) is automatically applied to each element of the array. This makes array operations faster and more efficient without writing loops.

Example 7.12: Write a program for broadcasting a 1D array to a 2D array

In this example, **arr2** is a 2D array with two rows and three columns. **arr1** is a 1D array with three elements. When **arr2 + arr1** is performed, NumPy broadcasts the 1D array across each row of the 2D array. Take a look at the following code:

```
import numpy as np
# 2D array with shape (2, 3)
arr2 = np.array([[11, 10, 20],
                 [20, 30, 30]])
# 1D array with shape (3,)
arr1 = np.array([1, 2, 3])
# Broadcasting: add arr1D to each row of arr2D
result = arr2 + arr1
print("Original 2D array:\n", arr2)
print("1D array:\n", arr1)
print("Result after broadcasting:\n", result)
```

Figure 7.14 shows the output of broadcasting a 1D array onto a 2D array:

```
Original 2D array:
 [[11 10 20]
 [20 30 30]]
1D array:
 [1 2 3]
Result after broadcasting:
 [[12 12 23]
 [21 32 33]]
```

***Figure 7.14**: Output of broadcasting a 1D array to a 2D array*

Reshaping arrays

Reshaping arrays is useful when changing the shape of an array without changing data. The concept of reshaping arrays is discussed in *Example 7.13*.

Example 7.13: Write a program for transforming 1D array into a 2D array using reshape() function

In this program, we start by importing the NumPy library as **`np`**. We then create a 1D NumPy array called **`arr1`** that contains the elements **`[11,12,23,24,35,46]`**. The key operation here is **`reshape((2,3))`**, which transforms the 1D array into a 2D array with two rows and three columns. The reshaping is possible because the total number of elements remains the same ($2 \times 3 = 6$). Finally, the original array and the reshaped array are printed. This demonstrates how the **`reshape()`** function in NumPy is used to reorganize the structure of an array without changing its data. Take a look at the following code:

```
import numpy as np
arr1 = np.array([11,12,23,24,35,46])
reshape_arr1 = arr1.reshape((2, 3))
print("Original array:", arr1)
print("Reshaped array (2x3):")
print(reshape_arr1)
```

The output is shown in *Figure 7.15*:

```
>>>
    ==================== RESTART: G:/DS
    Original array: [11 12 23 24 35 46]
    Reshaped array (2x3):
    [[11 12 23]
     [24 35 46]]
```

Figure 7.15: *Output of transforming 1D array into a 2D array using reshape() function*

NumPy for data preprocessing and statistical analysis

NumPy plays a vital role in data preprocessing and statistical analysis by offering a variety of powerful functions. Common preprocessing tasks include identifying unique elements and their frequency using **`np.unique()`**, detecting missing values with **`np.isnan()`**, and applying conditional logic using **`np.where()`**. Additionally, data transformation techniques like matrix transposition with **`.T`** help reshape data for further analysis. For summarizing data, NumPy provides statistical functions such as **`np.max()`**, **`np.min()`**, and **`np.mean()`** to quickly compute maximum, minimum, and average values. These operations are essential for preparing and understanding data before applying machine learning or advanced analytics.

Example 7.14: Write a program for finding unique elements and their counts

This program demonstrates how to find unique elements in a NumPy array and count how many times each unique element appears. This code is useful in data preprocessing when you want to understand the distribution or frequency of different values in your data. First, the NumPy library is imported using **`import numpy as np`**. An array **`arr1`** is created containing some repeated values: **`[12,22,3,22,14,14,25]`**. The function **`np.unique(arr1, return_counts=True)`** is used to extract all unique (non-repeated) elements from the array. Take a look at the following code:

```
import numpy as np
arr1 = np.array([12,22,3,22,14,14,25])
unique_values,count_value = np.unique(arr1,return_counts=True)
print("Unique elements:", unique_values)
print("Counts:", count_value)
```

The output of the code is shown in *Figure 7.16*:

```
>>>
    ===================== RESTART: G:/
    Unique elements: [ 3 12 14 22 25]
    Counts: [1 1 2 2 1]
```

Figure 7.16: Output of finding unique elements and their counts

Example 7.15: Write a program for checking for missing or NaN Values

Here, a NumPy array named **`arr1`** is created containing five elements. One of the elements is **`np.nan`**, which stands for not a number and is used to represent missing or undefined values. This prints the original array and then shows a Boolean array indicating whether each element is **`NaN`**. The program checks for missing values (**`NaN`**) in the array. It identifies that the third element is **`NaN`**, and returns **`True`** only at that position in the result. This technique is useful in data cleaning and preprocessing, especially when working with real-world datasets that may contain incomplete data. Take a look at the following code:

```
import numpy as np
arr1 = np.array([11,12,np.nan,14,15])
is_nan_val = np.isnan(arr1)
print("Original Array is:", arr1)
print("Finding a NaN value:", is_nan_val)
```

The output of checking missing or NaN values is shown in *Figure 7.17*:

```
>>>
    ==================== RESTART: G:/DS/Chapter 7/Exampl
    Original Array is: [11. 12. nan 14. 15.]
    Finding a NaN value: [False False  True False False]
```

Figure 7.17: Output of checking missing or NaN values

Example 7.16: Write a program using where() for conditional logic

This NumPy program demonstrates how to apply conditional logic on a NumPy array using the **np.where()** function. First, a 1D array **arr1** is created containing the elements **[10,15,25,35,40]**. The **np.where()** function is then used to evaluate each element of the array against a condition, specifically, whether each element is greater than 20. If the condition is true for an element, the string **Greater** is returned; otherwise, the string **Less** is returned. This results in a new array **result** that holds the outcome of the condition for each element in the original array. Finally, both the original and the conditionally evaluated arrays are printed. This type of operation is useful for data preprocessing, such as categorizing or labeling values based on certain thresholds. Take a look at the following code:

```
import numpy as np
arr1 = np.array([10,15,25,35,40])
result = np.where(arr1>20,"Greater","Less")
print("Original Array is:",arr1)
print("Result after condition is:",result)
```

The output of the code is shown in *Figure 7.18*:

```
>>>
    ==================== RESTART: G:/DS/Chapter 7/Example7.16.py ===========
    Original Array is: [10 15 25 35 40]
    Result after condition is: ['Less' 'Less' 'Greater' 'Greater' 'Greater']
```

Figure 7.18: Output of applying conditional logic on NumPy array

Example 7.17: Write a program for finding the transpose of a matrix

The transpose of a matrix is used in matrix algebra and data manipulation. This code demonstrates how to perform the transpose of a 2D NumPy array. A matrix named **arr1** is first created using NumPy with elements arranged as **[[1, 2], [3, 4]]**. The transpose of this matrix is then obtained using the **.T** attribute, which effectively swaps the rows and columns. As a result, the first row becomes the first column and the second row becomes the second column. The original matrix is displayed along with its transposed version. Transposing is a common operation in mathematical computations, especially in linear algebra and data analysis, where it helps in aligning data structures for operations like matrix multiplication or data transformation. Take a look at the following code:

```
import numpy as np
arr1 = np.array([[1, 2], [3, 4]])
transpose_matrix = arr1.T
print("Original Matrix:\n", arr1)
print("Transposed Matrix:\n", transpose_matrix)
```

The output of transposing a matrix is shown in *Figure 7.19*:

```
>>>
=====================
Original Matrix:
 [[1 2]
 [3 4]]
Transposed Matrix:
 [[1 3]
 [2 4]]
```

***Figure 7.19**: Output of transposing a matrix*

Example 7.18: Write a program for finding maximum, minimum, and mean using NumPy's built-in statistical methods

The given code demonstrates how to perform basic statistical operations using the NumPy library in Python. First, a 1D NumPy array **`arr1`** is created with the elements **`[23, 37, 42, 29, 21]`**. Using the **`np.max()`** function, the program identifies and prints the maximum value in the array, which is 42. Similarly, the **`np.min()`** function is used to find and print the minimum value, which is 21. Finally, the **`np.mean()`** function calculates the average (mean) of all elements in the array, which in this case is $(23 + 37 + 42 + 29 + 21)/5 = 30.4$. This example shows how NumPy can be used effectively for simple statistical analysis on numeric data:

```
import numpy as np
arr1 = np.array([23,37,42,29,21])
print("Maximum Value:", np.max(arr1))
print("Minimum Value:", np.min(arr1))
print("Mean Value:", np.mean(arr1))
```

The output of the code is shown in *Figure 7.20*:

```
>>>
=====================
Maximum Value: 42
Minimum Value: 21
Mean Value: 30.4
```

***Figure 7.20**: Output of finding maximum, minimum, and mean using built-in statistical methods*

Example 7.19: Write a program for creating a 2D NumPy array, checking its shape and data type

The given code demonstrates the use of NumPy to create and manipulate a 2D array. First, a 2D array **`arr1`** is created using **`np.array`** with two rows and three columns. The code then prints the shape of the array using **`arr1.shape`**, which returns (2,3), indicating two rows and three columns. It also prints the data type of the array elements using **`arr1.dtype`**, which typically shows **`int64`** because the elements are integers. Lastly, the code uses **`arr1.flatten`**

`()` to convert the 2D array into a 1D array (i.e., flatten it), resulting in a single list of values: **`[1,2,3,4,5,6]`**. This example highlights basic operations such as checking array shape, data type, and flattening multi-dimensional arrays into a simpler form using NumPy. Take a look at the following example:

```
import numpy as np
arr1 = np.array([[1, 2, 3], [4, 5, 6]])
print("Shape of Array:", arr1.shape)
print("Data Type of Array:", arr1.dtype)
print("Flattened Array:", arr1.flatten())
```

The output of creating a 2D NumPy array, checking its shape, and data type is shown in *Figure 7.21*:

```
>>>
==================== RESTART:
Shape of Array: (2, 3)
Data Type of Array: int32
Flattened Array: [1 2 3 4 5 6]
```

Figure 7.21*: Output of creating a 2D NumPy array, checking its shape and data type*

Conclusion

In this chapter, we explored the powerful features of the Python NumPy library, which is essential for numerical and scientific computing. Beginning with the creation of 1D and 2D arrays, we understood the structure and importance of ndarray. We covered key array attributes such as shape, size, and datatype, followed by basic operations like indexing, slicing, reshaping, and sorting.

We also discussed how to perform element-wise arithmetic operations, matrix operations, and utilize universal functions such as np.sqrt(), np.exp() for efficient computations. The concept of broadcasting was introduced to show how NumPy handles operations between arrays and scalars or differently shaped arrays.

Furthermore, we delved into Boolean indexing, filtering using conditions, and statistical analysis using functions like np.max(), np.min(), and np.mean(). We also learned how to handle data preprocessing tasks such as finding unique values, detecting missing (NaN) values, and using conditional functions like np.where().

By the end of this chapter, students should be comfortable with using NumPy to handle array-based data efficiently and perform a wide range of mathematical, logical, and preprocessing operations, forming a solid foundation for data analysis and machine learning applications in Python.

Points to remember

The following points are to be kept in mind:

- NumPy is a core library in Python for scientific computing. It introduces ndarray, a powerful n-dimensional array object that supports fast, vectorized (element-wise) operations, eliminating the need for explicit loops in many cases.
- Arrays in NumPy can be created using the np.array() function by passing Python lists or tuples. Additional functions like np.zeros(), np.ones(), np.arange(), and np.linspace() provide convenient ways to initialize arrays with specific patterns or values.
- NumPy supports arithmetic operations such as addition, subtraction, multiplication, and division directly on arrays. These operations are applied element-wise and are much faster due to NumPy's optimized implementation.
- Individual elements of an array can be accessed using indices. NumPy allows slicing, which means selecting a range of values from an array. In multi-dimensional arrays, indexing is done using comma-separated values (e.g., arr[1, 2]).
- Boolean indexing allows the selection of array elements that satisfy a particular condition. For example, arr[arr > 10] returns all elements greater than 10. It is a useful method for filtering or modifying data based on conditions.
- NumPy provides a set of universal functions (like np.sqrt(), np.exp(), np.mean(), np.max()) that operate element-wise on arrays. These functions are optimized and provide faster computation compared to loops.
- Broadcasting refers to NumPy's ability to perform arithmetic operations between arrays of different shapes. For example, adding a scalar value to a 1D array automatically expands the scalar to match the shape of the array.
- The shape of an array can be changed using the reshape() function, provided the total number of elements remains constant. This is helpful for converting 1D arrays into 2D structures or vice versa for matrix operations.
- NumPy includes several built-in functions for preparing data, such as np.unique() to find distinct values, np.isnan() to detect missing values, and np.where() for conditional logic. It also provides statistical methods like np.mean(), np.min(), and np.max() for summarizing data efficiently.

Key terms

- **Ndarray**: It is a powerful N-dimensional array object in NumPy used for storing and manipulating numerical data.
- **Vectorization**: Vectorization means performing operations on entire arrays without writing explicit loops. It leads to faster computations.

- **Arrays**: Arrays can be created using np.array(), and special arrays using np.zeros(), np.ones(), np.arange(), and np.linspace().
- **Array indexing**: It means accessing specific elements using their position. Multidimensional arrays use comma-separated indices.
- **Array slicing**: It extracts parts (sub-arrays) from arrays using the slice notation (: operator).
- **Boolean indexing**: It refers to selecting data from an array using conditional statements that return Boolean values (True/False).
- **Universal functions (ufuncs)**: These are fast element-wise operations like np.sqrt(), np.abs(), np.exp(), np.log(), np.mean().
- **Broadcasting**: It is a powerful feature that allows NumPy to perform operations on arrays of different shapes by automatically expanding the smaller array.
- **Reshape**: It means changing the shape of an array using reshape() or .T for transpose.
- **NaN (not a number)**: NaN is a special floating-point value used to denote missing or undefined values in an array.
- **np.unique()**: This function finds all unique elements in an array, often used in data cleaning and frequency counting.
- **np.where()**: It performs conditional checks and returns results based on the condition for each element.
- **Transpose**: Transpose means swapping rows and columns in a matrix, useful in mathematical and machine learning applications.
- **Statistical functions**: These are the useful functions like np.mean(), np.min(), np.max(), np.std() to analyze data trends and patterns.

Multiple choice questions

1. **Which function is used to create a NumPy array?**
   a. array()
   b. np.array()
   c. numpy.create()
   d. create_array()
2. **What does the np.arange(5) function return?**
   a. [1, 2, 3, 4, 5]
   b. [0, 1, 2, 3, 4]
   c. [0, 1, 2, 3, 4, 5]
   d. [1, 2, 3, 4]

3. **What is broadcasting in NumPy?**
   a. Combining two arrays
   b. Converting arrays into matrices
   c. Performing operations on arrays of different shapes
   d. Sorting arrays
4. **Which method is used to check for missing (NaN) values?**
   a. np.isnull()
   b. np.check_nan()
   c. np.isnan()
   d. np.isNaN()
5. **What is the output shape of np.array([1,2,3,4,5,6]).reshape(2,3)?**
   a. (3,2)
   b. (6,1)
   c. (2,3)
   d. (1,6)
6. **What will np.where(arr > 10, "Yes", "No") do?**
   a. Return Boolean values only
   b. Replace all values greater than 10 with Yes, others with No
   c. Delete values greater than 10
   d. None of the above
7. **Which function returns both unique elements and their counts?**
   a. np.count()
   b. np.unique()
   c. np.elements()
   d. np.value_count()
8. **What is the result of np.mean(np.array([1,2,3]))?**
   a. 2
   b. 3
   c. 1
   d. 6
9. **Which of the following is a universal function (ufunc) in NumPy?**
   a. np.read()
   b. np.write()
   c. np.sqrt()
   d. np.input()
10. **What does .T do to a NumPy matrix?**
    a. Deletes it
    b. Multiplies it
    c. Transposes it
    d. Flattens it

Answers

1	b
2	b
3	c
4	c
5	c
6	b
7	b
8	a
9	c
10	c

Questions

1. What is NumPy? What is an ndarray in NumPy?
2. List and explain at least three important attributes of a NumPy ndarray.
3. Explain how memory efficiency is achieved using NumPy ndarray over traditional lists.
4. Write a Python program to create a 1D ndarray and display its shape, data type, and size.
5. How can we create a 2D ndarray and reshape it into a 1D array? Illustrate with code.
6. Explain the concept of broadcasting in NumPy with a suitable example. Why is it useful in data processing?
7. What are ufuncs in NumPy? Demonstrate the use of at least three different ufuncs with code examples.
8. How do you perform Boolean indexing in NumPy?
9. Describe the steps involved in reshaping a NumPy array. What are the rules to follow while reshaping?
10. How can you handle missing data (NaN) in NumPy? Write a program that identifies missing values and replaces them.
11. What are the basic operations supported by NumPy arrays? Show examples of addition, multiplication, and comparison between arrays.
12. How can NumPy be used for basic statistical analysis? Write a program to calculate the maximum, minimum, mean, and standard deviation of a dataset.

Chapter 8
Introduction to Pandas Data Structure

Introduction

This chapter introduces the essential components of the Pandas library, a powerful and widely used tool for data manipulation and analysis in Python. It begins with an overview of Series and DataFrame, the fundamental data structures in Pandas, followed by practical techniques for accessing and modifying data using loc. The chapter also delves into real-world data preparation tasks, such as data cleaning and filtering, applying functions with apply(), and exploring datasets using methods like unique() and count(). Additionally, students will learn how to read data from external CSV files and write processed data back into files, making this chapter a practical foundation for data handling in Python.

Structure

The following topics are covered in this chapter:

- Introduction to Pandas Series and DataFrames
- Running Python programs in online and offline environments
- Other tools to run Python programs
- DataFrame and data selection
- Dropping entries
- apply() function for transformation
- Filtering rows based on conditions
- Reading and writing data
- Reading from a CSV file

Objectives

The objective of this chapter is to equip students with a foundational understanding of the Pandas library for data analysis. By the end of the chapter, students will be able to create and manipulate Series and DataFrames, perform data cleaning and filtering tasks, and apply functions to datasets using Pandas tools. They will also be proficient in reading data from CSV files and writing the cleaned or processed results back to external files. The chapter emphasizes hands-on examples to help students develop practical skills in handling and analyzing tabular data using Python.

Introduction to Pandas Series and DataFrames

Pandas is one of the most widely used Python libraries for data analysis and data manipulation, making it an essential tool for students working with real-world datasets. In practical scenarios, data is often messy, large, and stored in different file formats, and Pandas provides efficient structures and functions to clean, analyze, and transform such data with ease. Learning Pandas helps students bridge the gap between raw data and meaningful insights, which is a crucial step in any data-driven workflow. The Pandas library is a free, open-source tool in Python designed for data analysis and data modification. It offers quick, adaptable, and user-friendly data constructs such as Series for one-dimensional and DataFrame for two-dimensional, rendering it indispensable for handling organized data.

The primary characteristics of Pandas are:

- Pandas supports common data preprocessing tasks, including handling missing values, removing duplicates, and performing data transformations.
- Another key feature it offers is data filtering, which enables the selection of specific rows and columns based on certain conditions.
- It performs calculations such as sum, mean, and count, and so on, for data aggregation.
- Pandas are compatible with NumPy, Matplotlib, and other libraries.
- It also offers support for file handling, including reading and writing CSV files, Excel, JSON, and databases.

Although both Series and DataFrame are core Pandas data structures, they differ in terms of dimensionality, structure, and typical usage. To clearly highlight these differences, *Table 8.1* provides a comparison between a Pandas Series and a DataFrame:

Feature	Series	DataFrame
Data structure	One-dimensional	Two-dimensional
Shape	Single column	Rows and columns
Similar to	A single column in a table	A spreadsheet or SQL table
Indexing	Uses a single index	Uses row index and column labels
Example use	Storing marks of one subject	Storing marks of multiple subjects

***Table 8.1**: Comparison between Pandas Series and a DataFrame*

A Pandas Series can be compared to a list or a single column within a table. It comprises actual data values, with the index serving as labels for each corresponding value.

Conceptually, a Pandas Series can be thought of as a one-dimensional list of values, for example: `Series: [78, 85, 90]`. Similarly, a Pandas DataFrame can be thought of as a two-dimensional table with rows and columns, for example:

Math	Science	English
78	82	88

The examples using the Pandas library can be done in a Jupyter Notebook. The Jupyter Notebook is an open-source interactive environment for computing, enabling users to develop and distribute documents that incorporate live code, mathematical equations, visualizations, and explanatory writing. Jupyter supports various languages and executes code interactively, where scripts are divided into small blocks or cells and run individually, rather than running the entire script at one time. The Jupyter Notebook displays text, plots, tables, and multimedia content. It features data visualization capabilities that seamlessly integrate with libraries such as Matplotlib and Seaborn. The Jupyter Notebook file format, denoted by the **`.ipynb`** extension, can be exported in various formats, including HTML, PDF, or Python scripts.

Note: `.ipynb` and `.py` files differ in the following ways:

- **.ipynb (Jupyter Notebook): Used mainly for learning, experimentation, and data analysis. It allows code execution in cells along with text, equations, and visualizations, making it ideal for teaching and exploratory work.**
- **.py (Python Script): Used for writing complete Python programs and applications. It contains only code and is preferred for production, automation, and deployment.**

Follow these steps:

1. A Jupyter Notebook can be used to write and run Python code interactively. One way to access it is through the **Anaconda Navigator**, as shown in *Figure 8.1*:

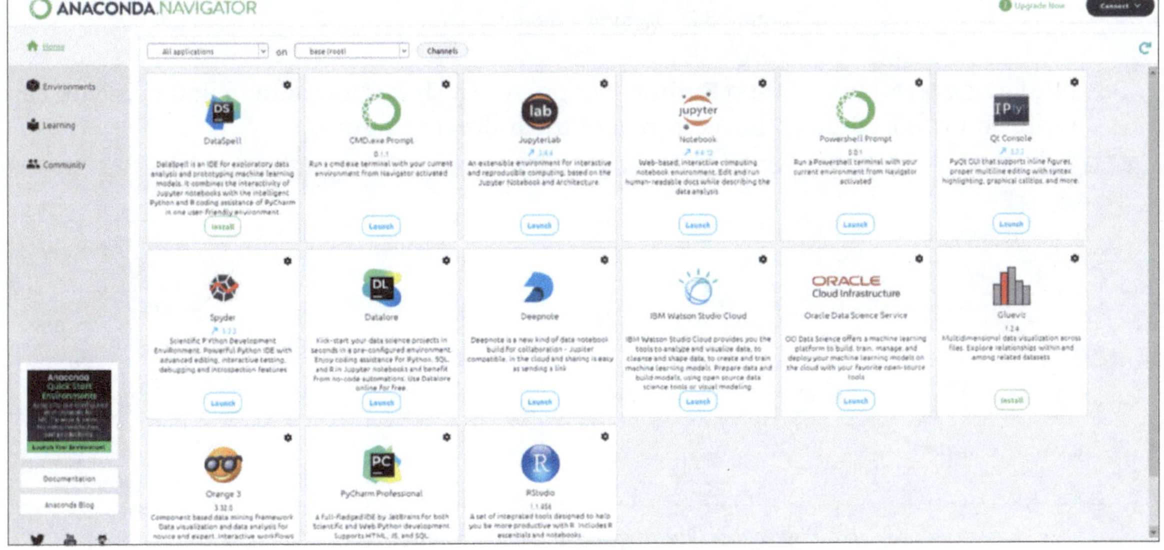

Figure 8.1: Anaconda Navigator Window for launching Jupyter Notebook

2. Alternatively, if Anaconda is not installed, you can download and install **Jupyter Notebook** using **`pip install notebook`** from the command prompt. After successful installation, you can open the Jupyter Notebook interface (refer to *Figure 8.2*).

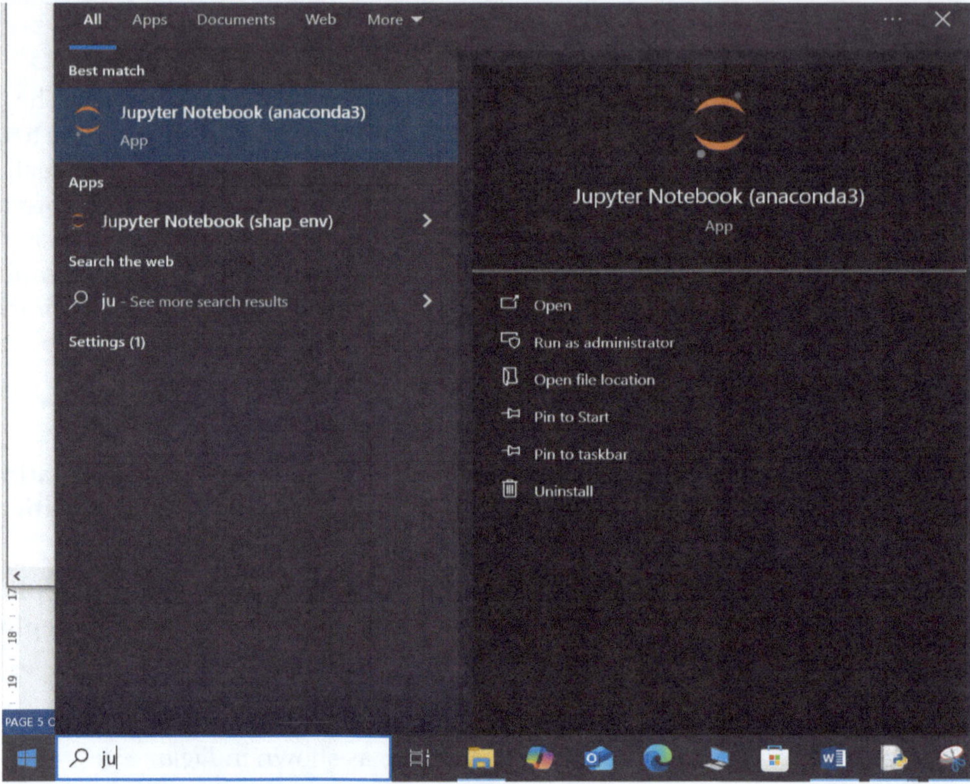

Figure 8.2: Opening a Jupyter Notebook

3. Next, click on **New** and then **Python 3** to open a fresh Python notebook where you can write and run Python code, as shown in the following figure:

Figure 8.3: Opening a new Python 3 notebook

Running Python programs in online and offline environments

Python programs can also be written and executed in online environments like Google Colab, which does not require any installation. Google Colab supports Python and comes with pre-installed libraries like **`pandas`**, **`numpy`**, **`matplotlib`**, and **`scikit-learn`**.

To begin with:

1. Visit **https://colab.research.google.com**.
2. Sign in with your Gmail account.
3. Click on **New notebook** (refer to *Figure 8.4*).

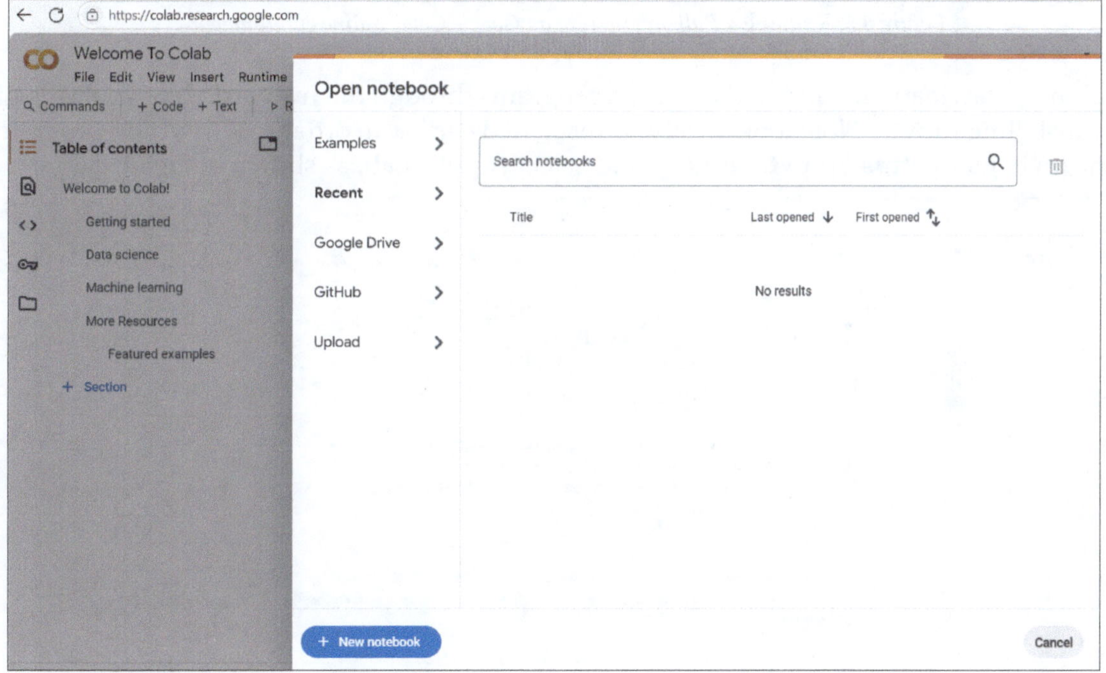

***Figure 8.4:** Open a notebook in Google Colab*

On clicking a **New notebook** tab, a Jupyter file with extension **`.ipynb`** opens, and learners can start writing code on it and obtain the output as shown in *Figure 8.5*. A new **`.ipynb`** file (Jupyter Notebook file) opens in your browser. You can now write and run Python code directly in this notebook.

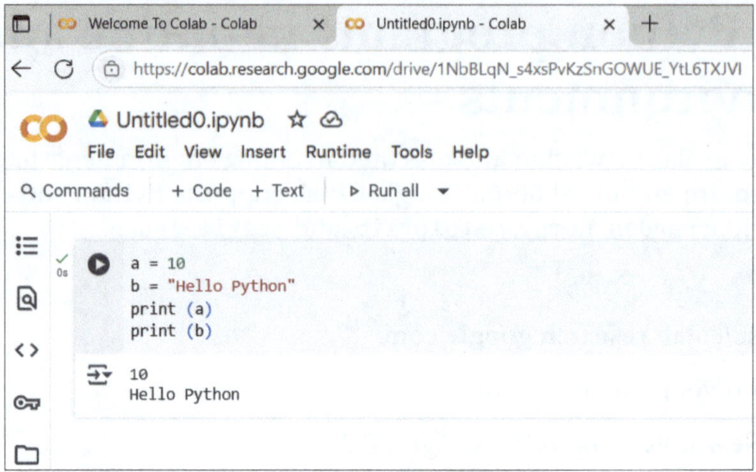

Figure 8.5: Running a Python program on Google Colab online environment

In a similar way, learners can run the Python programs through the **JupyterLab** official website or by installing Jupyter Notebook locally, as discussed earlier. In order to try Python programs online on it, go to **https://jupyter.org/try** and select **JupyterLab**, as shown in *Figure 8.6*:

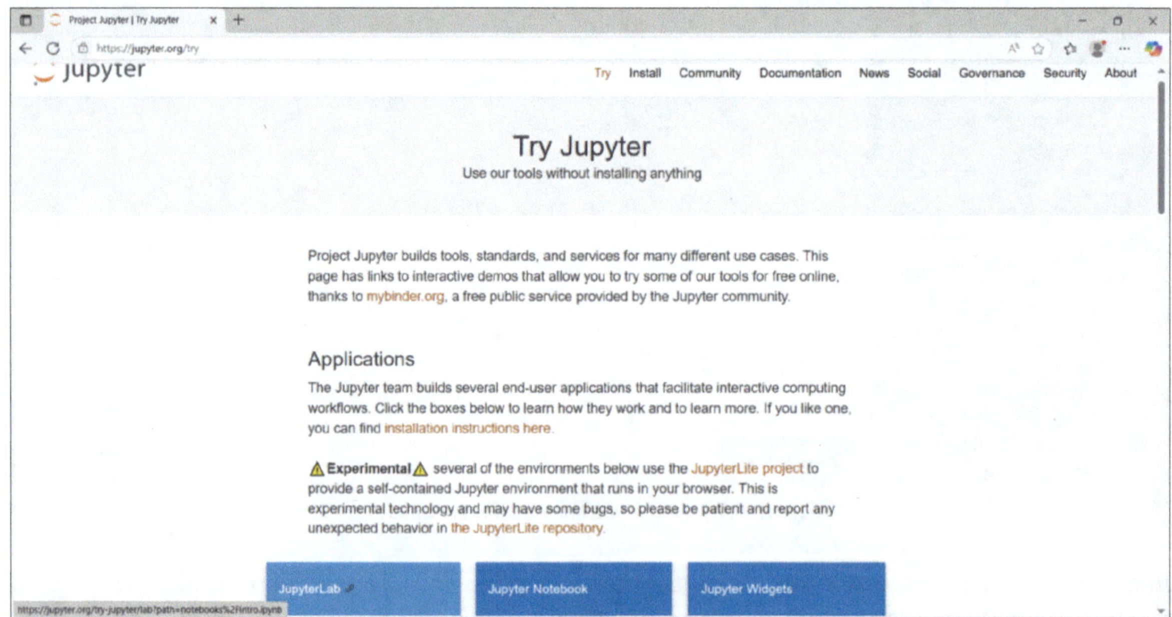

Figure 8.6: Try JupyterLab online

After clicking on the **JupyterLab**, open a **New Notebook** as shown in *Figure 8.7* to write and execute the Python program:

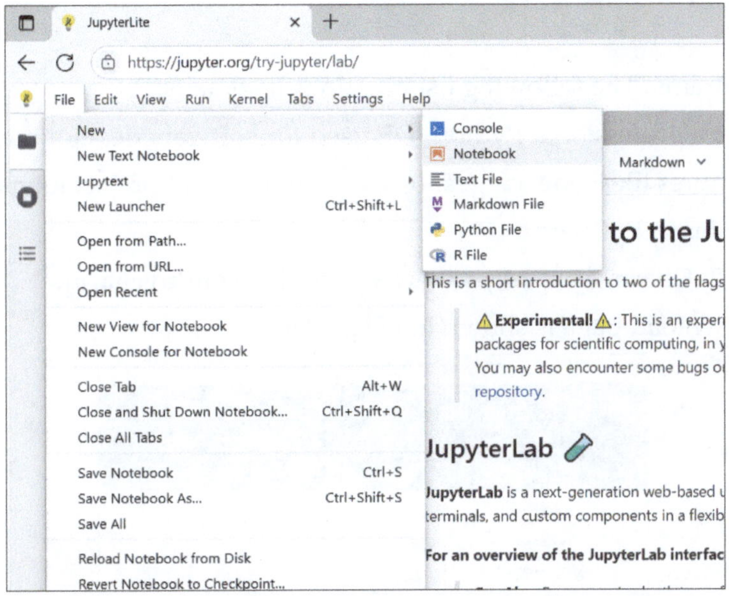

Figure 8.7: Opening a new notebook in the online JupyterLab environment

In this notebook, write a Python program in a cell and run the program to get the output as shown in *Figure 8.8*:

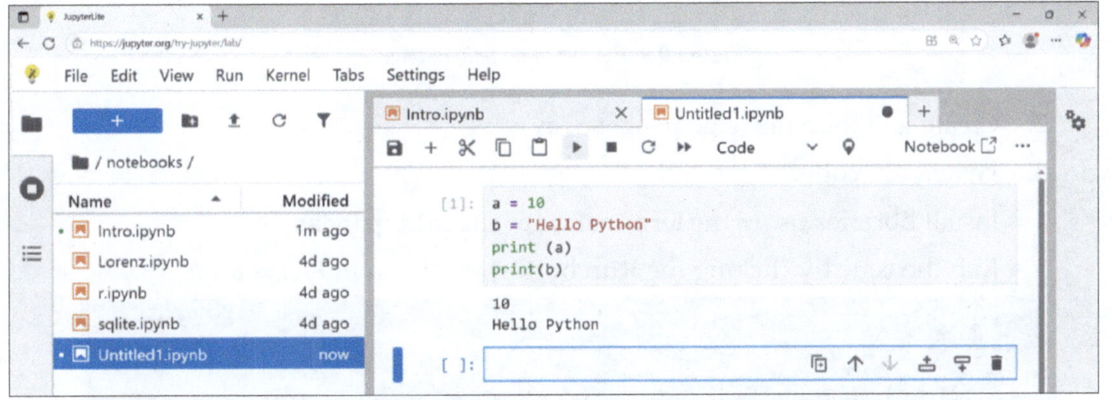

Figure 8.8: Writing a Python program in online JupyterLab environment and obtain output

Other tools to run Python programs

Apart from Jupyter Notebook, you can also run Python (and Pandas) programs using the following tools:

- PyCharm (by JetBrains)
- **Visual Studio Code** (**VS Code**)

Let us understand more about them.

PyCharm

PyCharm is by JetBrains. The following list mentions its details:

- PyCharm is a professional Python IDE used for software development.
- It offers features like code suggestions, debugging, and project management.
- To use Pandas in PyCharm:
  1. Install **PyCharm** from **https://www.jetbrains.com/pycharm**.

     The download page is shown in *Figure 8.9*:

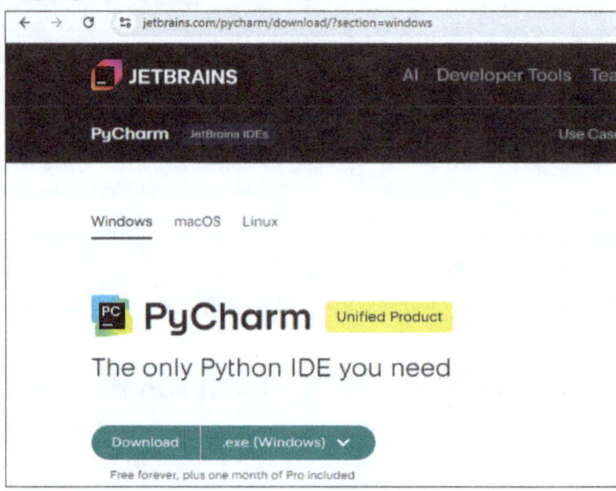

***Figure 8.9**: PyCharm download page*

  2. Create a Python file (e.g., `program.py`).
  3. Write your code.
  4. Install libraries using the terminal: `pip install pandas`
  5. Run the code by clicking the **Run** button as shown in *Figure 8.10*:

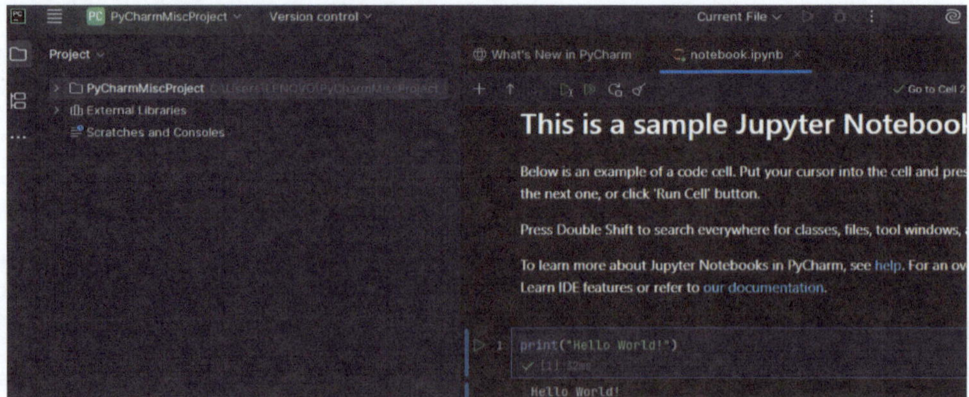

***Figure 8.10**: Running a Hello World program in PyCharm*

Visual Studio Code

The following list mentions the details of VS Code:

- VS Code is a lightweight and fast editor for many languages, including Python.
- It requires adding the Python extension from Microsoft.
- To use Pandas in VS Code:
    1. Download VS Code from **https://code.visualstudio.com**.
    2. Install the Python extension.
    3. Create a **`.py`** file.
    4. Install Pandas with: **`pip install pandas`**
    5. Run the code from the **Run** button or the terminal.

Note: When using VS Code for running Python programs, it is recommended to install the Python Extension for VS Code (by Microsoft). This extension provides essential features such as code execution, syntax highlighting, debugging support, IntelliSense (auto-completion), and integrated terminal support, making Python development easier and more efficient.

Earlier, we discussed how Python programs can be executed in both online and offline environments. Common online tools include Google Colab and JupyterLab, while offline execution is typically done using local Python installations. *Table 8.2* compares these environments in terms of usability and practical considerations:

Aspect	Online environment (Google Colab/JupyterLab)	Offline environment (local Python, Anaconda, VS Code)
Setup	No installation required	Requires installation of Python and libraries
Accessibility	Accessible from any device with internet	Limited to the installed system
Hardware support	Colab provides free **graphics processing unit** (GPUs)/ **tensor processing unit** (TPUs); JupyterLab depends on server	Depends on local machine hardware
Internet dependency	Continuous internet connection required	Works without internet after setup
Session persistence	Sessions may reset	Fully persistent

Aspect	Online environment (Google Colab/JupyterLab)	Offline environment (local Python, Anaconda, VS Code)
Data storage	Temporary unless saved to cloud or server	Permanent local storage
Best use	Learning, experimentation, demonstrations	Development, deployment, long-running tasks

Table 8.2: Comparison of online and offline environments

Note: Online platforms such as Google Colab automatically disconnect after a period of inactivity, which may result in loss of unsaved variables and files. JupyterLab sessions may also reset depending on server configuration. Users should regularly save their work or connect cloud storage (e.g., Google Drive) to avoid data loss. In practice, beginners often prefer online environments such as Colab or JupyterLab for quick experimentation, while offline environments are better suited for stable and long-term projects.

Example 8.1: Write a program for creating a series from a list using the Pandas library

In this example, **pd** is the object of **pandas**. A series from a list is created using the **Series()** method. By default, it assigns numerical indexes (0, 1, 2, ...).

The following code creates a Pandas Series from a simple list and prints it to show how Series store data with index labels:

```
import pandas as pd
# Creating a Series from a list
data1 = [15, 25, 30, 35]
series1 = pd.Series(data1)
print(series1)
```

The output of the code is shown in *Figure 8.11*:

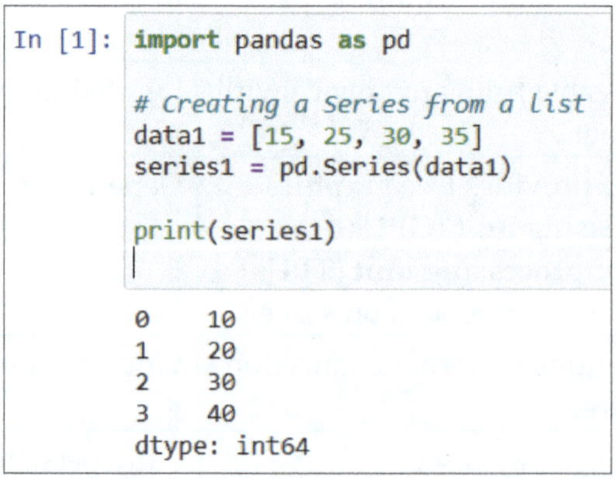

```
In [1]: import pandas as pd

        # Creating a Series from a list
        data1 = [15, 25, 30, 35]
        series1 = pd.Series(data1)

        print(series1)

        0    10
        1    20
        2    30
        3    40
        dtype: int64
```

Figure 8.11: Creating a Series from a list

DataFrame and data selection

A DataFrame resembles a table, with multiple series functioning as its columns. The item is composed of the following:

- Rows means index
- A column represents series and data represents values

Example 8.2: Write a program for a DataFrame

In this example, a DataFrame is created for three attributes, i.e., **Name**, **Age**, and **RegId**. With the help of the **pandas** library, a DataFrame will be displayed, as the following code shows:

```
import pandas as pd
data ={
'Name':['Anil','Vijay','Akash'],
'Age':[35,30,25],
'RegId':[101,102,103]
}
df=pd.DataFrame(data)
print(df)
```

The code window along with the output is shown in *Figure 8.12*:

```
import pandas as pd
data = {
    'Name': ['Anil', 'Vijay', 'Akash'],
    'Age': [35, 30, 25],
    'RegId': [101, 102, 103]
}

df = pd.DataFrame(data)
print(df)
```

```
    Name  Age  RegId
0   Anil   35    101
1  Vijay   30    102
2  Akash   25    103
```

***Figure 8.12**: Code window of a DataFrame*

The basic operations in DataFrame include accessing a particular column, or we can access a row using the keyword **loc** for location.

Pandas provides two commonly used methods for selecting data from a DataFrame: **.loc[]** and **.iloc[]**:

- **.loc[] (label-based indexing)**: Used to select rows and columns by their labels. For example, it selects data using row names or column names.

- **.iloc[] (integer-based indexing)**: Used to select rows and columns using integer positions, similar to array indexing starting from zero. **`.iloc[]`** uses positions, not labels. Here, counting always starts from 0, and it works like indexing in lists or NumPy arrays.

Example usage: **`.loc[2, 'Marks']`** selects the value in the row with label 2 and column Marks, whereas **`.iloc[2, 1]`** selects the value at the third row and second column position. The first number (2) refers to the row position. The second number (1) refers to the column position, and Indexing starts from 0.

Note: Each column of a Pandas DataFrame behaves like a Series. This means that individual columns can be accessed, indexed, and manipulated using Series operations, such as filtering, arithmetic operations, and statistical functions. Example: Accessing `df['Math']` returns a Series, allowing operations like df['Math'].mean().

Example 8.3: Write a program for accessing the age column

In this example, values from the **age** column are fetched:

```
import pandas as pd
data ={
'Name':['Anil','Vijay','Akash'],
'Age':[35,30,25],
'RegId':[101,102,103]
}
df=pd.DataFrame(data)
print(df['Age'])
```

The code window is shown in *Figure 8.13*:

```
import pandas as pd
data = {
    'Name': ['Anil', 'Vijay', 'Akash'],
    'Age': [35, 30, 25],
    'RegId': [101, 102, 103]
}

df = pd.DataFrame(data)
print(df['Age'])

0    35
1    30
2    25
Name: Age, dtype: int64
```

***Figure 8.13**: Code window for accessing values of the age column*

Note: Accessing a column using `df['Age']` returns a Series, not a DataFrame.

This distinction is important because Series and DataFrames differ in shape and behavior. Example:

`df['Age']` returns a Series

`df[['Age']]` returns a DataFrame

Example 8.4: Write a program for accessing a row using the loc keyword

In this example, a row can be accessed using a **`loc`** keyword. If we want to access a row at index 1, then we use **`df.loc[1]`** to fetch a row at index, as the following code shows:

```
import pandas as pd
data ={
'Name':['Anil','Vijay','Akash'],
'Age':[35,30,25],
'RegId':[101,102,103]
}
df=pd.DataFrame(data)
print(df.loc[1])
```

The code and output window are shown in *Figure 8.14*:

```
import pandas as pd
data = {
    'Name': ['Anil', 'Vijay', 'Akash'],
    'Age': [35, 30, 25],
    'RegId': [101, 102, 103]
}

df = pd.DataFrame(data)
print(df.loc[1])
```

```
Name      Vijay
Age          30
RegId       102
Name: 1, dtype: object
```

Figure 8.14: Code window for fetching a row at location 1

While **`.loc[]`** and **`.iloc[]`** are commonly used for selecting rows and columns, Pandas also provides **`.at[]`** and **`.iat[]`** for fast access to a single value (scalar). Use **`.at[]`** or **`.iat[]`** when accessing or updating a single cell repeatedly, as they are optimized for speed compared to **`.loc[]`** and **`.iloc[]`**.

- **.at[] (label-based)**: Used to access a single value using row and column labels. It is faster than **`.loc[]`** when only one value is required.
- **.iat[] (integer-based)**: Used to access a single value using row and column positions. It is faster than **`.iloc[]`** and is recommended for performance-critical code.

The following is an example usage:

`df.at[3, 'Age']` retrieves the value in the row labeled 3 and column **Age**.

`df.iat[3, 1]` retrieves the value at the 4th row and 2nd column position.

Example 8.5: Write a program for accessing a specific value

In this example, using DataFrame, a value is retrieved at row index 1 and column **RegId**:

```
import pandas as pd
data ={
'Name':['Anil','Vijay','Akash'],
'Age':[35,30,25],
'RegId':[101,102,103]
}
df=pd.DataFrame(data)
print(df.at[2, 'Name'])
```

The output and code window are shown in *Figure 8.15*:

```
import pandas as pd
data = {
    'Name': ['Anil', 'Vijay', 'Akash'],
    'Age': [35, 30, 25],
    'RegId': [101, 102, 103]
}
df = pd.DataFrame(data)
print(df.at[2, 'Name'])  # Get value at row index 2 and column 'Name'
```

```
Akash
```

***Figure 8.15**: Code window for retrieving value at row index 2 and column Name*

Dropping entries

The **drop()** method is employed to delete rows or columns from a DataFrame.

Example 8.6: Write a program to delete rows or columns from a DataFrame using drop() method

In this illustrative example, a row is dropped using **drop()** function for index 1. A column **RegId** is dropped using the same function, as the following code shows:

```
import pandas as pd
# Sample DataFrame
data1 = {
    'Name': ['Anil', 'Sunil', 'Akshay'],
    'Age': [25, 30, 35],
    'RegId': [101, 90, 95]
}
df = pd.DataFrame(data1)
# Dropping a row by index
```

```
drop_row = df.drop(index=1)
print("After Dropping Row with index 1:\n", drop_row)
# Dropping a column
drop_column = df.drop(columns='RegId')
print("\nAfter Dropping 'RegId' Column:\n", drop_column)
```

The following figure shows how the DataFrame looks after dropping the row with index 1 and then removing the **RegId** column using the **drop()** function in Pandas:

```
After Dropping Row with index 1:
      Name  Age  RegId
0     Anil   25    101
2   Akshay   35     95

After Dropping 'RegId' Column:
      Name  Age
0     Anil   25
1    Sunil   30
2   Akshay   35
```

***Figure 8.16:** Output of deleting rows or columns from a DataFrame using drop() method*

In Pandas, many operations such as dropping rows or columns do not modify the original DataFrame by default. Instead, they return a new DataFrame with the changes applied. For example, when rows or columns are removed using **drop()**, the original DataFrame remains unchanged unless specified otherwise. To apply changes directly to the existing DataFrame, the parameter **inplace=True** can be used. Dropping rows without **inplace=True** creates a new DataFrame, whereas using **inplace=True** updates the original DataFrame. By default, Pandas operations are non-destructive. This design allows safer data manipulation, as the original data is preserved unless explicitly modified.

Example usage:

- Dropping a column without **inplace=True** (creates a new DataFrame):

  ```
  df = df.drop('Age', axis=1)
  ```

- Dropping a column with **inplace=True** (modifies the same DataFrame):

  ```
  df.drop('Age', axis=1, inplace=True)
  ```

- Dropping a row using index with **inplace=True**:

  ```
  df.drop(2, inplace=True)
  ```

Note: inplace=True is to be used when memory usage needs to be reduced and when the original DataFrame no longer needs to be preserved and for performing step-by-step data cleaning workflows. Using inplace=True permanently modifies the DataFrame. Therefore, it is recommended to use it carefully, especially during exploratory data analysis.

In Pandas operations, the axis parameter specifies whether the action should be performed on rows or columns. The value **axis=0** refers to rows (operating vertically down the DataFrame), while **axis=1** refers to columns (operating horizontally across the DataFrame). When dropping data, **axis=0** removes rows based on index values, and **axis=1** removes columns based on column names. A small coding snippet is shown:

```
# Dropping a row (axis=0 → rows)
df.drop(2, axis=0, inplace=True)
# Dropping a column (axis=1 → columns)
df.drop('Age', axis=1, inplace=True)
```

In this snippet, **axis=0** removes the row with index 2, while **axis=1** removes the column named **Age**. The use of **inplace=True** ensures that the original DataFrame is modified directly.

Example 8.7: Write a program for data cleaning and filtering data using Pandas

This example demonstrates several essential data cleaning and filtering operations using the Pandas library. We begin by creating a DataFrame containing a mixture of valid data, missing entries (None), and duplicate rows. The first operation uses the **dropna()** function to remove any rows where one or more values are missing, which is useful when such data is incomplete or unreliable for analysis. Next, rather than discarding the missing data, we create a copy and apply the **fillna()** method to replace missing values in the **Age** column with the average age, ensuring the dataset remains consistent while retaining all records. We then eliminate duplicate rows using the **drop_duplicates()** method to avoid repeated data that might distort statistical results. Finally, we filter the DataFrame to extract only those entries where the individual's age is 25 or older. This is done using a simple conditional statement inside the DataFrame selection brackets. Together, these steps provide a foundation for preparing real-world data for analysis, where cleaning and filtering are often necessary before drawing meaningful conclusions.

The following code shows different data cleaning operations in Pandas, like removing missing values, filling missing values with the mean, removing duplicate entries, and filtering data based on a specific condition:

```
import pandas as pd
# Creating a DataFrame with missing values and duplicates
data = pd.DataFrame({
    'Name': ['Ajay', 'Binu', None, 'Ajay', 'Chetan'],
    'Age': [25, None, 22, 25, 22]
})
# Step 1: Removing rows with missing values
cleaned_data = data.dropna()
print("Data after dropping missing values:")
print(cleaned_data)
# Step 2: Filling missing values in 'Age' with the column's mean
```

```
data_filled = data.copy()
data_filled['Age'] = data_filled['Age'].fillna(data_filled['Age'].mean())
print("\nData after filling missing Age values with mean:")
print(data_filled)
# Step 3: Removing duplicate rows
unique_data = data_filled.drop_duplicates()
print("\nData after removing duplicates:")
print(unique_data)
# Step 4: Filtering rows where Age is 25 or more
filtered_data = unique_data[unique_data['Age'] >= 25]
print("\nFiltered data (Age >= 25):")
print(filtered_data)
```

The code and output window of the example are shown in *Figure 8.17*:

```
Data after dropping missing values:
     Name   Age
0    Ajay  25.0
3    Ajay  25.0
4  Chetan  22.0

Data after filling missing Age values with mean:
     Name   Age
0    Ajay  25.0
1    Binu  23.5
2    None  22.0
3    Ajay  25.0
4  Chetan  22.0

Data after removing duplicates:
     Name   Age
0    Ajay  25.0
1    Binu  23.5
2    None  22.0
4  Chetan  22.0

Filtered data (Age >= 25):
   Name   Age
0  Ajay  25.0
```

Figure 8.17: Output of data cleaning and filtering data using Pandas

apply() function for transformation

The **apply()** function is used when we want to apply a function to an entire row or column.

Example 8.8: Write a program using apply() function to an entire row or column

In this example, a DataFrame is created with a column named **RollNo** containing **[15, 25, 30]**. The **apply()** function takes each value(**x**) in the **RollNo** column and applies the function

x+5. The results are stored in a new column alias called **NewColumn**. A lambda function in Python is a short, unnamed function that can be created in a single line of code. This method is typically used for simple operations because creating a complete function with the **def** keyword would be overly complicated.

The following code demonstrates how to create a new column in a DataFrame by adding 5 to each value in the existing **RollNo** column using the **apply()** function with a lambda expression:

```
import pandas as pd
# Sample DataFrame
df = pd.DataFrame({'RollNo': [15, 25, 30]})
# Adding 5 to each number using apply()
df['NewColumn'] = df['RollNo'].apply(lambda x: x + 5)
print(df)
```

The output of the code is shown in *Figure 8.18*:

	RollNo	NewColumn
0	15	20
1	25	30
2	30	35

Figure 8.18*: Output of using the apply() function to an entire row or column*

The **applymap()** function in Pandas is used to apply a function to each individual element of a DataFrame. Unlike **apply()**, which works row-wise or column-wise, **applymap()** performs element-wise operations and is useful when the same transformation must be applied to every value in the dataset.

As shown in the following code snippet, the first statement applies an 18% tax to all numerical values, and the second statement performs normalization:

```
df_tax = df.applymap(lambda x: x * 0.18)
df_normalized = df.applymap(lambda x: x / 100)
```

applymap() is mainly used for numerical transformations and should be applied only to DataFrames, not Series.

Note: You can also use the map() function along with a lambda expression to apply transformations to a column. For example, classifying numbers as even or odd, as shown in Example 8.9.

Example 8.9: Write a program for classifying numbers as even or odd using lambda with map() function

In this example, a sample DataFrame is created, and numbers are initialized to some values. Lambda function checks if each number is even or odd and assigns the label, whereas **map()** applies it element-wise to the column. The Pandas library is first imported using the alias pd. A small DataFrame is then created with a single column named **Numbers** containing the values

12, **25**, and **35**. The goal is to classify each number as either **Even** or **Odd**. To achieve this, the **map()** function is used along with a lambda function. The lambda function takes each value **x** from the **Numbers** column and checks if it is divisible by 2 using the condition **x % 2 == 0**. If the condition is true, it returns **Even**; otherwise, it returns **Odd**. The **map()** function applies this logic to each element in the column and stores the result in a new column called **Result**. Finally, the updated DataFrame is printed, displaying both the original numbers and their corresponding classifications:

```
import pandas as pd
# Sample DataFrame
df = pd.DataFrame({'Numbers': [12, 25, 35]})
# Classify numbers as Even or Odd
df['Result'] = df['Numbers'].map(lambda x: 'Even' if x % 2 == 0 else 'Odd')
print(df)
```

The output window along with the code window is shown in *Figure 8.19*:

```
import pandas as pd
# Sample DataFrame
df = pd.DataFrame({'Numbers': [12, 25, 35]})
# Classify numbers as Even or Odd
df['Result'] = df['Numbers'].map(lambda x: 'Even' if x % 2 == 0 else 'Odd')

print(df)
```

```
   Numbers Result
0       12   Even
1       25    Odd
2       35    Odd
```

Figure 8.19: Output of the program for classifying numbers as even or odd using lambda with map() function

Filtering rows based on conditions

Pandas allow you to filter rows in a DataFrame based on specific conditions using comparison operators. This helps you display only the rows that meet certain criteria, such as values greater than a number or matching a particular text.

Example 8.10: Write a program for filtering rows based on a condition

In this example, a DataFrame is created with student names and their marks. We filter the rows where the marks are greater than 50 using a condition inside square brackets. The filtered result is stored in **filtered_data** and printed. Take a look at the following code:

```
import pandas as pd
df = pd.DataFrame({'Name': ['A', 'B', 'C'], 'Marks': [45, 78, 62]})
filtered_data = df[df['Marks'] > 50]
print(filtered_data)
```

The output of the code is shown in *Figure 8.20*:

```
   Name  Marks
1     B     78
2     C     62
```

Figure 8.20: Output of filtered rows based on a condition

Example 8.11: Write a program for using unique() and value_counts() on a column

This code creates a DataFrame of cities. The **unique()** function returns all distinct city names, and **value_counts()** returns how many times each city appears. These are useful for understanding the distribution of categorical data, as shown in the following code:

```
import pandas as pd
df = pd.DataFrame({'City': ['Delhi', 'Gujrat', 'Delhi', 'Chennai',
'Chennai']})
print("Unique cities:", df['City'].unique())
print("City counts:\n", df['City'].value_counts())
```

The output of the code is shown in *Figure 8.21*:

```
Unique cities: ['Delhi' 'Gujrat' 'Chennai']
City counts:
 City
Delhi      2
Chennai    2
Gujrat     1
Name: count, dtype: int64
```

Figure 8.21: Output using unique() and value_counts() function on a column

Example 8.12: Write a program for sorting a DataFrame by a column

The DataFrame contains student names and their marks. Using the **sort_values()** function, the data is sorted in descending order of marks, i.e., highest first. The sorted DataFrame is then printed, shown as follows:

```
import pandas as pd
df = pd.DataFrame({'Name': ['A', 'B', 'C'], 'Marks': [77, 89, 57]})
sorted_data = df.sort_values(by='Marks', ascending=False)
print(sorted_data)
```

The output of sorting a DataFrame by a column is shown in *Figure 8.22*:

```
  Name  Marks
1    B     89
0    A     77
2    C     57
```

Figure 8.22: Output of sorting a DataFrame by a column

Example 8.13: Write a program for finding unique values in a column using a pre-defined function

In this example, a pre-built **unique()** function is used to return all distinct, i.e., unique values in a column, as shown in *Figure 8.23*. The **unique()** function removes the duplicate values and extracts only distinct values, as shown in the following code:

```
import pandas as pd
# Creating a DataFrame
df = pd.DataFrame({'courses': ['php', 'python', 'java', 'java', 'dotnet',
'c']})
# Finding unique courses
unique_course = df['courses'].unique()
print("Unique courses are:", unique_course)
```

The output of finding unique values in a column using a pre-defined function is shown in *Figure 8.23*:

```
Unique courses are: ['php' 'python' 'java' 'dotnet' 'c']
```

Figure 8.23: Output of finding unique values in a DataFrame

Example 8.14: Write a program to count the values in a DataFrame

The occurrences of each value in a dictionary are counted using **value_counts()** function. It counts how many times each unique value appears in a column, as shown in *Figure 8.24*.

```
import pandas as pd
# Creating a DataFrame
df = pd.DataFrame({'courses': ['php', 'python', 'java', 'java', 'dotnet',
'c']})
# Finding unique courses
unique_course = df['courses'].unique()
print("Unique courses are:", unique_course)
# Counting occurrences of each course
coursecount = df['courses'].value_counts()
print(coursecount)
```

The output of counting the values in a DataFrame is shown in *Figure 8.24*:

```
Unique courses are: ['php' 'python' 'java' 'dotnet' 'c']
courses
java      2
php       1
python    1
dotnet    1
c         1
Name: count, dtype: int64
```

Figure 8.24: Output of finding unique values and their count

Example 8.15: Write a program for checking values in a column using isin() membership function

In order to check if each value in a column belongs to a given list, the **isin()** membership function is used. This function returns a true or false Boolean value for each row. Let us take a look at the following code:

```
import pandas as pd
# Creating a DataFrame
df = pd.DataFrame({'courses': ['php', 'python', 'java', 'java', 'dotnet',
'c']})
# Finding unique courses
unique_course = df['courses'].unique()
print("Unique courses are:", unique_course)
# Counting occurrences of each course
coursecount = df['courses'].value_counts()
print(coursecount)
# Check if each course is 'java' or 'python'
df['Is_Course_Available'] = df['courses'].isin(['php', 'python', 'java',
'java', 'dotnet', 'c++'])
print(df)
```

The output of the code is shown in *Figure 8.25*:

```
Unique courses are: ['php' 'python' 'java' 'dotnet' 'c']
courses
java      2
php       1
python    1
dotnet    1
c         1
Name: count, dtype: int64
  courses  Is_Course_Available
0     php                 True
1  python                 True
2    java                 True
3    java                 True
4  dotnet                 True
5       c                False
```

Figure 8.25: Output of checking values in a column using isin() membership function

The **value_counts()** function is commonly used to count unique values in a column. When the parameter **normalize=True** is used, it returns the relative frequency (percentage) of each value instead of absolute counts. After executing this code statement, the output shows the proportion of each grade in the dataset; for instance, a value of 0.40 indicates that 40% of the records belong to that grade:

```
df['Grade'].value_counts(normalize=True)
```

To convert the proportions into percentages, the result can be multiplied by 100:

```
df['Grade'].value_counts(normalize=True) * 100
```

Reading and writing data

Pandas make it easy to read from and write to external files such as CSV or text files. The **read_csv()** function is used to read data from a file into a DataFrame, allowing easy analysis and manipulation. Similarly, the **to_csv()** function helps write data from a DataFrame to a file, with options to choose separators and whether to include row indices. These functions are useful for handling real-world datasets in data science projects.

Example 8.16: Write a program for writing data into a file using pandas

This program demonstrates how to write data to a text file using pandas. First, the **pandas** library is imported. Then, a DataFrame is created using a dictionary that contains three columns: **Name**, **Age**, and **City**, with some sample data. The **to_csv()** function is used to save the DataFrame to a text file at the specified location (**F:\\students_data.txt**). The parameter **sep='\t'** ensures that the values are tab-separated, and **index=False** prevents pandas from writing row numbers into the file. Finally, a confirmation message **Data written successfully!** is printed. This example shows how **pandas** can easily export data from a DataFrame into external files for storage or sharing:

```
import pandas as pd
# Create a simple DataFrame
data = {
'Name': ['Anil', 'Sunil', 'Akshay', 'Vijay'],
        'Age': [25, 30, 35, 40],
        'City': ['Sml', 'Solan', 'Mandi', 'Hamirpur']}
df = pd.DataFrame(data)
# Save DataFrame to a text file (tab-separated)
df.to_csv('F:\\students_data.txt', sep='\t', index=False)
print("Data written successfully!")
```

The output is shown in *Figure 8.26*, where data in the DataFrame is written successfully in a file **students_data.txt** in **F:** drive:

```
Data written successfully!

students_data - Notepad
File  Edit  Format  View  Help
Name    Age     City
Anil    25      Sml
Sunil   30      Solan
Akshay  35      Mandi
Vijay   40      Hamirpur
```

Figure 8.26: Data written successfully into a file students_data.txt in F:\\ drive

Reading from a CSV file

Pandas provides a simple and efficient method to read data from **comma separated values** (**CSV**) files using the **read_csv()** function. This function loads the contents of a CSV file into a DataFrame, making it easy to analyze and manipulate structured data.

Example 8.17: Write a program to read a CSV file and display the top five rows

In this example, a **csv** file, which is also known as CSV is read using **pandas** library. A **csv** file is a common file format used to store tabular data. A **csv** file is loaded into a DataFrame which is a table-like data structure. **data.head()** displays the first five rows of the dataset, shown as follows:

```
import pandas as pd
df = pd.read_csv('D:\\students.csv')
print(df.head())
```

The output of reading and displaying the top 5 rows of a CSV file is shown in *Figure 8.27*:

	StudentID	Name	Department	Math	Science	English
0	1	Anil	Computer Science	85	90	88
1	2	Binu	Mathematics	78	82	85
2	3	Chetan	Physics	92	88	84
3	4	Divya	Chemistry	70	75	80
4	5	Eshaan	Biology	88	85	90

Figure 8.27: Reading and displaying the top 5 rows of a CSV file

Example 8.18: Another example of reading a CSV file and displaying rows and columns

This Python program uses the Pandas library to read and explore data from a CSV file named **students.csv**. The **pd.read_csv(file_path)** function loads the file into a DataFrame called data. The statement **data.head()** displays the first five rows of the dataset to give a quick overview. Then, using **data.shape**, the program determines the total number of rows and columns in the DataFrame, helping the user understand the size and structure of the dataset. Finally, it prints out this information for easy viewing. The code is as follows:

```
import pandas as pd
# Load the CSV file
file_path = 'D:\\students.csv'
data = pd.read_csv(file_path)
# Display the first 5 rows
print("First 5 rows of the dataset:")
print(data.head())
# Display number of rows and columns
rows, columns = data.shape
print(f"\nNumber of rows: {rows}")
print(f"Number of columns: {columns}")
```

The output of the example is shown in *Figure 8.28*:

```
First 5 rows of the dataset:
   StudentID    Name          Department  Math  Science  English
0          1    Anil  Computer Science    85       90       88
1          2    Binu       Mathematics    78       82       85
2          3  Chetan           Physics    92       88       84
3          4   Divya         Chemistry    70       75       80
4          5  Eshaan           Biology    88       85       90

Number of rows: 10
Number of columns: 6
```

***Figure 8.28**: Output of reading a CSV file and displaying rows and columns*

Example 8.19: Write a program for renaming columns in a DataFrame

In this example, a DataFrame with column names **A** and **B** are created. The **rename()** function is used to rename the columns to **Python** and **Java**. The **inplace=True** argument updates the DataFrame directly. The following code demonstrates how to change the names of columns in a DataFrame. Here, the columns **A** and **B** are renamed to **Python** and **Java** respectively using the **rename()** method:

```
import pandas as pd
df = pd.DataFrame({'A': [1, 2], 'B': [3, 4]})
df.rename(columns={'A': 'Python', 'B': 'Java'}, inplace=True)
print(df)
```

The output is shown in *Figure 8.29*:

```
   Python  Java
0       1     3
1       2     4
```

***Figure 8.29**: Output of renaming columns in a DataFrame*

Example 8.20: Write a program for descriptive Statistics on a CSV Dataset using Pandas

In this example, a dataset in the form of a **.csv** file is loaded using **pd.read_csv("filename")**. After reading a dataset, mean, median, mode is calculated on columns containing subject marks in numerical form. Here, **mean** is the average score for each subject, median is the middle value score and mode is the most frequent value. **describe()** function displays a full descriptive statistical summary. The results show the count, mean, standard deviation, min, max and quartile scores. The standard deviation shows how much the scores vary from the mean. A higher value means more variation. The following code demonstrates how to load a dataset from a CSV file using Pandas and compute summary statistics, including mean, median, mode, and other descriptive measures for numerical columns like Math, Science, and English:

```
import pandas as pd
# Load the CSV file
data = pd.read_csv('D:\students.csv')
```

```
# Display the first 5 rows (optional, for context)
print("First 5 rows of the dataset:")
print(data.head())
# Mean of each subject
print("\nMean scores:")
print(data[['Math', 'Science', 'English']].mean())
# Median of each subject
print("\nMedian scores:")
print(data[['Math', 'Science', 'English']].median())
# Mode of each subject
print("\nMode scores:")
print(data[['Math', 'Science', 'English']].mode())
# Full statistical summary
print("\nDescriptive statistics:")
print(data[['Math', 'Science', 'English']].describe())
```

In output, the mode is the most frequent score in each subject. In **`Math`**, 85.0 appeared most often, and in **`Science`** and **`English`**, many scores appear only once, so multiple modes are shown. The output of the code is shown in *Figure 8.30*:

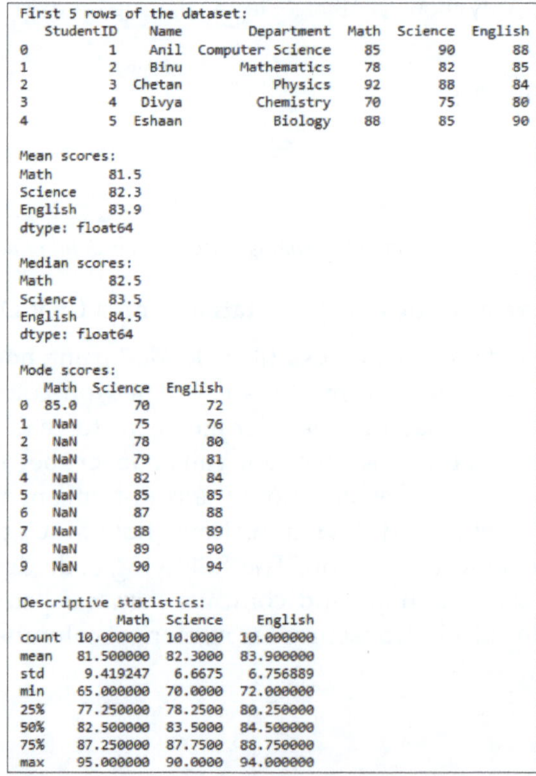

```
First 5 rows of the dataset:
   StudentID    Name         Department  Math  Science  English
0          1    Anil   Computer Science    85       90       88
1          2    Binu        Mathematics    78       82       85
2          3  Chetan            Physics    92       88       84
3          4   Divya          Chemistry    70       75       80
4          5  Eshaan            Biology    88       85       90

Mean scores:
Math       81.5
Science    82.3
English    83.9
dtype: float64

Median scores:
Math       82.5
Science    83.5
English    84.5
dtype: float64

Mode scores:
   Math  Science  English
0  85.0       70       72
1   NaN       75       76
2   NaN       78       80
3   NaN       79       81
4   NaN       82       84
5   NaN       85       85
6   NaN       87       88
7   NaN       88       89
8   NaN       89       90
9   NaN       90       94

Descriptive statistics:
            Math  Science    English
count  10.000000  10.0000  10.000000
mean   81.500000  82.3000  83.900000
std     9.419247   6.6675   6.756889
min    65.000000  70.0000  72.000000
25%    77.250000  78.2500  80.250000
50%    82.500000  83.5000  84.500000
75%    87.250000  87.7500  88.750000
max    95.000000  90.0000  94.000000
```

***Figure 8.30**: Output of descriptive statistics on a CSV dataset using Pandas*

Note: To explore and run the code examples covered in this chapter, you can open the Jupyter Notebook file named `Coding_Chapter8_Examples.ipynb` given with this book.

Follow these steps to view these programs in a notebook:

1. Make sure Jupyter Notebook is installed. You can launch it via open **Anaconda Navigator** and then click on **Launch** under Jupyter Notebook.

2. Once the Jupyter Notebook opens in your browser, navigate to the location using the **Upload** tab where the file **`Chapter8_Examples.ipynb`** is saved, as shown in *Figure 8.31*:

***Figure 8.31**: Navigate to the location using Upload tab for accessing programs*

3. On clicking the **Upload** tab, browse the file with extension **`.ipynb`** and upload it as shown in *Figure 8.32*:

***Figure 8.32**: Uploading a file Chapter8_Examples.ipynb*

4. All examples will come in a readable format. Click on the file to open it. You will now see all the examples inside. Click on each cell and press *Shift* + *Enter* to execute the code.

Conclusion

In this chapter, we introduced the essential data structures provided by the Pandas library Series and DataFrames, which are widely used for handling structured data in Python. Through practical and easy-to-follow examples, students learned how to create Series and DataFrames, access columns and rows using loc, filter rows based on conditions, and apply transformations using the apply() function. We also covered how to classify values using lambda with the map() function and how to add or remove columns or rows using the drop() method. In addition, we learned how to read data from a CSV file using read_csv() and write data to external files using to_csv(). To help explore and summarize data, we discussed useful built-in functions like head(), describe(), unique(), and value_count(). These functions are extremely helpful when getting an overview of any dataset. By the end of this chapter, students should feel confident working with small datasets using Pandas for selection, transformation, basic exploration, and file operations.

Points to remember

The following points are to be kept in mind:

- Pandas are a Python library used for data manipulation and analysis.
- The two main data structures in Pandas are:
    - o **Series**: a one-dimensional labeled array.
    - o **DataFrame**: a two-dimensional labeled table of data.
- Use pd.Series() to create a Series and pd.DataFrame() to create a DataFrame.
- Data from a DataFrame can be accessed using:
    - o Column name (e.g., df['Age'])
    - o Row label with .loc[] (e.g., df.loc[1])
    - o Specific cell using row and column (e.g., df.loc[1, 'Age'])
- The drop() function is used to delete rows or columns from a DataFrame.
- Filtering can be done by applying conditions on DataFrame columns.
- The apply() function is used to apply operations to entire rows or columns.
- The map() function with a lambda is helpful for element-wise operations.
- To read data from a CSV file: pd.read_csv('filename.csv')
- To write data to a file: df.to_csv('filename.csv')
- Useful functions to explore data:

- o **head()**: It displays the first few rows.
- o **describe()**: It gives summary statistics.
- o **unique()**: It shows unique values in a column.
- o **count()**: It counts non-missing entries in columns.

Key terms

- **Pandas**: A Python library used for working with structured data, especially for data analysis and manipulation.
- **Series**: A one-dimensional labeled array in Pandas that can hold any data type like numbers or strings.
- **DataFrame**: A two-dimensional table of data with labeled rows and columns, similar to an Excel sheet.
- **loc[]**: A label-based method to access a group of rows and columns from a DataFrame.
- **drop()**: A function used to remove rows or columns from a DataFrame.
- **apply()**: A function that applies a given function like sum, mean to each row or column.
- **map()**: A function used to apply a transformation to each element of a Series.
- **lambda**: A short, anonymous function in Python often used with apply() or map().
- **read_csv()**: Reads a CSV file and loads it into a DataFrame for analysis.
- **to_csv()**: Saves a DataFrame to a CSV file on your system.
- **head()**: Displays the first 5 rows (by default) of a DataFrame.
- **describe()**: Provides statistical summaries (like mean, min, max) of numerical columns.
- **unique()**: Returns the unique/distinct values present in a column.
- **count()**: Returns the number of non-null (non-missing) values in each column.

Multiple choice questions

1. **What is a Pandas Series?**

   a. A 2D table
   b. A labeled one-dimensional array
   c. A graph
   d. A chart

2. **Which function is used to create a DataFrame from a dictionary?**
   a. pd.series()
   b. pd.table()
   c. pd.frame()
   d. pd.DataFrame()

3. **Which of the following is an example of an online environment to run Python?**
   a. Jupyter Notebook
   b. Google Colab
   c. VS Code
   d. IDLE

4. **The function used to select a row using a label in a DataFrame is:**
   a. iloc[]
   b. select[]
   c. loc[]
   d. write[]

5. **What does df.iloc[1] return?**
   a. the row at index label 1
   b. the second row (based on position)
   c. all columns
   d. the first column

6. **What does the drop() function do in Pandas?**
   a. Deletes the entire DataFrame
   b. Drops missing values only
   c. Removes specified rows or columns
   d. Drops all data

7. **Which function is used to apply a transformation to each element in a column?**
   a. map()
   b. transform()
   c. apply()
   d. filter()

8. **Which condition will filter rows where Age is greater than 30?**
   a. df[df['Age'] > 30]
   b. df.Age > 30
   c. df['Age'] >= 30
   d. df['Age'] => 30

9. **What function is used to read data from a CSV file?**
   a. read.text()
   b. pd.read_csv()
   c. csv.read()
   d. pd.open_file()

10. **How can we write a DataFrame df to a text file in tab-separated format?**
    a. df.write()
    b. df.to_text('file.txt')
    c. df.to_csv('file.txt', sep='\t')
    d. df.to_file('file.txt')

Answers

1	b
2	d
3	b
4	c
5	b
6	c
7	c
8	a
9	b
10	c

Questions

1. What is a Pandas Series?
2. What is the difference between Pandas Series and DataFrame?
3. Which function is used to read a CSV file in Pandas?
4. What does the head() function do in Pandas?
5. What is the use of loc[] and iloc[] in Pandas?
6. How can you drop a column named City from a DataFrame?
7. What does the apply() function do?
8. Which method is used to write a DataFrame to a text file?
9. Name any two tools that can be used to run Python programs offline.

Join our Discord space

Join our Discord workspace for latest updates, offers, tech happenings around the world, new releases, and sessions with the authors:

https://discord.bpbonline.com

CHAPTER 9
Data Cleaning and Preparation

Introduction

Effective data preparation and cleaning are essential to ensure the accuracy and reliability of datasets used for in-depth analysis. One of the primary challenges in this process is handling missing data, which may arise due to factors such as incomplete data collection or faulty data entry. If not managed appropriately, missing values can lead to biased results and inaccurate predictions. Common approaches for addressing missing data include imputation, where missing values are estimated using statistical measures such as mean, median, or mode, and deletion, where records or attributes with missing values are removed. To further improve data quality, advanced techniques such as machine learning based imputation and interpolation methods can also be employed.

Structure

The following topics are covered in this chapter:

- Introduction to data cleaning
- Handling missing data
- Imputation
- Removing duplicate data
- Data type conversion
- Renaming columns
- Analyzing rows and columns using indexing
- Filtering rows using conditions
- String cleaning
- Binning or categorizing data
- Combining columns

Objectives

The objective of this chapter is to provide students with a foundational understanding of data preprocessing for effective data analysis. The chapter introduces techniques for handling missing and duplicate data, correcting inconsistent values, converting data types, and improving data clarity through column renaming and string cleaning. Students will also learn methods for data filtering, indexing, categorization, and column combination. Through practical examples and exercises, the chapter aims to develop essential skills for preparing clean, reliable, and analysis-ready datasets.

Introduction to data cleaning

Data cleaning is a crucial step in the data preprocessing phase of data science and machine learning. Raw data collected from various sources is often messy, incomplete, or inconsistent, which can lead to inaccurate results during analysis or model training. Common issues in raw datasets include missing values, duplicate records, incorrect data types, inconsistent formats, and typographical errors. Data cleaning aims to detect and correct (or remove) these errors to improve data quality and reliability. For example, in a customer transaction dataset used by an e-commerce company, missing values in purchase amounts, duplicate customer records, or inconsistent date formats can significantly affect sales analysis and demand forecasting if left unaddressed. Without proper cleaning, even the most advanced analytical tools or algorithms may fail to produce meaningful insights. Therefore, data cleaning is not just a technical requirement; it is a foundational process that ensures the validity, accuracy, and effectiveness of any data-driven decision-making process.

Handling missing data

In the data cleaning process, addressing missing data is a critical step due to the common presence of incomplete or null values in real-world datasets. The missing values can result from data entry mistakes or incomplete surveys. Properly addressing these issues can prevent inaccurate analysis and misleading results. The methods for dealing with missing data often involve eliminating rows or columns that contain null values, or alternatively, replacing them using statistical procedures like the mean, median, or mode. The choice of method depends on the nature of the data and the impact of the missing values on the analysis. However, missing data should not be removed when the proportion of missing values is high or when the missingness itself carries meaningful information, as removal in such cases may introduce bias and distort the overall data distribution. In such situations, imputation or other estimation techniques are generally preferred. By effectively handling missing data, we ensure that our dataset is reliable and ready for further processing.

Example 9.1: Write a program for handling missing values

The given code demonstrates how to identify missing values in a dataset using the Pandas library. First, a dictionary containing student names and their marks is created, where some values are missing. This dictionary is then converted into a DataFrame using **`pd.DataFrame()`**. The **`isnull()`** function is applied to the DataFrame to detect any missing data. It returns a new DataFrame of the same shape, where each cell shows **`True`** if the corresponding value is missing (either **`None`** or **`NaN`**) and **`False`** if the value is present. This technique is useful in data cleaning as it helps identify incomplete records that may require further handling, such as imputation or removal:

```
import pandas as pd
data1 = {'Name': ['Anil', 'Sunil', None], 'Marks': [78, None, 89]}
df = pd.DataFrame(data1)
print(df.isnull())
```

The output of the code is shown in *Figure 9.1*, where the **`None`** or **`NaN`** values in that respective column are shown as **`True`**, whereas non-missing values are shown as **`False`**:

```
    Name  Marks
0  False  False
1  False   True
2   True  False
```

Figure 9.1*: Output of handling missing values*

Imputation

It is the process of replacing missing or null values in a dataset with substituted values so that the data can be analyzed or processed effectively. It helps to maintain the completeness of the dataset and avoid errors in data analysis or machine learning models. It can be done using various methods, such as replacing missing values with the mean, median, or mode of the column, a specific constant value, etc. However, the choice of imputation method can influence the results of analysis or model performance, as simple techniques may reduce data variability or introduce bias, while more appropriate methods help preserve underlying data patterns. Therefore, selecting a suitable imputation strategy is essential to ensure reliable and meaningful outcomes.

Example 9.2: Write a program for handling missing data by replacing it with the mean in Pandas

This example demonstrates how to handle missing values in a dataset using the Pandas library. First, a dataset is created with the names of students and their marks in Math and English, where some marks are missing (represented by **`None`**). This data is then converted into a DataFrame. The original dataset is printed to show the missing values. Next, the **`.isnull().sum()`** function is used to count the number of missing values in each column. After identifying the missing entries, the code replaces them with the average (mean) of the respective column using the **`.fillna()`** function. This is done separately for both **`Math_Marks`** and **`English_Marks`** columns. Finally, the cleaned dataset is printed, showing all missing values filled with the computed mean, ensuring no loss of data and maintaining data consistency. The following code demonstrates how to identify and handle missing values in a Pandas DataFrame. It checks for null entries using **isnull().sum()** and fills them with the mean value of each column using **fillna()**:

```
import pandas as pd
# Step 1: Create a dataset with missing values
data = {
    "Student": ["A", "B", "C", "D", "E"],
    "Math_Marks": [78, None, 92, 70, 88],
    "English_Marks": [80, 75, None, 72, 90]
}
df = pd.DataFrame(data)
print("Original Dataset with Missing Values:")
print(df)
# Step 2: Check for missing values
print("\nMissing Values Count:")
print(df.isnull().sum())
# Step 3: Fill missing values with the mean
df["Math_Marks"].fillna(df["Math_Marks"].mean(), inplace=True)
df["English_Marks"].fillna(df["English_Marks"].mean(), inplace=True)
print("\nDataset After Filling Missing Values with Mean:")
print(df)
```

The output of the code is shown in *Figure 9.2*:

```
Original Dataset with Missing Values:
  Student  Math_Score  English_Score
0       A        78.0           80.0
1       B         NaN           75.0
2       C        92.0            NaN
3       D        70.0           72.0
4       E        88.0           90.0

Missing Values Count:
Student          0
Math_Score       1
English_Score    1
dtype: int64

Dataset After Filling Missing Values with Mean:
  Student  Math_Score  English_Score
0       A        78.0          80.00
1       B        82.0          75.00
2       C        92.0          79.25
3       D        70.0          72.00
4       E        88.0          90.00
```

Figure 9.2: *Output of handling missing values using pandas*

Example 9.3: Write a program for handling missing data by replacing it with the median

In this example, a dataset containing missing values is created using a dictionary and converted into a **pandas** DataFrame. The dataset has two subject columns, **Math_Marks** and **English_Marks**, with some **None** (missing) values. The code first prints the original dataset and uses the **isnull().sum()** function to count how many missing values are present in each column. To handle these missing entries, the imputation technique used here is median imputation. The **fillna()** function is applied to both columns, where each missing value is replaced with the median of the respective column. Using the median is often more robust than the mean, especially when the data contains outliers.

Note: An outlier is a value that is much higher or lower than the other values in a dataset. For example, in the data [10,13,14,16,300], the value 300 is an outlier because it is far from the rest of the values.

The code is as follows:

```
import pandas as pd
# Step 1: Create a dataset with missing values
data = {
    "Student": ["A", "B", "C", "D", "E"],
    "Math_Marks": [78, None, 92, 70, 88],
    "English_Marks": [80, 75, None, 72, 90]
}
df = pd.DataFrame(data)
print("Original Dataset with Missing Values:")
print(df)
# Step 2: Check for missing values
print("\nMissing Values Count:")
print(df.isnull().sum())
# Step 3: Fill missing values with the median
df["Math_Marks"].fillna(df["Math_Marks"].median(), inplace=True)
df["English_Marks"].fillna(df["English_Marks"].median(), inplace=True)
print("\nDataset After Filling Missing Values with Median:")
print(df)
```

The final dataset, after imputation, shows all missing values successfully filled with the column medians as shown in *Figure 9.3*:

```
Original Dataset with Missing Values:
  Student  Math_Marks  English_Marks
0       A        78.0           80.0
1       B         NaN           75.0
2       C        92.0            NaN
3       D        70.0           72.0
4       E        88.0           90.0

Missing Values Count:
Student          0
Math_Marks       1
English_Marks    1
dtype: int64

Dataset After Filling Missing Values with Median:
  Student  Math_Marks  English_Marks
0       A        78.0           80.0
1       B        83.0           75.0
2       C        92.0           77.5
3       D        70.0           72.0
4       E        88.0           90.0
```

Figure 9.3: Output with median imputation

Example 9.4: Write a program for handling missing values by imputation using a constant value

The missing values in a dataset can also be handled by performing imputation using constant values instead of the mean or median. Here, `fillna(0)` replaces all missing `None` or `NaN` values in the column with a constant value (in this case, it is 0). You can replace the `0` value with any other constant value as well. The imputation using constant values is useful when we want to highlight that the value is missing clearly. The code is as follows:

```
import pandas as pd
# Step 1: Create a dataset with missing values
data = {
    "Student": ["A", "B", "C", "D", "E"],
    "Math_Marks": [78, None, 92, 70, 88],
    "English_Marks": [80, 75, None, 72, 90]
}
df = pd.DataFrame(data)
print("Original Dataset with Missing Values:")
print(df)
# Step 2: Check for missing values
print("\nMissing Values Count:")
print(df.isnull().sum())
# Step 3: Fill missing values using a constant value (e.g., 0 or any default)
df["Math_Marks"].fillna(0, inplace=True)
df["English_Marks"].fillna(0, inplace=True)
```

```
print("\nDataset After Filling Missing Values with Constant Value:")
print(df)
```

The output of the code after imputation using constant values is shown in *Figure 9.4*:

```
Original Dataset with Missing Values:
  Student  Math_Marks  English_Marks
0       A        78.0           80.0
1       B         NaN           75.0
2       C        92.0            NaN
3       D        70.0           72.0
4       E        88.0           90.0

Missing Values Count:
Student          0
Math_Marks       1
English_Marks    1
dtype: int64

Dataset After Filling Missing Values with Constant Value:
  Student  Math_Marks  English_Marks
0       A        78.0           80.0
1       B         0.0           75.0
2       C        92.0            0.0
3       D        70.0           72.0
4       E        88.0           90.0
```

***Figure 9.4**: Output of imputation using constant values*

Example 9.5: Write a program for dropping missing values

In this example, to drop missing values from a DataFrame, **`dropna()`** function is used in Pandas. In this example, a dictionary is first created with two columns, **`Name`** and **`Marks`**, where some values are missing (represented by **`None`**). This dictionary is converted into a DataFrame. The **`dropna()`** function is then applied with **`inplace=True`**, which means the original DataFrame will be updated by removing any rows that contain at least one missing value. As a result, only the rows with complete data are retained. In this case, the final output will only display the row where both the **`Name`** and **`Marks`** values are present, effectively cleaning the dataset by removing incomplete entries. The code is:

```
import pandas as pd
# Create a dictionary with some missing (None) values
data = {'Name': ['Anil', 'Sunil', None], 'Marks': [80, None, 90]}
# Convert it into a DataFrame
df = pd.DataFrame(data)
# Drop rows with any missing values
df.dropna(inplace=True)
# Display the cleaned DataFrame
print(df)
```

The output of dropping missing values from a DataFrame is shown in *Figure 9.5*:

	Name	Marks
0	Anil	80.0

***Figure 9.5:** Output of dropping missing values in a DataFrame*

Removing duplicate data

Removing duplicate values is a crucial step in data preprocessing because duplicates can lead to misleading analysis, inflated results, and incorrect model training. Duplicate records occur when the same data appears more than once, either due to data entry errors or merging datasets. In addition to exact duplicate rows, duplicates may also exist when key attributes (such as IDs, names, or dates) are repeated with slight variations caused by formatting differences or typographical errors. By identifying and removing such duplicates using relevant attributes or key columns, we ensure that each observation is unique, which improves the quality and reliability of the data. This step helps maintain data integrity and ensures accurate insights during data analysis and machine learning tasks.

Example 9.6: Write a program for removing duplicate data

In this example, a DataFrame is created with two columns: **`Name`** and **`Marks`**. The row **`['Sunil', 44]`** appears twice, which is a duplicate value. The **`drop_duplicates(inplace=True)`** function removes the second occurrence of any duplicate row. In code, **`inplace=True`** modifies the original DataFrame directly. The following code shows how to clean a dataset by removing duplicate rows using the **`drop_duplicates()`** function in Pandas:

```
import pandas as pd
df = pd.DataFrame({'Name': ['Vijay','Sunil','Sunil'], 'Marks': [3, 44, 44]})
df.drop_duplicates(inplace=True)
# Display the cleaned DataFrame
print(df)
```

The output of removing duplicate data and displaying the final DataFrame is shown in *Figure 9.6*:

	Name	Marks
0	Vijay	3
1	Sunil	44

***Figure 9.6:** Removing duplicate data and displaying the final DataFrame*

Data type conversion

Data type conversion is an essential step in data preprocessing, where data is transformed from one type to another, such as converting strings to integers or floats to categorical types. This ensures that each data column is in the appropriate format required for analysis or modeling. Incorrect data types can lead to errors in computation, prevent statistical operations, or produce inaccurate results. Converting data to suitable types allows efficient memory usage, accurate calculations, and ensures compatibility with machine learning algorithms that expect specific data formats.

Example 9.7: Write a program for data type conversion

In this example, the **Age** column initially contains values as strings (object type). By using **.astype(int)**, we convert it to an **integer** data type. This conversion is important because numerical operations like averaging or comparison will not work correctly if the values are stored as strings:

```
import pandas as pd
# Create a DataFrame with 'Age' column as string type
data = {'Name': ['Anil', 'Sunita', 'Raj'], 'Age': ['25', '30', '22']}
df = pd.DataFrame(data)
# Check data types before conversion
print("Before Conversion:")
print(df.dtypes)
# Convert 'Age' column from string to integer
df['Age'] = df['Age'].astype(int)
# Check data types after conversion
print("\nAfter Conversion:")
print(df.dtypes)
```

The following output shows the data types of each column before and after converting the **Age** column from string to integer:

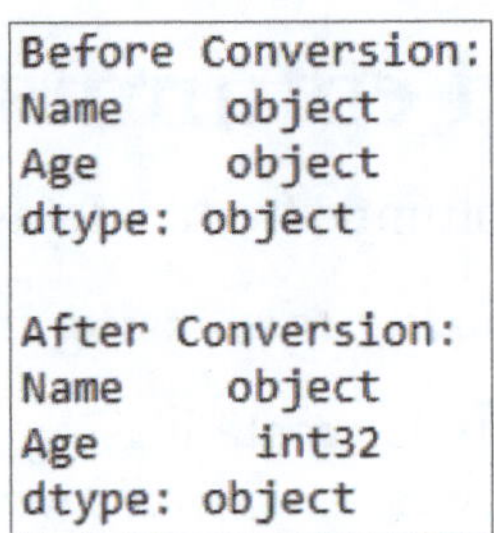

```
Before Conversion:
Name     object
Age      object
dtype: object

After Conversion:
Name     object
Age       int32
dtype: object
```

Figure 9.7: Output of a program converting a string to an integer data type

Renaming columns

Renaming columns is important for data preprocessing because it improves the clarity, consistency, and usability of the dataset. Often, raw data comes with unclear, inconsistent, or non-standard column names (e.g., spaces, typos, abbreviations). By renaming columns to meaningful, standardized names, we make the data easier to understand, analyze, and share. It also helps prevent errors in data analysis and ensures that code using column names is readable and less prone to mistakes. Clear column names are especially useful when combining datasets, applying machine learning models, or generating reports.

Example 9.8: Write a program for renaming columns

The renaming operation is especially useful in data cleaning and preparation when you want more meaningful or standardized column names. The process of renaming columns is commonly used in data preprocessing. In this example, a simple DataFrame is created using Pandas with two columns, i.e., **Name** and **Marks**, and a single row containing the values **'Vijay'** and **3**. The **rename()** function is then used to change the column names. Specifically, **Name** is renamed to **FirstName**, and **Marks** is renamed to **RegId**. The parameter **columns= {'Name': 'FirstName', 'Marks': 'RegId'}** specifies the mapping of old column names to new ones. By setting **inplace=True**, the original DataFrame is modified directly without the need to assign it to a new variable, as shown in the following code:

```
import pandas as pd
df = pd.DataFrame({'Name': ['Vijay'], 'Marks': [3]})
df.rename(columns={'Name': 'FirstName', 'Marks': 'RegId'}, inplace=True)
print(df)
```

After renaming, the DataFrame will have the updated column names and will look like this, as shown in *Figure 9.8*:

```
  FirstName  RegId
0     Vijay      3
```

***Figure 9.8**: Renaming columns in a DataFrame*

Analyzing rows and columns using indexing

In order to extract specific rows and columns from a dataset for analysis, we use indexing.

Example 9.9: Write a program for selecting rows using indexing

In *Example 9.6*, a simple DataFrame **df** is created using the **pandas** library. The DataFrame consists of two columns, **Name** and **Marks**, and two rows with data for students **Vijay** and **Sunil**. The first print statement, **df.loc[0]**, uses label-based indexing to access the row with label 0, which corresponds to the first row of the DataFrame. It will print the details of the first student, **Vijay**, with **74** marks. The second print statement, **df.iloc[1]**, uses position-based indexing to access the second row (index 1) of the DataFrame. It will print the details of the second student, **Sunil**, with **75** marks. Both **loc** and **iloc** are commonly used to retrieve specific rows from a DataFrame: **loc[]** retrieves by row label, while **iloc[]** retrieves by row position. Since the DataFrame has two rows, both statements will execute correctly without any errors:

```
import pandas as pd
df = pd.DataFrame({'Name': ['Vijay', 'Sunil'], 'Marks': [74,75]})
print(df.loc[0]) # Access by label
print(df.iloc[1]) # Access by position
```

The output of the code is shown in *Figure 9.9*:

```
Name      Vijay
Marks        74
Name: 0, dtype: object
Name      Sunil
Marks        75
Name: 1, dtype: object
```

***Figure 9.9**: Selecting rows and columns using indexing*

Example 9.10: Write a program for converting a dictionary to a DataFrame and fetching rows, columns using indexing

In *Example 9.10*, a dictionary is defined with three columns and is converted into a structured Pandas DataFrame named **df**, enabling efficient data manipulation. The example demonstrates how to use **.iloc** for positional indexing. The line **gender_data = df.iloc[:3, 1]** retrieves the first three rows (i.e., rows at index 0, 1, and 2) from the second column (index 1), which corresponds to the **Gender** column. This extracts the first three gender values from the dataset. The statement **subset = df.iloc[1:4, 1:]** selects rows from index 1 to 3 (excluding 4), and columns starting from index 1 to the end. This means it retrieves the data from rows 2 to 4 (i.e., entries **B**, **A**, and **C**) and includes only the **Gender** and **Grade** columns.

```
import pandas as pd
# Create a dataset
data = {
    "Student": ["A", "B", "C", "D", "E"],
    "Gender": ["Female", "Male", "Male", "Male", "Female"],
    "Grade": ["A", "B", "A", "C", "B"]
}
# Convert to a DataFrame
df = pd.DataFrame(data)
# Display the dataset
print("Original Dataset:")
print(df)
# Select the first 3 rows and the "Gender" column
gender_data = df.iloc[:3, 1]
print("\nFirst 3 rows of the 'Gender' column:")
print(gender_data)
```

```
# Select rows 2 to 4 and the last two columns
subset = df.iloc[1:4, 1:]
print("\nRows 2 to 4 and the last two columns:")
print(subset)
```

The output shows the selected subset of data based on row and column index positions, as shown in *Figure 9.10*:

```
Original Dataset:
  Student  Gender Grade
0       A  Female     A
1       B    Male     B
2       C    Male     A
3       D    Male     C
4       E  Female     B

First 3 rows of the 'Gender' column:
0    Female
1      Male
2      Male
Name: Gender, dtype: object

Rows 2 to 4 and the last two columns:
  Gender Grade
1   Male     B
2   Male     A
3   Male     C
```

***Figure 9.10**: Output of selecting rows and columns using indexing*

Note: Although both `loc` and `iloc` are used for selecting rows and columns in a DataFrame, they differ in how indexing is applied. The loc method is label-based and selects data using row and column names, whereas `iloc` is position-based and selects data using integer indices. Understanding this distinction helps avoid confusion and reduces repetition when applying these methods across multiple examples.

Filtering rows using conditions

Filtering rows in a DataFrame using a conditional statement is also an important part of preprocessing. Condition-based filtering is very useful in data analysis to isolate specific data based on criteria.

Example 9.11: Write a program for filtering rows using a condition

The given code demonstrates how to filter rows in a DataFrame using a conditional statement. A DataFrame **`df`** is created using the **`pandas`** library, containing two columns: **`Name`** and **`Marks`**. It includes three students with their respective marks. The line **`filtered_df = df[df['Marks'] > 80]`** applies a filtering condition to select only those rows where the value in the **`Marks`** column is greater than 80. This results in a new DataFrame **`filtered_df`** that includes only the students who scored more than 80 marks. Finally, the filtered data is printed.

In this case, the output will display the rows for **Vijay** (**81** marks) and **Sumit** (**85** marks):

```
import pandas as pd
df = pd.DataFrame({'Name': ['Vijay','Sunil','Sumit'], 'Marks': [81, 75, 85]})
filtered_df = df[df['Marks'] > 80]
# Display the filtered rows using conditions
print(filtered_df)
```

The output of the code displaying filtered rows using conditions is shown in *Figure 9.11*:

```
    Name  Marks
0  Vijay     81
2  Sumit     85
```

***Figure 9.11**: Output of displaying filtered rows using condition*

Note: While the examples above demonstrate basic filtering, multiple conditions can be applied using logical operators such as AND (&) and OR (|) to create more refined filters. This approach is commonly used in real-world data analysis. The general syntax is as mentioned as follows:

```
df[(condition1) & (condition2)]   # AND condition
df[(condition1) | (condition2)]   # OR condition
```

String cleaning

String cleaning is an essential part of data preprocessing because textual data often contains inconsistencies such as extra spaces, inconsistent letter cases, or hidden characters that can negatively affect analysis. For example, strings like **Anil** and **anil** might refer to the same person but would be treated as different values by a program. To ensure consistency and accuracy, string cleaning techniques such as trimming whitespace, converting to lower or upper case, and removing unwanted characters are applied. In addition, encoding and locale considerations are important when working with text data. Incorrect character encoding (e.g., non-UTF formats) can result in unreadable text, and locale settings may affect the interpretation of characters, date formats, or numeric separators. Addressing these issues ensures that string data is standardized and can be reliably processed across different systems. These techniques help standardize the data, making it more reliable for operations like filtering, grouping, and matching.

Example 9.12: Write a program for trimming whitespaces in a string

The **str.strip()** function removes any leading and trailing spaces from the string values in the **Name** column. This ensures consistency in names and avoids mismatches during analysis (e.g., filtering, comparing, etc.). Take a look at the following code:

```
import pandas as pd
# Sample data with extra spaces
names = {'Name': ['Ajay  ','    Anil',' Binu  ']}
df = pd.DataFrame(names)
print("The names before trimming:")
print(df)
# Trimming leading and trailing whitespace
df['Name'] = df['Name'].str.strip()
print("\nThe names after trimming:")
print(df)
```

The output after trimming the whitespaces in a string is shown in *Figure 9.12*:

```
The names before trimming:
       Name
0    Ajay
1      Anil
2    Binu

The names after trimming:
   Name
0  Ajay
1  Anil
2  Binu
```

Figure 9.12: Output after trimming the whitespaces in a string

Example 9.13: Write a program for converting string to lowercase and uppercase

In this example, converting strings from lowercase to uppercase and uppercase to lowercase is essential in data preprocessing to reduce variations due to inconsistent case usage, and it helps standardize text data for searching, comparison, and grouping. In the code, we start by creating a small dataset using a dictionary with a column called **Name**, which contains names with a mix of uppercase and lowercase letters like **Anil**, **ANIL**, and **AniL**. We convert this dictionary into a **pandas** DataFrame called **df**. To clean the text data and make it consistent, string case conversion is done. **df[Name].str.lower()** is used to convert all names to lowercase (e.g., **Anil** becomes **anil**), and the result is stored in a new column called **lcase_name. df['Name'].str.upper()** is used to convert all names to uppercase (e.g., **Anil** becomes **ANIL**), and this is stored in another new column called **ucase_Name**. This step is useful in data preprocessing to ensure uniformity in text fields, which helps avoid errors in filtering, sorting, or comparing data:

```
import pandas as pd
# Sample data
data = {'Name': ['Anil','ANIL','AniL']}
df = pd.DataFrame(data)
```

```
print("Original Data without conversion:")
print(df)
# Convert to lowercase
df['lcase_name'] = df['Name'].str.lower()
# Convert to uppercase
df['ucase_Name'] = df['Name'].str.upper()
print("\nAfter Converting to Lowercase and Uppercase:")
print(df)
```

The output of the string conversion is shown in *Figure 9.13*:

```
Original Data without conversion:
   Name
0  Anil
1  ANIL
2  AniL

After Converting to Lowercase and Uppercase:
   Name lcase_name ucase_Name
0  Anil       anil       ANIL
1  ANIL       anil       ANIL
2  AniL       anil       ANIL
```

***Figure 9.13**: Output of string conversion*

Example 9.14: Write a program for removing unwanted characters

Removing unwanted characters is an essential part of data cleaning, especially when preparing textual data for tasks such as name matching, text classification, and ensuring data consistency. In the given example, the **pandas** library is used to organize the data in a tabular format using a DataFrame. The **re** (regular expressions) module helps define a pattern to identify and eliminate unwanted characters. A dictionary containing a list of names with special characters is first created and then converted into a DataFrame. The **str.replace(r'[^a-zA-Z]', '', regex=True)** function is applied to the column, where the regular expression pattern matches any character that is not a lowercase (a to z) or uppercase (A to Z) letter. As a result, all non-alphabet characters such as **@**, **!**, **#**, **$**, **^**, and ***** are removed, leaving only clean alphabetical names. Take a look at the following:

```
import pandas as pd
import re
# Sample data with unwanted characters
data = {'Name': ['@Anil!','A#jit$','Bi^nu*']}
df = pd.DataFrame(data)
# Remove special characters using regex
df['Correct_Data'] = df['Name'].str.replace(r'[^a-zA-Z]', '', regex=True)
# Display the result
print(df)
```

The output of the code after removing the special characters from a string is shown in *Figure 9.14*:

	Name	Correct_Data
0	@Anil!	Anil
1	A#jit$	Ajit
2	Bi^nu*	Binu

***Figure 9.14**: Output after removing the special characters from a string*

Binning or categorizing data

Binning or categorizing data refers to the process of converting continuous numerical values into discrete categories or groups. This technique is commonly used in data preprocessing to simplify data analysis, reduce the impact of minor observation errors, and help machine learning models perform better by grouping values into ranges or bins. For example, suppose you have students' marks, and you want to categorize them into performance levels like poor, average, and good. While the bin ranges in examples may seem arbitrary, they can be chosen statistically using methods such as equal-width bins (dividing the range into intervals of the same size), equal-frequency bins (ensuring each bin contains roughly the same number of observations), or based on domain knowledge and data distribution. Selecting appropriate bins helps maintain meaningful distinctions between categories and ensures robust analysis.

Example 9.15: Write a program to categorize continuous numerical data into specific bins using binning

Binning is particularly useful when you want to simplify continuous data for easier interpretation or when certain algorithms perform better with categorical inputs. In this example, we begin by creating a dictionary with student names and their corresponding marks, which is then converted into a pandas DataFrame called **df**. The **bins** define the boundaries of each category, for instance, marks from 0 to 40 are labeled as **Poor**, 50 to 70 as **Average**, and 70 to 100 as **Good**. The **labels** specify the category names assigned to these ranges. The **pd.cut()** function is used to divide the **Marks** column according to the defined bins. Each student's marks are categorized as **Poor**, **Average**, or **Good**, and the results are stored in a new column called **Grade**, shown as follows:

```
import pandas as pd
# Sample data
data = {'Student': ['A','B','C','D','E'],
        'Marks': [55,68,89,75,85]}
df = pd.DataFrame(data)
# Define bins and labels
bins = [0,40,70,100]
labels = ['Poor','Average','Good']
# Apply binning
```

```
df['Grade']= pd.cut(df['Marks'], bins=bins, labels=labels)
print(df)
```

The output of the code for categorizing continuous numerical data into specific bins using the binning technique is shown in *Figure 9.15*:

	Student	Marks	Grade
0	A	55	Average
1	B	68	Average
2	C	89	Good
3	D	75	Good
4	E	85	Good

***Figure 9.15**: Output of categorizing continuous numerical data into specific bins*

Note: The term cut in `pandas.cut()` comes from the idea of cutting a continuous range of data into slices or intervals. It means slicing the continuous numerical data into bins or discrete groups. So, `pd.cut()` is literally cutting the data into categories.

Example 9.16: Write a program on binning using age groups

We can use binning to categorize a continuous variable like age into meaningful groups. Suppose we have a dataset of individuals with their ages. We can group these ages into categories like child, teen, adult, and senior to make the data more interpretable. First, we create a dictionary with names and their corresponding ages, then convert it into a **pandas** DataFrame. We define **bins** as the boundaries for age ranges. For example, 0–12 for **Child**, 13–19 for **Teenager**, 20–59 for **Adult**, and 60 and above for **Senior**. Using **pd.cut()**, the **Age** column is divided into these specified bins, and each individual is assigned to one of the categories. The categorized results are stored in a new column named **AgeGroup**. Take a look at the following:

```
import pandas as pd
# Sample data
data = {
    'Name': ['A','B','C','D','E'],
    'Age': [10, 17, 26, 60, 41]
}
df = pd.DataFrame(data)
# Define bins and labels
bins = [0,13,20,59,100]
labels = ['Child','Teenager','Adult','Senior']
# Perform binning
df['AgeGroup'] = pd.cut(df['Age'], bins=bins, labels=labels)
print(df)
```

The output of the code for binning use age groups is shown in *Figure 9.16*:

```
  Name  Age  AgeGroup
0    A   10     Child
1    B   17  Teenager
2    C   26     Adult
3    D   60    Senior
4    E   41     Adult
```

***Figure 9.16:** Output of categorizing age groups using binning*

Combining columns

Combining columns in data preprocessing refers to the process of merging two or more columns in a dataset to create a single, more meaningful column. This is especially useful when the data is split across multiple columns but represents a single concept. For example, a dataset might store a person's first and last names in separate columns, but for reporting or matching purposes, it is more helpful to combine them into a full name column. Combining columns is important in preprocessing because it helps to:

- Reduce redundancy and improve data readability.
- Create derived features for machine learning (e.g., combining date and time into a datetime column).
- Prepare data for exporting or formatting in reports.

Example 9.17: Write a program for combining columns

A Python dictionary is created named data with two keys, i.e., **`FirstName`** and **`LastName`**. Each key has a list of values, which represent the first name and last name. The statement **`df = pd.DataFrame(data)`** converts the dictionary into a **`pandas`** DataFrame called **`df`**. Now, the data is in tabular form with columns **`FirstName`** and **`LastName`**. The statement **`df['FullName'] = df['FirstName'] + ' ' + df['LastName']`** combines the values in the **`FirstName`** and **`LastName`** columns for each row using string concatenation. The result is stored in a new column called **`'FullName'`**:

```
import pandas as pd
# Sample data
data = {
    'FirstName': ['Anil', 'Sunita', 'Raj'],
    'LastName':  ['Kumar', 'Verma', 'Sharma']
}

df = pd.DataFrame(data)
# Combine columns to create a full name
```

```
df['FullName'] = df['FirstName'] + ' ' + df['LastName']
print(df)
```

The output of the example for combining two columns is shown in *Figure 9.17*:

```
  FirstName LastName      FullName
0      Anil    Kumar    Anil Kumar
1    Sunita    Verma  Sunita Verma
2       Raj   Sharma    Raj Sharma
```

***Figure 9.17**: Output of combining columns*

Note: This technique ensures that the dataset is better structured for tasks like name matching, sorting, searching, and visualization.

Example 9.18: Write a program for concatenating the course and marks for student reports

In this example, the **`course`** and **`marks`** columns are combined into a new column **`grade`**. The numeric marks are converted to a string using **`.astype(str)`** before combining:

```
import pandas as pd
# Sample data of students
data = {
    'StudentName': ['Amit', 'Vinod', 'Sanjay'],
    'Course': ['Math','Science','English'],
    'Marks': [85, 92, 78]
}
# Create DataFrame
df = pd.DataFrame(data)
# Combine Course and Marks into a single column
df['Grade'] = df['Course'] + ': ' + df['Marks'].astype(str)
# Display the updated DataFrame
print(df)
```

The output of the program for combining the columns **`Course`** and **`Marks`** is shown in *Figure 9.18*:

```
  StudentName   Course  Marks         Grade
0        Amit     Math     85      Math: 85
1       Vinod  Science     92   Science: 92
2      Sanjay  English     78   English: 78
```

***Figure 9.18**: Output of combining columns Course and Marks into a single column Grade*

Note: While the examples above demonstrate string concatenation, column combination can also be applied to numeric or date-time data. For instance, numeric columns can be summed or averaged, and date and time columns can be merged to create a complete timestamp. Understanding these possibilities helps generalize the concept of column combination for different data types.

Example 9.19 demonstrates how date and time data can be merged to create a proper timestamp for time-based analysis.

Example 9.19: Write a program for combining numeric and date-time columns in a DataFrame

In this example, a sample DataFrame is created containing numeric columns (**Math** and **Science**) and string columns for **Date** and **Time**. A new numeric column, **Total_Score**, is generated by adding the **Math** and **Science** columns, illustrating how numeric data can be combined to produce aggregated values. Additionally, the **Date** and **Time** columns are concatenated and converted into a single datetime column, **Full_Timestamp**, using **pd.to_datetime()**. The final DataFrame shows the original data along with these newly created columns, highlighting how column combination techniques can be applied to different data types for preprocessing and analysis.

```
import pandas as pd
# Sample data
data = {
    'Math': [80, 90, 75],
    'Science': [85, 95, 70],
    'Date': ['2025-11-28', '2025-11-29', '2025-11-30'],
    'Time': ['10:30:00', '14:45:00', '09:15:00']
}
df = pd.DataFrame(data)
# Numeric combination: sum of scores
df['Total_Score'] = df['Math'] + df['Science']
# Date-time combination: create complete timestamp
df['Full_Timestamp'] = pd.to_datetime(df['Date'] + ' ' + df['Time'])
print(df)
```

The output of the program for combining the numeric and date-time columns is shown in *Figure 9.19*:

```
>>>
= RESTART: C:/Users/DELL/AppData/Local/Programs/Python/Python311/Example9.19.py
   Math  Science        Date      Time  Total_Score      Full_Timestamp
0    80       85  2025-11-28  10:30:00          165 2025-11-28 10:30:00
1    90       95  2025-11-29  14:45:00          185 2025-11-29 14:45:00
2    75       70  2025-11-30  09:15:00          145 2025-11-30 09:15:00
```

Figure 9.19: Output of combining numeric and date-time columns

Conclusion

In this chapter, we explored the foundational aspects of data cleaning and preparation, a crucial step in the data analysis pipeline. Starting with an introduction to why data cleaning is important, we delved into methods for handling missing data through techniques like imputation, as well as the removal of duplicate values to maintain data accuracy. We also looked at data type conversion and column renaming, both essential for ensuring that data is in the right format and easily interpretable. The chapter demonstrated how to analyze and filter data using indexing and conditions, which helps in focusing on relevant subsets. Further, we learned the importance of string cleaning, including trimming spaces and changing text case to maintain uniformity. The chapter also covered how to categorize continuous data using binning and the significance of combining columns to enhance the meaning of raw data. Best practices include carefully handling missing and duplicate data, standardizing data types and column names, and cleaning string data for consistency. Applying filtering, indexing, and binning techniques enables focused and meaningful analysis, while combining columns can enhance interpretability. Awareness of encoding, locale issues, and understanding indexing methods (loc versus iloc) further ensures data integrity. By following these practices, students can prepare clean, consistent, and analysis-ready datasets that support accurate, insightful, and robust data-driven decision-making. Together, these techniques form the backbone of effective data preprocessing, ensuring that the dataset is clean, consistent, and ready for meaningful analysis or modeling.

Points to remember

The following points are to be kept in mind:

- **Data cleaning**: It is the process of fixing or removing incorrect, incomplete, duplicate, or improperly formatted data.
- **Missing data**: Missing data can be handled by removal or by imputation (filling in values using mean, median, mode, or constant).
- **Imputation**: Imputation helps retain the dataset size and reduce bias caused by missing values.
- **Duplicate values**: It can cause errors in analysis and should be identified and removed.
- **Data type conversion**: Data type conversion ensures that each column has the appropriate data type (e.g., integer, float, string) for analysis.
- **Renaming columns**: Renaming columns improves readability and consistency in datasets.
- **Indexing and filtering**: This allows us to access specific rows/columns or subsets of data using conditions.

- **String cleaning**: String cleaning like trimming whitespace or changing case is important for maintaining consistency in textual data.
- **Binning**: Binning means categorizing data and transforms continuous variables into discrete categories, useful for analysis and visualization.
- **Combining columns**: Combining columns helps in creating new, meaningful data such as full names, complete addresses, etc.

Key terms

- **Data cleaning**: The process of detecting and correcting or removing errors and inconsistencies in data to improve its quality.
- **Missing data**: Information not recorded or unavailable in a dataset, often represented as NaN in pandas.
- **Imputation**: The technique of filling missing values using statistical methods like mean, median, mode, or a constant value.
- **fillna()**: A pandas function used to replace missing values (NaN) in a DataFrame with specified values (e.g., mean, median, constant).
- **Duplicate values**: Rows in the dataset that are repeated, which can bias analysis and must often be removed using .drop_duplicates().
- **Data type conversion**: Changing the type of data (e.g., from string to integer or float) using .astype() to ensure correct operations.
- **Renaming columns**: Changing column headers using .rename() to make them clear, readable, and standardized.
- **Indexing**: Accessing data from a DataFrame using row/column positions or labels. Two main types:
  - o **loc[]**: Label-based indexing (e.g., df.loc[2, 'Name'])
  - o **iloc[]**: Position-based indexing (e.g., df.iloc[2, 0])
- **String cleaning**: Preparing text data by:
  - o Trimming extra spaces (str.strip())
  - o Changing case (str.lower(), str.upper())
  - o Removing special characters using regex
- **Binning**: Grouping continuous numerical data into categories using pd.cut().
- **Categorical data**: Data that represents distinct categories or groups like gender, grade, or department.

- **Combining columns**: Merging two or more columns to create a new one (e.g., combining first and last name into full name).
- **read_csv()**: A Pandas function used to read data from a CSV file into a DataFrame for analysis.

Multiple choice questions

1. **Which function is used in Pandas to replace missing values in a DataFrame?**
   a. replace() b. dropna()
   c. fillna() d. isnull()
2. **What does the drop_duplicates() function do in Pandas?**
   a. Deletes columns with null values
   b. Removes repeated rows
   c. Drops specified rows
   d. Renames columns
3. **Which of the following functions reads a CSV file into a DataFrame?**
   a. readfile() b. pd.load()
   c. pd.read_csv() d. read.data()
4. **What is the role of the cut() function in Pandas?**
   a. To remove missing data
   b. To delete columns
   c. To categorize continuous data into bins
   d. To trim text columns
5. **The method str.strip() is used to:**
   a. Convert strings to uppercase
   b. Remove special characters
   c. Remove whitespace from both ends of a string
   d. Combine strings
6. **Which indexing method uses integer positions to access data in Pandas?**
   a. loc[] b. iloc[]
   c. index[] d. axis[]

7. **Which method would you use to change the data type of a column in Pandas?**
   a. typecast()
   b. convert()
   c. astype()
   d. to_type()

8. **Why is renaming columns useful in preprocessing?**
   a. To delete rows
   b. To make column names more readable and meaningful
   c. To change data types
   d. To remove missing values

9. **What is an outlier in a dataset?**
   a. A missing value
   b. A duplicate row
   c. A value that significantly differs from other observations
   d. A categorical variable

10. **What does the str.lower() function do in Pandas?**
    a. Converts text to uppercase
    b. Removes extra spaces
    c. Converts text to lowercase
    d. Combines multiple strings

11. **A dataset of students' test scores has several missing values in the Math column due to absent students. You want to ensure that the dataset remains usable for calculating average scores and training a predictive model.**

    Which approach is most appropriate in this scenario?
    a. Delete the entire Math column.
    b. Delete only the rows with missing Math values.
    c. Replace missing Math values with the mean of the column.
    d. Leave the missing values as they are.

12. **While merging two customer databases, you notice that some customers appear twice with minor differences in the spelling of their names.**

    Which method is the best way to handle these duplicates without losing valid information?

    a. Remove only exact duplicate rows.

    b. Remove all duplicates regardless of variation.

    c. Use key identifiers or similarity checks to identify and merge near-duplicate records.

    d. Ignore duplicates, as they rarely affect analysis

13. **You have a dataset with separate Date and Time columns, and you want to create a single timestamp column for analysis of events over time.**

    Which of the following approaches is correct?

    a. Concatenate the date and time columns as strings without conversion.

    b. Combine date and time columns using pd.to_datetime() to create a datetime column.

    c. Sum the date and time values directly.

    d. Remove the time column and keep only the date.

Answers

1	c
2	b
3	c
4	c
5	c
6	b
7	c
8	b
9	c
10	c
11	c
12	c
13	b

Questions

1. What is a Pandas Series?
2. What is the difference between Pandas Series and DataFrame?
3. Which function is used to read a CSV file in Pandas?
4. What does the head() function do in Pandas?
5. What is the purpose of the fillna() function in data cleaning?
6. How can we remove duplicate rows from a DataFrame?
7. What is the use of astype() function in Pandas?
8. What is the difference between loc[] and iloc[] indexing?
9. Why is it important to rename columns in a dataset?
10. What is the role of dropna() in data preprocessing?
11. What is binning, and how is it helpful in categorizing data?
12. How can you combine two or more columns in Pandas?
13. What does str.strip() do when applied to a text column?
14. Why is string cleaning important during data preprocessing?
15. How do you convert a string column to lowercase in Pandas?

Chapter 10
Data Visualization Using Matplotlib

Introduction

This chapter focuses on data visualization using the Matplotlib library in conjunction with Pandas. While Pandas offers robust tools for managing and analyzing structured data, Matplotlib enables users to present that data visually through various types of charts, which is essential for interpreting results in real-world applications such as business analytics and research reporting. By utilizing Pandas' built-in integration with Matplotlib, users can generate plots directly from Series and DataFrames with minimal effort. The chapter introduces the fundamentals of creating common visualizations such as line plots, bar charts, pie charts, histograms, and scatter plots using matplotlib.pyplot alongside Pandas. It also discusses techniques for customizing plot elements, including titles, axis labels, legends, and colors, to improve the readability and impact of visual representations.

Structure

The following topics are covered in this chapter:

- Introduction to Matplotlib with Pandas
- Basic plotting with Series and DataFrames
- Histograms and scatter plots for distribution visualization
- Customizing plots with titles, labels, and legends
- Enhancing visuals with colors, styles, and markers
- Using subplots for multiple visualizations
- Exporting visualizations as image files

Objectives

The objective of this chapter is to equip students with practical skills for analyzing and visualizing data effectively using Matplotlib in combination with Pandas. Students will generate and compare various types of plots, such as line plots, bar charts, pie charts, histograms, and scatter plots, directly from Pandas Series and DataFrames. They will also customize and evaluate visual elements such as titles, axis labels, legends, colors, and markers to enhance clarity and interpretability. Additionally, the chapter introduces how to create and manage multiple plots using subplots and how to export visualizations as image files. By the end of this chapter, students will be able to present and interpret data clearly and meaningfully for data analysis, reporting, and decision-making in real-world contexts.

Introduction to Matplotlib with Pandas

The combination of Pandas and Matplotlib makes data visualization easier in Python. While Pandas is mainly used for handling and analyzing data, it also offers built-in support for creating basic plots using Matplotlib in the background. This allows users to generate charts such as line graphs, bar charts, and histograms directly from DataFrames or Series with very little code. By using the **`.plot()`** function in Pandas, students can quickly turn raw data into meaningful visual representations without needing to learn all the details of Matplotlib right away. While Pandas **`.plot()`** method is suitable for quick and standard visualizations, direct use of Matplotlib functions is required for advanced customization, complex layouts, fine-grained control over plot elements, and publication-quality figures. This integration is helpful for both beginners and data analysts who want to understand patterns and trends in their data more clearly. A simple example of plotting a line chart from a DataFrame using Pandas and Matplotlib is shown in *Example 10.1*.

Example 10.1: Plotting a simple line chart from a DataFrame using Pandas and Matplotlib

In this example, we begin by creating a DataFrame using Pandas, which contains sales data for five consecutive months. The **`plot()`** function from Pandas is used to generate a line graph by specifying **`kind='line'`**. This method internally uses Matplotlib, which means we do not need to directly call **`plt.plot()`** for simple cases. We set the **`Month`** column as the x-axis and **`Sales`** as the y-axis. The **`marker='o'`** adds circular markers at each data point, while **`color='blue'`** defines the line color. A title is given to the plot using the **`title`** argument, and additional labeling is done using **`plt.xlabel()`** and **`plt.ylabel()`** to clearly describe the axes. Finally, **`plt.grid(True)`** is added to make the plot easier to read. This basic line plot demonstrates how easily we can visualize time-based or sequential data using Pandas and Matplotlib together. It is a foundational step in building more complex plots. This code illustrates how to generate a line chart from a Pandas DataFrame using the **`plot()`** function and Matplotlib for visualization:

```
import pandas as pd
import matplotlib.pyplot as plt
# Creating a simple DataFrame
data = pd.DataFrame({
    'Month': ['Jan', 'Feb', 'Mar', 'Apr', 'May'],
    'Sales': [200, 250, 300, 280, 320]
})
# Plotting the data using the built-in plot() method
```

```
data.plot(x='Month', y='Sales', kind='line', marker='o', color='blue', ti-
tle='Monthly Sales')
# Displaying the plot
plt.xlabel('Month')
plt.ylabel('Sales in Units')
plt.grid(True)
plt.show()
```

The line plot illustrates the monthly sales trend over time, showing a general increase from January to May with a slight decline in April, which may indicate a temporary fluctuation or seasonal variation in sales. Such visualizations help in identifying overall trends and short-term changes when comparing values across categories. It is important to note that the x-axis assumes the data is ordered chronologically; therefore, real-world datasets should be explicitly sorted to avoid misleading interpretations. Additionally, the y-axis uses a linear scale, which is appropriate for moderate variations in sales, but alternative scaling may be required when dealing with data that spans a wider range of values.

The output of the example for creating a simple line plot from Pandas data is shown in *Figure 10.1*:

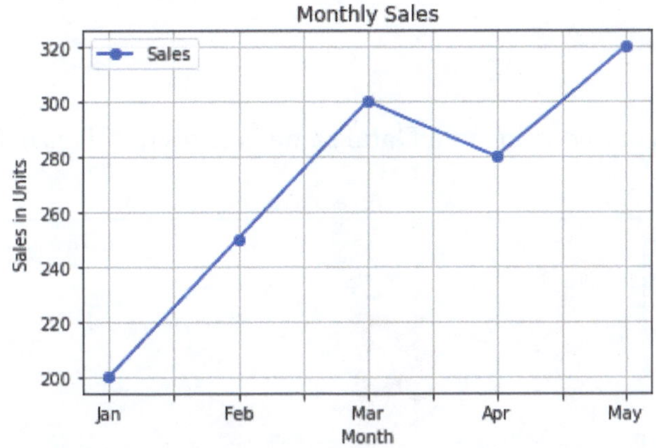

***Figure 10.1**: Output of creating a simple line plot from Pandas data*

Example 10.2: Plotting a bar chart from a DataFrame

In this example, we use Pandas to create a DataFrame that stores the number of units sold for four different products. We then create a bar chart by setting **`kind='bar'`** in the **`plot()`** function. The **`Product`** column is used for the x-axis, and **`Quantity Sold`** represents the height of each bar.

The bars are displayed in orange for visual clarity. We use **`plt.xlabel()`** and **`plt.ylabel()`** to label the axes appropriately and **`plt.grid(axis='y')`** to add horizontal grid lines for better readability. The function **`plt.tight_layout()`** ensures that labels and elements are neatly arranged and do not overlap. Finally, **plt.show()** renders the chart. A bar chart is ideal for comparing quantities across different categories, and this example shows how easily such charts can be generated directly from Pandas using Matplotlib as the backend:

```
import pandas as pd
import matplotlib.pyplot as plt
# Creating a DataFrame with product sales data
data = pd.DataFrame({
    'Fruits': ['Apples', 'Bananas', 'Cherries', 'Oranges'],
    'Quantity Sold': [120, 90, 60, 30]
})
# Plotting a vertical bar chart
data.plot(x='Fruits', y='Quantity Sold', kind='bar', color='orange',
title='Sale of Fruits')
# Adding axis labels
plt.xlabel('Fruits')
plt.ylabel('Units Sold')
# Displaying the plot
plt.grid(axis='y')
plt.tight_layout()
plt.show()
```

The output of plotting a bar chart from a DataFrame is shown in *Figure 10.2*:

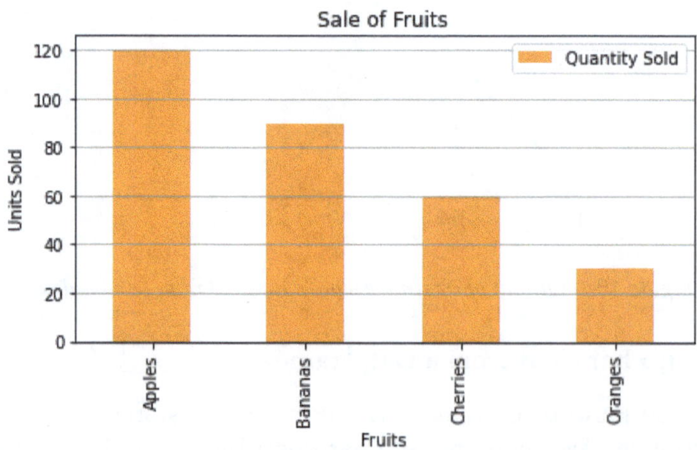

Figure 10.2*: Output of plotting a bar chart from a DataFrame*

Example 10.3: Write a program for plotting a pie chart for course enrollment distribution

In this example, we represent the number of students enrolled in various academic courses using a pie chart. The data is organized in a Pandas DataFrame, where each row contains a course name and the corresponding number of enrolled students. To create the pie chart, we use Matplotlib's **plt.pie()** function. The **labels** parameter is linked to the course names, and **autopct='%1.1f%%'** displays percentage labels on each segment of the pie. The **startangle=90** rotates the chart for a better initial visual layout, and **plt.axis('equal')** ensures the pie appears as a perfect circle. Pie charts are effective for illustrating the proportion of a whole, making them especially useful for understanding how student enrollment is distributed across multiple subjects. The following Python program visualizes course-wise student enrollment using a pie chart created with Pandas and Matplotlib:

```
import pandas as pd
import matplotlib.pyplot as plt
# Creating a DataFrame for course enrollment
data = pd.DataFrame({
    'Course': ['Mathematics','Physics','Computer Science','English','Biolo-
gy'],
    'Enrolled Students': [45, 30, 60, 25, 40]
})
# Generating a pie chart
plt.figure(figsize=(6,6))
plt.pie(data['Enrolled Students'], labels=data['Course'], au-
topct='%1.1f%%', startangle=90)
plt.title('Course-wise Student Enrollment')
plt.axis('equal') #Ensures pie is drawn as a circle
plt.show()
```

The output for plotting a pie chart is shown in *Figure 10.3*:

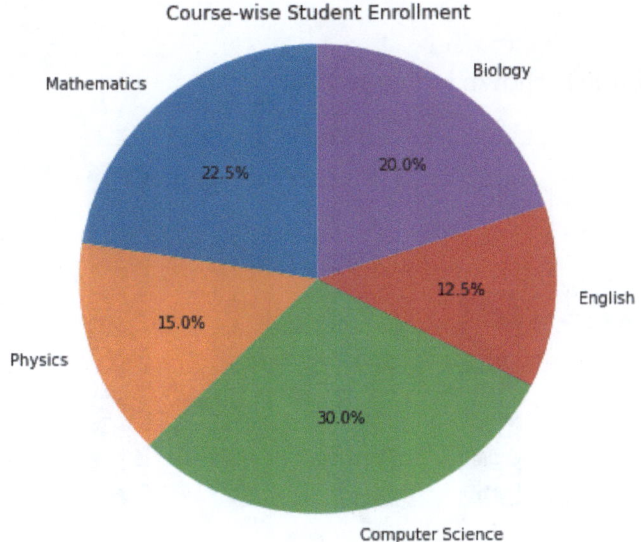

***Figure 10.3**: Output of plotting a pie chart*

Basic plotting with Series and DataFrames

Pandas makes it easy to visualize data by allowing direct plotting from Series and DataFrame objects using the **.plot()** method. This built-in function internally uses Matplotlib, so users do not have to write complex code to generate plots. When working with a Series, a simple line plot can be created by just calling **.plot()** on it. Similarly, DataFrames can produce more complex plots by specifying columns for the x and y axes and choosing the plot type. This direct integration streamlines the visualization process, making it convenient for quick data exploration and analysis. A Series represents a single variable and therefore produces a plot with one set of values, making it suitable for visualizing individual trends or distributions. In contrast, a DataFrame can contain multiple columns, and plotting a DataFrame typically results in multiple data series being displayed within the same figure, either as grouped elements or separate lines, depending on the plot type. This distinction allows Series plots to focus on isolated patterns, while DataFrame plots are more effective for comparing relationships and variations across multiple variables within a dataset.

Example 10.4: Write a program for plotting directly from a Series or a DataFrame

We can plot directly from a Series or a DataFrame using **.plot()**, simplifying the process of generating visuals:

```
import pandas as pd
import matplotlib.pyplot as plt
s = pd.Series([20, 15, 27, 32])
s.plot(kind='bar', title='Simple Bar Chart')
plt.xlabel('Index')
plt.ylabel('Values')
plt.show()
```

The output of the example is shown in *Figure 10.4*:

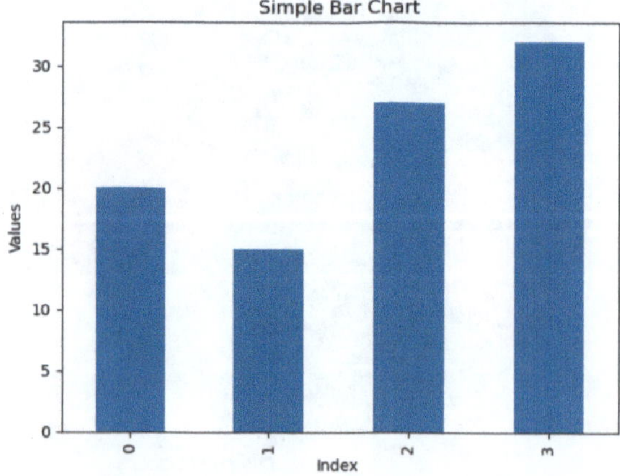

***Figure 10.4**: Output of plotting directly from a Series or a DataFrame*

Histograms and scatter plots for distribution visualization

Histograms and scatter plots are two powerful tools used to understand the distribution and relationships within a dataset. A histogram is helpful when you want to see how values are spread across different intervals. It groups data into ranges (called bins) and displays the frequency of values within each bin, making it easy to spot patterns such as skewness, peaks, or gaps. On the other hand, a scatter plot is used to visualize the relationship between two numerical variables. Each point in a scatter plot represents an observation in the dataset, positioned according to its values on the x and y axes. These plots are especially useful for identifying trends, clusters, or outliers in the data.

Example 10.5: Write a program for plotting a histogram of random integer values

In this example, a histogram is created to visualize the distribution of students' marks. The program starts by importing the **`numpy`** library and using **`np.random.randint(0, 100, 50)`** to generate 50 random integers between 0 and 100. These values represent the marks of students and are stored in a Pandas DataFrame named **`df`**. The **`.plot()`** function with **`kind='hist'`** creates a histogram from this data. The **`bins=10`** parameter divides the entire range of marks into 10 equal-width intervals, and the frequency of marks falling into each bin is displayed. The color of the bars is set to light green. A title and x-axis label are added for better readability. Finally, **`plt.show()`** displays the plot. This type of chart helps to understand how the marks are spread across different score ranges.

```
import numpy as np
df = pd.DataFrame({'Marks': np.random.randint(0, 100, 50)})
df['Marks'].plot(kind='hist', bins=10, color='lightgreen')
plt.title('Marks Distribution')
plt.xlabel('Marks')
plt.show()
```

The histogram represents the distribution of students' marks and helps in identifying the overall pattern of the data. The concentration of bars around certain ranges indicates clustering, revealing where most students' scores are grouped. Any noticeable asymmetry in the distribution suggests skewness, which may indicate whether lower or higher scores are more prevalent. Such visual analysis is useful for assessing performance trends, identifying outliers, and understanding the spread of marks before applying further statistical analysis.

The output of plotting a histogram of random integer values is shown in *Figure 10.5*:

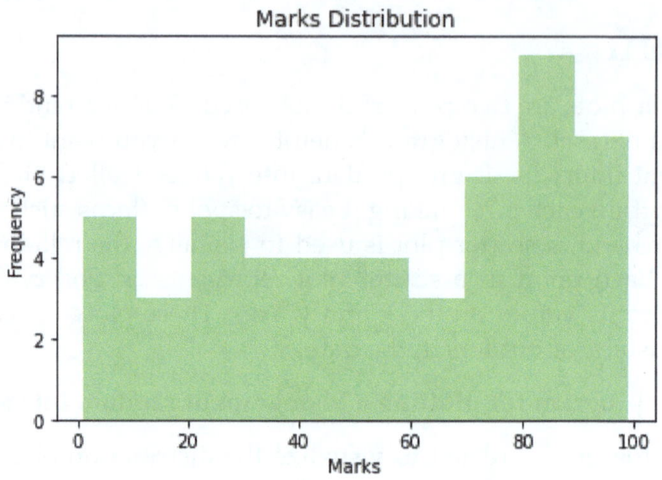

***Figure 10.5**: Output of plotting a histogram of random integer values*

Example 10.6: Write a program for plotting a scatter plot

This example demonstrates how to create a scatter plot to visualize the relationship between students' scores in **`Maths`** and **`Science`**. The program starts by creating a Pandas DataFrame **`df`** containing two columns: **`Maths`** and **`Science`**, with five scores each. The **`.plot()`** function is used with **`kind='scatter'`**, where the x-axis is set to **`Maths`** and the y-axis to **`Science`**. This means each point in the scatter plot represents a student's **`Maths`** and **`Science`** scores as coordinates (x, y). A title is added for clarity using **`plt.title()`**, and **`plt.show()`** is used to display the plot. This scatter plot helps in visually identifying any trend or correlation between the two subjects, such as whether students who score high in **`Maths`** also tend to score high in **`Science`**:

```
import numpy as np
df = pd.DataFrame({
    'Maths': [65, 75, 86, 95, 71],
    'Science': [68, 75, 89, 90, 80]
})
df.plot(kind='scatter', x='Maths', y='Science')
plt.title('Maths vs Science Scores')
plt.show()
```

The output of the example is shown in *Figure 10.6*:

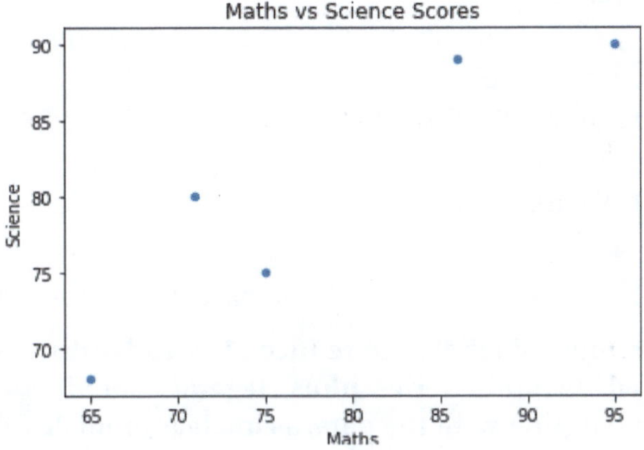

***Figure 10.6**: Output window of plotting a scatter plot*

Customizing plots with titles, labels, and legends

Customizing plots is essential to make data visualizations clear, informative, and easy to interpret. The titles help in describing what the graph represents, axis labels explain the meaning of values on each axis, and legends help identify different data series in the plot. Matplotlib allows us to customize these elements using functions like **`plt.title()`**, **`plt.xlabel()`**, **`plt.ylabel()`**, and **`plt.legend()`**. Clear and concise titles and axis labels with appropriate font sizes improve plot readability. Legends should be used only when necessary and positioned to avoid overlapping with data. Limiting colors and visual elements helps reduce clutter and results in cleaner, more effective visualizations. A proper use of these customizations enhances the readability and effectiveness of data presentations.

Example 10.7: Write a program for adding a title and axis labels

In this example, **`data.plot(...)`** plots a line chart of enrollments over months, and **`marker='o'`** adds circular markers at each data point. Here, **`color='purple'`** changes the line color. The statements **`plt.title()`**, **`plt.xlabel()`**, and **`plt.ylabel()`** are used to enhance readability with a proper chart title and labeled axes, as shown in the following code:

```
import pandas as pd
import matplotlib.pyplot as plt
# Creating a DataFrame for student enrollments
data = pd.DataFrame({
    'Month': ['Jan','Feb','March','April','May'],
    'Enrollments': [20, 35, 50, 75, 80]
```

```
})
# Plotting the enrollments data
data.plot(x='Month', y='Enrollments', kind='line', marker='o', color='purple')
# Adding a title and axis labels
plt.title('Monthly Student Enrollments')
plt.xlabel('Month')
plt.ylabel('Number of Enrollments')
plt.grid(True)
plt.show()
```

Note: Excessive or overcrowded labels can reduce plot readability, especially when many categories are displayed. In multi-series plots, legends should be clearly labeled and positioned to avoid overlapping with the data, as unclear or misleading legends may lead to misinterpretation.

The output of the program for adding a title and axis labels is shown in *Figure 10.7*:

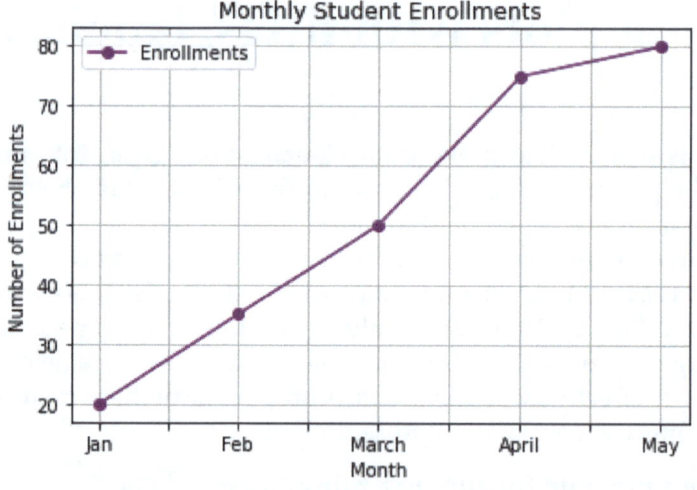

***Figure 10.7**: Output of adding a title and axis labels*

Example 10.8: Write a program for a legend with multiple lines

This example demonstrates how to create a line plot comparing marks in two subjects, i.e., `Maths` and `Science`, for four students using a Pandas DataFrame and Matplotlib. The DataFrame contains scores for each student, labeled from `Student1` to `Student4`. The `plot()` function is used with the `kind='line'` parameter and `marker='o'` to display the data points as circles connected by lines. The plot is then customized with a title, axis labels, and a legend titled `Subjects` to distinguish between the two subjects. Grid lines are added using `plt.grid(True)` to enhance readability. This visual representation helps compare performance in each subject across students, making the data easier to interpret and analyze:

```
import pandas as pd
import matplotlib.pyplot as plt
df = pd.DataFrame({
    'Maths': [75, 80, 95, 71],
    'Science': [66, 81, 82, 72]
}, index=['Student1', 'Student2', 'Student3', 'Student4'])

df.plot(kind='line', marker='o')
plt.title('Marks Comparison')
plt.xlabel('Students')
plt.ylabel('Marks')
plt.legend(title='Subjects')
plt.grid(True)
plt.show()
```

The output of the program for legends with multiple lines is shown in *Figure 10.8*:

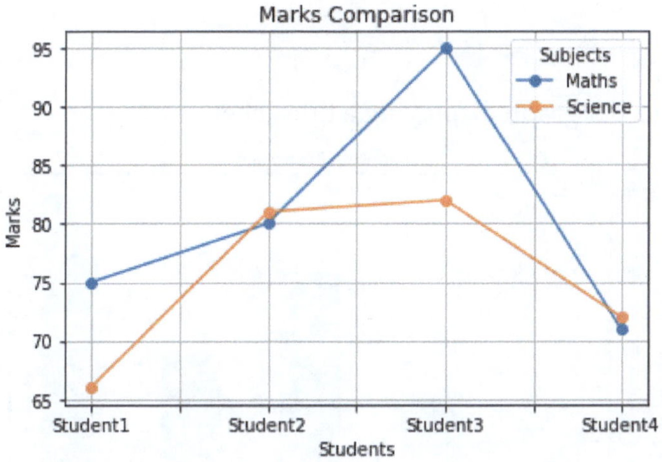

Figure 10.8: Output of legends with multiple lines

Example 10.9: Write a program for plotting a bar graph displaying a title, label, and legends

In this example, a bar chart is used to represent the number of student enrollments over five months. The visualization is enhanced by adding a title using **`plt.title`**, and labeling the x-axis and y-axis using **`plt.xlabel`** and **`plt.ylabel`**, respectively. A legend is added with **`plt.legend`**, including a custom title, **`Data Type`**, to clarify the meaning of the bars. The use of **`plt.grid()`** adds horizontal grid lines, which improves the readability of the values. Finally, **`plt.tight_layout()`** is applied to ensure that all elements of the plot are neatly arranged without overlapping. This code demonstrates how to plot monthly enrollment figures as a bar chart while customizing the title, axis labels, grid lines, and legend using Matplotlib:

```
import pandas as pd
import matplotlib.pyplot as plt

# Creating a DataFrame for monthly enrollment data
df = pd.DataFrame({
    'Month': ['Jan', 'Feb', 'Mar', 'Apr', 'May'],
    'Enrollments': [40, 50, 80, 60, 100]
})
# Plotting the data
df.plot(x='Month', y='Enrollments', kind='bar', color='skyblue', legend=False)
plt.title('Monthly Enrollments')       # Adding a title
plt.xlabel('Month')                    # Customizing X-axis label
plt.ylabel('Number of Enrollments')    # Customizing Y-axis label
plt.xticks(rotation=0)                 # Keeping month names horizontal
plt.grid(axis='y', linestyle='--', alpha=0.7)   # Adding grid lines for clarity
plt.legend(['Enrollments'], title='Data Type')  # Custom legend with a title
plt.tight_layout()
plt.show()
```

The output of plotting a bar graph displaying a title, label, and legends is shown in *Figure 10.9*:

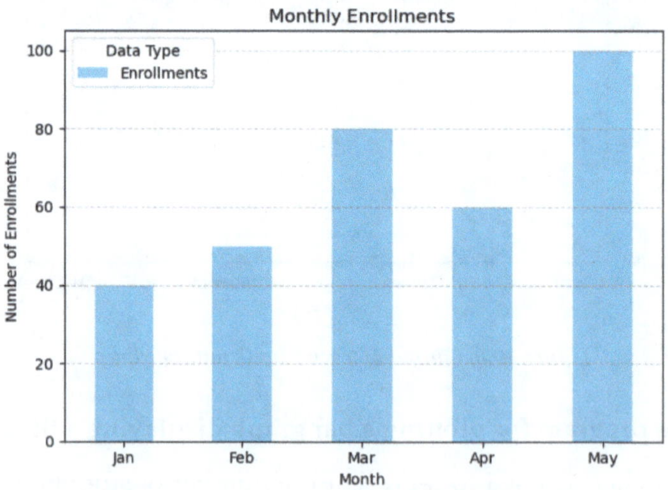

Figure 10.9*: Output of plotting a bar graph displaying a title, label, and legends*

Enhancing visuals with colors, styles, and markers

To make charts more visually appealing and easier to understand, we can enhance them using different colors, line styles, and markers. Colors help distinguish between different data sets, while styles like dashed or dotted lines can make plots clearer. The markers, such as circles or squares, highlight specific data points on a line chart. These customizations not only improve the look of a graph but also help the viewer quickly understand the information being presented. When enhancing visualizations with colors, styles, and markers, accessibility should be taken into account. Color-blind friendly palettes and sufficient contrast help ensure that plots remain interpretable for all viewers. Over-styling through excessive colors, patterns, or markers should be avoided, as it can distract from the data and reduce clarity.

Example 10.10: Write a program for enhancing a line plot with colors, styles, and markers

This example shows how many students were present each day of the week. The line is in green color, uses a dash-dot pattern, i.e., **`linestyle='-.'`**, and has circular markers (**`marker='o'`**) for each day. These visual enhancements make the chart more colorful, easier to follow, and visually engaging for students, as shown in the following code:

```
import pandas as pd
import matplotlib.pyplot as plt
# Data of attendance over 5 school days
data = pd.DataFrame({
    'Day': ['Monday', 'Tuesday', 'Wednesday', 'Thursday', 'Friday'],
    'Attendance': [45, 47, 44, 48, 46]
})
# Line plot with customized color, style, and marker
plt.plot(data['Day'], data['Attendance'],
         color='green', linestyle='-.', marker='o', label='Attendance')
# Customizing the plot
plt.title('Student Attendance During the Week')
plt.xlabel('Day')
plt.ylabel('Number of Students Present')
plt.legend()
plt.grid(True)
plt.tight_layout()
plt.show()
```

The output of visualizing a line plot with colors, styles, and markers is shown in *Figure 10.10*:

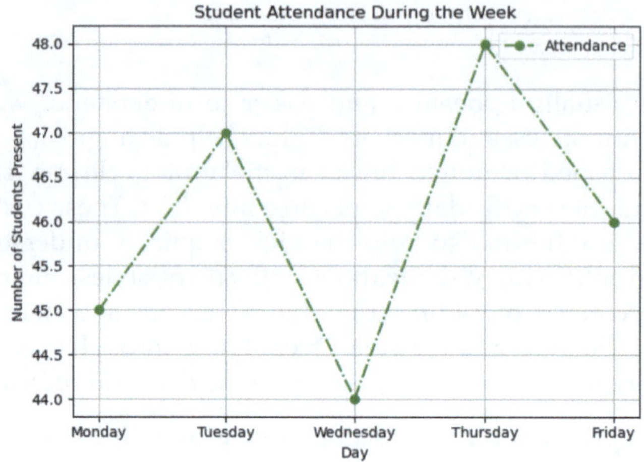

***Figure 10.10**: Output of visualizing line plot with colors, styles, and markers*

Example 10.11: Write a program for plotting a bar graph displaying students' performance in different subjects

In this example, a bar chart is used to show a student's scores in five different subjects. The bars are filled with a sky blue color (**`color='skyblue'`**) and have black edges (**`edgecolor='black'`**) for clarity. A dashed horizontal grid is added for better readability using **`plt.grid(axis='y')`**. The plot is neatly laid out using **`plt.tight_layout()`**.

```
import pandas as pd
import matplotlib.pyplot as plt
# Sample data: test marks of a student in different subjects
data = pd.DataFrame({
    'Subjects': ['Maths', 'Science', 'English', 'History', 'Computer'],
    'Scores': [85, 90, 78, 88, 92]
})
# Bar chart with custom color and bar edge style
plt.bar(data['Subjects'], data['Scores'],
        color='skyblue', edgecolor='black')
# Customizing the plot
plt.title('Test Scores in Different Subjects')
plt.xlabel('Subjects')
plt.ylabel('Scores')
plt.grid(axis='y', linestyle='--', alpha=0.7)  # Grid only on Y-axis
plt.tight_layout()
plt.show()
```

The output of plotting a bar graph displaying students' performance in different subjects is shown in *Figure 10.11*:

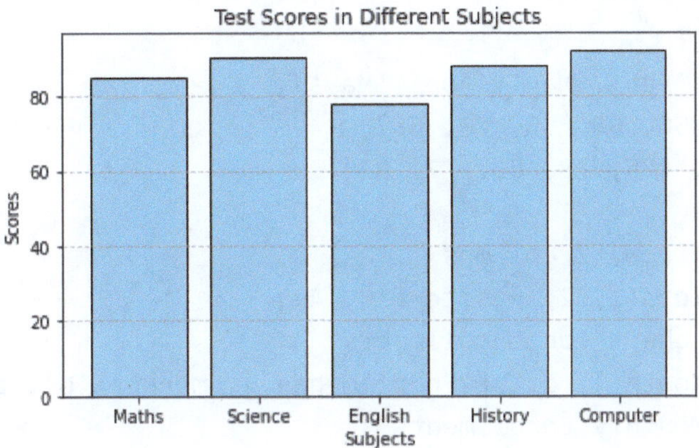

***Figure 10.11**: Output of plotting a bar graph displaying students' performance in different subjects*

Using subplots for multiple visualizations

Subplots allow us to display multiple plots within a single figure. This is useful when we want to compare different aspects of data side by side. Instead of showing each chart separately, we can organize them in rows and columns using the **`plt.subplot()`** or **`plt.subplots()`** function from Matplotlib. This makes it easier to analyze related plots together, saving space and improving clarity.

Example 10.12: Write a program demonstrating subplots for multiple visualizations

In this example, we use **`plt.subplots(1, 2)`** to create two plots side by side. The first plot displays how student enrollments change each month using a line chart, while the second plot shows average scores for the same months using a bar chart. The titles, axis labels, and gridlines are added to make the plots more readable and informative. The statement **`plt.tight_layout()`** ensures that the plots do not overlap and fit neatly within the figure area. When we use **`plt.subplots()`**, it returns two objects:

- **fig**: The overall figure or canvas.
- **axes**: A list (or array) of individual subplots.

By writing **`fig, axes = plt.subplots(1, 2)`**, we are creating one row and two columns of subplots, meaning two plots arranged horizontally. Here, **`axes[0]`** refers to the first (left) plot, and **`axes[1]`** refers to the second (right) plot. This allows us to customize each subplot individually. The following code illustrates how to create multiple visualizations using Matplotlib subplots, representing monthly enrollments with a line chart and average marks with a bar chart:

```
import pandas as pd
import matplotlib.pyplot as plt
# Creating sample data
data = pd.DataFrame({
    'Month': ['Jan','Feb','Mar','Apr','May'],
    'Enrollments': [50, 60, 55, 70, 65],
    'Average Marks': [75, 78, 80, 77, 82]
})
# Create subplots: 1 row, 2 columns
fig, axes = plt.subplots(1, 2, figsize=(10, 4))
# First plot - Line chart for enrollments
axes[0].plot(data['Month'], data['Enrollments'], marker='o', color='blue')
axes[0].set_title('Monthly Enrollments')
axes[0].set_xlabel('Month')
axes[0].set_ylabel('Number of Students')
axes[0].grid(True)
# Second plot - Bar chart for average scores
axes[1].bar(data['Month'], data['Average Marks'], color='green')
axes[1].set_title('Average Marks')
axes[1].set_xlabel('Month')
axes[1].set_ylabel('Marks')
axes[1].grid(True)
# Adjust layout
plt.tight_layout()
plt.show()
```

The choice of subplot layout depends on the type of comparison required. A horizontal layout (more columns than rows) is suitable when comparing different metrics across the same categories, while a vertical layout is often preferable when emphasizing trends over a shared axis. A proper alignment between subplots is important to ensure consistent spacing and label visibility; functions such as **`tight_layout()`** help prevent overlapping titles, labels, and axes, which is a common issue when working with multiple plots.

The output of subplots for displaying monthly enrollments and average marks of students is shown in *Figure 10.12*:

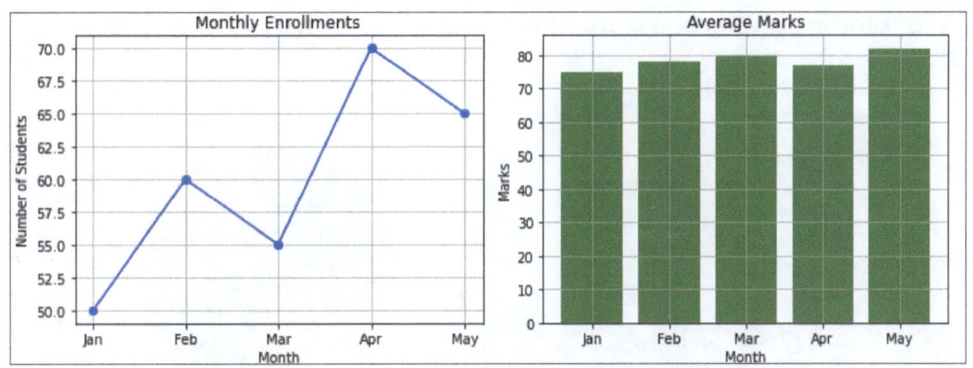

Figure 10.12: Output of subplots for displaying monthly enrollments and average marks of students

Example 10.13: Write a program for plotting marks of a student with bar and pie charts using subplots

This example uses **`plt.subplots(1, 2)`** to create two visualizations side by side. The left chart (**`axes[0]`**) is a bar chart that displays **`Maths`** marks for four students, while the right chart (**`axes[1]`**) is a pie chart that shows how **`Science`** marks are distributed among the same students. Gridlines and axis labels are added to the bar chart for better readability. The **`autopct`** parameter in the pie chart displays percentage values inside each slice. Finally, **`plt.tight_layout()`** ensures that the plots have proper spacing and do not overlap. The following code illustrates how to use Matplotlib subplots to represent students' marks in different subjects through a bar chart for **`Maths`** and a pie chart for **`Science`**:

```
import matplotlib.pyplot as plt
# Sample data
students = ['Aman','Bina','Chetan','Divya']
maths_marks = [85, 92, 78, 88]
science_marks = [80, 91, 70, 90]
# Create 1 row and 2 columns of subplots
fig, axes = plt.subplots(1, 2, figsize=(10, 5))
# First subplot: Bar chart for Maths Scores
axes[0].bar(students, maths_marks, color='skyblue')
axes[0].set_title('Maths Marks')
axes[0].set_xlabel('Students')
axes[0].set_ylabel('Marks')
axes[0].grid(True)
# Second subplot: Pie chart for Science Marks
axes[1].pie(science_marks, labels=students, autopct='%1.1f%%', startangle=90)
axes[1].set_title('Science Score Distribution')
# Improve spacing between plots
plt.tight_layout()
plt.show()
```

The output for plotting marks of a student with bar and pie charts using subplots is shown in *Figure 10.13*:

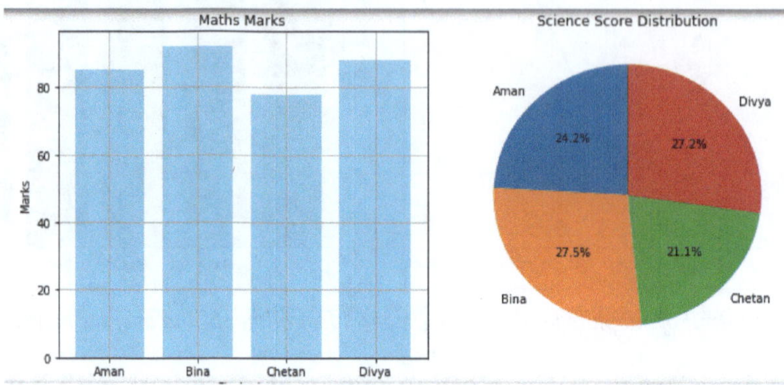

***Figure 10.13**: Output of plotting marks of a student with bar and pie charts using subplots*

Exporting visualizations as image files

Exporting visualizations as image files is an important feature that allows users to save their plots for future use in reports, presentations, or sharing with others. In Python's Matplotlib library, this can be done easily using the **`plt.savefig()`** function. You can save a plot as a **`.png`**, **`.jpg`**, **`.pdf`**, or other supported formats. For example, **`plt.savefig('plot.png')`** saves the current plot as a PNG image. To ensure high-quality images, you can also specify the resolution using the dpi parameter, such as **`dpi=300`**. It is important to call **`plt.savefig()`** before **`plt.show()`**, otherwise the saved image might be blank. This feature makes it simple to preserve and reuse your visual work outside of Python.

Example 10.14: Demonstrate with the help of an example for saving the plot as an image file

In this example, a line chart is created to show how student enrollments change over five months, i.e., January to May. The **`plt.plot()`** function is used to create the line chart, where months are shown on the X-axis, enrollment of the number of students is shown on the Y-axis, **`marker='o'`** adds a circular point at each data value, and **`color='green'`** sets the line color to green. The **`plt.title()`**, **`plt.xlabel()`**, and **`plt.ylabel()`** functions are used to add a title and axis labels to make the chart easier to understand. The **`plt.grid(True)`** adds horizontal and vertical grid lines for better readability. Here, before displaying the chart using **`plt.show()`**, the code saves the chart as an image file (**`chart1.png`**) on the **`F: drive`** using the **`plt.savefig()`** function. The **`dpi=300`** makes sure the image is saved in high resolution. It is important to save the plot before calling **`plt.show()`** to avoid saving a blank image. The following code illustrates how to visualize monthly enrollment trends of students using a line chart and save the output as an image file in Matplotlib:

```
import matplotlib.pyplot as plt
months = ['Jan', 'Feb', 'Mar', 'Apr', 'May']
enrollments = [45, 50, 55, 48, 60]
```

```
plt.plot(months, enrollments, marker='o', color='green')
plt.title('Monthly Enrollments')
plt.xlabel('Month')
plt.ylabel('Number of Students')
plt.grid(True)
# Save the plot as an image file before displaying it
plt.savefig('F:\\chart1.png', dpi=300)
plt.show()
```

Note: Avoid using absolute file paths like `F:\chart1.png` because they may not exist on other computers. Instead, use relative paths (e.g., `chart1.png`) or ensure the folder exists before saving the plot.

The output of saving a plot as an image file is shown in *Figure 10.14*:

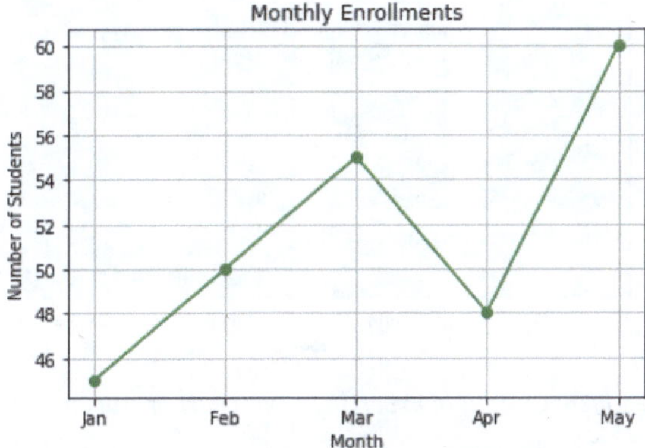

***Figure 10.14**: Output of saving a plot as an image file*

Example 10.15: Write a program for exporting a bar chart of students' marks

This code creates a bar chart to display the marks of four students. The **`plt.bar()`** function is used for the bar chart, with a soft blue color. The chart is customized with a title and axis labels. The statement **`plt.grid(axis='y')`** adds horizontal lines for better readability. Again, before showing the chart, **`plt.savefig()`** is used to save the image to **`F:\student_marks.png`** in high resolution (300 dpi). Finally, **`plt.show()`** displays the chart on screen. The following Python program creates a bar chart to display students' marks and saves the chart as an image file using Matplotlib:

```
import matplotlib.pyplot as plt
# Sample data
students = ['Aman', 'Bina', 'Chirag', 'Divya']
marks = [85, 90, 78, 92]
# Create a bar chart
plt.bar(students, marks, color='skyblue')
```

```
plt.title('Student Marks')
plt.xlabel('Students')
plt.ylabel('Marks')
plt.grid(axis='y')  # Add horizontal grid lines
# Save the bar chart as an image file
plt.savefig('F:\\student_marks.png', dpi=300)
# Show the plot
plt.show()
```

The output of exporting a bar chart of students' marks is shown in *Figure 10.15*:

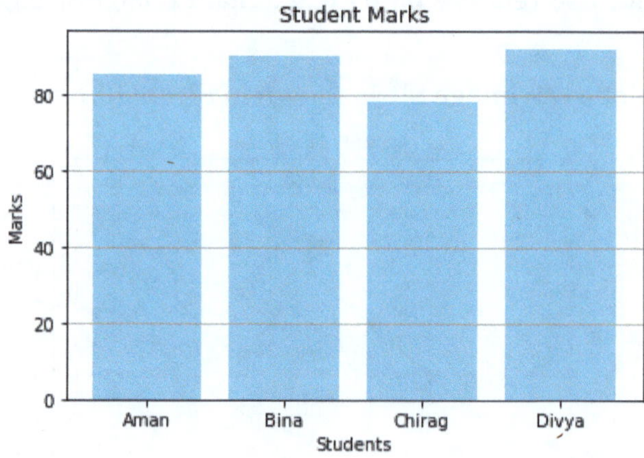

***Figure 10.15**: Output of exporting a bar chart of students marks*

Conclusion

In this chapter, we explored how to use Matplotlib in combination with Pandas to create clear, informative, and visually appealing data visualizations. Starting with basic plotting using Pandas Series and DataFrames, we learned how to generate line plots, bar charts, and pie charts to represent categorical and numerical data effectively. We then examined histograms and scatter plots to understand data distribution and relationships between variables. Further, we explored how to customize plots by adding titles, axis labels, legends, and grid lines, making our visualizations more readable and meaningful. By using colors, line styles, and markers, we enhanced the visual appeal of plots and made them more distinguishable. We also learned how to create multiple plots in a single figure using subplots, which is useful when comparing different types of data side-by-side.

Lastly, we discovered how to export our plots as image files, making it easy to include visualizations in reports and presentations. Overall, this chapter provided a strong foundation in creating and customizing plots with Matplotlib and Pandas, helping students and analysts turn raw data into powerful visual insights.

Points to remember

The following points are to be kept in mind:

- Matplotlib is a powerful library used to create different types of charts and graphs in Python.
- Pandas work well with Matplotlib for visualizing data stored in Series and DataFrames.
- Use the plot() function to create simple line plots with Series or DataFrames.
- Bar charts show comparisons between different groups; pie charts show parts of a whole.
- Histograms display the frequency distribution of numerical data.
- Scatter plots show relationships between two numeric variables.
- Use plt.title(), plt.xlabel(), and plt.ylabel() to add titles and axis labels.
- Use plt.legend() to add a legend to describe what the plot lines or bars represent.
- Customize your plots using colors, line styles, and markers to make them more readable.
- Use plt.subplots() to create multiple plots in a single figure.
- The plt.grid(True) function adds grid lines to help read values more easily.
- plt.tight_layout() avoids overlapping of plots in subplots.
- Use plt.savefig('filename.png') to save your plots as image files before using plt.show().
- Always display the plot at the end using plt.show().

Key points

- **Matplotlib**: It is a widely used Python library for creating visualizations like line plots, bar charts, and more.
- **Pandas**: It allows easy plotting of data stored in Series and DataFrames using built-in .plot() function.
- **Line plots**: These are useful for showing trends over time, such as monthly enrollments or sales, etc.
- **Bar charts**: Bar charts are effective for comparing categories like student marks or product sales.
- **Pie charts**: They represent parts of a whole and are best for showing percentage distributions.

- **Histograms**: Histograms are used to show the frequency distribution of continuous data.
- **Scatter plots**: These plots help visualize the relationship or correlation between two numeric variables.
- **Customize plots**: You can customize plots using titles, axis labels, legends, grid lines, and tick marks.

  Enhance the appearance using colors, line styles ('--', ':'), and markers ('o', '*', 's').
- **Subplots**: Subplots allow multiple visualizations to be shown in one figure using plt.subplots().
- **plt.tight_layout()**: Use plt.tight_layout() to automatically adjust subplot spacing and avoid overlaps.
- **plt.savefig**: Save your visualizations using plt.savefig('filename.png') before displaying them with plt.show().

Multiple choice questions

1. **Which Python library is commonly used for creating visualizations with Pandas?**
   a. NumPy
   b. Matplotlib
   c. TensorFlow
   d. OpenCV
2. **What does the plot() function do in Pandas or Matplotlib?**
   a. Saves the figure
   b. Creates a visualization
   c. Imports data
   d. Adds a title to a chart
3. **Which function is used to show the plot window in Matplotlib?**
   a. plt.draw()
   b. plt.open()
   c. plt.show()
   d. plt.run()
4. **What type of chart is best for comparing quantities across different categories?**
   a. Line chart
   b. Bar chart
   c. Pie chart
   d. Histogram
5. **In a pie chart, what does the parameter autopct='%1.1f%%' do?**
   a. Sets the color
   b. Adds percentage labels
   c. Adds gridlines
   d. Sets title

6. **Which method is used to add a title to a plot?**
   a. plt.label()
   b. plt.name()
   c. plt.heading()
   d. plt.title()

7. **What does plt.xlabel('Month') do?**
   a. Plots the x-values
   b. Adds label to X-axis
   c. Sets chart title
   d. Draws a pie chart

8. **What is the use of plt.grid(True) in a plot?**
   a. It changes background color
   b. It displays gridlines
   c. It highlights a legend
   d. It saves the plot

9. **What does plt.savefig('chart.png') do?**
   a. Shows the chart
   b. Deletes the chart
   c. Saves the chart as an image file
   d. Plots a bar chart

10. **Which keyword is used to create multiple plots in one figure?**
    a. subplot()
    b. subfig()
    c. plt.multi()
    d. plt.group()

11. **What does marker='o' do in a line plot?**
    a. Changes line color
    b. Adds circles at data points
    c. Adds a legend
    d. Adds a grid

12. **Which of the following is used to plot histograms in Matplotlib?**
    a. plt.hist()
    b. plt.bar()
    c. plt.scatter()
    d. plt.pie()

13. **Which plot is best for visualizing trends over time?**
    a. Pie chart
    b. Line plot
    c. Bar chart
    d. Scatter plot

14. **How many plots are created using plt.subplots(1, 2)?**
    a. 1
    b. 2
    c. 3
    d. None

15. **In Matplotlib, what is the full form of plt?**
    a. Pandas label table
    b. Python line tool
    c. Pyplot module
    d. Plotting terminal

Answers

1	b
2	b
3	c
4	b
5	b
6	d
7	b
8	b
9	c
10	a
11	b
12	a
13	b
14	b
15	c

Questions

1. What is the purpose of the plot() function in Pandas or Matplotlib?
2. How do you display a plot in Matplotlib?
3. Which function is used to create multiple visualizations in the same figure?
4. How can you add labels to the x-axis and y-axis in a plot?
5. What does the marker='o' argument do in a line plot?
6. How can you save a chart as an image file in Matplotlib?
7. What is the use of the autopct argument in a pie chart?
8. Which plot type is best suited to show data distribution?
9. What is the role of plt.title() in customizing a plot?
10. Why is plt.tight_layout() used when working with subplots?

CHAPTER 11
Introduction to ML and Supervised Learning

Introduction

Machine learning (ML) is a branch of **artificial intelligence** (AI) that allows computers to learn from data and improve their performance without being directly programmed. Instead of giving step-by-step instructions, we feed data to the computer and let it discover patterns and make decisions on its own. From voice assistants like *Alexa* to personalized recommendations on *YouTube* and *Amazon*, all of this is possible because of ML. A personalized recommendations on YouTube or Amazon are examples of supervised learning, where the system learns from historical labeled data (e.g., past user preferences) to predict future choices; grouping customers by purchasing behavior illustrates unsupervised learning, which finds hidden patterns without labels; and training a robot to navigate a maze using rewards demonstrates reinforcement learning, where an agent learns through trial and error. This chapter introduces the basic idea of ML, how it works, and the different types of learning: supervised learning, unsupervised learning, and a brief overview of reinforcement learning.

Structure

The following topics are covered in this chapter:

- Introduction to machine learning
- Importance and applications of machine learning
- Types of machine learning
- Types of ML problems
- Examples of supervised learning
- Model evaluation metrics

Objectives

The objective of this chapter is to provide students with a practical and beginner-friendly introduction to the fundamental concepts of ML. By the end of the chapter, students will be able to differentiate between supervised, unsupervised, and reinforcement learning, explain how machines learn from data and make decisions without explicit programming, compare the approaches used in the three types of learning, illustrate real-world applications such as recommendation systems, customer segmentation, and autonomous agents, and identify commonly used machine learning algorithms along with their basic purposes.

Introduction to machine learning

ML is a branch of AI that enables computers to learn from data and make decisions or predictions without being explicitly programmed. It is widely used in applications like search engines, recommendation systems, spam filters, and more. Broadly, machines can learn in three main ways. These form the three categories of ML:

- **Supervised learning**: This uses labeled datasets, where the input comes with correct output labels. For example, if we want to teach a machine to recognize fruits, we give it examples like *This is an apple, This is a banana,* etc. The machine learns from these examples. Example algorithms are linear regression, decision trees, **k-nearest neighbors** (**KNN**), **support vector machine** (**SVM**), etc. These algorithms are commonly used when labeled data is available, such as for prediction or classification tasks, where the output value or class is known in advance.

- **Unsupervised learning**: This works on unlabeled data, where the machine tries to find hidden patterns or groupings by itself. For example, grouping customers by purchasing behavior without knowing anything about them in advance. The example algorithms are K-means clustering, hierarchical clustering, etc. Such algorithms are useful when the structure of the data is unknown, and the goal is to discover hidden patterns or natural groupings.

- **Reinforcement learning**: In this type, the machine learns by trial and error, based on feedback from its actions, similar to how we learn through rewards and punishments. It keeps improving its decisions based on the feedback it receives. For example, game-playing agents that improve over time by learning from outcomes. Reinforcement learning is most appropriate for sequential decision-making problems where an agent must learn optimal actions through feedback over time.

Traditional ML algorithms often face performance limits as the dataset grows. However, a deep learning method, which is a subset of ML, can scale better and improve with more data. Unlike traditional machine learning algorithms, which usually rely on manually designed features, deep learning models use multi-layer neural networks that automatically learn complex features from raw data. This makes deep learning particularly suitable for tasks such as image recognition, speech processing, and natural language understanding.

Importance and applications of machine learning

ML is a branch of AI and computer science that focuses on teaching computers how to learn from data, just like humans learn from experience. Instead of being directly programmed for each specific task, ML algorithms allow computers to learn by identifying patterns in data and using those patterns to make decisions or predictions. Over time, as more data is provided, these algorithms can gradually improve their accuracy and performance. The importance of ML lies in its ability to handle large amounts of data and extract meaningful insights without human intervention. This makes it useful in solving complex problems and automating repetitive tasks. ML saves time, increases productivity, and helps in making smarter decisions in various fields. There are many real-world applications of ML. In *healthcare*, it helps doctors detect diseases, recommend treatments, and predict patient outcomes. In *education*, it can analyze how students are performing and suggest personalized learning paths. In *finance*, it is used for detecting fraud, predicting stock trends, and managing risks. In *marketing*, ML helps recommend products and show relevant advertisements based on user behavior. In *agriculture*, it assists in predicting crop yields and identifying plant diseases. As ML continues to grow, it is becoming an essential part of everyday technologies and transforming the way we live, learn, and work.

Types of machine learning

ML is broadly classified into three main types based on how a machine is trained with data. These are:

- Supervised learning
- Unsupervised learning
- Reinforcement learning

Supervised learning

In supervised learning, a labeled dataset is used to train the machine. Each piece of data has a label, or the right response, when it is labeled. In order to enable the model to predict the correct label for fresh, unseen data, supervised learning aims to learn from this data. Here, the data used for training is labeled, meaning both the input and the correct output are provided. The primary goal is to predict the output for new, unseen data based on this training. A simple example is predicting a student's exam score from the number of hours studied.

It is similar to learning from an instructor. In order to train the student (the machine) to solve comparable problems on its own, the teacher gives those questions and the right solutions. The examples of supervised learning algorithms are:

- **Linear regression**: Predicts continuous values (e.g., predicting marks based on study hours).

- **Support vector machine (SVM)**: Classifies data into categories (e.g., classifying emails as spam or not spam).
- **KNN**: Finds patterns based on closeness to labeled data points.
- **Decision trees**: Follow rules to make predictions based on the features of the data.

Note: **Classification is a type of supervised learning where the goal is to categorize input data into predefined classes or labels.**

The common applications of classification include the following:

- Classifying emails as spam or not spam
- Predicting student performance, such as whether a student will pass or fail
- Diagnosing diseases based on symptoms
- Recognizing handwritten characters or digits

Unsupervised learning

Unsupervised learning uses unlabeled data. This implies that the machine must find patterns, similarities, or contrasts in the data on its own without being instructed what to look for. The objective is to simplify or group data without any kind of direction.

It is similar to learning without an instructor, or another example is grouping customers into segments based on their purchasing behavior. A machine attempts to figure out the data's structure on its own. Here, the data is unlabeled, so the algorithm explores the structure of the data to find patterns or groupings without predefined outputs.

Common examples of unsupervised learning algorithms are:

- **K-means clustering**: Groups similar data points into clusters (e.g., grouping students by learning habits).
- **Hierarchical clustering**: Builds a hierarchy of clusters.
- **Principal component analysis (PCA)**: PCA reduces data dimensions while keeping important information. In many real-world datasets, a large number of features can make data difficult to visualize, slow to process, and prone to noise. Dimensionality reduction techniques help simplify such data by reducing the number of variables while retaining the most important information, making analysis, visualization, and learning more efficient. Unlike clustering methods, which group similar data points into clusters, PCA does not create groups but instead transforms the data into a smaller set of new variables that capture the maximum variance present in the original features. Intuitively, PCA can be understood as rotating the data to find new axes that best represent its spread. For example, when data points are distributed diagonally in two dimensions, PCA identifies a new axis along that direction, allowing the same information to be represented using fewer dimensions.

Note: **Clustering is an unsupervised learning technique used to group similar data points together, based on features, without knowing labels.**

The common applications of clustering include the following:

- Grouping students based on their study patterns.
- Organizing news articles by topic or automatically sorting documents and images.
- Customer segmentation in marketing, such as grouping customers based on their purchase history.
- Grouping similar items in online stores to improve recommendations.

Reinforcement learning

Reinforcement learning is a distinct sort of learning in which the computer learns by interacting with its surroundings. It learns through trial and error, with incentives for correct behaviors and penalties for incorrect ones. It improves its decision-making abilities over time in order to maximize the payoff.

It is like teaching a youngster how to play a game. The youngster learns which activities result in winning or losing and modifies their behavior accordingly. Another example can be like training a robot to walk, where it receives positive feedback for successful steps and negative feedback for falling. The system learns through feedback-based data, where actions are taken in an environment, and the algorithm receives rewards or penalties in return. The goal is to maximize rewards over time.

Examples of reinforcement learning algorithms are:

- **Q-learning**: Learns the value of actions to take in different situations.
- **Deep Q-networks (DQN)**: Combines deep learning with reinforcement learning.
- **State-Action-Reward-State-Action (SARSA)**: Learns from the actions taken and their outcomes.

Common applications of reinforcement learning include:

- Training robots to walk or pick objects
- Teaching computers to play games like chess or video games
- Self-driving cars that learn how to navigate roads safely

In reinforcement learning, the agent observes the current state, takes an action, and receives a reward, which helps it learn which actions lead to better long-term outcomes. While supervised and unsupervised learning focus on learning from existing datasets, reinforcement learning introduces a decision-making perspective that builds on these concepts. To better understand this interaction, reinforcement learning can be viewed in terms of three core components in

Table 11.1: the state of the environment, the action taken by the agent, and the reward received as feedback.

Component	Example (game agent)
State	Current position of the agent
Action	Move left, move right, jump
Reward	+1 for success, −1 for failure

***Table 11.1**: Conceptual view of the reinforcement learning process*

At each step, the agent observes the current state, selects an action, and receives a reward, which guides future decisions toward better performance.

Types of ML problems

ML problems for supervised learning are broadly divided into two main types:

- Classification
- Regression

Classification

Classification is about predicting a category or label, where the output is discrete (from a fixed set of possible values). It is used when the answer must be one of the predefined options. The examples are as follows:

- Predicting whether an email is *Spam* or *Not Spam*.
- Classifying animals as *Cat*, *Dog*, or *Rabbit*.
- Predicting whether a student will *Pass* or *Fail* based on study hours.

The output of classification problems is always in the form of categories or classes (e.g., *Pass/Fail*, *Yes/No*, *Red/Blue/Green*). The algorithms used in classification are logistic regression, decision trees, SVM, and KNN.

Regression

Regression is about predicting a number. The output is continuous (can take any value within a range). It is to be used when the answer is a quantity, price, or measurement. The examples are as follows:

- Predicting house prices based on size and location.
- Estimating a student's exam score based on study hours.
- Predicting the temperature for the next day.

The output of regression values is in numerical form, i.e., marks, price, temperature (e.g., 85, 2000, 32°C). The algorithm used in regression is linear regression.

Note: **Some problems fall between these two categories, such as ordinal classification, where the output consists of ordered categories (e.g., low, medium, high), combining aspects of both classification and regression.**

Examples of supervised learning

Let us understand supervised learning with the help of a few popular algorithms. We will start with logistic regression, followed by linear regression to see how it predicts continuous values, and then move on to algorithms like SVM, KNN, and decision trees to perform classification. In each case, we will imagine a dataset where the inputs (features) and the correct answers (labels) are already known. By using these examples, you will see how supervised learning models learn from labelled data to make predictions.

Logistic regression

Logistic regression is a classification algorithm used when the output is categorical (e.g., Yes/No, Pass/Fail, Spam/Not Spam). Unlike linear regression, which predicts a continuous number, logistic regression predicts the probability that something belongs to a certain class. It uses a special S-shaped curve called the sigmoid function to convert predictions into values between 0 and 1. If the probability is ≥ 0.5, we predict one class (e.g., Pass), and if it is < 0.5, we predict the other class (e.g., Fail). Given is a program to predict whether a student will pass or fail an exam based on the number of study hours. We use a simple dataset and apply a basic classification algorithm, such as logistic regression, to display the prediction for a given input.

Intuitively, the sigmoid function maps any input value to a range between 0 and 1, allowing the model's output to be interpreted as a probability. Large positive values are pushed close to 1, large negative values close to 0, while values near zero map to probabilities around 0.5, making the function well-suited for binary classification. Although a threshold of 0.5 is commonly used, it is not fixed and can be adjusted depending on the problem requirements, such as prioritizing precision over recall or handling class imbalance.

Example 11.1: Write a program for classifying whether a student passed or failed based on the number of study hours using the logistic regression algorithm

In this example, we use **`LogisticRegression`** from the **`scikit-learn (sklearn)`** library, which is a common algorithm for classification tasks where the output has fixed categories, such as **`Pass`** or **`Fail`**. First, we prepare the training dataset with **`X`** as the input values (number of study hours) and **`y`** as the output labels (0 for **`Fail`** and 1 for **`Pass`**). We then create an empty logistic regression model and train it using **`model.fit(X, y)`**, which enables the model to learn the relationship between study hours and the pass/fail outcome. Once trained, the model understands that studying for more hours generally increases the likelihood of passing. To make a prediction, we use **`model.predict([[6]])[0]`**, where **`[[6]]`** represents the input (6 study hours) and **`[0]`** extracts the single predicted value from the list-like output. The model returns **`1`** for Pass or **`0`** for Fail, which can be further mapped to user-friendly text for better readability, as shown in the following code:

```
from sklearn.linear_model import LogisticRegression
# Training data
X = [[1], [2], [3], [4], [5]]  # Study hours
y = [0, 0, 0, 1, 1]            # 0 = Fail, 1 = Pass
# Create and train the model
model = LogisticRegression()
model.fit(X, y)
# Predict for 6 study hours
pred_output = model.predict([[6]])[0]
# Map the numeric result to text
result = "Pass" if pred_output == 1 else "Fail"
print(f"Predicted result for 6 hours of study: {result}")
```

The Jupyter Notebook code window, along with its output, is shown in *Figure 11.1*:

```
In [2]: #Example 11.1
        from sklearn.linear_model import LogisticRegression
        # Training data
        X = [[1], [2], [3], [4], [5]]  # Study hours
        y = [0, 0, 0, 1, 1]            # 0 = Fail, 1 = Pass
        # Create and train the model
        model = LogisticRegression()
        model.fit(X, y)
        # Predict for 6 study hours
        pred_output = model.predict([[6]])[0]
        # Map the numeric result to text
        result = "Pass" if pred_output == 1 else "Fail"
        print(f"Predicted result for 6 hours of study: {result}")

        Predicted result for 6 hours of study: Pass
```

***Figure 11.1**: Output of classification using logistic regression algorithm*

Linear regression

Before jumping into the example, let us understand where linear regression fits in. In many real-world situations, we need to predict a numeric value based on some input features. For example, predicting the price of a house based on its area or estimating the marks a student might score based on study hours.

Linear regression is one of the simplest and most widely used algorithms for such tasks because it assumes a straight-line relationship between the input (independent variable) and the output (dependent variable).

Example 11.2: Write a Python program to implement linear regression using a sample dataset

Suppose we have a sample dataset (shown in *Table 11.2*) of students where **`Study_Hours`** is the input feature (labelled data, denoted as **`X`**) and **`Marks_Obtained`** is the output label (denoted as **`y`**).

Study_Hours	Marks_Obtained
2	50
3	60
4	65
5	70
6	80

***Table 11.2**: Sample dataset*

The objective of using linear regression is to find the relationship between study hours and marks obtained so that we can predict marks for any given number of study hours.

How linear regression works: The algorithm plots the data points on a graph and draws the *best-fit* straight line through them. The equation of this line is:

$$Y = mX + c$$

Here:

- m is the slope, representing how marks change with each additional study hour.
- c is the intercept, representing the marks obtained when study hours are zero.

The model learns this relationship from the dataset. Once the line is determined, we can use it to predict marks for a new (random) study hour value.

In this program:

- We first import the **`LinearRegression`** class from the scikit-learn library (**`from sklearn.linear_model import LinearRegression`**) and NumPy (**`import numpy as np`**), which is used for handling numerical data, which is already discussed in detail in *Chapter 7, NumPy Library*.
- The **`X`** variable stores the values of **`Study_Hours`**, and the **`y`** variable stores the values of **`Marks_Obtained`**.
- The **`reshape()`** function ensures that the data is in the correct format (2D array) for training.
- After preparing the **`X`** and **`y`** variables, we create a model object using **`LinearRegression()`** and train it with **`model.fit(X, y)`**.
- Finally, after training, we use **`model.predict()`** to predict marks for any new given value of study hours.

To demonstrate how machine learning can be used to predict outcomes based on historical data, we use a simple linear regression model. In this example, we analyze the relationship between the number of hours a student studies and the marks they achieve. Using Python's scikit-learn library, a linear regression model is trained on sample data representing study hours and corresponding scores. After training the model, we use it to predict the expected marks for a student who studies for 7 hours:

```
from sklearn.linear_model import LinearRegression
import numpy as np
# Study hours (input) and marks (output)
X = np.array([2, 3, 4, 5, 6]).reshape(-1, 1)
y = np.array([50, 60, 65, 70, 80])
# Create and train the model
model = LinearRegression()
model.fit(X, y)
# Predict marks for 7 study hours
predicted_marks = model.predict([[7]])
print("Predicted marks for 7 study hours:", predicted_marks[0])
```

The code and output window of predicting marks for any new given value of study hours is shown in *Figure 11.2*:

```
from sklearn.linear_model import LinearRegression
import numpy as np

# Study hours (input) and marks (output)
X = np.array([2, 3, 4, 5, 6]).reshape(-1, 1)
y = np.array([50, 60, 65, 70, 80])

# Create and train the model
model = LinearRegression()
model.fit(X, y)

# Predict marks for 7 study hours
predicted_marks = model.predict([[7]])
print("Predicted marks for 7 study hours:", predicted_marks[0])
```

```
Predicted marks for 7 study hours: 86.0
```

Figure 11.2: *Output of predicting marks for any new given value of study hours using linear regression*

After exploring linear regression for predicting continuous outcomes and logistic regression for classifying data into discrete categories, it is clear that both methods rely on finding a line (or curve) that best fits the data. However, not all classification problems can be solved effectively with logistic regression, especially when the data points are not easily separated by a simple boundary. This is where SVMs come in. SVMs take classification a step further by finding the optimal decision boundary, called a hyperplane, that maximizes the margin between different classes, making them powerful for complex datasets where the separation between categories is not straightforward.

Note: Linear regression works well only when certain basic conditions are met. The relationship between input and output should be roughly straight-line in nature, the data points should be independent of each other, and the spread of errors should remain fairly constant. In addition, the input variables should not be too strongly related to one another. If these conditions are not satisfied, the model's results may become less reliable or harder to interpret.

Support vector machine

SVM is a supervised learning algorithm used for classification and regression, but it is mainly famous for classification. The main idea is to find a decision boundary (line or plane) that separates the classes as clearly as possible. SVM tries to place this boundary so that it is as far as possible from the nearest data points of both classes; these points are called support vectors. Geometrically, a hyperplane can be understood as a boundary that separates data points belonging to different classes. In two dimensions, this boundary is simply a line, and in three dimensions, it becomes a plane. The goal of SVM is to find the boundary that not only separates the classes but does so with the maximum possible margin, meaning the greatest distance from the nearest data points on either side.

In SVM with a linear kernel, the decision boundary can be written as:

$$w \,.\, x + b = 0$$

Where:

- w is the weight (controls the slope of the line)
- x is the input value(s)
- b is the bias (controls the position of the line)

The prediction rule is:

$$If\ (w \cdot x + b) \geq 0 \Rightarrow Class\ 1\ (Pass)$$
$$If\ (w \cdot x + b) < 0 \Rightarrow Class\ 0\ (Fail)$$

SVM chooses w and b such that the separation between the two classes is as wide as possible, meaning it finds the maximum margin between the closest data points from each class.

Note: Kernel functions help SVMs work with data that cannot be separated by a straight line. They do this by viewing the data in a different way, where separation becomes possible, without actually changing the data itself. This allows SVMs to draw curved or more complex boundaries between classes.

Example 11.3: Write a program for classifying fruits using SVM algorithm

In this example, we use a dataset containing examples of apples and oranges, each described by two features, i.e., **`weight`** and **`size`**. The labels are assigned as 0 for **`Apple`** and 1 for **`Orange`**.

We create the model using **svm.SVC(kernel='linear')**, which instructs the SVM to use a straight-line decision boundary. The **model.fit(X, y)** step trains the model to find the optimal line (or plane) that separates apples from oranges with the maximum possible margin. Finally, we test the model on a fruit with a weight of 145g and a size of 6.9cm. If the prediction is 0, it is classified as an **Apple**; if it is 1, it is classified as an **Orange**.

To illustrate how machine learning can be applied to classification problems, the following code uses a SVM model to distinguish between apples and oranges based on their physical characteristics, such as weight and size. Using a small training dataset with labeled examples, the SVM learns patterns that separate the two types of fruits. Once trained, the model is used to predict the type of a new fruit based on its measurements:

```
from sklearn import svm
# Example dataset: [weight (gms), size (cm)]
X = [
    [150, 7],   # Apple
    [170, 7.5], # Apple
    [140, 6.8], # Apple
    [130, 6.5], # Orange
    [120, 6.2], # Orange
    [110, 6.0]  # Orange
]
# Labels: 0 = Apple, 1 = Orange
y = [0, 0, 0, 1, 1, 1]
# Create and train the SVM model
model = svm.SVC(kernel='linear')
model.fit(X, y)
# Predict for a new fruit
prediction = model.predict([[145, 6.9]])[0]
# Output in human-readable form
if prediction == 0:
    print("The fruit is likely an Apple.")
else:
    print("The fruit is likely an Orange.")
```

In scikit-learn, **support vector classification** (**SVC**) is the class used to implement the SVM algorithm specifically for classification tasks. It works by finding the best decision boundary (line, plane, or hyperplane) that separates different classes in the dataset with the maximum margin. In scikit-learn, **svm.SVC()** allows you to choose the kernel type (**linear**, **poly**, **rbf**, etc.) to handle both linear and non-linear classification problems.

The output of classifying a fruit using the SVM algorithm is shown in *Figure 11.3*:

```
In [1]: # Example 11.3
        from sklearn import svm
        # Example dataset: [weight (gms), size (cm)]
        X = [
            [150, 7],    # Apple
            [170, 7.5], # Apple
            [140, 6.8], # Apple
            [130, 6.5], # Orange
            [120, 6.2], # Orange
            [110, 6.0]  # Orange
        ]
        # Labels: 0 = Apple, 1 = Orange
        y = [0, 0, 0, 1, 1, 1]
        # Create and train the SVM model
        model = svm.SVC(kernel='linear')
        model.fit(X, y)
        # Predict for a new fruit
        prediction = model.predict([[145, 6.9]])[0]
        # Output in human-readable form
        if prediction == 0:
            print("The fruit is likely an Apple.")
        else:
            print("The fruit is likely an Orange.")

        The fruit is likely an Apple.
```

Figure 11.3: *Output of classifying a fruit using SVM algorithm*

Note: SVC means finding the clearest boundary between classes.

Example 11.4: Write a program for predicting students' result using SVM

In this example, we import a library, **SVC**. We have a dataset of students with features **Study_Hours(X)** and **Result(y)** that is whether they **Pass** or **Fail(y)**. The goal is to train an SVM model that predicts whether a student will pass or fail based on their study hours. In this example, we use SVM to decide if a student will pass or fail based on how many hours they studied. We tell the model that **kernel='linear'** means it will try to separate the data with a straight line. First, we give the model with some training data, which includes **Study_Hours** and **Result** using the **fit()** function. Then, we ask the model to predict the result for a student who studied for 5 hours. The model looks at the line it created (decision boundary) and says whether the student will pass or fail. The following example demonstrates how a SVM classifier can be used to predict student performance based on the number of study hours. Using a small dataset that labels students as either **Pass** or **Fail**, the model learns to identify the boundary that separates the two outcomes. After training the model with study-hour data, we use it to predict whether a new student who studies for 5 hours is likely to pass or fail:

```
from sklearn.svm import SVC
import numpy as np
# Step 1: Input feature (study hours)
X = np.array([[1], [2], [3], [4], [5], [6], [7], [8]])
```

```
# Step 2: Output labels (Pass or Fail)
y = ['Fail', 'Fail', 'Fail', 'Fail', 'Pass', 'Pass', 'Pass', 'Pass']
# Step 3: Create SVM model with linear kernel
model = SVC(kernel='linear')
# Step 4: Train the model
model.fit(X, y)
# Step 5: Predict result for a new student
prediction = model.predict([[5.0]])
print("Predicted result:", prediction[0])
```

The output of classification using SVM is shown in *Figure 11.4*:

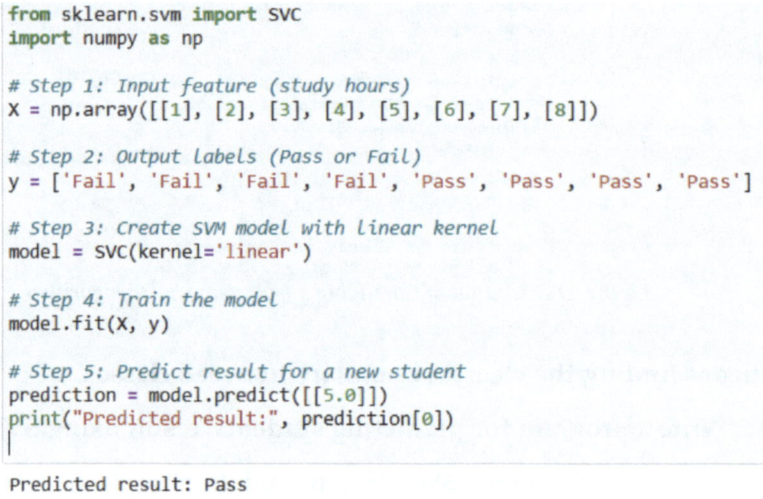

```
from sklearn.svm import SVC
import numpy as np

# Step 1: Input feature (study hours)
X = np.array([[1], [2], [3], [4], [5], [6], [7], [8]])

# Step 2: Output labels (Pass or Fail)
y = ['Fail', 'Fail', 'Fail', 'Fail', 'Pass', 'Pass', 'Pass', 'Pass']

# Step 3: Create SVM model with linear kernel
model = SVC(kernel='linear')

# Step 4: Train the model
model.fit(X, y)

# Step 5: Predict result for a new student
prediction = model.predict([[5.0]])
print("Predicted result:", prediction[0])

Predicted result: Pass
```

***Figure 11.4**: Output of classification using SVM*

Decision tree

A decision tree is an ML algorithm that makes decisions by splitting data into branches based on conditions, similar to a flowchart. Each internal node represents a question (e.g., *Is it sunny?*), each branch represents the answer (*Yes* or *No*), and each leaf node gives the final decision or prediction (e.g., *Play Outside* or *Stay Inside*). Decision trees are easy to understand because they mimic how humans make decisions step-by-step.

Decision tree criteria for selecting the best split

When building a tree, the algorithm looks for the best question to split the data so that each group is as *pure* as possible (meaning most of the items belong to the same class).

A Gini impurity of 0 represents perfect purity, meaning all data points in a set belong to a single class. Higher values up to 0.5 for binary classes or nearly 1.0 for many classes indicate a more diverse or impure mix of data. It is often compared to **entropy**, another common measure of purity/disorder.

Note: **One common measure of purity is Gini impurity.**

Gini impurity formula is mentioned as follows:

$$G = 1 - \sum_{i=1}^{n} (p_i)^2$$

In this formula, p_i is the proportion of class i in the group and n is the number of classes.

Here, we take an example for mathematical calculation. Suppose we have 10 days of weather data: 6 days were *Play Outside* and 4 days were *Stay Inside*:

$$p_{play\_outside} = \frac{6}{10} = 0.6, p_{stay\_inside} = \frac{4}{10} = 0.4$$

Now, Gini impurity is calculated:

$$G = 1 - (0.6^2 + 0.4^2) = 1 - (0.36 + 0.16) = 1 - 0.52 = 0.48$$

A Gini value of 0 means the group is perfectly pure (all same decision), and higher values mean more mixed decisions. The decision tree will try different questions like *Is it sunny?*, *Is there humidity?*, *Is it rainy?*, *Is it windy*, etc., and choose the one that reduces impurity the most; this improvement is called **information gain**.

Information gain is another measure used to decide how a decision tree splits the data. It evaluates how well a feature separates the data into purer groups after a split. A feature that results in clearer and more similar groups is considered more informative and is preferred for splitting. While Gini impurity measures how mixed the classes are, information gain focuses on how much improvement a split brings in terms of data separation.

Example 11.5: Write a program to classify data using the decision tree algorithm

In this example, for a decision *Should children play outside?*, we have a dataset as shown in *Table 11.3*. Here, the weather can be **`Sunny`**, **`Humid`**, or **`Rainy`**. The decision tree uses the Gini impurity method to split the data in a way that best separates the **`Yes`** and **`No`** decisions. First, it might split based on whether the weather is **`Rainy`** or not, then check the temperature for further decisions. When given **`[Sunny, 20°C]`**, the model follows the learned rules and predicts **`Play Outside!`**. The following dataset illustrates how different weather conditions and temperature levels influence the decision of whether children play outside or not. It contains several instances showing the relationship between weather type, temperature, and the corresponding outcome. This sample dataset will be used to demonstrate how decision tree algorithms analyze categorical and numerical features to make predictions:

Weather	Temperature (°C)	Play outside
Sunny	25	Yes
Sunny	22	Yes
Humid	20	Yes
Rainy	18	No
Rainy	15	No
Humid	23	Yes
Sunny	19	No
Rainy	21	No

Table 11.3: *Sample dataset*

Programmatically, we first import the **`tree`** library from scikit-learn. The dataset contains two features: **`Weather`** and **`Temperature`**. Weather is represented numerically as: **`Sunny = 0`**, **`Humid = 1`**, **`Rainy = 2`**. Here, **`X`** represents the independent variables (features or predictors), and **`y`** is the target variable (output), where **`Yes`** is represented by 1 and **`No`** by 0. Next, we create a decision tree model using **`DecisionTreeClassifier`** with the **`criterion='gini'`**, and train it using the **`fit()`** function. Finally, we use the **`predict()`** function with input **`[Sunny (0), 20]`**. If the predicted value is 1, the message **`Play Outside`** is printed; otherwise, **`Stay Inside`** is displayed.

```
from sklearn import tree
# Features: [Weather, Temperature]
# Weather: Sunny=0, Humid=1, Rainy=2
X = [
    [0, 25],
    [0, 22],
    [1, 20],
    [2, 18],
    [2, 15],
    [1, 23],
    [0, 19],
    [2, 21]
]
# Labels: Yes=1, No=0
y = [1, 1, 1, 0, 0, 1, 0, 0]
# Create Decision Tree model
clf = tree.DecisionTreeClassifier(criterion='gini')
clf = clf.fit(X, y)
# Test: Weather = Sunny (0), Temp = 20°C
```

```
prediction = clf.predict([[0, 20]])
if prediction[0] == 1:
    print("Decision: Play Outside!")
else:
    print("Decision: Stay Inside!")
```

The output of classifying data using the decision tree algorithm is shown in *Figure 11.5*:

```
#Example 11.5
from sklearn import tree
# Features: [Weather, Temperature]
# Weather: Sunny=0, Humid=1, Rainy=2
X = [
    [0, 25],
    [0, 22],
    [1, 20],
    [2, 18],
    [2, 15],
    [1, 23],
    [0, 19],
    [2, 21]
]
# Labels: Yes=1, No=0
y = [1, 1, 1, 0, 0, 1, 0, 0]
# Create Decision Tree model
clf = tree.DecisionTreeClassifier(criterion='gini')
clf = clf.fit(X, y)
# Test: Weather = Sunny (0), Temp = 20°C
prediction = clf.predict([[0, 20]])
if prediction[0] == 1:
    print("Decision: Play Outside!")
else:
    print("Decision: Stay Inside!")

Decision: Play Outside!
```

***Figure 11.5**: Classifying data using decision tree algorithm*

Note: Categorical variables are converted into numerical values because decision tree algorithms perform numerical comparisons; the assigned numbers are used only to represent categories and do not imply any inherent order or ranking. The categories are mapped to numbers only to allow the algorithm to process them, not to indicate any numerical importance.

K-nearest neighbors

K-nearest neighbors is a simple, non-parametric ML algorithm used for both classification and regression:

- In classification, it predicts the class of a new data point by looking at the K nearest points (neighbors) in the training data.
- The idea is that similar data points tend to be close to each other.

The following is how it works (classification case):

1. Choose the number K (e.g., K = 3).
2. Measure the distance between the new point and all points in the training set (often using Euclidean distance).
3. Pick the K nearest points.
4. The majority class among these K points is the prediction.

Mathematically, here we calculate Euclidean Distance. For two points *A(x1, y1)* and *B(x2, y2)*, the distance is:

$$Distance = \sqrt{(x_1 - x_2)^2 + (y_1 - y_2)^2}$$

This formula tells us how far two points are in a 2D space.

Example 11.6: Write a program for performing classification using KNN algorithm

In this example, we have a dataset (*Table 11.4*) of fruits described by their weight (in grams) and size (in cm). Label 0 represents an **`Apple`**, while label 1 represents an **`Orange`**. The statement **`KNeighborsClassifier(n_neighbors=3)`** tells the model to look at the three nearest neighbors when making a prediction. The **`fit(X, y)`** step stores the training data unlike decision trees, KNN does not train in the traditional sense; it simply remembers the examples. When we give the input (145g, 6.9cm), the model calculates the distance from this fruit to all fruits in the dataset, finds the three closest ones, and chooses the majority label. If most of these neighbours are **`Apples`**, the model predicts **`Apple`**; if most are **`Orange`**, it predicts **`Orange`**. Take a look at the following table:

Weight (g)	Size (cm)	Fruit
150	7.0	Apple (0)
170	7.5	Orange (1)
140	6.8	Apple (0)
180	7.8	Orange (1)

***Table 11.4**: Sample dataset*

To determine the class of a new fruit using the KNN algorithm, the Euclidean distance is computed between the new input sample and each sample in the dataset. This distance helps identify which existing data points are closest to the new observation and therefore most influential in determining its classification. The following steps illustrate the distance calculation process for the input values:

1. Mathematically, Euclidean distance is calculated as follows for the input values **`[145, 6.9]`**:

$$Distance = \sqrt{(x_1 - x_2)^2 + (y_1 - y_2)^2}$$

Where:

- $x1, y1$ are the features of the new point (145, 6.9)
- $x2, y2$ are the features of a point in the dataset

2. Now, we calculate the distances from a dataset for each row:
   - For (150, 7.0) Apple (0):

$$\sqrt{(145-150)^2+(6.9-7.0)^2}=5.0$$

   - For (170, 7.5) Orange (1):

$$\sqrt{(145-170)^2+(6.9-7.5)^2}=25.0$$

   - For (140, 6.8) Apple (0):

$$\sqrt{(145-140)^2+(6.9-6.8)^2}=5.0$$

   - For (180, 7.8) Orange (1):

$$\sqrt{(145-180)^2+(6.9-7.8)^2}=35.0$$

3. Then, we sort by distance as shown in *Table 11.5*:

Fruit	Distance
Apple (0)	5.0
Apple (0)	5.0
Orange (1)	25.0
Orange (1)	35.0

Table 11.5: Sort by distance

4. Then, we assume with $k = 3$ nearest neighbors: Apple, Apple, Orange, i.e., 2 Apples, and 1 Orange. The majority is of Apple (0); therefore, the predicted fruit is Apple.

```
from sklearn.neighbors import KNeighborsClassifier
# Features (weight(gms), size(cm))
X = [[150, 7.0], [170, 7.5], [140, 6.8], [180, 7.8]]
# Labels: 0 = Apple, 1 = Orange
y = [0, 1, 0, 1]
# Create KNN model with K=3
model = KNeighborsClassifier(n_neighbors=3)
model.fit(X, y)
# Predict fruit type for weight=145g, size=6.9cm
prediction = model.predict([[145, 6.9]])
```

```
if prediction[0] == 0:
    print("It's an Apple!")
else:
    print("It's an Orange!")
```

The output of performing a classification using the KNN algorithm is shown in *Figure 11.6*:

```
# Example 11.6
from sklearn.neighbors import KNeighborsClassifier
# Features (weight(gms), size(cm))
X = [[150, 7.0], [170, 7.5], [140, 6.8], [180, 7.8]]
# Labels: 0 = Apple, 1 = Orange
y = [0, 1, 0, 1]
# Create KNN model with K=3
model = KNeighborsClassifier(n_neighbors=3)
model.fit(X, y)
# Predict fruit type for weight=145g, size=6.9cm
prediction = model.predict([[145, 6.9]])
if prediction[0] == 0:
    print("It's an Apple!")
else:
    print("It's an Orange!")

It's an Apple!
```

***Figure 11.6**: Data classification using KNN algorithm*

Note: **The value of K determines how many nearest neighbors are considered when making a prediction. A small value of K makes the model sensitive to noise and individual data points, while a larger value of K produces smoother decisions but may overlook local patterns. Therefore, the choice of K depends on the dataset and is usually selected through experimentation or validation rather than being fixed. Choosing K is a balance: too small can be noisy, too large can be too general.**

We explored several ML algorithms like linear regression, logistic regression, SVM, decision trees, and KNN, each having its strengths and limitations. However, regardless of the algorithm chosen, one important challenge in ML is ensuring that the model generalizes well to unseen data.

Two common problems that can occur are overfitting and underfitting.

Note: **Overfitting versus underfitting:**

- **Overfitting: The model learns too much from the training data even noise and unnecessary details. Works great on training data but performs poorly on unseen (test) data.**
- **Underfitting: The model is too simple to learn the patterns in the data. It performs poorly on both training and test data.**

Naïve Bayes

Naïve Bayes is a simple yet powerful ML algorithm that is mainly used for classification problems. It is based on Bayes' theorem, which deals with conditional probability. The term *Naïve* is used because the algorithm assumes that all features (attributes) are independent of each other, even though in reality they may not be. Naïve Bayes works well, especially for text classification tasks such as spam email detection.

Mathematically, Bayes' theorem is written as:

$$P(A \mid B) = \frac{P(B \mid A) \cdot P(A)}{P(B)}$$

Here:

- **P(A|B)**: Probability of event *A* given that event *B* has occurred, also known as Posterior probability.
- **P(B|A)**: Probability of event B given that event *A* has occurred, known as likelihood.
- **P(A)**: Probability of event *A*, also known as prior probability.
- **P(B)**: Probability of event *B* known as evidence.

In the case of Naïve Bayes classification:

- *A* represents the class (e.g., Apple or Orange).
- *B* represents the features (e.g., Color of the fruit).

The algorithm calculates the probability of each class given the features and assigns the class with the highest probability. Let us understand this with a simple fruit example. Suppose we have two fruits: an Apple which is Red and an Orange which is Orange in color. If we now see a fruit that is Red, we want to predict whether it is an Apple or an Orange. Imagine we want to classify whether a fruit is an Apple or an Orange based on a simple feature: Color (Red/Orange). We have two pieces of training data as shown in *Table 11.6*:

Fruit	Color
Apple	Red
Orange	Orange

***Table 11.6**: Sample dataset for Naïve Bayes classification*

Now, suppose we observe a fruit that is Red and want to predict whether it is an Apple or an Orange. The following are the steps:

1. **Calculate prior probabilities**:
   - **Probability of Apple (P(Apple))**: There is 1 Apple out of 2 fruits, so:

     P(Apple)=1/2=0.5

- **Probability of Orange (P(Orange))**: There is 1 Orange out of 2 fruits, so:

$$P(Orange)=1/2=0.5$$

2. **Calculate likelihoods**:

- **Probability of seeing Red given Apple (P(Color=Red | Apple))**: It happened once, so:

$$P(Color=Red|Apple)=1/1=1$$

- **Probability of seeing Red given Orange (P(Color=Red | Orange))**: It never happened, so:

$$P(Color=Red|Orange)=0/1=0$$

3. **Apply Bayes' theorem**: Now we calculate the posterior probabilities for Apple and Orange given that the fruit is Red:

- $P(Apple|Red) \propto P(Apple) \times P(Red|Apple)=0.5 \times 1=0.5$
- $P(Orange|Red) \propto P(Orange) \times P(Red|Orange)=0.5 \times 0=0$

This step is explained in detail:

- **For Apple**:
  - **Prior**: $P(Apple)=0.5$ (half of the fruits are apples).
  - **Likelihood**: $P(Red \mid Apple)=1$(all apples are red).

  So, $P(Apple \mid Red) \propto 0.5 \times 1=0.5$

- **For Orange**:
  - **Prior**: $P(Orange)=0.5$ (half of the fruits are oranges).
  - **Likelihood**: $P(Red \mid Orange)= 0$ (oranges are not red).

  So, $P(Orange \mid Red) \propto 0.5 \times 0=0$

- **Now it is interpreted as**:
  - Apple gets a probability of 0.5.
  - Orange gets a probability of 0.

Since Apple has a higher probability, we predict Apple if the fruit is red.

4. **Classify**: Since $P(Apple|Red)$ is higher than $P(Orange|Red)$, we predict that the fruit is an Apple.

Example 11.7: Write a program for classifying a fruit using Naïve Bayes

This code demonstrates how Naive Bayes classification works using a simple fruit example. We start by defining the prior probabilities of **`Apple`** and **`Orange`**, which are both 0.5 since there is one **`Apple`** and one **`Orange`** in the dataset. Next, we calculate the *likelihoods* of the fruit being

`Red`, given it is an **`Apple`** or an **`Orange`**. Since the **`Apple`** is red, this likelihood is 1, while for the **`Orange`** it is 0 because it is not red. Using Bayes' theorem, we then calculate the posterior probabilities by multiplying the prior with the likelihood. For **`Apple`**, the result is $0.5 \times 1 = 0.5$, and for **`Orange`** it is $0.5 \times 0 = 0$. Finally, we compare these posterior probabilities: because **`Apple`** has a higher probability than **`Orange`**, the model predicts that a red fruit is most likely an **`Apple`**.

```
# Naive Bayes: Predict if fruit is Apple or Orange based on Color
#  Priors
Prob_Apple = 1/2   # 1 Apple out of 2 fruits
Prob_Orange = 1/2  # 1 Orange out of 2 fruits
print("P(Apple) =", Prob_Apple)
print("P(Orange) =", Prob_Orange)
# Likelihoods
Prob_Red_given_Apple = 1  # Apple is red
Prob_Red_given_Orange = 0 # Orange is not red
print("\nP(Red | Apple) =", Prob_Red_given_Apple)
print("P(Red | Orange) =", Prob_Red_given_Orange)
# Posterior (Prior * Likelihood)
Prob_Apple_given_Red = Prob_Apple * Prob_Red_given_Apple
Prob_Orange_given_Red = Prob_Orange * Prob_Red_given_Orange
print("\nP(Apple | Red) =", Prob_Apple_given_Red)
print("P(Orange | Red) =", Prob_Orange_given_Red)
# Classify
if Prob_Apple_given_Red > Prob_Orange_given_Red:
    print("\nPredicted Fruit: Apple")
else:
    print("\nPredicted Fruit: Orange")
```

The output of classifying a fruit as an apple or an orange using Naïve Bayes is shown in *Figure 11.7*:

```
P(Apple) = 0.5
P(Orange) = 0.5

P(Red | Apple) = 1
P(Red | Orange) = 0

P(Apple | Red) = 0.5
P(Orange | Red) = 0.0

Predicted Fruit: Apple
```

***Figure 11.7**: Classifying a fruit using Naïve Bayes*

Model evaluation metrics

AI models are evaluated using various performance metrics. In classification tasks, these metrics commonly include the confusion matrix along with measures such as accuracy, precision, recall, and the F1-score.

Confusion matrix

When we train a classification model, we need to evaluate how well it predicts the categories also called as classes. One of the simplest and most useful tools for this is the confusion matrix. It is a table that compares the actual values with the predicted values. It helps us see not just how many predictions are correct, but also what kinds of mistakes the model makes.

For a binary classification problem, there are two classes: **`Positive`** and **`Negative`**. The confusion matrix is shown in *Table 11.7*:

	Predicted Positive	Predicted Negative
Actual Positive	**True Positive (TP)** Model correctly predicted positive.	**False Negative (FN)** Model wrongly predicted negative (Type II Error)
Actual Negative	**False Positive (FP)** Model wrongly predicted positive (Type I Error)	**True Negative (TN)** Model correctly predicted negative.

Table 11.7: Confusion matrix

Note: **A confusion matrix is a tabular method used to evaluate the performance of a classification model. It compares the model's predicted outputs with the actual (true) outcomes, providing a clear summary of correct and incorrect predictions.**

In this context, actual values are the true results observed or measured in the dataset, and predicted values are the outcomes generated by the AI model based on its learning and algorithm. By organizing these values into a table, the confusion matrix helps in identifying not just overall accuracy but also the types of errors made by the model.

It is essential to understand a few key terms associated with the confusion matrix:

- **TP**: When the model correctly predicts a positive outcome, i.e., both the predicted value and the actual value are positive.
- **TN**: When the model correctly predicts a negative outcome, i.e., both the predicted value and the actual value are negative.
- **FP**: Also known as a *Type I Error*, this occurs when the model predicts a positive outcome, but in reality, the actual value is negative.

- **FN**: Also known as a *Type II Error*, this occurs when the model predicts a negative outcome, but the actual value is positive.

These terms form the foundation for calculating important evaluation measures such as accuracy, precision, recall, and F1-score.

Using the confusion matrix, we can derive several important measures to evaluate the performance of an AI model.

Accuracy rate

Accuracy indicates how often the model makes correct predictions out of all predictions made. It is calculated as the proportion of correctly classified cases (both TP and TN) to the total number of observations:

$$Accuracy = \frac{Number\ of\ correct\ predictions\ (TP + TN)}{Total\ number\ of\ predictions\ (TP + TN + FP + FN)}$$

While accuracy is a useful starting point, it is not always a reliable indicator of model performance, especially when the dataset is imbalanced (i.e., one class has far more samples than the other). In such cases, accuracy can be misleading, and additional evaluation metrics must be considered.

Precision rate

Precision measures how many of the instances predicted as positive are actually correct. In other words, it tells us the proportion of TP among all predicted positives (TP + FP), shown as follows:

$$Precision = \frac{TP}{(TP + FP)} * 100\%$$

A model with high precision ensures that when it predicts a positive case, it is usually correct. This makes precision particularly important in applications where false positives can be costly e.g., diagnosing a disease in healthy patients.

Recall

Recall, also known as sensitivity or true positive rate, measures how many of the actual positive cases are correctly identified by the model. It answers the question: *Out of all the instances that are truly positive, how many did the model correctly predict as positive?*

The formula to compute recall is:

$$Recall = \frac{TP}{(TP + FN)}$$

In datasets with class imbalance, precision and recall can behave very differently. For example, in a disease detection scenario where only 10 out of 100 patients are sick, a model that predicts only 5 patients as sick might get all 5 correct. This gives high precision (all predicted positives are correct) but low recall (it missed 5 actual sick patients). Conversely, if the model predicts 50 patients as sick to catch more true cases, it may correctly identify 8 sick patients but also label many healthy patients as sick. This gives high recall (most sick patients are detected) but low precision (many false positives). Understanding this trade-off is essential when evaluating models on imbalanced data. In such cases, the F1-score provides a balanced measure that considers both precision and recall.

F1-score

The F1-score, also called the F-measure, is a metric that provides a balance between precision and recall. It is particularly useful when both FP and FN carry equal importance, and a trade-off between precision and recall is needed. The F1-score is the harmonic mean of precision and recall, ensuring that the model performs well on both aspects rather than excelling at one while neglecting the other. It is computed as per the following formula:

$$F1 = \frac{2 * (Precision * Recall)}{Precision + Recall}$$

A high F1-score indicates that the model maintains a good balance between correctly identifying positive cases and avoiding incorrect positive predictions.

While accuracy, precision, recall, and F1-score all measure model performance, the choice of metric depends on the problem context. Precision is more important when false positives are costly, such as marking legitimate emails as spam. Recall is preferred when missing a positive case is more harmful, such as failing to detect a disease. The F1-score is useful when both precision and recall are important, and a balance between them is required, especially when dealing with imbalanced datasets.

Note: **Precision is prioritized when false alarms should be minimized, recall is prioritized when missing true cases is risky, and F1-score is preferred when a balanced performance between precision and recall is required.**

The following example demonstrates how classification models can be applied in real-world scenarios, such as identifying whether an email should be labeled as Spam or Not Spam.

Let us consider an illustrative example. Suppose we are building a model to classify whether emails are Spam or Not Spam.

We test the model on 20 emails and get the following results, as shown in *Table 11.8*:

	Predicted: Spam	Predicted: Not Spam
Actual: Spam	7 (TP)	3 (FN)
Actual: Not Spam	2 (FP)	8 (TN)

***Table 11.8**: Confusion matrix for email classification*

To evaluate the performance of a classification model, we compare its predictions with the actual outcomes. The results are summarized using four key metrics: TP, TN, FP, and FN. These values indicate how accurately the model identifies spam and non-spam emails, and they help assess the model's reliability and types of errors it makes. The interpretation of each metric is given as follows:

- **TP = 7**: 7 emails were actually spam and correctly predicted as spam.
- **TN = 8**: 8 emails were not spam and correctly predicted as not spam.
- **FP = 2**: 2 emails were not spam but wrongly predicted as spam.
- **FN = 3**: 3 emails were spam but wrongly predicted as not spam.

The other metrics are calculated as follows:

- **Accuracy**: $\frac{(TP + TN)}{(TP + TN + FP + FN)} = (7 + 8) / 20 = 0.75 \text{ or } 75\%$
- **Precision**: $\frac{TP}{(TP + FP)} = 7 / (7 + 2) = 0.78 \text{ or } 78\%$
- **Recall**: $\frac{TP}{(TP + FN)} = 7 / (7 + 3) = 0.70 \text{ or } 70\%$
- **F1-score**: $\frac{2 \times (Precision \times Recall)}{(Precision + Recall)} = 2 \times (0.78 \times 0.70) / (0.78 + 0.70) \approx 0.74$

Example 11.8: Write a program to classify if an email is spam or not

This Python code demonstrates how to evaluate a classification model for detecting whether emails are **Spam** or **Not Spam**. First, we define two lists: **y_actual** contains the true labels of 10 emails, while **y_predicted** contains the labels predicted by the model. Using the **confusion_matrix** function from **sklearn.metrics**, we calculate the confusion matrix, which summarizes the counts of TP, FN, FP, and TN. The code then computes several key performance metrics: **accuracy** measures the proportion of correct predictions overall, **precision** measures the proportion of correctly predicted **Spam** emails out of all emails predicted as **Spam**, **recall** measures the proportion of actual **Spam** emails that were correctly identified, and F1-score provides a balance between **precision** and **recall**. This example helps students understand how a simple confusion matrix translates into commonly used evaluation metrics for classification problems:

```
from sklearn.metrics import confusion_matrix, accuracy_score, precision_score,
recall_score, f1_score
# Actual labels
y_actual = ['Spam', 'Spam', 'Spam', 'Not Spam', 'Not Spam', 'Spam', 'Not
Spam', 'Not Spam', 'Spam', 'Not Spam']
# Predicted labels by the model
y_predicted = ['Spam', 'Not Spam', 'Not Spam', 'Not Spam', 'Not Spam', 'Spam',
'Spam', 'Not Spam', 'Spam', 'Not Spam']
# Confusion Matrix
```

```
conf_mat = confusion_matrix(y_actual, y_predicted, labels=['Spam', 'Not Spam'])
print("Confusion Matrix:")
print(conf_mat)
# Accuracy
accuracy = accuracy_score(y_actual, y_predicted)
print("\nAccuracy:", accuracy)
# Precision
precision = precision_score(y_actual, y_predicted, pos_label='Spam')
print("Precision:", precision)
# Recall
recall = recall_score(y_actual, y_predicted, pos_label='Spam')
print("Recall:", recall)
# F1-Score
f1 = f1_score(y_actual, y_predicted, pos_label='Spam')
print("F1-Score:", f1)
```

The output of classifying an email as spam or not in the form of a confusion matrix and other metrics is shown in *Figure 11.8*:

```
Confusion Matrix:
[[3 2]
 [1 4]]

Accuracy: 0.7
Precision: 0.75
Recall: 0.6
F1-Score: 0.6666666666666665
```

***Figure 11.8**: Confusion matrix and other evaluation metrics*

To better understand how classification models are applied in real-world decision-making; consider the case of medical diagnosis. Machine learning techniques are often used to predict the presence or absence of a disease based on patient data, allowing healthcare professionals to make informed decisions. The following example illustrates how a predictive model can classify medical test results into two categories.

Let us consider an illustrative example. Suppose a medical test is used to predict whether a patient has *Diabetes* or *Not Diabetes*. There are two instances where:

- **Positive**: Patient has Diabetes
- **Negative**: Patient does not have Diabetes

Now, in the form of a confusion matrix, it is shown in *Table 11.9*:

	Predicted Positive (Diabetes)	**Predicted Negative (Not Diabetes)**
Actual Positive (Diabetes)	**08** **TP**: Patient actually has diabetes and the test correctly detects it.	**02** **FN**: Patient actually has diabetes, but the test fails to detect it.
Actual Negative (Not Diabetes)	**02** **FP**: Patient does not have diabetes, but the test wrongly predicts diabetes.	**08** **TN**: Patient does not have diabetes and the test correctly predicts it.

Table 11.9: Confusion matrix for diabetic disease classification

Let us understand these better in the form of steps:

1. From a confusion matrix, it can be interpreted as:
   - **TP**: Diabetic patient is correctly identified, and it is good for treatment. Here, eight patients with diabetes were correctly predicted as diabetic patients.
   - **TN**: Healthy patient correctly identified, and therefore avoids unnecessary treatment. TN value of 8 shows that healthy patients were correctly predicted.
   - **FP**: Healthy patient wrongly told they have diabetes, which causes stress, unnecessary tests, or treatment. It is derived from the confusion matrix that 2 healthy patients were predicted as diabetic.
   - **FN**: Diabetic patient wrongly told they are healthy, which is very risky, as diabetes remains untreated. Here, two patients with diabetes were predicted as not diabetic.

   Note: Now, in this case, it is noted that doctors usually want to reduce FNs because missing diabetes can delay treatment and worsen health. That is why recall (sensitivity) is often more important than precision in medical diagnosis.

2. Now, we will calculate metrics as follows:
   - **Accuracy**: $\frac{(TP + TN)}{(TP + TN + FP + FN)} = (8 + 8) / 20 = 0.80 \text{ or } 80\%$
   - **Precision**: $\frac{TP}{(TP + FP)} = 8 / (8 + 2) = 0.80 \text{ or } 80\%$
   - **Recall**: $\frac{TP}{(TP + FN)} = 8 / (8 + 2) = 0.80 \text{ or } 80\%$
   - **F1-score**: $\frac{2 \times (Precision \times Recall)}{(Precision + Recall)} = 2 \times (0.80 \times 0.80) / (0.80 + 0.80) \approx 0.80 = 80\%$

Example 11.9: Write a program for diabetic disease classification and obtain a confusion matrix

This code demonstrates how to evaluate a diabetes detection test using a confusion matrix and standard performance metrics. First, we create the actual labels: **`y_actual`** representing whether

20 patients truly have diabetes or not, and the predicted labels: **y_predicted** representing the test results. These are designed to match the case where TPs = 8, FNs = 2, FPs = 2, and TNs = 8. Using the **confusion_matrix** function from **sklearn.metrics**, the code generates a 2×2 table that summarizes correct and incorrect predictions. Then, it calculates accuracy, which is overall correctness, precision that shows how many predicted diabetic cases were actually correct, recall, which means how many actual diabetic cases were correctly identified, and the F1-score is a balance between precision and recall. The results show that the test has 80% accuracy, precision, recall, and F1-score:

```
from sklearn.metrics import confusion_matrix, accuracy_score, precision_score,
recall_score, f1_score
# Actual labels (ground truth)
y_actual = ['Diabetes']*10 + ['Not Diabetes']*10   # 10 with diabetes, 10 without
# Predicted labels by the test (based on TP=8, FN=2, FP=2, TN=8)
y_predicted = ['Diabetes']*8 + ['Not Diabetes']*2 + ['Diabetes']*2 + ['Not
Diabetes']*8
# Confusion Matrix
conf_matrix = confusion_matrix(y_actual, y_predicted, labels=['Diabetes', 'Not
Diabetes'])
print("Confusion Matrix:")
print(conf_matrix)
# Performance Metrics
print("\nPerformance Metrics are:")
print("Accuracy :", accuracy_score(y_actual, y_predicted))
print("Precision:", precision_score(y_actual, y_predicted, pos_
label='Diabetes'))
print("Recall   :", recall_score(y_actual, y_predicted, pos_label='Diabetes'))
print("F1-Score :", f1_score(y_actual, y_predicted, pos_label='Diabetes'))
```

The output of the confusion matrix and other performance metrics for classifying a diabetic patient is shown in *Figure 11.9*:

```
Confusion Matrix:
[[8 2]
 [2 8]]

Performance Metrics are:
Accuracy : 0.8
Precision: 0.8
Recall   : 0.8
F1-Score : 0.8000000000000002
```

***Figure 11.9**: Confusion matrix and performance metrics for classifying a diabetic patient*

Conclusion

In this chapter, we explored the foundational concepts and algorithms of machine learning, focusing on both their working principles and practical applications. Rather than viewing each algorithm in isolation, it is useful to compare their strengths and suitable scenarios: linear regression provides a simple and interpretable approach for predicting continuous values, logistic regression extends this idea to probability-based classification, SVM excels at finding optimal boundaries in complex or high-dimensional datasets, decision trees offer intuitive, rule-based predictions, KNN relies on similarity to known examples for decision-making, and Naive Bayes combines prior knowledge with observed evidence for efficient probabilistic classification. Evaluating models using metrics such as accuracy, precision, recall, and F1-score further reinforces understanding of their performance, especially in situations with imbalanced data. By synthesizing these insights, learners are now better prepared to explore unsupervised learning techniques in upcoming chapters, where the focus shifts to discovering patterns and structure in unlabeled data.

Points to remember

The following points are to be kept in mind:

- **Machine learning (ML)**: ML is the ability of computers to learn patterns from data without being explicitly programmed.
- **Main types of ML are**:
  - o **Supervised learning**: Uses labeled data (input + output).
  - o **Unsupervised learning**: Works with unlabeled data to find patterns.
  - o **Reinforcement learning**: Learns by trial and error, receiving rewards/penalties.
- **Applications of ML**: It includes spam detection, stock price prediction, medical diagnosis, recommendation systems, self-driving cars, and speech recognition.
- **Linear regression**: Linear regression predicts continuous values (e.g., predicting salary from years of experience). It uses the equation (where *m* is slope, *c* is intercept). It finds the best-fitting straight line by minimizing errors.
- **Logistic regression**: Logistic regression is used for classification (Yes/No, 0/1) and outputs probabilities using the sigmoid function. There is a decision boundary with probability ≥ 0.5 is considered as class 1, else class 0.
- **Support vector machine (SVM)**: SVM is a powerful classifier that finds the best hyperplane separating classes. Margin means the distance between the hyperplane and the nearest points (support vectors). It works well for both linear and non-linear data (via kernels).
- **Decision tree**: Decision tree predicts outcomes by splitting data into branches based on feature values. The splits chosen using Gini impurity or information gain.

- **K-nearest neighbors (KNN)**: KNN classifies a data point based on the majority label among its k closest points. A distance usually measured with Euclidean distance formula. There is no actual training phase, it stores data and computes during prediction.
- **Key ML terms are**:
  - **Feature**: An input variable (e.g., weight, size).
  - **Label/Target**: The output variable to be predicted.
  - **Training data**: Data used to teach the model.
  - **Test data**: Data used to evaluate the model.
- **Features of a dataset are also called**:
  - Independent variables
  - Attributes
  - Predictors
- **Output feature is also called**:
  - Dependent variable
  - Target variable
  - Output class/label
- **Overfitting**: Model performs well on training data but poorly on new data.
- **Underfitting**: Model is too simple to capture data patterns.
- General ML workflow includes the following:
  - Collect and prepare the dataset.
  - Choose the right ML algorithm.
  - Train the model with training data.
  - Evaluate performance on test data.
  - Use the model for predictions.
- **Confusion matrix**: It is a table that summarizes classification results into four categories: TP, TN, FP, and FN.
- **Accuracy**: Accuracy measures the overall correctness of a model.
- **Precision**: Precision shows how many of the predicted positive values were actually correct.
- **Recall**: Recall is also called sensitivity or true positive rate. It shows how many of the actual positive values were correctly identified.
- **F1-score**: F1-score is also called F-measure gives a balance between precision and recall by taking their harmonic mean.

Key terms

- **Machine learning (ML)**: It is a branch of AI that enables systems to learn patterns from data and make predictions without being explicitly programmed.
- **Supervised learning**: It is a type of ML where the model is trained on labeled data (input-output pairs).
- **Unsupervised learning**: It is a type of ML where the model finds patterns or groups in unlabeled data.
- **Features**: Features are the independent variables or attributes used as input to the model.
- **Labels/target variable**: These are the output or dependent variable the model predicts.
- **Linear regression**: Linear regression is a supervised learning algorithm used for predicting continuous values.
- **Logistic regression**: It is a supervised learning algorithm used for binary classification problems.
- **Support vector machine (SVM)**: SVM is an algorithm that finds the best boundary (hyperplane) to separate different classes.
- **Kernel**: Kernel is a function used in SVM to transform data into a higher-dimensional space for better separation.
- **Decision tree**: It is a model that makes decisions by splitting data based on conditions, forming a tree-like structure.
- **Gini impurity**: It is a measure of how often a randomly chosen element would be incorrectly classified in a dataset split.
- **Information gain**: It is a measure of improvement in purity after a split in a decision tree.
- **K-nearest neighbors (KNN)**: KNN is a simple algorithm that classifies a data point based on the majority class among its closest neighbors.
- **Distance metric**: It is a mathematical formula (e.g., Euclidean distance) to measure closeness between points in KNN.
- **Training data**: It is the sample dataset used to teach the model.
- **Testing data**: It is the dataset used to evaluate the model's performance.
- **Overfitting**: Overfitting means that a model learns the training data too well, including noise, and fails to generalize to new data.
- **Underfitting**: Underfitting means that a model is too simple to capture the patterns in the data.

- **Confusion matrix**: A table used to evaluate the performance of a classification model by comparing actual and predicted outcomes.
- **True Positive (TP)**: Cases where the model correctly predicts the positive class.
- **True Negative (TN)**: Cases where the model correctly predicts the negative class.
- **False Positive (FP)**: Cases where the model incorrectly predicts positive (also called *Type I Error*).
- **False Negative (FN)**: Cases where the model incorrectly predicts negative (also called *Type II Error*).
- **Accuracy**: The ratio of correctly predicted cases (both positive and negative) to the total number of cases.
- **Precision**: The ratio of correctly predicted positives (TP) to all predicted positives (TP + FP).
- **Recall (sensitivity/true positive rate)**: The ratio of correctly predicted positives (TP) to all actual positives (TP + FN).
- **Specificity (true negative rate)**: The ratio of correctly predicted negatives (TN) to all actual negatives (TN + FP).
- **F1-score (F-measure)**: The harmonic mean of precision and recall, giving a balance between the two.
- **Type I error**: Mistakenly predicting a positive when it is actually negative (FP).
- **Type II error**: Mistakenly predicting a negative when it is actually positive (FN).
- **Class imbalance**: A situation where one class (positive or negative) has far more samples than the other, making accuracy less reliable.

Multiple choice questions

1. **Which of the following is an example of supervised learning?**
    a. Grouping news articles by topic without labels
    b. Predicting student marks using past data
    c. Finding patterns in shopping carts without predefined categories
    d. Detecting anomalies in bank transactions without historical data
2. **In linear regression, the output variable is:**
    a. Categorical
    b. Continuous
    c. Boolean
    d. None of the above

3. **Which algorithm is best suited for predicting whether an email is spam or not?**
    a. Linear regression
    b. Logistic regression
    c. K-means clustering
    d. Principal component analysis

4. **In SVM, the term maximum margin refers to**:
    a. The largest distance between the decision boundary and the closest data points
    b. The largest number of features in the dataset
    c. The number of support vectors used
    d. The width of the dataset in pixels

5. **Decision trees choose splits based on measures like**:
    a. Gradient descent
    b. Gini impurity or information gain
    c. Euclidean distance
    d. Kernel functions

6. **K in KNN refers to**:
    a. Number of features in the dataset
    b. Number of neighbors considered for classification
    c. Number of decision boundaries
    d. Kernel size used in training

7. **Which of the following is not a supervised learning algorithm?**
    a. SVM
    b. Decision tree
    c. KNN
    d. K-means clustering

8. **Overfitting in ML means**:
    a. The model performs well on training data but poorly on new data
    b. The model is too simple to capture the patterns in data
    c. The dataset has too many missing values
    d. The algorithm has too many iterations

9. **In logistic regression, which function is commonly used to map predictions to probabilities?**
    a. Sigmoid function
    b. Linear function
    c. Step function
    d. None of these

10. **Which of the following statements about KNN is true?**
    a. It requires a training phase with gradient descent
    b. It stores all training data and makes predictions based on proximity
    c. It builds a decision boundary during training
    d. It can only be used for regression problems

Answers

1.	b
2.	b
3.	b
4.	a
5.	b
6.	b
7.	d
8.	a
9.	a
10.	b

Questions

1. What are the three main types of machine learning?
2. Which algorithm is best suited for predicting continuous values?
3. In logistic regression, what function is used to map values to probabilities?
4. What is the main idea behind SVM?
5. How does a decision tree decide where to split the data?
6. In KNN, what does the parameter n_neighbors represent?
7. Differentiate between overfitting and underfitting in machine learning.
8. Write the applications of machine learning in different sectors.

Chapter 12
Introduction to Unsupervised and Reinforcement Learning

Introduction

In the previous chapter, we explored supervised learning, where the model learns from labeled data. However, not all real-world problems come with ready-made labels. For instance, businesses often have large amounts of customer data without predefined categories, making it difficult to extract meaningful insights. Sometimes, the data is unlabeled, and we want the model to discover hidden patterns; this is where unsupervised learning comes into play. In other situations, an intelligent agent learns by interacting with its environment, making decisions, and receiving feedback in the form of rewards or penalties, such as in robotics or game playing. This is the essence of reinforcement learning. Together, these approaches extend the capabilities of **machine learning** (**ML**) to solve problems ranging from customer segmentation to strategic decision-making in dynamic environments.

Structure

The following topics are covered in this chapter:

- Unsupervised learning
- Reinforcement learning
- Machine learning versus deep learning

Objectives

By the end of this chapter, students will have a clear understanding of the concepts of unsupervised learning and reinforcement learning. They will be able to differentiate these approaches from supervised learning and identify where each method is most applicable in real life. Students will learn how clustering algorithms, such as K-means, can group unlabelled data into meaningful categories, and how reinforcement learning enables an agent to make decisions based on rewards and penalties. They will gain hands-on experience by implementing simple Python programs for clustering, and will understand the key elements, such as agents, actions, environments, and rewards, that form the foundation of reinforcement learning. This will equip them with both theoretical knowledge and practical skills to apply these techniques in various problem-solving scenarios.

Unsupervised learning

Unsupervised learning is a type of machine learning where the model works with unlabelled data. This means the data does not have a predefined output or category. Instead, the algorithm tries to find hidden patterns, similarities, or groupings within the data. Unlike supervised learning, there is no correct answer, as such, provided during training, the machine must organize the data on its own.

The key features of unsupervised learning work entirely with unlabelled data, meaning there are no predefined target values for the algorithm to learn from. Its main purpose is to automatically discover patterns, relationships, and groupings within the data without prior guidance. This approach is often used for exploration and understanding of datasets, and in many cases, it serves as a preprocessing step before applying more complex algorithms. Since there is no correct answer, the focus is on identifying structure rather than making direct predictions.

In real-life scenarios, unsupervised learning has a wide range of real-world applications. In marketing, it is commonly used for customer segmentation, where customers are grouped based on their purchasing behavior. E-commerce platforms use it to group similar products together, making recommendations more effective. In image processing, it is applied for image compression, which reduces file size while retaining essential details. Another example is where news platforms can also use it to automatically organize articles by topic, even when categories are not provided in advance.

Clustering

Clustering is one of the most common techniques in unsupervised learning, where the goal is to group similar data points together based on their features. The algorithm tries to place items in the same group, called a cluster, if they are more alike to each other than to items in other groups. The key idea is that data within a cluster should be as similar as possible, while data from different clusters should be as different as possible. A popular clustering method is K-means clustering. In this method, you first choose the number of clusters, denoted as K. The algorithm then assigns each data point to the nearest cluster center, typically measured using a distance metric such as Euclidean or Manhattan distance, and repeatedly adjusts these centers to minimize the difference between points in the same cluster. Before clustering, feature scaling is often applied to ensure that all features contribute equally to the distance calculations. Over time, the groups become more distinct. For example, a teacher could use clustering to group students based on their exam scores in different subjects. One cluster might contain students who perform well in both math and science, while another might have students who are stronger in arts and languages. This helps in identifying patterns in performance and planning personalized teaching strategies.

K-means clustering

The steps for performing K-means clustering on a sample dataset are shown in *Table 12.1*:

Person	Height(cm)	Weight (kgs)
A	160	55
B	165	60
C	170	65
D	180	80

***Table 12.1**: Sample dataset for K-means clustering*

In this example, we have three features: *Person*, *Height*, and *Weight*. We aim to group these into two clusters based on height and weight.

The steps are as follows:

1. **Choose the number of clusters (K = 2)**: The objective is to group people into two categories: *shorter and lighter* versus *taller and heavier*.
2. **Initialize the centroids**: We randomly select two points from the dataset as the starting centroids:
   - *Centroid 1 (C1) = Person A with values (160, 55)*
   - *Centroid 2 (C2) = Person D with values (180, 80)*
3. **Assign each point to the nearest centroid**: To determine the nearest centroid, we use the Euclidean distance formula:

$$Distance = \sqrt{(x_2 - x_1)^2 + (y_2 - y_1)^2}$$

   - **For Person A (160, 55):**

$$Distance\ to\ centroid\ C1 = \sqrt{((160 - 160)^2 + (55 - 55)^2)} = 0$$

$$Distance\ to\ centroid\ C2 = \sqrt{((160 - 180)^2 + (55 - 80)^2)} = 32.0$$

     Here, distance is closest to C1.

   - **For Person B (165, 60):**

$$Distance\ to\ C1 = \sqrt{((165 - 160)^2 + (60 - 55)^2)} = 7.0$$

$$Distance\ to\ C2 = \sqrt{((165 - 180)^2 + (60 - 80)^2)} = 25$$

Here, distance is closest to C1.

- **For Person C (170, 65):**

$$\text{Distance to C1} = \sqrt{((170-160)^2 + (65-55)^2)} = 14.14$$

$$\text{Distance to C2} = \sqrt{((170-180)^2 + (65-80)^2)} = 18.03$$

Here, distance is closest to C1.

- **For Person D (180, 80):**

$$\text{Distance to C1} = \sqrt{((180-160)^2 + (80-55)^2)} = 32.0$$

$$\text{Distance to C2} = \sqrt{((180-180)^2 + (80-80)^2)} = 0$$

Here, distance is closest to C2.

- **Cluster assignment after Step 3:**
  - o **Cluster 1:** A, B, C
  - o **Cluster 2:** D

4. **Update the centroids:**
   - **Cluster 1 average:**

$$\text{Height} = (160 + 165 + 170) / 3 = 165$$

$$\text{Weight} = (55 + 60 + 65) / 3 = 60$$

Updated centroid C1 values are (165, 60).

   - **Cluster 2 average:**

$$\text{Height} = (180) / 1 = 180$$

$$\text{Weight} = (80) / 1 = 80$$

Updated centroid C2 values are (180, 80).

5. **Repeat steps 3 and 4:** We check distances again, but in this case, the assignments will not change, so the algorithm stops.

   The final clusters are:

   - **Cluster 1 is of shorter and lighter persons:** A (160, 55), B (165, 60), C (170, 65)
   - **Cluster 2 is of taller and heavier persons:** D (180, 80)

Example 12.1: Write a program for performing K-means clustering on persons grouped by height and weight

This code demonstrates K-means clustering using a small dataset of four people, where each person is represented by their height and weight. First, the dataset is created as a NumPy array, with each row containing the values for height and weight. Then, a K-means model is created with two clusters (**n_clusters=2**), meaning we want to divide the people into two groups based on their height and weight. The model is trained using the **fit()** function, which assigns each person to the nearest cluster. After fitting, the cluster labels (which indicate the group each person belongs to) and the cluster centers (average points of each group) are obtained. Finally, the data points are plotted on a scatter plot using Matplotlib, where different colors represent the two clusters. The centroids are also highlighted on the plot, showing how the algorithm has grouped the people into two categories.

The following Python code demonstrates how the K-means clustering algorithm can be used to group individuals based on their height and weight. Using a small dataset of four persons, the program applies K-means with two clusters to identify natural groupings in the data. After training the model, it retrieves cluster labels and centroid positions and visualizes the results on a scatter plot. Each person is represented as a point, colored according to its assigned cluster, while the centroids are highlighted to show the center point of each group.

```
import matplotlib.pyplot as plt
from sklearn.cluster import KMeans
import numpy as np
# Step 1: Create data [Height(cm), Weight(kg)]
persons = np.array([
    [160, 55],  # Person A
    [165, 60],  # Person B
    [170, 65],  # Person C
    [180, 80],  # Person D
])
# Step 2: Create KMeans model with 2 clusters
kmeans = KMeans(n_clusters=2, random_state=0)
# Step 3: Fit the model
kmeans.fit(persons)
# Step 4: Get cluster labels
labels = kmeans.labels_
# Step 5: Get centroids
centers = kmeans.cluster_centers_
# Step 6: Plot results
plt.scatter(persons[:, 0], persons[:, 1], c=labels, cmap='rainbow', s=100)
plt.scatter(persons[:, 0], persons[:, 1], c='red', marker='X', s=200,
label='Centroids')  # centroids
plt.title("Persons grouped by Height & Weight")
plt.xlabel("Height (cm)")
plt.ylabel("Weight (kg)")
plt.show()
```

The output of performing K-means clustering on persons grouped by height and weight is shown in *Figure 12.1*. K-means works by placing centroids (red crosses) as the average point of each group, and then assigning each person (purple dots) to the nearest centroid. In the output graph, every dot represents a person with their height and weight, while the red crosses represent the centers of the groups. This helps us see which people are similar in terms of height and weight. For example, one cluster may represent short and light people, another cluster medium height and weight people, and another cluster tall and heavy people.

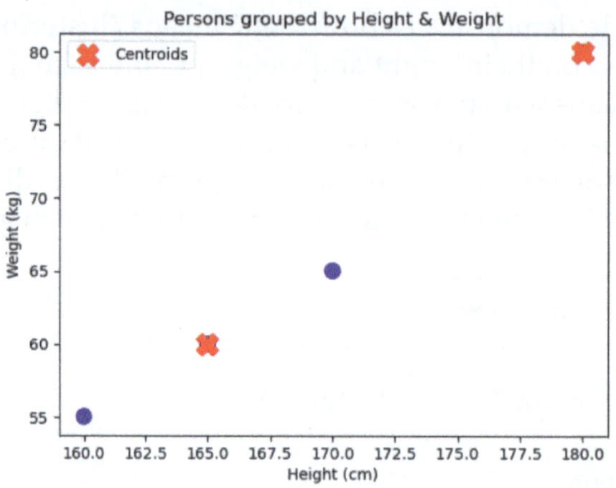

***Figure 12.1**: Output of performing K-means clustering*

Example 12.2: Write a program for clustering student groups based on their marks

This code demonstrates how K-means clustering can be applied to group students based on their Math and Science scores. First, a small dataset of six students' scores is created, where some students have high scores above 80, and others have low scores around 40–55. The K-means algorithm is then applied with **`n_clusters=2`**, meaning we want to divide the students into two groups, i.e., high performers and low performers. After fitting the data, the algorithm assigns each student a cluster label (0 or 1) and calculates the centroid (center point) of each group. In the plot, students' scores are shown as colored points where the color represents their cluster, and the centroids are shown as large black **`X`** marks. The result clearly separates students into two performance groups, helping us understand how clustering can be used to categorize data based on similarity:

```
# Step 1: Import libraries
import matplotlib.pyplot as plt
from sklearn.cluster import KMeans
import numpy as np
# Step 2: Create a small dataset of (Math, Science) scores
scores = np.array([
    [83, 91], [84, 85], [93, 84],    # High performers
    [55, 45], [53, 45], [42, 51]     # Low performers
```

```
])
# Step 3: Apply K-Means clustering for 2 groups
kmeans = KMeans(n_clusters=2, random_state=0)
kmeans.fit(scores)
# Step 4: Get the cluster labels
labels = kmeans.labels_
# Step 5: Get cluster centers
centers = kmeans.cluster_centers_
# Step 6: Plot the scores
plt.scatter(scores[:, 0], scores[:, 1], c=labels, cmap='coolwarm', s=100)
plt.scatter(centers[:, 0], centers[:, 1], c='black', marker='X', s=200,
label='Centroids')
plt.xlabel("Math Score")
plt.ylabel("Science Score")
plt.title("Clustering Student Scores")
plt.legend()
plt.show()
```

This plot shows the result of K-means clustering applied to student scores in Math and Science. Each point represents a student, where the x-axis is the Math score, and the y-axis is the Science score. The students have been divided into two groups: The red points represent students with high performance in both Math and Science (scores clustered around 80–90). The blue points represent students with lower performance in both subjects (scores clustered around 40–55). The large black **X** markers represent the centroids, or the average point of each cluster, which act as the center of the groups. One centroid lies near the high-performing group, and the other near the low-performing group.

The output of clustering students based on the students' marks is shown in *Figure 12.2*:

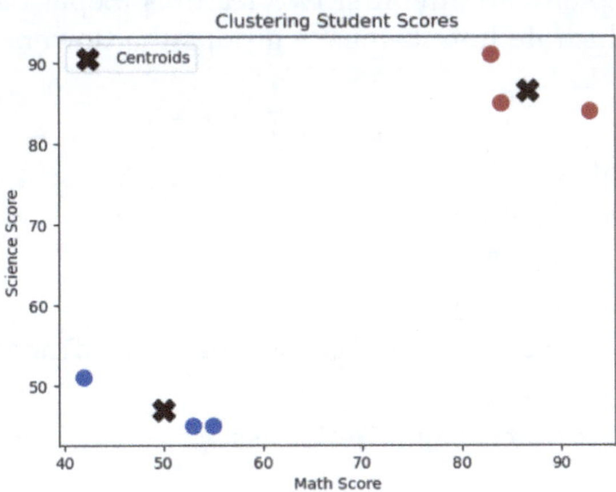

***Figure 12.2**: Output of clustering group of students based on subject marks*

Example 12.3: Write a program for performing K-means clustering on a dataset

In this example, we have taken a dataset **`Iris.csv`** which is one of the famous datasets in machine learning and can be freely obtained from the **University of California, Irvine (UCI)** machine learning repository. The repository is maintained by the information and computer sciences department at the UCI, and is one of the most widely used sources for publicly available datasets for machine learning research and education. It contains measurements of 150 flowers from three different species: Setosa, Versicolor, and Virginica. Each flower in the dataset includes four measurements (features), also known as independent variables, attributes, or predictors:

- **Sepal Length** (cm)
- **Sepal Width** (cm)
- **Petal Length** (cm)
- **Petal Width** (cm)

In addition, there is one label, Species, which indicates the type of Iris flower. The Species represents the dependent variable, also referred to as the target variable, output class, or label.

The sample dataset is shown in *Table 12.2*:

SepalLength	SepalWidth	PetalLength	PetalWidth	Species
5.1	3.5	1.4	0.2	setosa
7.0	3.2	4.7	1.4	versicolor
6.3	3.3	6.0	2.5	virginica

***Table 12.2**: Example rows from Iris.csv dataset*

The following code demonstrates how to apply the K-means clustering algorithm to the Iris dataset using Python. After loading the dataset from a CSV file, the program selects the four numeric feature columns and performs clustering by assuming three groups, corresponding to the three Iris species. The predicted cluster labels are then added to the dataset, and the results are visualized in a scatter plot using the first two features (Sepal Length and Sepal Width). This visualization helps illustrate how K-means groups the flowers based on similarities in their measurements:

```
import pandas as pd
import matplotlib.pyplot as plt
from sklearn.cluster import KMeans
# Step 1: Load dataset from CSV
df = pd.read_csv("F:\\iris.csv")
# Step 2: Select only the features (not the species column)
X = df.drop("species", axis=1)
# Step 3: Apply K-Means clustering (let's assume 3 clusters since Iris has 3 
species)
kmeans = KMeans(n_clusters=3, random_state=42)
```

```
df['cluster'] = kmeans.fit_predict(X)
# Step 4: Plot clusters (use first two features just for visualization)
plt.scatter(X.iloc[:, 0], X.iloc[:, 1], c=df['cluster'], cmap='viridis')
plt.xlabel("Sepal Length")
plt.ylabel("Sepal Width")
plt.title("Iris Dataset clustered using K-Means")
plt.show()
```

In this program, we use the **`pandas`** library to read and handle the dataset (like working with tables in Excel), **`matplotlib.pyplot`** to draw graphs, and **`KMeans`** as a machine learning algorithm for clustering. The dataset **`iris.csv`** is first loaded into a DataFrame (**`df`**), which is just like a table of rows and columns. Since clustering is done only on numbers, we remove the **`species`** column (the label that contains Setosa, Versicolor, Virginica), and keep only the numerical features: Sepal Length, Sepal Width, Petal Length, and Petal Width. K-means is then applied to group the flowers into 3 clusters because there are three species. For easier visualization, we only plot the first two features (Sepal Length and Sepal Width) on a scatter plot, where each flower is shown as a point. The points are colored based on the cluster assigned by K-means. The statement **`plt.scatter(X.iloc[:, 0], X.iloc[:, 1], c=df['cluster'], cmap='viridis')`** makes a scatter plot, i.e., dots on a graph. **`X.iloc[:, 0]`** selects the first column of **`X`** (Sepal Length), and it goes on the x-axis. **`X.iloc[:, 1]`** selects the second column of **`X`** (Sepal Width), and it goes on the y-axis. The statement **`c=df['cluster']`** colors each point based on the cluster number assigned by K-means (0, 1, or 2). The statement **`cmap='viridis'`** decides the color scheme. The output of the K-means clustering on **`Iris.csv`** dataset is shown in *Figure 12.3*:

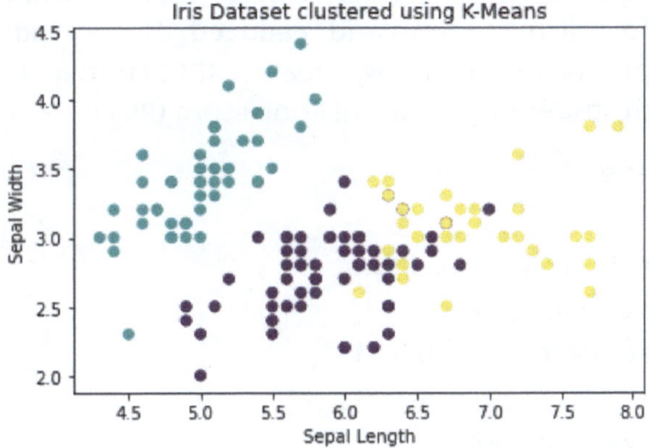

***Figure 12.3**: Output of K-means clustering on Iris.csv dataset*

Note: It is important to note that K-means does not know the actual species names; it only groups flowers by similarity in measurements, so the clusters may or may not exactly match the real species.

Dimensionality reduction

In dimensionality reduction, we do not provide labels (answers). The algorithm only tries to reduce the number of features (columns) while keeping the most important information. Since no labels are given, it is a part of unsupervised learning. A common example is **principal component analysis** (**PCA**), which creates new, smaller features that still explain most of the data. Dimensionality reduction is mainly used to simplify datasets with many features and to remove noise and redundancy. The main idea is to simplify the dataset by removing less useful or redundant features while still capturing the overall pattern of the data. A popular technique for dimensionality reduction is PCA, which transforms the data into a smaller set of new variables called principal components. These components are combinations of the original features but still explain most of the variation in the dataset. For example, if we have a dataset with 100 features, PCA may reduce it to just two or three features, making it much easier to visualize and work with. Dimensionality reduction is especially helpful when dealing with very large datasets, as it reduces complexity, speeds up machine learning algorithms, and removes noise. In real-world applications, it is used in image compression, data visualization, and preparing datasets before applying other algorithms.

Example 12.4: Write a program for dimensionality reduction of converting two features into one feature

In this example, we first import the libraries and make a small dataset with scores of five students in two subjects: Math and Science. This is stored in a Pandas DataFrame called **`df`**. The statements **`pca=PCA(n_components=1)`**, **`X_reduced = pca.fit_transform(df)`** reduce the two features into one feature (**`PC1`**). PC1 is a new combined score created by PCA, chosen so it captures the maximum variation in the students' performance. A statement **`fit_transform()`** calculates PC1 values for each student and **`reduced_df = pd.DataFrame(X_reduced, columns=["PC1"])`** will put the reduced single feature (**`PC1`**) into a new DataFrame. So instead of Math and Science, each student now has just one score (**`PC1`**).

Take a look at the following:

```
import pandas as pd
from sklearn.decomposition import PCA
import matplotlib.pyplot as plt
# Step 1: Small dataset with 2 subjects
data = {
    "Math": [80, 85, 78, 90, 88],
    "Science": [75, 82, 79, 92, 85]
}
df = pd.DataFrame(data)
print("Original Data:\n", df)
# Step 2: Apply PCA to reduce 2 features into 1 feature
pca = PCA(n_components=1)
```

```
X_reduced = pca.fit_transform(df)
# Step 3: Create a new DataFrame
reduced_df = pd.DataFrame(X_reduced, columns=["PC1"])
print("\nReduced Data:\n", reduced_df)
# Step 4: Plot original vs reduced
plt.scatter(df["Math"], df["Science"], color="blue", label="Original Data")
plt.scatter(reduced_df.index, reduced_df["PC1"], color="red", label="Reduced
(PC1)")
plt.xlabel("Index")
plt.ylabel("Values")
plt.legend()
plt.title("PCA Dimensionality Reduction")
plt.show()
```

In this example, a student achieved marks in Math and Science. PCA looks at both subjects together. The Math and Science scores are highly related, i.e., students who do well in Math usually do well in Science too; therefore, PCA will make a new single score (**`PC1`**) that captures most of the variation in both subjects instead of keeping both columns. After applying PCA, we get a new column, **`PC1`**. The values obtained in the output of **`PCA1`** can be negative or positive. It does not represent bad or good, it just shows the relative position of students along the new **`PC1`** line. It is like rotating the 2D plot (Math versus Science) into a single line. Here, students to the left of that line get negative values, and students to the right get the positive values. After PCA, each student represents one number, and it makes the dataset simpler while keeping most of the information. In output, the blue dots show the original 2-dimensional data, i.e., Maths versus Science. The red dots show the reduced 1-dimensional data (**`PC1`** values) plotted against the student index.

Note: **PCA helps us reduce multiple features into fewer features without losing too much important information. The sign itself does not matter in PCA; it is just a direction on the new axis. So the negative values only indicate position relative to the new axis, not that the student has negative marks. The important part is how far the points are from zero (spread/variance), not the sign itself.**

The output using PCA dimensionality reduction of converting two columns into a single column is shown in *Figure 12.4*:

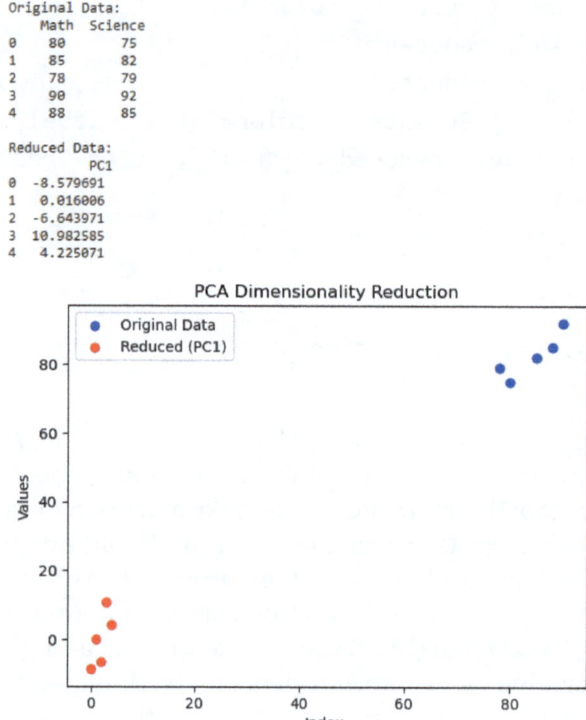

***Figure 12.4**: Output using PCA dimensionality reduction of converting 2 columns into a single column*

In the output shown, these two scores are related because students who perform well in Math often also do well in Science. Instead of keeping both features separately, we use PCA to combine them into one new feature called **`PC1`**. The **`PC1`** values like **`-8.57`**, **`0.01`**, **`10.98`** are the combined scores that capture the overall academic performance of each student in both subjects. A negative **`PC1`** value means the student's scores are lower than the group's average, while a positive **`PC1`** value means the student's scores are higher than average. So, instead of describing a student with two numbers (Math and Science), we can now describe them with one number (**`PC1`**) that reflects their overall performance in both subjects, as depicted in *Table 12.2*:

Math	Science	PC1 (approx. meaning)
80	75	-8.58: Lower performance
85	82	0.01: Around average
78	79	-6.64: Slightly below average
90	92	10.98: Much higher performance
88	85	4.23: Above average

***Table 12.3**: Output of PCA example for easier understanding*

Example 12.5: Write a program to convert two features (Height and Weight) into one (PC1) using PCA

In this example, we first take a sample dataset with two features: **`Height`** and **`Weight`**. Using PCA, we reduce these two features into a single feature called **`PC1`**. This new feature captures the overall body size pattern. Instead of describing a person separately by **`Height`** and **`Weight`**, we now describe them with a single combined score (**`PC1`**). In simple words, PCA helps us summarize the relationship between **`Height`** and **`Weight`** in just one dimension. The following code demonstrates how PCA can be used to reduce dimensionality by converting two related features, **`Height`** and **`Weight`** into a single principal component. After creating a small dataset and applying PCA with one component, the transformed data is displayed and visualized. The plot compares the original two-dimensional values with the reduced one-dimensional representation, illustrating how PCA compresses information while retaining the most significant variation:

```
import pandas as pd
from sklearn.decomposition import PCA
import matplotlib.pyplot as plt
# Step 1: A Small dataset with Height (cm) and Weight (kg)
data = {
    "Height": [150, 160, 170, 180, 190],
    "Weight": [50, 60, 65, 80, 90]
}
df = pd.DataFrame(data)
print("Original Data:\n", df)
# Step 2: Apply PCA to reduce 2 features into 1 feature
pca = PCA(n_components=1)
X_reduced = pca.fit_transform(df)
# Step 3: Store reduced feature
reduced_df = pd.DataFrame(X_reduced, columns=["PC1"])
print("\nReduced Data:\n", reduced_df)
# Step 4: Plot
plt.scatter(df["Height"], df["Weight"], color="blue", label="Original Data")
plt.scatter(reduced_df.index, reduced_df["PC1"], color="red", label="Reduced
(PC1)")
plt.xlabel("Index")
plt.ylabel("Values")
plt.legend()
plt.title("Height & Weight Features converted into one Feature: PC1")
plt.show()
```

The output of converting two features (**Height** and **Weight**) into one (**PC1**) using PCA is shown in *Figure 12.5*:

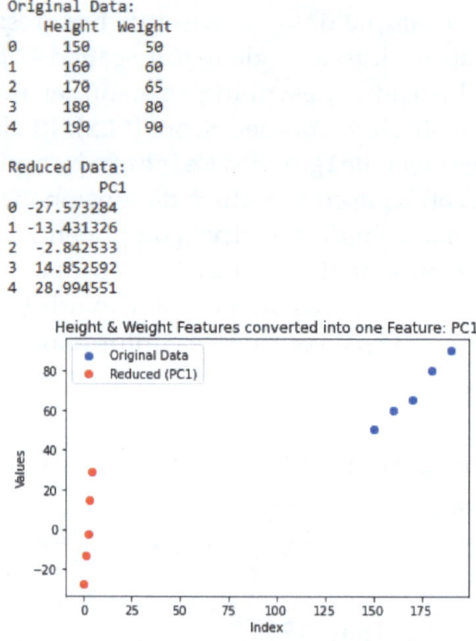

```
Original Data:
   Height  Weight
0     150      50
1     160      60
2     170      65
3     180      80
4     190      90

Reduced Data:
         PC1
0 -27.573284
1 -13.431326
2  -2.842533
3  14.852592
4  28.994551
```


Figure 12.5: *Output of converting two features (Height and Weight) into one (PC1) using PCA*

In output, PCA finds a new axis (direction) in the data, called **PC1**, which captures the maximum variation. Each person's data (**Height**, **Weight**) is then projected onto this axis to give a single number (**PC1** score). The negative and positive values that appeared in the output are **PC1** values (like **-27.57**, **14.85**) and are coordinates along this new axis. They do not directly mean cm or kg anymore. Instead, they are a weighted combination of **Height** and **Weight**. If the combination is less than average, the score can be negative (like **-27.57**). If the combination is more than average, the score can be positive (like **14.85**). So, negative does not mean height or weight is negative; it just means the person's overall size (**Height** and **Weight** combined) is smaller than the average pattern. In simple terms, a positive value means larger than average. So, the **PC1** score is like a single body size index where lower (negative) values mean smaller, higher (positive) values mean larger. The output shown in *Figure 12.4* is depicted in *Table 12.3*:

Height	Weight	PC1 (approx. meaning)
150	50	-27.57: Much smaller body size
160	60	-13.43: Smaller than average
170	65	-2.84: Near average
180	80	14.85: Larger than average
190	90	28.99: Much larger body size

Table 12.4: *Output of PCA example for easier understanding*

Reinforcement learning

Reinforcement learning (RL) is a branch of **artificial intelligence** (AI) where a computer program or a machine learns to make decisions by trial and error. Just like humans learn from experience, RL agents learn by trying actions, observing the results, and receiving rewards or penalties. The goal is to maximize rewards over time.

Example: A child learns to play a video game. In the beginning, they may lose often (penalty), but slowly they understand which moves give more points (reward). Over time, they become better at the game.

Basic elements of reinforcement learning

There are four important elements in RL:

- **Agent**: The learner or the decision maker. For example, a robot, a software program, or a player in a video game.
- **Environment**: The world in which the agent operates. For example, the road for a self-driving car, or the chessboard for a chess-playing AI.
- **Actions**: The choices the agent can make. For example, a robot can move left, right, forward, or backward. In chess, an action is moving a piece on the board.
- **Rewards**: The feedback signal given to the agent after an action. Positive reward means good action, and a negative reward means bad action. For example, a robot reaching its goal is rewarded with +10 points, and a robot hitting an obstacle is penalized with -10 points.

Note: **Reinforcement learning can be described more formally as a process where an agent interacts with an environment through actions, observes states, and receives rewards or penalties. The agent's goal is to learn a policy, a strategy that maximizes cumulative rewards using algorithms such as Q-learning networks, which provide a systematic method for decision-making based on the observed data.**

Real-life examples

Let us understand the concept of reinforcement learning with the help of real-life examples.

Example 1: Child learning to ride a bicycle is one of the real-life examples. The following are the important elements:

- **Agent**: The child
- **Environment**: The bicycle and the road
- **Actions**: Pedal, steer, balance

- **Rewards**:
  - Falls down means negative reward (–1)
  - Rides without falling means positive reward (+1)

Note: **The advantage of this approach is that, over time, the child improves by learning from past mistakes.**

Example 2: A self-driving car at traffic lights is another example explained with the following important elements:

- **Agent**: The self-driving car
- **Environment**: The road with traffic signals
- **Actions**: Stop, Go, or Slow down
- **Rewards**:
  - Stops at red light means +1 reward point
  - Crosses on red light will deduct –5 reward points (penalty)
  - Goes on green light means +2 reward point

Note: **Over time, the car learns the safest and best way to behave at traffic signals.**

Applications of reinforcement learning

RL has a wide range of applications across industries, where it enables agents to learn optimal strategies through interactions and feedback:

- **Robotics**: RL trains robots to perform physical tasks by trial and error, optimizing actions to achieve specific goals. For example, a robot learning to walk receives positive rewards when it maintains balance and moves forward, and penalties when it falls, gradually improving its gait. This allows robots to adapt to complex environments without explicit programming of every movement.
- **Self-driving cars**: RL helps autonomous vehicles make safe driving decisions in dynamic traffic conditions. By rewarding correct maneuvers, such as stopping at red lights, and penalizing mistakes, like collisions or traffic violations, RL agents learn to navigate safely and efficiently, improving over time through continuous interaction with the environment.
- **Gaming**: In board games and video games, RL trains AI agents to find optimal strategies through repeated play. By evaluating the outcomes of different moves as rewards or penalties, agents learn to anticipate opponent strategies and maximize cumulative success, as demonstrated in games like *Chess* and *Go*.

- **Recommendation systems**: RL enables personalized recommendations by learning user preferences from interactions. Positive rewards are given when users engage with content (clicks, watches, or purchases), while negative feedback occurs when content is ignored. This adaptive approach improves user engagement and satisfaction on platforms like *Netflix* and *YouTube*.
- **Healthcare**: RL assists in treatment planning by helping agents recommend optimal dosages or therapies. By receiving feedback based on patient outcomes, RL systems can suggest strategies that maximize efficacy while minimizing risks, supporting doctors in decision-making.
- **Finance**: RL is used in stock trading and portfolio management to maximize profit. Agents learn to buy or sell assets based on reward signals such as price increases or decreases, enabling dynamic decision-making in complex financial markets.
- **Industrial automation**: RL optimizes manufacturing processes by adjusting machine parameters in real-time. For example, a factory robot can learn to vary speed and power to reduce energy consumption while maintaining output quality.
- **Energy management**: In smart grids, RL helps schedule energy usage efficiently. Agents learn the best times to run or stop heavy machinery, reducing overall consumption and improving sustainability.
- **Personal assistants**: Virtual assistants like *Siri*, *Alexa*, and *Google Assistant* use RL to enhance user interactions. By learning patterns in user behavior (e.g., setting alarms or reminders), the system improves its suggestions and anticipates user needs.
- **Education (adaptive learning systems)**: RL personalizes e-learning experiences by adapting lessons based on student performance. If a student struggles with a topic, the system provides additional practice, optimizing learning outcomes through continuous feedback.

Example 12.6: Write a simple program to demonstrate reinforcement learning (agent moving towards a goal)

Through this simple trial-and-error process, the example demonstrates how reinforcement learning works: the agent interacts with the environment, takes actions, and learns from the feedback provided by rewards. This program is a simple example of reinforcement learning where an agent tries to reach a goal in a straight line of five positions numbered from 0 to 4.

The line **`import random`** in Python means we are using the **`random`** module, which is a built-in library in Python that helps us generate random numbers or make random choices. The agent always starts at position 0 (**`position = 0`**), and at each step it randomly decides to move left or right using (**`action = random.choice([-1, 1])`**). It randomly picks either -1 (move left) or 1 (move right). This makes the agent's movement unpredictable, just like real-life situations where actions may not always be fixed. The new location after moving is stored in a variable called **`revised_position`**, and boundary checks ensure that the agent never goes outside the range 0 to 4. The learning process is guided by rewards: if the agent reaches the goal at position 4 (**`if revised_position == goal_state:`**), it earns a reward of +10; otherwise, for every other move it receives a penalty of –1 (**`reward = -1`**). The program repeats this process for 10 steps, printing the position and reward at each move, and finally displaying all collected rewards and the total score (**`print("Total Score:", sum(rewards))`**). The following code provides a simple demonstration of reinforcement learning concepts using a random-movement agent. The environment consists of five states, with the agent starting at position 0 and attempting to reach the goal state at position 4. At each step, the agent randomly chooses to move left or right, receives rewards based on its new position, and updates its state accordingly. After ten steps, the accumulated rewards and final score are displayed, illustrating how actions and feedback drive learning in RL environments:

```
import random
# Environment setup
states = [0, 1, 2, 3, 4]   # 0 = Start, 4 = Goal
goal_state = 4
# Agent starts at position 0
position = 0
rewards = []
print("Agent starts at position:", position)
# Run for 10 steps
for step in range(10):
    # Action: Move Left (-1) or Right (+1)
    action = random.choice([-1, 1])
    revised_position = position + action
    # Keep agent within bounds
    if revised_position < 0:
        revised_position = 0
    if revised_position > 4:
        revised_position = 4
    # Reward system
    if revised_position == goal_state:
        reward = 10
        print(f"Step {step+1}: Moved to {revised_position} Goal reached!
Reward = {reward}")
    else:
        reward = -1
        print(f"Step {step+1}: Moved to {revised_position} Reward = {reward}")
    rewards.append(reward)
    position = revised_position  # Update agent's position
print("\nAll Rewards:", rewards)
print("Total Score:", sum(rewards))
```

The output of the reinforcement learning program of an agent moving towards a goal is shown in *Figure 12.6*:

```
Agent starts at position: 0
Step 1: Moved to 0 Reward = -1
Step 2: Moved to 1 Reward = -1
Step 3: Moved to 2 Reward = -1
Step 4: Moved to 3 Reward = -1
Step 5: Moved to 4 Goal reached! Reward = 10
Step 6: Moved to 4 Goal reached! Reward = 10
Step 7: Moved to 3 Reward = -1
Step 8: Moved to 4 Goal reached! Reward = 10
Step 9: Moved to 4 Goal reached! Reward = 10
Step 10: Moved to 3 Reward = -1

All Rewards: [-1, -1, -1, -1, 10, 10, -1, 10, 10, -1]
Total Score: 34
```

***Figure 12.6**: Output of the reinforcement learning program of an agent moving towards a goal*

Machine learning versus deep learning

ML is a branch of artificial intelligence that allows computers to learn from data and improve their performance using algorithms. It mainly involves three types of learning: supervised learning, where the model is trained on labeled data (like predicting student grades based on past performance), unsupervised learning, where the system finds hidden patterns or groups in unlabeled data (like clustering customers by shopping habits), and reinforcement learning, where an agent learns by interacting with an environment and receiving rewards or penalties (like a robot learning to walk). In ML, human experts often decide which features are important for solving a problem, and the algorithms usually work well with smaller datasets and require less computational power. For example, in predicting house prices, features like the number of rooms, location, and area are chosen manually. ML techniques work well even with smaller datasets and require less computational power.

Deep learning (**DL**), on the other hand, is a specialized branch of ML that uses artificial neural networks with multiple layers (input, hidden, and output layers) to automatically extract features from raw data. These neural networks are inspired by how the human brain processes information. Unlike traditional ML models, where features often need to be selected and engineered manually, DL models can learn complex features directly from large datasets. For example, **convolutional neural networks** (**CNNs**) are widely used in image recognition, while **recurrent neural networks** (**RNNs**) are applied in sequential tasks like speech and language processing. Since deep learning requires a lot of computational power, it often relies on **graphics processing units** (**GPUs**) to handle the heavy processing. Thus, while ML offers simpler methods suitable for smaller datasets, DL with neural networks provides powerful techniques for solving highly complex tasks. While classical algorithms like regression, SVM, and KNN are sufficient for smaller datasets, neural networks are better suited for complex, large-scale data.

From a practical perspective, the choice between machine learning and deep learning is not only conceptual but also depends on factors such as dataset size, data type, model interpretability, and computational cost. While traditional ML models are often preferred when transparency and limited data are important, deep learning becomes advantageous when handling large-scale, unstructured data where automatic feature extraction outweighs interpretability concerns. Thus, the selection of ML or DL should be guided by problem complexity and resource availability rather than accuracy alone.

Conclusion

In this chapter, we explored important branches of machine learning beyond supervised learning. We learned about unsupervised learning, where the system works without labeled data and instead discovers hidden patterns on its own. Two key types were introduced: clustering, such as K-means, which groups similar data points together, and dimensionality reduction, such as PCA, which simplifies large datasets while keeping essential information. We also studied reinforcement learning, where an agent interacts with an environment, performs actions, and receives rewards to learn the best strategy over time. Finally, we compared ML with DL. ML includes approaches like supervised, unsupervised, and reinforcement learning, while DL, powered by neural networks with many layers (e.g., CNNs), relies heavily on GPUs for handling complex tasks such as image recognition and natural language processing. Together, these concepts provide a strong foundation to understand how machines can learn, adapt, and solve real-world problems in different ways.

Points to remember

The following points are to be kept in mind:

- Unsupervised learning enables pattern discovery in unlabeled data through techniques such as clustering and dimensionality reduction.
- K-means clustering groups similar data points, while PCA reduces feature dimensionality without significant loss of information.
- RL focuses on learning optimal actions through interaction, rewards, and penalties.
- Traditional ML methods are suitable for structured data and smaller datasets, whereas deep learning excels in complex, large-scale, and unstructured data scenarios.
- Understanding the strengths and limitations of ML and DL helps in selecting appropriate techniques for real-world problem-solving.
- Unsupervised learning deals with unlabeled data where the system finds hidden patterns or structures without predefined output.

- Clustering like K-means group similar data points together, while dimensionality reduction like PCA simplifies data by reducing features while keeping important information.
- RL is based on an agent, environment, actions, and rewards, where learning happens through trial and error.
- In ML, models learn from data using approaches such as supervised, unsupervised, and reinforcement learning.
- DL is a subset of ML that relies on neural networks with multiple layers, capable of automatically extracting features from large datasets.
- ML usually works well with smaller datasets and manual feature engineering, while DL requires big data and high computational power (GPUs).
- CNNs are popular in image recognition tasks, while RNNs are widely used in sequential data like text and speech.
- Neural networks are the foundation of DL, consisting of layers of interconnected nodes, also known as neurons, that enable models to automatically learn complex patterns and representations from data.

Key terms

- **Unsupervised learning**: A type of learning where the algorithm works with unlabeled data to discover patterns or structures; commonly used in customer segmentation, anomaly detection, and data exploration.
- **Clustering**: The process of grouping similar data points together, such as using K-means; widely applied in market analysis, student performance grouping, and image segmentation.
- **Dimensionality reduction**: A technique that reduces the number of input features while preserving important information, such as PCA; used to simplify large datasets, improve visualization, and reduce computational cost.
- **Reinforcement learning**: A learning method where an agent interacts with an environment and learns through actions and rewards; applied in robotics, game playing, and autonomous systems.
- **Agent**: The learner or decision-maker in reinforcement learning that selects actions; for example, a robot, software program, or autonomous vehicle controller.
- **Environment**: The external system with which the agent interacts; this could be a physical world (robot navigation) or a simulated setting (games or trading systems).

- **Action**: The choices made by the agent at each step; such as moving forward, selecting a strategy, or recommending an item.
- **Reward**: Feedback given to the agent based on its action; positive rewards encourage desirable behavior, while negative rewards discourage poor decisions.
- **Machine learning (ML)**: A broad field that includes supervised, unsupervised, and reinforcement learning; used for predictive tasks such as classification, regression, and pattern recognition.
- **Deep learning (DL)**: A subset of ML that uses neural networks with multiple layers to automatically learn complex features; especially effective for image, speech, and natural language processing.
- **Neural network**: A computational model inspired by the human brain, consisting of interconnected layers of neurons; used to model complex relationships in data.
- **Convolutional neural network (CNN)**: A deep learning architecture designed to process grid-like data such as images; widely used in image classification, object detection, and facial recognition.
- **Graphics processing unit (GPU)**: A hardware component that accelerates the training of deep learning models; essential for handling large datasets and deep neural networks efficiently.

Multiple choice questions

1. **In unsupervised learning, the data used is**:
    a. Labeled
    b. Unlabeled
    c. Both labeled and unlabeled
    d. None of these
2. **Which of the following is an example of clustering?**
    a. Predicting house prices
    b. Grouping customers by buying behavior
    c. Detecting spam emails
    d. Classifying animals as cats or dogs
3. **The main goal of dimensionality reduction is**:
    a. To increase the number of features
    b. To reduce features while keeping important information
    c. To remove noise from the dataset
    d. To create new labels for the dataset

4. **PCA stands for:**
   a. Principal classification analysis
   b. Principal component analysis
   c. Primary component arrangement
   d. Partial cluster analysis

5. **In RL, who interacts with the environment?**
   a. Dataset
   b. Agent
   c. Reward system
   d. Neural network

6. **The feedback given to the agent in RL is called:**
   a. Label
   b. Feature
   c. Reward
   d. Cluster

7. **Machine learning includes which types of learning?**
   a. Supervised and deep learning
   b. Unsupervised and reinforcement learning
   c. Supervised, unsupervised, and reinforcement learning
   d. Only supervised learning

8. **Deep learning mainly relies on:**
   a. Clustering methods
   b. Neural networks
   c. PCA
   d. Decision trees

9. **Which of the following is commonly used for image recognition tasks?**
   a. PCA
   b. CNN
   c. Decision tree
   d. K-means

10. **GPUs are mainly used in deep learning to:**
    a. Increase dataset size
    b. Train neural networks faster
    c. Reduce the number of neurons
    d. Create labels automatically

11. **A retail company has a large dataset containing customer purchase history, browsing behavior, and visit frequency, but no predefined customer categories. The company wants to group customers with similar behavior patterns to design targeted marketing strategies.**

    Which machine learning approach is most appropriate for this task?

    a. Supervised learning using linear regression

    b. Unsupervised learning using K-means clustering

    c. Reinforcement learning using Q-learning

    d. Deep learning using convolutional neural networks

12. **A data scientist is working with a dataset containing 120 features related to sensor readings. The dataset is difficult to visualize, and training machine learning models on it is slow. The goal is to reduce complexity while preserving most of the important information.**

    Which technique should be applied first?

    a. K-means clustering

    b. Principal component analysis

    c. Decision tree classification

    d. Q-learning

13. **An autonomous delivery robot operates in a warehouse. It must decide which path to take to deliver packages efficiently while avoiding obstacles. The robot receives positive feedback for faster deliveries and penalties for collisions or delays.**

    Which learning paradigm best fits this scenario?

    a. Supervised learning

    b. Unsupervised learning

    c. Reinforcement learning

    d. Clustering

Answers

1	b
2	b
3	b
4	b

5	b
6	c
7	c
8	b
9	b
10	b
11	b
12	b
13	c

Questions

1. What is machine learning? Explain the three main types of learning with suitable examples.
2. Differentiate between machine learning and deep learning. Give at least two real-world applications of each.
3. What is unsupervised learning? Write a short Python program using sklearn to perform clustering with K-means on a small dataset.
4. What is dimensionality reduction? Explain PCA with a simple example.
5. Define reinforcement learning. Describe the terms agent, environment, and reward with a simple example.
6. What is deep learning? How is it different from traditional machine learning? Give one real-world example where deep learning performs better.
7. What is CNN? Mention one example where CNN is widely used.
8. Compare clustering and classification with examples. Write a small Python code snippet that demonstrates classification using KNN.
9. Assume that a company is developing two different systems:
   - System A analyzes a small, structured dataset of student marks and attendance to predict final grades, where the input features are clearly defined and limited in number.
   - System B processes thousands of images captured by traffic cameras to automatically detect vehicles and pedestrians in real time.

   Which combination of learning approaches is most appropriate for System A and System B, respectively? Justify.

Join our Discord space

Join our Discord workspace for latest updates, offers, tech happenings around the world, new releases, and sessions with the authors:

https://discord.bpbonline.com

Appendix A: Simple Projects Using Pandas

Introduction

This appendix presents a collection of small applications that demonstrate how to use the Pandas library in Python for analyzing data stored in CSV files. Each example is designed to be simple, clear, and practical so that readers can easily follow and apply the concepts. The applications include analyzing students' performance, summarizing sales records, and extracting insights from employee salary data. Examples also show how Python data structures such as lists, tuples, and dictionaries can be converted into DataFrames and then saved or used as CSV files for further analysis. Through these hands-on exercises, readers are introduced to essential analytical techniques that form the foundation of data-driven decision making, which is a key component of modern data science workflows. By learning how to load, manipulate, and interpret real datasets using pandas, readers gain initial exposure to practical skills used widely in academic research, business analytics, and industry-level data processing.

Additional case studies cover library book records, sports data analysis to identify the highest score player and average scores, and social media data to find the most engaging platforms. The appendix also includes the widely known Iris dataset, where basic statistical analysis such as minimum, maximum, averages, and correlations is performed.

By working through these examples, readers will learn how CSV files serve as a common format for datasets and how Pandas provides powerful yet simple functions to explore, summarize, and gain insights from them.

Data analysis examples using Python and Pandas

The following examples illustrate a variety of practical data analysis tasks that can be performed using the **pandas** library in Python. Each example demonstrates how different types of data, such as student grades, sales records, employee information, and well-known datasets like Iris, can be read, processed, analyzed, and interpreted. These examples progressively introduce essential operations, including reading data from CSV files, converting Python data structures into DataFrames, filtering and grouping data, computing summary statistics, and generating visualizations. Through these hands-on demonstrations, readers can develop a better understanding of how pandas simplifies real-world data analysis and enables meaningful insights from raw datasets.

Example Appendix A.1: Write a program for analyzing students' performance

In *Example Appendix A.1*, we are working with a small dataset stored in the form of a **comma separated values** (**CSV**) file, as shown in *Table Appendix A.1*:

Name	Math	English	Science
Amit	78	80	85
Rita	90	85	88
Karan	60	70	65
Sita	85	95	92

Table Appendix A.1*: Sample dataset*

A CSV file is a simple text file that stores data in a tabular format using rows and columns. Each row represents a record (for example, one student), and the values in each row are separated by commas. Although the actual file uses commas to separate values, for clarity and better readability, the data is displayed here in a table format. In this dataset, Name is one of the columns (also called a feature), and each student's marks are recorded across the row corresponding to their name.

Need for CSV files: CSV files are one of the most widely used formats for storing and sharing data because they are:

- **Simple**: Use of just plain text, easy to read and edit.
- **Portable**: Supported by almost all software, including Excel, Google Sheets, and programming languages like Python.
- **Lightweight**: Much smaller in size compared to databases.
- **Flexible**: Can be used for storing different types of data (numbers, text, categories).

To demonstrate how pandas can read and analyze data from a CSV file where data is stored as text and commas separate individual values (columns) within each row. Here, we have used a sample dataset named **`students.csv`**. This dataset contains the academic performance of four students in three subjects: Mathematics, English, and Science. Each row represents an individual student, while the columns store their respective subject marks. The dataset is small and easy to understand, making it suitable for beginners to practice data loading, summary statistics, and basic data manipulation operations in **`pandas`**. The contents of the file are as follows:

Filename: **`students.csv`**:

```
Name,Math,English,Science
Amit,78,80,85
Rita,90,85,88
Karan,60,70,65
Sita,85,95,92
```

The code statement **`import pandas as pd`** imports the **`pandas`** library, which is used to work with tabular data (rows and columns). **`pd.read_csv("d:\\students.csv")`** reads the data from a CSV file named **`students.csv`** and stores it in a DataFrame (**`df`**). A DataFrame is just like an Excel sheet in Python. **`df[["Math","Science","English"]]`** selects these three columns. A statement **`.mean(axis=1)`** calculates the mean row-wise (i.e., per student). **`df["Average"]`** creates a new column in the DataFrame called **`"Average"`**. The **`df["Average"].idxmax()`** gives the row index of the student with the maximum average, and **`df.loc[...]`** fetches that student's full row with all their details. The code statement **`sorted_df = df.sort_values(by="Average", ascending=False)`** sorts all students in descending order of their average marks. Take a look at the following code:

```
import pandas as pd
# Read a csv file
df = pd.read_csv("d:\\students.csv")
# Average score for each student
df["Average"] = df[["Math", "Science", "English"]].mean(axis=1)
# Find the student who scored highest marks
top_scorer = df.loc[df["Average"].idxmax()]
# Sort by average
sorted_df = df.sort_values(by="Average", ascending=False)
print("Student Data with Averages:\n", df)
print("\nTop Scorer:\n", top_scorer)
print("\nStudents Sorted by Average:\n", sorted_df)
```

The output of the program for analyzing students' performance is shown in *Figure Appendix A.1*:

```
Student Data with Averages:
    Name  Math  English  Science    Average
0   Amit    78       80       85  81.000000
1   Rita    90       85       88  87.666667
2  Karan    60       70       65  65.000000
3   Sita    85       95       92  90.666667

Top Scorer:
 Name            Sita
Math              85
English           95
Science           92
Average    90.666667
Name: 3, dtype: object

Students Sorted by Average:
    Name  Math  English  Science    Average
3   Sita    85       95       92  90.666667
1   Rita    90       85       88  87.666667
0   Amit    78       80       85  81.000000
2  Karan    60       70       65  65.000000
```

***Figure Appendix A.1**: Output of analyzing students' performance*

Example Appendix A.2: Write a program to analyze and summarize sales using Pandas

In this example, we are taking a small dataset in the form of a **`.csv`** file, as shown in *Table Appendix A.2*:

Day	Product	Sales
Monday	Apples	50
Monday	Oranges	30
Tuesday	Apples	40
Tuesday	Oranges	35
Wednesday	Apples	60
Wednesday	Oranges	45

***Table Appendix A.2**: Sample dataset*

In this program, we are analyzing a small sales dataset stored in a CSV file named **`sales.csv`**. After importing the required libraries (**`pandas`** for data handling and **`matplotlib.pyplot`** for visualization), the dataset is read into a DataFrame **`df`**. Using the **`groupby()`** function, the program first calculates the total sales for each product by grouping rows based on the **`"Product"`** column and summing the **`"Sales"`** values. Similarly, it calculates the total sales for each day by grouping data based on the **`"Day"`** column. Both results are displayed on the screen. To make the analysis more understandable, a bar chart is drawn for daily sales using Matplotlib, where the x-axis shows the days and the y-axis shows the corresponding sales values. This way, the program not only summarizes sales data but also provides a simple visual representation.

To further illustrate how **`pandas`** can be used for business-related data analysis, the following example uses a small dataset stored in a file named **`sales.csv`**. This dataset contains daily sales records for two fruit products: **`Apples`** and **`Oranges`** across three days of the week (Monday to Wednesday). Each row represents the sales quantity of a particular product on a given day. This dataset is useful for demonstrating operations such as filtering, grouping, calculating total or average sales, and visualizing sales trends. The contents of the file are shown as follows:

Filename: **`sales.csv`**:

```
Day,Product,Sales
Monday,Apples,50
Monday,Oranges,30
Tuesday,Apples,40
Tuesday,Oranges,35
Wednesday,Apples,60
Wednesday,Oranges,45
```

The following Python script demonstrates how to read the **sales.csv** file using the **pandas** library and perform basic data analysis. The code calculates the total sales for each product and the total sales for each day of the week using the **groupby()** function. It then displays the results and visualizes daily sales values using a bar chart created with **matplotlib**. This example helps readers understand how **pandas** can summarize real-world business data and present it in a graphical form:

```
import pandas as pd
import matplotlib.pyplot as plt
df = pd.read_csv("d:\\sales.csv")
# Total sales by product using groupby()
product_sales = df.groupby("Product")["Sales"].sum()
# Daily sales
daily_sales = df.groupby("Day")["Sales"].sum()
print("Sales by Product:\n", product_sales)
print("\nSales by Day:\n", daily_sales)
# Visualization
daily_sales.plot(kind="bar", title="Daily Sales")
plt.show()
```

The output of analyzing and summarizing sales using Pandas is shown in *Figure Appendix A.2*:

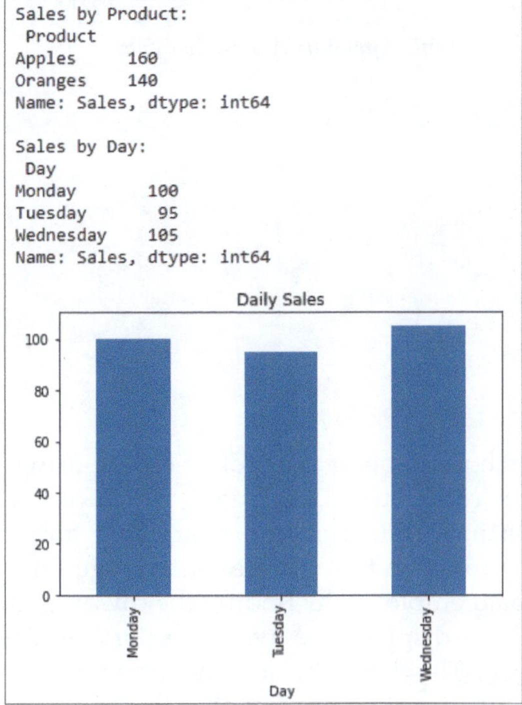

***Figure Appendix A.2**: Output of analyzing and summarizing sales using Pandas*

The bar chart titled **`Daily Sales`** represents the total sales amount for each day. On the x-axis, the chart displays different days, while the y-axis shows the corresponding total sales values aggregated using the **`groupby()`** and **`sum()`** functions. Each bar indicates the cumulative sales recorded on a particular day. From the chart, variations in sales across different days can be easily observed. Days with taller bars indicate higher sales, whereas shorter bars reflect lower sales performance. This visualization helps in identifying daily sales trends, comparing performance across days, and recognizing peak or low sales periods. Overall, the bar chart provides a clear and intuitive representation of daily sales distribution, making it easier to analyze patterns and support data-driven decision-making.

Example Appendix A.3: Write a program to analyze employee salary data and find insights

Again, we are using a dataset named **`employees.csv`**, which contains three features: **`Name`**, **`Department`**, and **`Salary`**. For better readability, the data is displayed in tabular form in *Table Appendix A.3*:

Name	Department	Salary
Ajay	HR	40000
Ritesh	IT	55000
Sameer	Finance	50000
Kiran	IT	60000
Pooja	HR	42000

***Table Appendix A.3**: Sample dataset*

The contents of the file are shown as follows:

Filename: **`employees.csv`**:

```
Name,Department,Salary
Ajay,HR,40000
Ritesh,IT,55000
Sameer,Finance,50000
Kiran,IT,60000
Pooja,HR,42000
```

This program demonstrates how to analyze employee data using the **`pandas`** library. First, the dataset **`employees.csv`** is read into a DataFrame, which contains employee details such as **`Name`**, **`Department`**, and **`Salary`**. To understand salary distribution across departments, the program uses the **`groupby()`** function to calculate the average salary for each department. It then identifies the highest-paid employee by finding the row with the maximum salary using **`idxmax()`**. Finally, the program displays the average salary by department and the details of the highest-paid employee. This helps in quickly summarizing the salary structure and spotting top earners within the organization.

The following Python code demonstrates how to analyze employee salary information stored in the **employees.csv** file using the **pandas** library. The script reads the dataset into a DataFrame and then calculates the average salary for each department using the **groupby()** function. It also identifies the highest-paid employee in the company by locating the row with the maximum salary. This example shows how pandas can be used to summarize workplace data and extract meaningful insights for decision-making:

```
import pandas as pd
df = pd.read_csv("d:\\employees.csv")
# Average salary by department
avg_salary = df.groupby("Department")["Salary"].mean()
# Highest paid employee
highest_paid = df.loc[df["Salary"].idxmax()]
print("Average Salary by Department:\n", avg_salary)
print("\n Highest Paid Employee:\n", highest_paid)
```

The code statement **groupby("Department")["Salary"].mean()** groups the data by department and then finds the average of the **Salary** column. **idxmax()** finds the index, i.e., row number of the maximum value in a column, here used to find the employee with the highest salary. The output of analyzing employee salary data is shown in *Figure Appendix A.3*:

```
Average Salary by Department:
 Department
Finance    50000.0
HR         41000.0
IT         57500.0
Name: Salary, dtype: float64

 Highest Paid Employee:
 Name          Kiran
Department      IT
Salary        60000
Name: 3, dtype: object
```

***Figure Appendix A.3**: Output of analyzing employees' salary data*

While the above example focuses on computing the average salary by department, relying solely on mean values may hide important salary differences among employees. In practice, salary variability and outliers should also be examined to obtain a more comprehensive understanding of compensation patterns.

This can be achieved using measures such as standard deviation and by identifying extreme salary values, illustrated as follows:

```
# Salary variability within each department
df.groupby("Department")["Salary"].std()
# Identifying a potential salary outlier (highest-paid employee)
df.loc[df["Salary"].idxmax()]
```

The standard deviation reflects how widely salaries are distributed within a department, while the highest salary highlights potential outliers that may significantly influence the average.

Example Appendix A.4: Write a program for using a List with pandas

In this example, a Python list is converted into a **pandas** DataFrame, and **pandas** functions like **`.sum()`** are applied to calculate the total sales.

```
import pandas as pd
# List of sales amounts
sales = [250, 350, 150, 450, 200]
# Convert list into a DataFrame
df = pd.DataFrame(sales, columns=["Sales"])
print("Sales Data:")
print(df)
print("\nTotal Sales:", df["Sales"].sum())
```

The output of using a list with **pandas** is shown in *Figure Appendix A.4*:

```
Sales Data:
   Sales
0    250
1    350
2    150
3    450
4    200

Total Sales: 1400
```

***Figure Appendix A.4**: Output of using a list with pandas*

This example demonstrates a basic sales aggregation scenario commonly encountered in small retail or daily transaction tracking systems. The list of sales values can be interpreted as individual transaction amounts recorded over a short time period, such as daily sales in a small store or point-of-sale system. Converting the list into a DataFrame reflects how raw transaction data is structured for further analysis in real-world applications. The calculation of total sales is a fundamental operation used in business reporting, inventory planning, and revenue analysis. Although simplified for instructional purposes, the example mirrors the initial data processing step typically performed before applying more advanced analytics such as trend analysis or forecasting. In practical applications, sales data is usually collected from files or databases and may include additional attributes such as date, product, or region. The same operation can be extended.

An example of a real-world extension is shown as follows:

```
df["Sales"].sum()
```

This aggregation forms the basis for generating business insights such as daily revenue reports or monthly performance summaries.

Example Appendix A.5: Write a program for using a list of tuples with pandas

We import the **pandas** library to work with data in a structured way (tables like Excel). This code begins by importing the **pandas** library, which is used to handle data in tabular form. A list of tuples is then created, where each tuple represents an employee with their name, age, and department. For example, the tuple **("Anil", 25, "HR")** means that Anil is 25 years old and works in the HR department. This list of tuples is converted into a **pandas** DataFrame using **pd.DataFrame()**, and column names are specified as **Name**, **Age**, and **Department**, which organizes the data neatly into a table format. When the DataFrame is printed, it displays the employee information in a structured way similar to a spreadsheet. Finally, the program selects the **"Age"** column from the DataFrame and applies the **.mean()** function to calculate the average age of all employees, resulting in the output **27.67**. Thus, the code demonstrates how Python data structures like lists and tuples can be integrated with **pandas** to perform data analysis easily.

The following example demonstrates how a list of tuples in Python can be converted into a **pandas** DataFrame without reading from a CSV file. Each tuple represents an employee with their name, age, and department. After creating the DataFrame, the code displays the employee data and calculates the average age of the employees using the **mean()** function. This example shows how **pandas** can efficiently handle structured data created directly within a Python program:

```
import pandas as pd
# List of tuples (Name, Age, Department)
employees = [
    ("Anil", 25, "HR"),
    ("Binu", 30, "IT"),
    ("Chetan", 28, "Finance")
]
# Convert list of tuples into DataFrame
df = pd.DataFrame(employees, columns=["Name", "Age", "Department"])
print("Employee Data:")
print(df)
# Find average age of employees
print("\nAverage Age:", df["Age"].mean())
```

The output of using a tuple with **pandas** is shown in *Figure Appendix A.5*:

```
Employee Data:
     Name  Age Department
0    Anil   25         HR
1    Binu   30         IT
2  Chetan   28    Finance

Average Age: 27.666666666666668
```

***Figure Appendix A.5**: Output of using a tuple with Pandas*

Example Appendix A.6: Write a program for using a dictionary with Pandas

This code starts by importing the **pandas** library, which is widely used for handling and analyzing data in Python. A dictionary named **data** is created, where each key represents a column name (**Name**, **Marks**, and **Subject**), and the corresponding values are lists containing the data for that column. For example, under the key **"Name"**, the list contains the values **["Divya","Sunil","Vinod"]**, representing three students. This dictionary is then converted into a pandas DataFrame using **pd.DataFrame(data)**, which organizes the data into a tabular structure similar to a spreadsheet. When the DataFrame is printed, it displays the student names, their marks, and their subjects in a clear format. Finally, the program accesses the **"Marks"** column and applies the **.max()** function to determine the highest marks scored among the students, which in this case is 92. This example shows how a Python dictionary containing lists can be easily converted into a DataFrame for structured representation and simple analysis using pandas.

Note: A dictionary is one of the most common ways to create DataFrames. The keys of the dictionary become column names. Each list inside the dictionary becomes a column of values.

The following example shows how a dictionary containing lists can be converted into a **pandas** DataFrame. Each key in the dictionary represents a column name, and the corresponding list holds the values for that column. After constructing the DataFrame, the code prints the student records and calculates the highest marks using the **max()** function. This example demonstrates how **pandas** can easily transform Python dictionary data into a structured format suitable for analysis:

```
import pandas as pd
# Dictionary with lists
data = {
    "Name": ["Divya", "Sunil", "Vinod"],
    "Marks": [80, 91, 70],
    "Subject": ["Math", "Science", "English"]
}
# Convert dictionary into DataFrame
df = pd.DataFrame(data)
print("Student Data:")
print(df)
# Find maximum marks
print("\nHighest Marks:", df["Marks"].max())
```

The output of using a dictionary with **pandas** is shown in *Figure Appendix A.6*:

```
Student Data:
    Name  Marks  Subject
0  Divya     80     Math
1  Sunil     91  Science
2  Vinod     70  English

Highest Marks: 91
```

***Figure Appendix A.6**: Output of a dictionary with Pandas*

In practical applications, student data is often retrieved from files or databases and may include additional attributes such as roll number, semester, or grades. The same logic can be applied to larger datasets to support tasks like ranking students or generating performance reports.

```
# Identifying top-performing student
df.loc[df["Marks"].idxmax()]
```

Example Appendix A.7: Write a program to perform data analysis on the library books dataset

In this example, we consider a dataset shown in *Table Appendix A.4*, saved as a CSV file:

Book	Genre	Borrowed
HarryPotter	Fantasy	120
Sherlock	Mystery	80
Narnia	Fantasy	95
Python101	Education	110

***Table Appendix A.4**: Library books dataset (Books, Genre, and Borrowed count)*

The contents of the file are shown as follows:

Filename: `library.csv`:

```
Book,Genre,Borrowed
HarryPotter,Fantasy,120
Sherlock,Mystery,80
Narnia,Fantasy,95
Python101,Education,110
```

The program begins by importing the **pandas** library, which is widely used for data analysis in Python. The dataset named **library.csv** is then loaded into a DataFrame called **df**. This DataFrame contains information about books in a library, such as their titles, genres, and the number of times they have been borrowed. The first print statement displays the complete dataset to give an overview of the library records. Next, the code identifies the most borrowed book by finding the row with the highest value in the **Borrowed** column using **idxmax()**. It then calculates the average number of borrowings across all books using the **mean()** function. Finally, the code determines the most popular genre by grouping the dataset by the **Genre** column, summing the borrow counts for each genre, and selecting the one with the highest total. This simple program demonstrates how **pandas** can be used to perform basic data analysis tasks on a real-world dataset like library records:

```
import pandas as pd
# Load CSV file
df = pd.read_csv("d:\\library.csv")
# Show the data
print("Data of Library Books:\n", df)
# Most borrowed book
print("\nMost Borrowed Book:", df.loc[df['Borrowed'].idxmax(), 'Book'])
# Average borrowed count
print("Average Borrowed:", df['Borrowed'].mean())
# Most popular genre
print("Most Popular Genre:")
print(df.groupby("Genre")['Borrowed'].sum().idxmax())
```

The output of analyzing library books data is shown in *Figure Appendix A.7*:

```
Data of Library Books:
          Book      Genre  Borrowed
0  HarryPotter    Fantasy       120
1     Sherlock    Mystery        80
2       Narnia    Fantasy        95
3    Python101  Education       110

Most Borrowed Book: HarryPotter
Average Borrowed: 101.25
Most Popular Genre:
Fantasy
```

***Figure Appendix A.7**: Output of library books data*

Example Appendix A.8: Program to analyze player scores using sports data

In this example, we will analyze a sports dataset to determine the highest scoring player, calculate the average score, and count the number of players in each sport. A sample CSV file in the form of a dataset is shown in *Table Appendix A.5*:

Player	Sport	Score
Virat	Cricket	95
Ronaldo	Football	88

Player	Sport	Score
Messi	Football	91
Sachin	Cricket	120
Roger	Tennis	100

Table Appendix A.5: Sample dataset of sports

The contents of the file are shown as follows:

Filename: **`sports.csv`**:

```
Player,Sport,Score
Virat,Cricket,95
Ronaldo,Football,88
Messi,Football,91
Sachin,Cricket,120
Roger,Tennis,100
```

This program demonstrates how to analyze a sports dataset using Pandas. First, the CSV file named **`sports.csv`** is read into a DataFrame, allowing us to work with the data in a table-like structure. The dataset is displayed to give an overview of the sports data. Next, the code finds the player with the highest score by locating the row with the maximum value in the **`Score`** column and printing the corresponding player's name. It then calculates the average score for each sport by grouping the data based on the **`Sport`** column and taking the mean of the scores in each group. Finally, it counts the number of players in each sport using the **`value_counts()`** function on the **`Sport`** column. This provides insights into player performance and the distribution of players across different sports:

```
import pandas as pd
# Load CSV file
df = pd.read_csv("d:\\sports.csv")
print("Sports Data:\n", df)
# Highest score player
print("\nTop Player:", df.loc[df['Score'].idxmax(), 'Player'])
# Average score by sport
print("\nAverage Score by Sport:\n", df.groupby("Sport")['Score'].mean())
# Count of players in each sport
print("\nPlayers per Sport:\n", df['Sport'].value_counts())
```

The output of analyzing sports data is shown in *Figure Appendix A.8*:

```
Sports Data:
    Player     Sport  Score
0    Virat   Cricket     95
1  Ronaldo  Football     88
2    Messi  Football     91
3   Sachin   Cricket    120
4    Roger    Tennis    100

Top Player: Sachin

Average Score by Sport:
 Sport
Cricket     107.5
Football     89.5
Tennis      100.0
Name: Score, dtype: float64


Players per Sport:
 Sport
Cricket     2
Football    2
Tennis      1
Name: count, dtype: int64
```

Figure Appendix A.8: Output of analyzing sports data

Example Appendix A.9: Write a program for social media data analysis using Pandas

In this example, using Pandas, we will analyze the social media dataset in the form of a CSV file to find:

- The platform with the most likes
- The average number of shares
- The platform with the highest total engagement, i.e., likes and shares

In this example, engagement is defined as the combined effect of likes and shares, which are two commonly used indicators of user interaction on social media platforms. Likes represent immediate user appreciation, while shares indicate deeper engagement by redistributing content to a wider audience. By summing likes and shares, a simple but effective engagement metric is obtained, allowing comparison of overall audience interaction across platforms. Although real-world social media analytics may include additional factors such as comments, reach, or impressions, this simplified definition is sufficient for demonstrating basic data aggregation and comparison techniques.

The sample dataset for social media data analysis is shown in *Table Appendix A.6*:

Platform	Likes	Shares
YouTube	500	200
Instagram	700	300
Twitter	250	150
Facebook	400	180

***Table Appendix A.6**: Social media data analysis*

The contents of the file are shown as follows:

Filename: **`social.csv`**:

```
Platform,Likes,Shares
YouTube,500,200
Instagram,700,300
Twitter,250,150
Facebook,400,180
```

The given program demonstrates how to analyze a social media dataset using the **`pandas`** library in Python. First, the dataset is read from a CSV file named **`social.csv`** and displayed to the user. Then, the program identifies the platform with the highest number of likes using the **`idxmax()`** function, which returns the index of the maximum value. Next, it calculates the average number of shares across all platforms by applying the **`mean()`** function on the **`Shares`** column. To measure overall engagement, a new column called **`Total`** is created by adding likes and shares for each platform. Finally, the program finds the platform with the highest total engagement and displays it as the most popular platform. This example shows how **`pandas`** can be used to perform simple but meaningful data analysis on real-world datasets:

```
import pandas as pd
# Load CSV file
df = pd.read_csv("social.csv")
print("Social Media Data:\n", df)
# Platform with most likes
print("\nMost Liked Platform:", df.loc[df['Likes'].idxmax(), 'Platform'])
# Average shares
print("Average Shares:", df['Shares'].mean())
# Platform with highest total engagement (Likes + Shares)
df['Total'] = df['Likes'] + df['Shares']
print("Most Popular Platform:", df.loc[df['Total'].idxmax(), 'Platform'])
```

The output of social media analysis using **pandas** is shown in *Figure Appendix A.9*:

```
Social Media Data:
     Platform  Likes  Shares
0     YouTube    500     200
1   Instagram    700     300
2     Twitter    250     150
3    Facebook    400     180

Most Liked Platform: Instagram
Average Shares: 207.5
Most Popular Platform: Instagram
```

Figure Appendix A.9*: Output of social media analysis*

Note: In real-world analytics, engagement is often calculated as a composite metric. For introductory analysis, engagement can be defined as:

Engagement = likes + shares

Example Appendix A.10: Write a program for data analysis on Iris flower dataset

The Iris dataset is one of the most famous datasets used in data science and machine learning. It contains 150 rows (records) and 5 columns (attributes). The four numerical attributes are Sepal Length, Sepal Width, Petal Length, and Petal Width, which are called independent variables (also known as features or predictors). The fifth attribute is species, which represents the type of iris flower and acts as the dependent variable (also called the target class). There are three species in the dataset: **`Iris-setosa`**, **`Iris-versicolor`**, and **`Iris-virginica`**, with 50 samples each. The sample Iris flower dataset, shown in *Table Appendix A.7*, contains attributes such as Sepal Length, Sepal Width, Petal Length, and Petal Width, which are considered independent variables (features or predictors). The species column represents the output class or target class, also known as the dependent variable. In this example, we will analyze the dataset using Pandas to find:

- Count of each species
- Average values (grouping by species)
- Minimum and maximum feature values

Table Appendix A.7 is as follows:

sepal_length	sepal_width	petal_length	petal_width	species
5.1	3.5	1.4	0.2	setosa
7.0	3.2	4.7	1.4	versicolor
6.3	3.3	6.0	2.5	virginica

Table Appendix A.7*: Sample dataset of Iris flower dataset*

In this example, the Iris dataset is first loaded into a DataFrame using the **pd.read_csv()** function. To understand the distribution of the dataset, the **value_counts()** function is applied on the species column, which shows how many samples belong to each species of iris flower. Next, the **groupby()** function is used along with the mean operation to compute the average petal length for each species, helping us compare differences among them. To determine which species has the largest average sepal width, the **idxmax()** function is applied to the grouped data. Finally, the **min()** and **max()** functions are used to display the minimum and maximum values of all numeric features, giving insights into the overall range of the dataset's measurements.

The following example demonstrates how pandas can be used to analyze the well-known *Iris dataset*, a widely used dataset in machine learning and data science education. The dataset contains measurements of Sepal Length, Sepal Width, Petal Length, and Petal Width for three species of iris flowers. This code reads the **iris.csv** file into a DataFrame, displays the first five records, and performs several statistical operations, including counting the occurrences of each species, computing the average Petal Length for each species, identifying the species with the highest average Sepal Width, and determining the minimum and maximum values for each numeric feature. This example illustrates how **pandas** simplifies exploratory data analysis using real-world scientific data:

```
import pandas as pd
#  Load the Iris dataset
df = pd.read_csv("d:\\iris.csv")
print("First 5 Rows of Iris Dataset:\n", df.head())
# Count of each species
print("\nCount of each species:\n", df['species'].value_counts())
#  Average petal length by species
print("\nAverage Petal Length by Species:\n", df.groupby('species')['petal_
length'].mean())
# Species with maximum average sepal width
avg_sepal_width = df.groupby('species')['sepal_width'].mean()
print("\nSpecies with Max Average Sepal Width:", avg_sepal_width.idxmax())
# Minimum and Maximum values of each feature
print("\nMinimum values of each column:\n", df.min(numeric_only=True))
print("\nMaximum values of each column:\n", df.max(numeric_only=True))
```

The output of analyzing the Iris flower dataset is shown in *Figure Appendix A.10*:

```
First 5 Rows of Iris Dataset:
   sepal_length  sepal_width  petal_length  petal_width      species
0           5.1          3.5           1.4          0.2  Iris-setosa
1           4.9          3.0           1.4          0.2  Iris-setosa
2           4.7          3.2           1.3          0.2  Iris-setosa
3           4.6          3.1           1.5          0.2  Iris-setosa
4           5.0          3.6           1.4          0.2  Iris-setosa

Count of each species:
 species
Iris-setosa        50
Iris-versicolor    50
Iris-virginica     50
Name: count, dtype: int64

Average Petal Length by Species:
 species
Iris-setosa        1.464
Iris-versicolor    4.260
Iris-virginica     5.552
Name: petal_length, dtype: float64

Species with Max Average Sepal Width: Iris-setosa

Minimum values of each column:
 sepal_length    4.3
sepal_width     2.0
petal_length    1.0
petal_width     0.1
dtype: float64

Maximum values of each column:
 sepal_length    7.9
sepal_width     4.4
petal_length    6.9
petal_width     2.5
dtype: float64
```

***Figure Appendix A.10**: Analysis of Iris flower dataset using pandas*

Conclusion

In this chapter, we explored a variety of small but meaningful applications of data analysis using Pandas. Through practical examples, students learned how to work with different types of datasets and extract useful insights. We began with analyzing students' performance by calculating averages and identifying top scorers, followed by sales data summarization to understand product and day-wise trends. Employee salary analysis was used to highlight grouping and aggregation, while separate examples demonstrated how Python structures like lists, tuples, and dictionaries can be seamlessly integrated into Pandas DataFrames for further analysis. Additional real-life datasets, such as library books, sports scores, and social media interactions, illustrated how pandas can be applied to find the most borrowed book, the highest-scoring players, or the most popular social media platform based on engagement. Finally, we extended our practice to the well-known Iris dataset, performing statistical analysis to identify averages, ranges, and correlations across species. Together, these applications provided students with a hands-on introduction to Pandas and showed how even simple datasets can yield valuable insights when analyzed systematically. By working through these examples, students not only strengthened their understanding of data manipulation and aggregation in Pandas but also gained confidence in applying Python skills to practical data analysis tasks. This foundation will help them as they move on to more advanced projects and larger datasets in subsequent studies.

Points to remember

The following points are to be kept in mind:

- Data science is a multidisciplinary approach that integrates programming expertise, statistical techniques, and analytical reasoning to investigate data and reveal significant patterns, trends, and findings. It converts raw data into useful information that facilitates decision-making and real-world problem solving.
- Pandas is a powerful Python library for handling and analyzing structured data.
- Data can be loaded from CSV files using pd.read_csv().
- Functions like groupby(), value_counts(), mean(), max(), min(), and idxmax() help in summarizing and comparing data.
- Python data structures such as lists, tuples, and dictionaries can be easily converted into pandas DataFrames for analysis.
- Functions like mean(), max(), and min() help find averages and top/bottom scores.
- Pandas can quickly summarize sales with groupby() and sum().
- mean(), median(), and max() are useful for salary distribution insights.
- A simple Python list can be converted to a DataFrame using pd.DataFrame().
- Tuples (immutable lists) can also be converted into DataFrames.
- Dictionaries map directly into column-based DataFrames (keys to columns). This is one of the most common ways to create a DataFrame manually.

Key terms

- **Pandas**: A Python library for data manipulation and analysis.
- **DataFrame**: A two-dimensional labeled data structure in Pandas, like a table.
- **Series**: A one-dimensional labeled array in pandas.
- **CSV**: A common file format used to store tabular data.

- **pd.read_csv()**: Function used to load data from a CSV file into a DataFrame.
- **Index**: The row labels in a Pandas DataFrame.
- **groupby()**: Function used to group data based on column values for aggregation.
- **value_counts()**: Function that counts unique values in a column.
- **mean()**: Function to compute the average of values in a column.
- **max()/min()**: Functions to find the maximum and minimum values in a column.
- **idxmax()**: Function that returns the index (row) of the maximum value.
- **Features/predictors**: Independent variables used to describe the dataset.
- **Target/classs**: Dependent variable or output to be predicted in a dataset.

Join our Discord space

Join our Discord workspace for latest updates, offers, tech happenings around the world, new releases, and sessions with the authors:

https://discord.bpbonline.com

Appendix B: Simple Projects Using Matplotlib

Introduction

This appendix presents a collection of small applications that demonstrate how to use the Matplotlib library in Python for visualizing data stored in CSV files. Each example is designed to be simple, clear, and practical so that readers can easily follow and apply the concepts. The applications include plotting students' marks using a line chart, visualizing product sales through bar charts, and examining employee salary distribution with histograms. Examples also illustrate how to represent students' interests in different subjects using pie charts, and how to extend this analysis by comparing interests between boys and girls with grouped bar charts.

Additional case studies cover weather data visualization, analysis of shopping categories, attendance tracking of students over several months, and borrowing patterns of library books by category. These examples combine real-world scenarios with effective visual techniques, allowing readers to see how charts and plots can turn raw data into meaningful insights.

By working through these examples, readers will learn how Matplotlib provides versatile and easy-to-use plotting functions to create a variety of visualizations. They will also understand how visual representation helps in interpreting trends, comparing categories, and identifying distributions in datasets.

Example applications using Matplotlib

The following section presents a series of practical, real-world example programs that demonstrate how Matplotlib can be used to visualize datasets across different domains. These examples include plotting students' academic performance using line charts, analyzing product sales with bar charts, examining salary distribution through histograms, and representing students' subject preferences using pie charts and grouped bar charts. Additional applications explore weather trend analysis, visualization of shopping categories, tracking student attendance across months, and analyzing library book borrowing patterns by category. The examples further extend to visualizing training course outcomes, predicting student performance using a decision tree with a confusion matrix, and performing diabetes prediction using the **k-nearest neighbors** (**KNN**) machine learning algorithm. Together, these hands-on exercises illustrate how graphical and analytical techniques transform raw data into meaningful insights and support effective decision-making.

Example Appendix B.1: Write a program for plotting students' marks using a line chart

This program demonstrates how to create a simple line plot using Matplotlib. First, two lists are defined: **students_name**, which contains the names of students, and marks, which holds their corresponding scores. The **plt.plot()** function is then used to draw a line graph with students' names on the x-axis and their marks on the y-axis, while the argument **marker='o'** ensures that each data point is highlighted with a circular marker. The **plt.title()**, **plt.xlabel()**, and **plt.ylabel()** functions are used to add a title to the graph and label the axes appropriately for better readability. Finally, **plt.show()** displays the plot window, allowing us to visually analyze how students performed based on their marks. We will use Matplotlib to create a simple line plot that shows the marks of students. Line plots are useful for visualizing trends or comparisons across different categories, such as student performance.

The following program shows how a simple line chart can be created in Matplotlib by mapping students' names on the x-axis and their corresponding marks on the y-axis:

```
import matplotlib.pyplot as plt
students_name = ["A", "B", "C", "D", "E"]
marks = [78, 85, 69, 90, 74]
plt.plot(students_name, marks, marker='o')
plt.title("Students' Marks")
plt.xlabel("Students Name")
plt.ylabel("Marks")
plt.show()
```

Although the x-axis represents categorical data (student names), a line chart is used here to illustrate the relative progression and comparison of marks across students. The connecting line helps visualize how marks increase or decrease from one student to the next, making it easier to observe overall performance trends. This approach is appropriate when the categories have a meaningful order, such as roll numbers or alphabetical listing, and when the emphasis is on identifying variations rather than isolated values.

The output of plotting students' marks using a line chart is shown in *Figure Appendix B.1*:

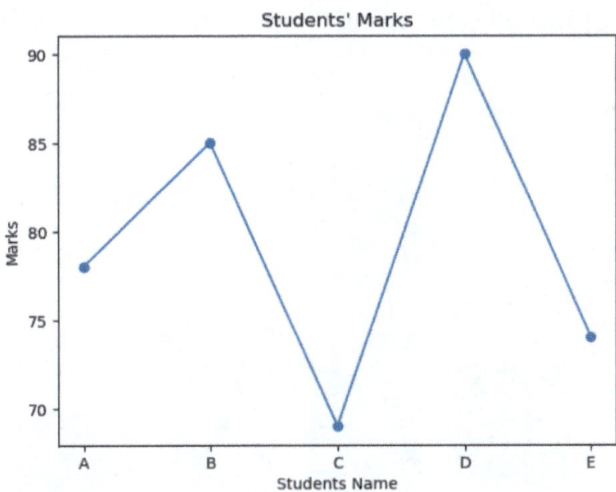

***Figure Appendix B.1**: Output of plotting students' marks using a line chart*

A bar chart is typically preferred for independent categorical comparisons, whereas a line chart is useful when the goal is to highlight changes or trends across an ordered set of categories. In this example, the line chart emphasizes performance variation across students. If individual comparison is the primary objective, a bar chart can also be used.

```
# Alternative visualization
plt.bar(students_name, marks)
```

Example Appendix B.2: Write a program for visualizing product sales using a bar chart

This program illustrates how to create a bar chart using Matplotlib to analyze product sales data. A list named **`products`** is defined to represent different product categories, while another list named **`sales`** contains the corresponding number of units sold for each product. The **`plt.bar()`** function is used to generate the bar chart, where the x-axis shows the product names and the y-axis displays the sales figures. The bars are colored light blue for better visualization. Additionally, **`plt.title()`**, **`plt.xlabel()`**, and **`plt.ylabel()`** are used to add a descriptive title and axis labels, making the chart easy to interpret. Finally, **`plt.show()`** is called to display the chart, allowing us to clearly compare sales performance across different products. The following program visualizes product sales using a bar chart:

```
import matplotlib.pyplot as plt
products = ["Laptop", "Mobile", "Tablet", "Headphones"]
sales = [120, 300, 150, 90]
plt.bar(products, sales, color="skyblue")
plt.title("Product Sales")
plt.xlabel("Products")
plt.ylabel("Units Sold")
plt.show()
```

The output of visualizing product sales using a bar chart is shown in *Figure Appendix B.2*:

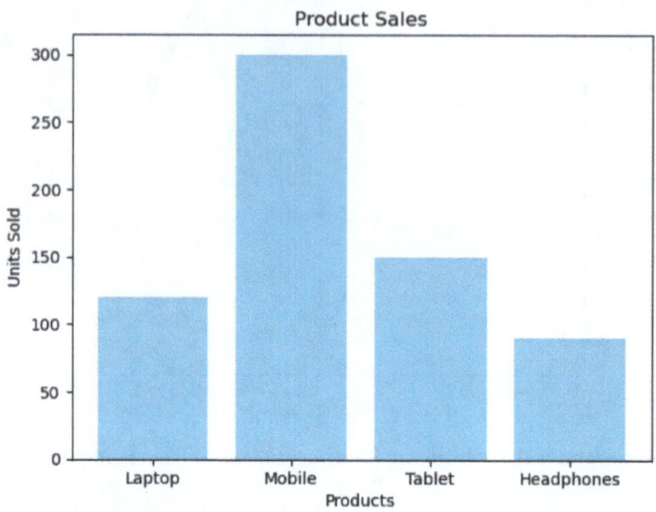

***Figure Appendix B.2**: Output of visualizing product sales using a bar chart*

Example Appendix B.3: Write a program for the distribution of employee salaries using a histogram

This program demonstrates how to create a histogram using Matplotlib to visualize the distribution of employee salaries. A list named **`salaries`** contains the salary values of different employees. The **`plt.hist()`** function is used to plot the histogram, where the data is divided into five intervals (bins) as specified by the parameter **`bins=5`**. The bars are filled with orange color, and black edges are added to make them more distinct. The x-axis represents salary ranges, while the y-axis shows the frequency, i.e., how many employees fall into each salary range. To make the chart more descriptive, **`plt.title()`**, **`plt.xlabel()`**, and **`plt.ylabel()`** are used to add a title and axis labels. Finally, **`plt.show()`** displays the histogram, allowing us to quickly analyze how salaries are distributed among employees. This program plots a histogram that shows how employee salaries are distributed across different ranges:

```
import matplotlib.pyplot as plt
salaries = [25000, 30000, 28000, 35000, 40000, 37000, 32000, 29000]
plt.hist(salaries, bins=5, color="orange", edgecolor="black")
plt.title("Employee Salary Distribution")
plt.xlabel("Salary")
plt.ylabel("Frequency")
plt.show()
```

In this example, the number of bins is set to five to provide a balanced visualization of the salary distribution for a small dataset. Using fewer bins may oversimplify the distribution, while too many bins could result in sparsely populated intervals that obscure overall patterns.

The chosen bin size enables clear observation of salary grouping and frequency without introducing unnecessary complexity. For larger datasets, bin selection can be optimized using data-driven methods; however, a fixed bin value is appropriate here for instructional clarity.

The output of the distribution of employees' salaries using a histogram is shown in *Figure Appendix B.3*:

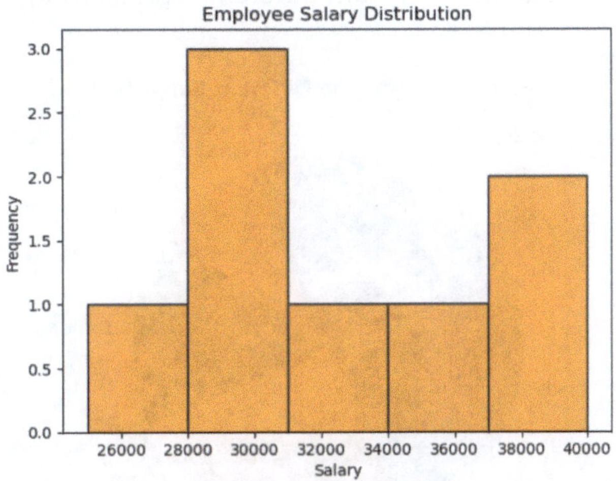

***Figure Appendix B.3**: Output of employees' salary distribution*

Example Appendix B.4: Write a program for visualizing students' interest in different subjects using a pie chart

This program uses a pie chart to show the distribution of students' interests across different subjects. The list **`subjects`** contains the names of the subjects, while the list **`students`** indicates the number of students who like each subject. The **`plt.pie()`** function creates the pie chart, where labels specify the categories and **`autopct="%1.1f%%"`** displays the percentage of students for each subject on the chart. The **`startangle=140`** rotates the chart slightly to make it look balanced. Finally, a title is added with **`plt.title()`**, and the chart is displayed using **`plt.show()`**. This visualization helps us quickly identify which subject is the most or least popular among students:

```
import matplotlib.pyplot as plt
subjects = ["Math", "Science", "English", "History", "Computer Science"]
students = [35, 30, 20, 10, 25]
plt.pie(students, labels=subjects, autopct="%1.1f%%", startangle=140)
plt.title("Students' Interest in Different Subjects")
plt.show()
```

This pie chart clearly shows the proportion of students interested in different subjects. Each slice of the chart represents a subject, and its size indicates how many students prefer that subject compared to the total. This makes it easy to visualize which subjects are most popular and how students' interests are distributed. However, pie charts have known limitations. They are less effective when comparing many categories or when values are close in magnitude, as visual comparison of angles can be difficult. In such cases, alternative visualizations such as bar charts provide clearer comparisons.

The output of visualizing students' interest in different subjects using a pie chart is shown in *Figure Appendix B.4*:

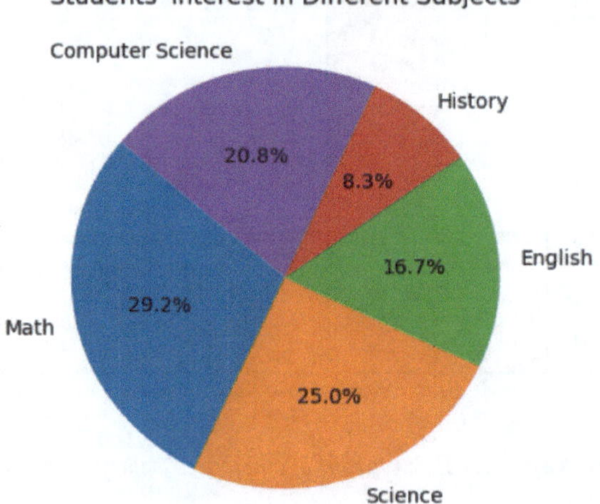

***Figure Appendix B.4**: Output using a pie chart*

Note: Pie charts should be used cautiously and primarily for:

- **Displaying parts of a whole**
- **Datasets with few categories**
- **Situations where approximate comparison is sufficient**

Example Appendix B.5: Write a program for finding students' interest in subjects by gender using a grouped bar chart

This program uses a grouped bar chart to compare boys' and girls' interests in different subjects. The subjects list stores the subject names, while the boys and girls lists record the number of boys and girls who prefer each subject. Using NumPy's **`arange()`**, positions for each subject are created. Then, two bars are plotted side by side for each subject: blue for boys and pink for girls. The **`plt.xticks()`** function ensures that subject names appear correctly under the bars. A legend is added to distinguish between boys and girls, and a title is displayed to describe the chart. To visualize how boys and girls differ in their subject preferences, the following program uses a grouped bar chart where each subject displays two bars representing the number of interested students.

```
import matplotlib.pyplot as plt
import numpy as np
subjects = ["Math", "Science", "English", "History", "Computer Science"]
# Number of boys and girls interested in each subject
boys = [20, 15, 10, 5, 12]
girls = [15, 15, 10, 5, 13]
x = np.arange(len(subjects))  # positions for subjects
width = 0.35  # width of each bar
# Plotting bars for boys and girls
plt.bar(x - width/2, boys, width, label="Boys", color="skyblue")
plt.bar(x + width/2, girls, width, label="Girls", color="lightpink")
# Adding labels and title
plt.title("Students' Interest in Subjects by Gender")
plt.xlabel("Subjects")
plt.ylabel("Number of Students")
plt.xticks(x, subjects)
plt.legend()
# Show chart
plt.show()
```

In a statement **`x = np.arange(len(subjects))`**, **`subjects`** is the list of subject names (like Math, Science, English, etc.), and **`len(subjects)`** gives the total number of subjects. **`np.arange(len(subjects))`** creates an array of positions [0, 1, 2, …] for plotting bars.

So, if there are four subjects, **`x`** will be **`[0, 1, 2, 3]`**. These numbers are the positions on the x-axis.

`width = 0.35` sets how thick each bar should be. A smaller value makes bars thinner, while a larger value makes them wider. **`plt.bar(x - width/2, boys, width, label="Boys", color="skyblue")`**. **`x - width/2`** shifts the boys' bars a little to the left of each position, boys is the list of values (number of boys interested in each subject), width makes sure the bars are not too wide, label and color add a legend name and set the color of the bars.

In a statement, **`plt.bar(x + width/2, girls, width, label="Girls", color="lightpink")`**, **`x + width/2`** shifts the girls' bars a little to the right of each position. This way, boys' and girls' bars appear side by side for easy comparison.

Note: **`x` creates positions, width controls thickness, and shifting with ± `width/2` places boys' and girls' bars neatly side by side for each subject.**

The visualization shown in *Figure Appendix B.5* makes it easy to compare how subject preferences vary between genders:

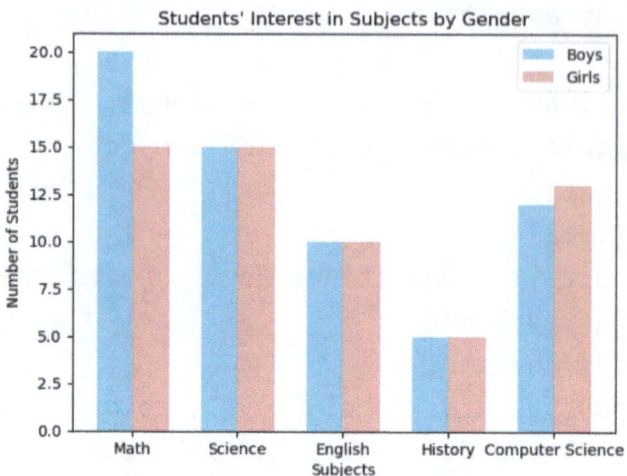

Figure Appendix B.5: Visualizing how subject preferences vary between genders

Example Appendix B.6: Write a program for weather data analysis using visualization

In this program, we created a dataset representing the weather conditions for one week, where the list **`days`** contains the names of the days, **`temperature`** stores the temperature values in Celsius, and **`rainfall`** holds the amount of rainfall in millimeters. Using Matplotlib, the temperature values are plotted as a red line chart with circular markers to highlight daily changes, while rainfall is displayed as a light blue bar chart to show how much rain was received each day. The **`plt.title()`**, **`plt.xlabel()`**, and **`plt.ylabel()`** functions are used to add a descriptive title and axis labels, and the **`plt.legend()`** function distinguishes between temperature and rainfall on the same plot. This visualization makes it easier to observe patterns, such as the gradual drop in temperature over the week and higher rainfall occurring toward the weekend.

Let us now create a simple project where we analyze weather data for a week by visualizing both temperature and rainfall using Matplotlib:

```
import matplotlib.pyplot as plt
# Sample dataset
days = ["Mon", "Tue", "Wed", "Thu", "Fri", "Sat", "Sun"]
temp = [29, 31, 32, 27, 29, 26, 25]  # in Celsius
rainfall = [6, 12, 1, 5, 19, 21, 11]       # in mm
# Plotting temperature as a line chart
plt.plot(days, temp, marker="o", color="red", label="Temperature (°C)")
# Plotting rainfall as a bar chart
plt.bar(days, rainfall, color="skyblue", alpha=0.6, label="Rainfall (mm)")
# Adding title and labels
plt.title("Weather Data Analysis (Temperature & Rainfall)")
plt.xlabel("Days of the Week")
```

```
plt.ylabel("Values")
plt.legend()
plt.show()
```

The output of visualizing the weather data for a week is shown in *Figure Appendix B.6*:

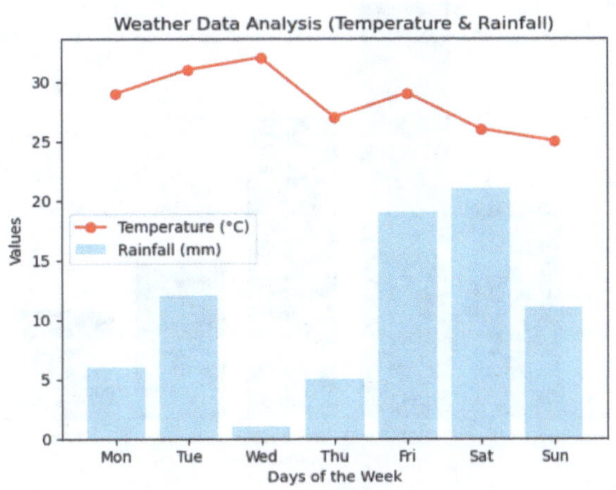

***Figure Appendix B.6**: Visualizing weather data for a week*

Example Appendix B.7: Write a program for visualizing and analyzing shopping categories

The program starts by creating two lists: one containing different shopping categories, such as **`Electronics`**, **`Clothing`**, **`Groceries`**, **`Books`**, and **`Toys`**, and another containing the number of purchases for each category. Using the **`matplotlib.pyplot`** library, a bar chart is drawn with **`plt.bar()`**, where the categories are shown on the x-axis and the purchase counts on the y-axis. The chart is customized with a title, and axis labels to make it more understandable. From the visualization, we can quickly see which shopping category is the most popular among customers, making it easier to analyze buying patterns. This program illustrates the use of a bar chart in Matplotlib to display the distribution of purchases among five major product categories:

```
import matplotlib.pyplot as plt
# Categories and their purchase counts
products = ["Electronics", "Clothing", "Groceries", "Books", "Toys"]
purchases = [130, 250, 180, 95, 65]
# Plotting the bar chart
plt.bar(products, purchases, color="teal")
plt.title("Online Shopping Categories")
plt.xlabel("Categories")
plt.ylabel("Number of Purchases")
plt.show()
```

The program uses a bar chart shown in *Figure Appendix B.7* to display the number of purchases made in different shopping categories. This visualization helps us easily compare customer preferences across categories and identify which types of products are most popular:

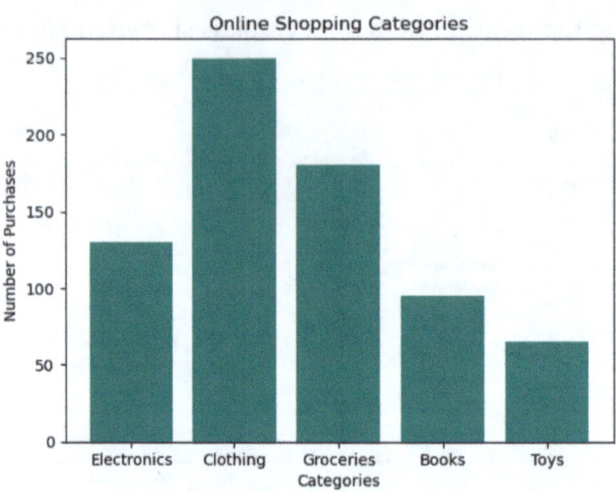

Figure Appendix B.7: Visualizing online shopping categories

Example Appendix B.8: Write a program for students' attendance tracking and visualization

This example uses an attendance dataset stored in a CSV file, which records the number of days attended by four students across six consecutive months. The file contains rows for each student and columns representing monthly attendance values from January to June. This CSV dataset provides a basis for visualizing attendance trends and comparing individual student participation over time:

Filename: `attendance.csv`:

```
Student,Jan,Feb,Mar,Apr,May,Jun
A,20,18,22,19,21,20
B,18,20,19,21,20,18
C,22,21,20,18,19,21
D,19,17,21,20,22,19
```

This program is designed to track and visualize students' monthly attendance using Python, Pandas, and Matplotlib. First, a dataset is created that stores each student's attendance from January to June. A line chart is then generated where each student's attendance trend is plotted across the months, making it easy to compare patterns such as consistency or sudden drops. The code uses a loop to plot each student's attendance values across the months, labeling them separately for clarity. After this, a new column is added to calculate the total attendance of each student, and a histogram is plotted to show the overall distribution of attendance totals among all students. This way, the program not only highlights individual performance trends but also provides an overall picture of attendance behavior in the group.

In a statement **`for student in df['Student']:`** goes through each student in the dataset one by one. The **`df.columns[1:]`** command selects only the month columns from January to June, which are used as the **`x-axis`** values. For each student, **`df.loc[df['Student'] == student]`** extracts the row of attendance data that belongs to them. The statement **`.values[0][1:]`** then converts that row into a list and removes the student's name, leaving only the attendance numbers to be used as the y-axis values. Finally, **`plt.plot(..., label=student)`** plots a line graph where the x-axis represents the months, the y-axis shows the attendance counts, and the label ensures that each student's line is clearly identified in the legend. This allows the program to display the attendance trends of all students together in one chart for easy comparison. The code for visualizing and tracking students' monthly attendance is shown as follows:

```
import pandas as pd
import matplotlib.pyplot as plt

# Load CSV file
df = pd.read_csv("attendance.csv")
print("Attendance Data:\n", df)

# Loops through each student's name in the "Student" column(A,B,C,D) in a dataset
# Line chart for attendance trend of each student
# df.columns gives all column names i.e.["Student","Jan","Feb","Mar","Apr",
#"May","Jun"]
# df.columns[1:] skips the "Student" column, keeping only months i.e. ["Jan",
#"Feb","Mar","Apr","May","Jun"]. This will be the x-axis (months).
# .values[0] converts that row into a list/array (like
# ["A",20,18,22,19,21,20]).
# [1:] removes the first element ("A") and keeps only the numbers [20, 18, 22, 19,
# 21, 20]. This is the y-axis (attendance values).
# plt.plot(..., label=student).It plots the line for that student with the months
# on the x-axis and attendance values on the y-axis.

for student in df['Student']:
    plt.plot(df.columns[1:], df.loc[df['Student'] == student].values[0][1:],
label=student)
plt.title("Monthly Attendance Trend")
plt.xlabel("Month")
plt.ylabel("Attendance Days")
plt.legend()
plt.show()
```

The output of students' monthly attendance tracking is shown in *Figure Appendix B.8*:

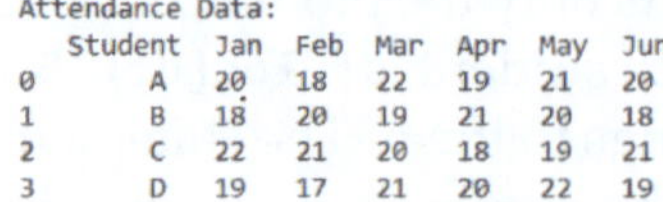

Attendance Data:

	Student	Jan	Feb	Mar	Apr	May	Jun
0	A	20	18	22	19	21	20
1	B	18	20	19	21	20	18
2	C	22	21	20	18	19	21
3	D	19	17	21	20	22	19

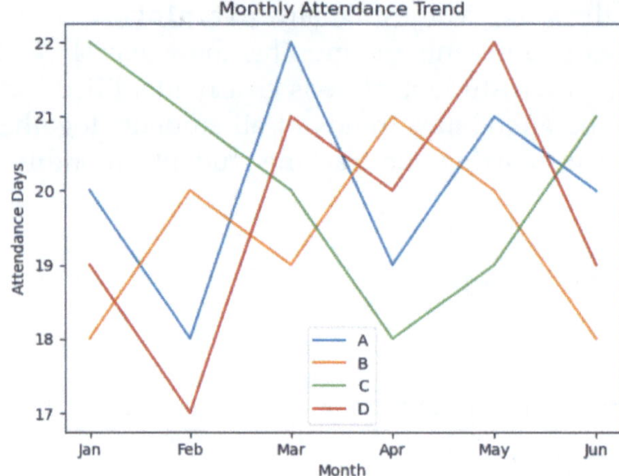

***Figure Appendix B.8**: Students' monthly attendance tracking*

Example Appendix B.9: Write a program to analyze library book borrowing data

This program performs a simple data analysis of library book borrowing using a CSV file. We will assume a dataset of borrowed books by category in the form of a CSV file, as shown:

Filename: **`library_books.csv`**:

```
Category,Books_Borrowed
Science,180
Literature,250
Technology,190
History,90
Arts,110
```

First, the dataset is loaded with **`pandas`** from a file named **`library_books.csv`**, which contains two columns: **`Category`** (such as **`Science`**, **`Literature`**, **`Technology`**, etc.) and **`Borrowed`** (the number of books borrowed in each category). The program extracts these two columns and uses them for visualization. A **bar chart** is then created with book categories on the x-axis and the number of books borrowed on the y-axis, making it easy to compare borrowing patterns across different categories. After that, a **pie chart** is generated using the same data to show the percentage distribution of borrowed books among categories, where each slice represents a category and its proportion of the total borrowing. This combination of bar and pie charts provides both numerical comparison and percentage-based insights, making the analysis visually clear and easy to interpret.

The code for analyzing library book borrowing data is as follows:

```
import pandas as pd
import matplotlib.pyplot as plt
# Load dataset from CSV file
df = pd.read_csv("d:\\library_books.csv")
# Extract data
categories = df["Category"]
books_borrowed = df["Books_Borrowed"]
# --- Bar Chart ---
plt.bar(categories, books_borrowed, color="skyblue")
plt.title("Books Borrowed by Category")
plt.xlabel("Book Categories")
plt.ylabel("Number of Books Borrowed")
plt.show()
# --- Pie Chart ---
plt.pie(
    books_borrowed,
    labels=categories,
    autopct="%1.1f%%",
    startangle=140,
    colors=["lightgreen", "lightblue", "orange", "pink", "violet"]
)
plt.title("Percentage Distribution of Borrowed Books")
plt.show()
```

The output of analyzing library books borrowing data in the form of bar and pie charts is shown in *Figure Appendix B.9* and *Figure Appendix B.10*:

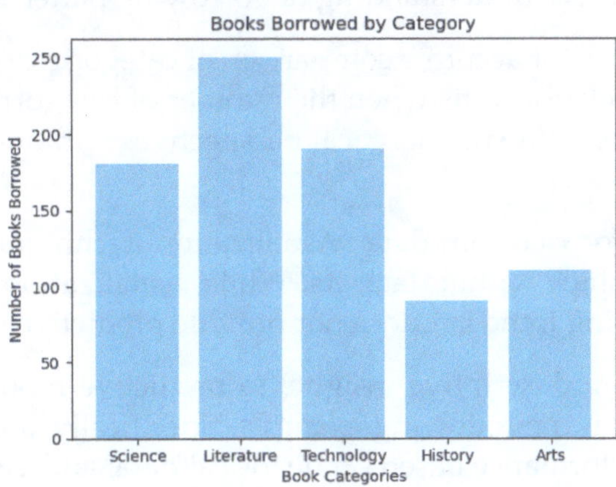

***Figure Appendix B.9**: Output of analyzing library books borrowing data using a bar plot*

The output in the form of a pie chart is shown in the following figure:

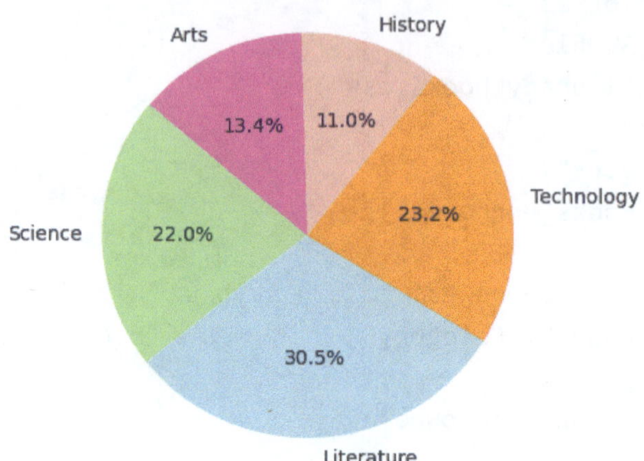

***Figure Appendix B.10**: Output of analyzing library books borrowing data using a pie plot*

Two different visualizations are used in this example to highlight complementary aspects of the same library dataset.

The **bar chart** is employed to compare the absolute number of books borrowed across different book categories. Bar charts are well-suited for categorical data where precise comparison of quantities is required, making it easy to identify categories with higher or lower borrowing counts.

The **pie chart**, on the other hand, is used to represent the relative proportion of borrowed books contributed by each category. By expressing values as percentages of the total, the pie chart provides an intuitive overview of how borrowing is distributed across categories. Together, these charts offer both an exact comparison (bar chart) and proportional insight (pie chart), enabling a more comprehensive understanding of borrowing patterns in the library dataset.

While bar charts are preferred for accurate comparison of categories, pie charts are effective for illustrating part-to-whole relationships when the number of categories is limited. Using both visualizations helps address different analytical perspectives without altering the underlying data.

The previous examples focused on data visualization techniques to explore patterns, distributions, and relationships within datasets. While visualization helps in understanding historical data and identifying trends, it does not provide predictive capability.

To extend this analysis from descriptive insights to predictive modeling, machine learning techniques are introduced in the following example. Specifically, a decision tree classifier is used to predict student performance based on historical data, and visualization tools such as plots and a confusion matrix are employed to evaluate the model's performance.

Example Appendix B.10: Write a program for analyzing training course data using Matplotlib

This program analyzes a training course dataset (**`courses_details.csv`**) containing details such as attendance, dropouts, trained candidates, certifications, total students, and average age. A bar chart is first used to compare the total number of students enrolled in each course. A stacked bar chart then shows the attendance distribution by gender. Dropouts for both males and females are compared using a line chart. Certification outcomes are visualized through a grouped bar chart, while the average age distribution is represented using a bar chart. Finally, a pie chart displays the overall percentage of male and female participants who achieved certification. These visualizations together provide a holistic view of training participation, dropout trends, certifications, and demographic patterns.

We will assume a dataset of training courses in the form of a CSV file, shown as follows:

Filename: **`courses_details.csv`**:

```
CourseName,Females_Attended,Males_Attended,Females_Dropped,Males_Dropped,Females_Trained,Males_Trained,Females_Certified,Males_Certified,Total_Students,Average_Age
Data Science,45,55,5,8,40,47,35,42,100,23
Web Development,60,70,6,12,54,58,50,55,130,22
AI & ML,30,40,4,5,26,35,22,30,70,24
Cyber Security,25,45,2,6,23,39,20,34,70,25
Cloud Computing,35,50,3,7,32,43,28,38,85,26
```

For better understanding, this is displayed in *Table Appendix B.1*:

CourseName	Females_Attended	Males_Attended	Females_Dropped	Males_Dropped	Females_Trained	Males_Trained	Females_Certified	Males_Certified	Total_Students	Average_Age
Data Science	45	55	5	8	40	47	35	42	100	23
Web Development	60	70	6	12	54	58	50	55	130	22
AI & ML	30	40	4	5	26	35	22	30	70	24
Cyber Security	25	45	2	6	23	39	20	34	70	25
Cloud Computing	35	50	3	7	32	43	28	38	85	26

***Table Appendix B.1**: Sample dataset of training course data*

The practical case study, with the help of a code, demonstrates how visualization helps in understanding educational and training program outcomes in a clear and meaningful way:

```
import pandas as pd
import matplotlib.pyplot as plt
# Load dataset
df = pd.read_csv("d:\\courses_details.csv")
print("Training Course Data:\n", df)
# ----Bar chart: Total students in each course ---
plt.figure(figsize=(8,5))
plt.bar(df["CourseName"], df["Total_Students"], color="skyblue")
plt.title("Total Students Enrolled per Course")
plt.xlabel("Course")
plt.ylabel("Total Students")
plt.show()
# ---Stacked bar chart: Attendance by gender ---
plt.figure(figsize=(8,5))
plt.bar(df["CourseName"], df["Males_Attended"], label="Males",
color="lightblue")
plt.bar(df["CourseName"], df["Females_Attended"], bottom=df["Males_Attended"],
label="Females", color="lightpink")
plt.title("Attendance by Gender")
plt.xlabel("Course")
plt.ylabel("Number of Attendees")
plt.legend()
plt.show()
# --- Line chart: Dropouts by gender ---
plt.figure(figsize=(8,5))
plt.plot(df["CourseName"], df["Males_Dropped"], marker='o', label="Males
Dropped", color="blue")
plt.plot(df["CourseName"], df["Females_Dropped"], marker='o', label="Females
Dropped", color="red")
plt.title("Dropouts by Gender")
plt.xlabel("Course")
plt.ylabel("Number of Dropouts")
plt.legend()
plt.show()
# --- Grouped bar chart: Certifications by gender ---
plt.figure(figsize=(8,5))
width = 0.35
indices = range(len(df))
plt.bar([i - width/2 for i in indices], df["Males_Certified"], width=width,
```

```
label="Males Certified", color="navy")
plt.bar([i + width/2 for i in indices], df["Females_Certified"], width=width,
label="Females Certified", color="purple")
plt.xticks(indices, df["CourseName"])
plt.title("Certified Candidates by Gender")
plt.xlabel("Course")
plt.ylabel("Number Certified")
plt.legend()
plt.show()
# --- Bar Plot: Average Age of Participants by Course ---
plt.figure(figsize=(8,5))
plt.bar(df["CourseName"], df["Average_Age"], color="orange",
edgecolor="black")
plt.title("Average Age of Participants by Course")
plt.xlabel("Course Name")
plt.ylabel("Average Age")
plt.show()
# --- Pie chart: Total certifications by gender ---
plt.figure(figsize=(6,6))
certifications = [df["Males_Certified"].sum(), df["Females_Certified"].sum()]
labels = ["Males Certified", "Females Certified"]
colors = ["skyblue", "lightcoral"]
plt.pie(certifications, labels=labels, autopct="%1.1f%%", colors=colors,
startangle=140)
plt.title("Percentage of Certifications by Gender")
plt.show()
```

The output of the visualization of course participation and certification data is shown in *Figures Appendix B.11* to *Appendix B.16*:

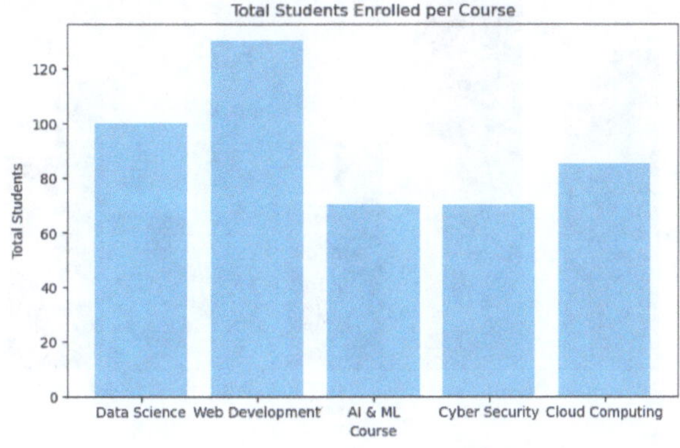

***Figure Appendix B.11**: Visualizing total students in each course*

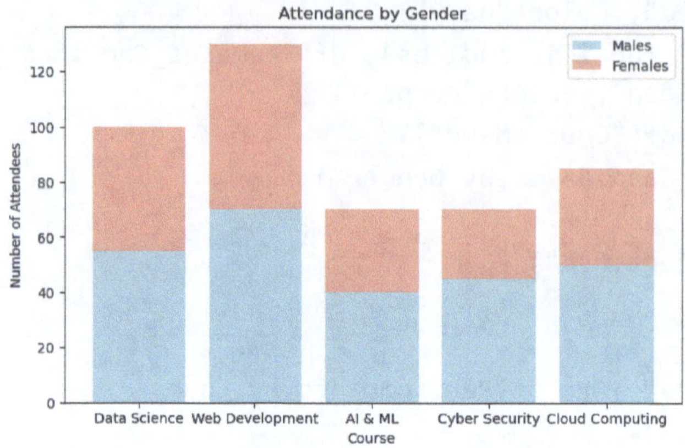

***Figure Appendix B.12**: Attendance by gender using a stacked bar chart*

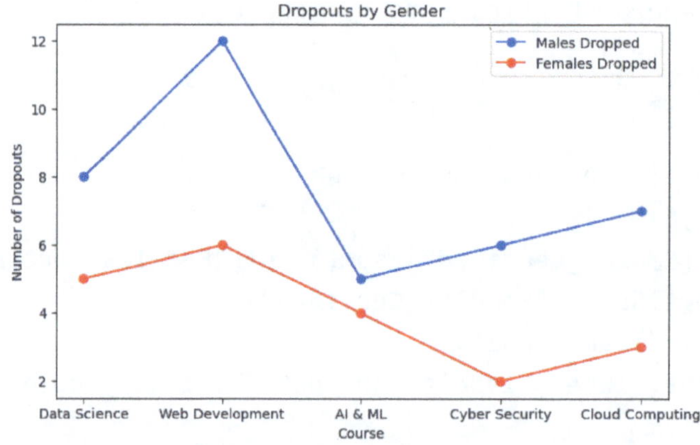

***Figure Appendix B.13**: Displaying dropouts by gender using a line chart*

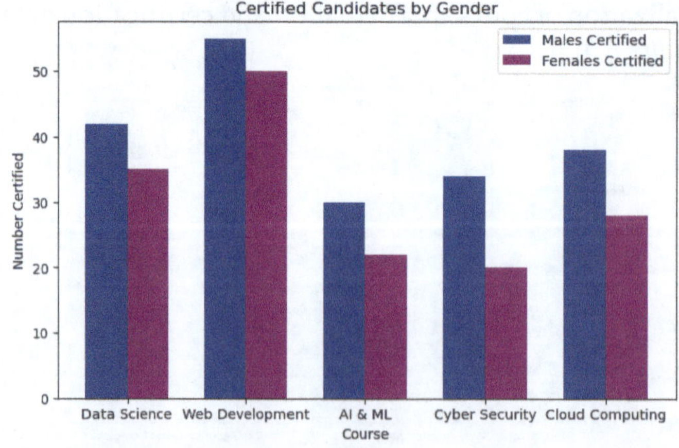

***Figure Appendix B.14**: Displaying certifications by gender using a grouped bar chart*

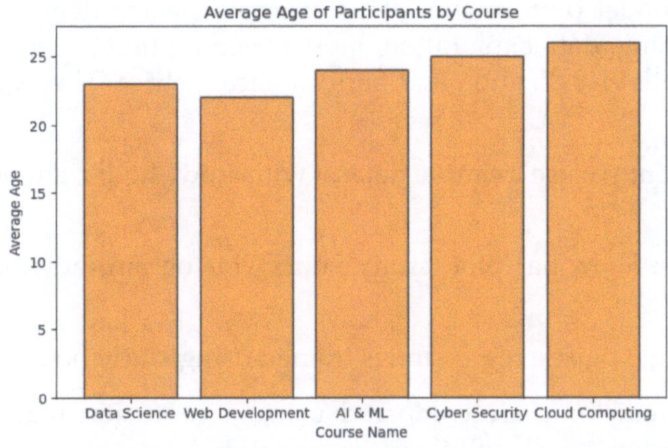

***Figure Appendix B.15**: Average age of participants by course using bar plot*

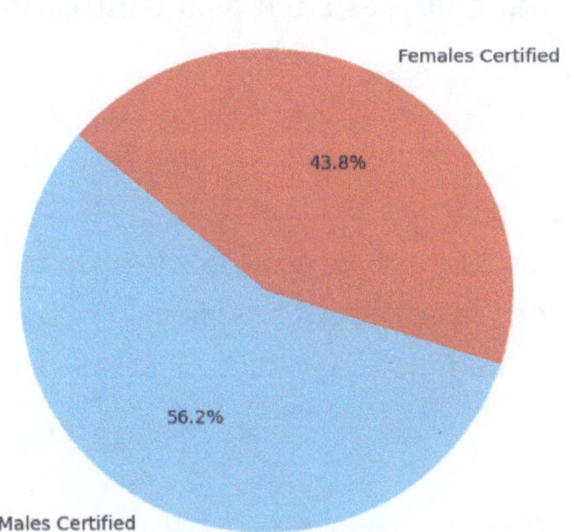

***Figure Appendix B.16**: Total certifications by gender using a pie chart*

Example Appendix B.11: Write a program for student performance prediction with visualization and a confusion matrix using a decision tree

This program demonstrates a simple application of machine learning using a small student performance dataset. The dataset includes study hours, attendance percentage, and the outcome (pass or fail). To begin, visualizations are used to explore the data: a bar chart shows the study hours of each student, a histogram illustrates the distribution of attendance, and a pie chart highlights the ratio of students who passed versus failed. Next, a decision tree classifier is created and trained using the **`fit()`** function, where study hours and attendance are the input features and pass/fail is the target. After training, the **`predict()`** function is applied to test data to generate predictions of student results. These predictions are compared with the actual outcomes using a confusion matrix, which summarizes correct and incorrect classifications. Finally, evaluation metrics such as accuracy, precision, recall, and F1-score are calculated to assess model performance. This example clearly demonstrates the complete cycle of machine learning: data exploration, model training (**fit()**), testing (**predict()**), and evaluation through both visualization and performance metrics. The explanation flow of the program is as follows:

- **Dataset creation**: We use a simple dataset with study hours, attendance, and pass/fail labels.
- **Visualizations**: Show bar plot (study hours), histogram (attendance), and pie chart (pass/fail).
- **Model training**: Logistic regression is trained using study hours and attendance.
- **Evaluation**: Predictions are compared using a confusion matrix, and metrics like accuracy, precision, recall, and F1-score are printed.

This example illustrates the application of a decision tree machine learning model for predicting whether a student will pass or fail, using hours studied and attendance as predictive features. The program also includes visual analyses such as a confusion matrix and additional charts for deeper insight:

```
# Import Libraries
import pandas as pd
import matplotlib.pyplot as plt
from sklearn.model_selection import train_test_split
from sklearn.tree import DecisionTreeClassifier
from sklearn.metrics import confusion_matrix, classification_report,
ConfusionMatrixDisplay

# Create dataset
data = {
    "Hours_Studied": [2,4,5,6,8,9,1,7,3,10,6,2],
    "Attendance":    [20,40,45,70,80,85,15,75,30,95,70,40],
    "Passed":        [0,0,1,1,1,1,0,1,0,1,0,1]   # 1 = Passed, 0 = Failed
}
df = pd.DataFrame(data)
# Split features and labels
X = df[["Hours_Studied", "Attendance"]]  # features
y = df["Passed"]                         # target variable

# Split into training (70%) and testing (30%)
X_train, X_test, y_train, y_test = train_test_split(X, y, test_size=0.3,
random_state=42)
```

```
# Train Decision Tree Model
model = DecisionTreeClassifier(random_state=42)
model.fit(X_train, y_train)  # training
# Predict on test data
y_pred = model.predict(X_test)
# Confusion Matrix and Metrics
conf_matrix = confusion_matrix(y_test, y_pred, labels=[0, 1])
disp = ConfusionMatrixDisplay(confusion_matrix=conf_matrix, display_
labels=["Fail", "Pass"])
disp.plot(cmap="Blues")
plt.title("Confusion Matrix")
plt.show()
print("Classification Report:")
print(classification_report(y_test, y_pred, target_names=["Fail", "Pass"]))
#  Visualizations
# Bar chart - Hours studied vs. Attendance
plt.figure(figsize=(8,5))
plt.bar(df["Hours_Studied"], df["Attendance"], color="skyblue",
edgecolor="black")
plt.title("Hours Studied vs Attendance")
plt.xlabel("Hours Studied")
plt.ylabel("Attendance (%)")
plt.show()
# Pie chart - Distribution of Passed vs Failed
pass_counts = df["Passed"].value_counts()
plt.pie(pass_counts, labels=["Failed", "Passed"], autopct="%1.1f%%",
        colors=["red", "green"], startangle=140)
plt.title("Overall Student Results")
plt.show()
# Histogram - Hours Studied
plt.hist(df["Hours_Studied"], bins=5, color="orange", edgecolor="black")
plt.title("Distribution of Hours Studied")
plt.xlabel("Hours Studied")
plt.ylabel("Frequency")
plt.show()
```

The confusion matrix and classification report summarize how well the decision tree model predicted students' pass or fail outcomes. The confusion matrix shows that out of three students who actually failed, the model correctly identified 1 student as fail (True Negative) but incorrectly predicted two students as pass (False Positives). Similarly, out of 1 student who actually passed, the model correctly predicted the result as pass (True Positive) with no false negatives. From the classification report, we can see that the precision for fail is 1.00, meaning whenever the model predicted a student would fail, it was always correct. However, its recall for fail is only 0.33, showing that it missed many actual failures. For pass, the recall is perfect (1.00), but the precision drops to 0.33 because some failures were wrongly predicted as passes. Overall, the accuracy of the model is 50%, meaning it correctly classified half of the students in the test set. These results highlight that while the model can identify passes well, it struggles with consistently detecting failures.

The output of student performance prediction with visualization and confusion matrix using a decision tree machine learning model is shown in *Figures Appendix B.17* to *Appendix B.20*:

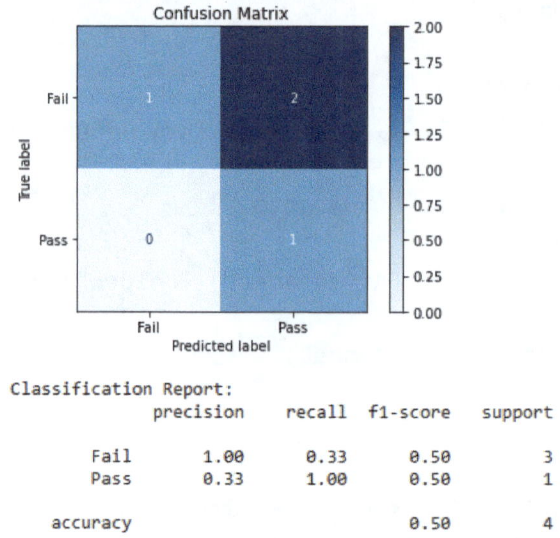

Classification Report:

	precision	recall	f1-score	support
Fail	1.00	0.33	0.50	3
Pass	0.33	1.00	0.50	1
accuracy			0.50	4

***Figure Appendix B.17**: Confusion matrix and classification report*

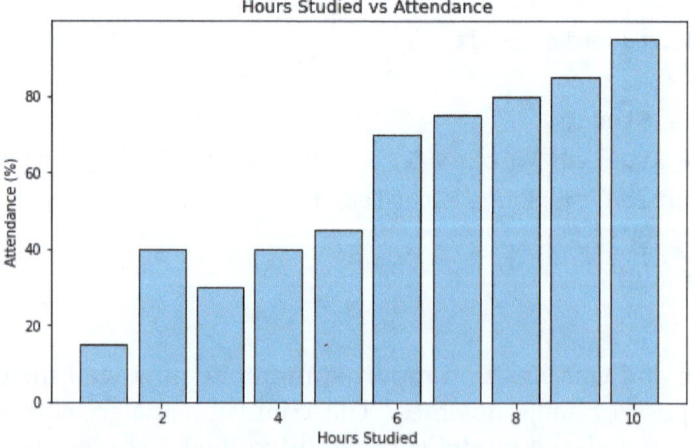

***Figure Appendix B.18**: Bar chart of hours studied and attendance*

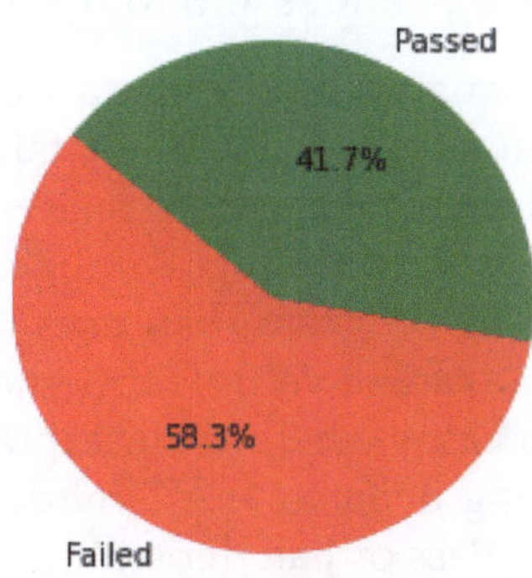

***Figure Appendix B.19**: Pie chart of overall students result*

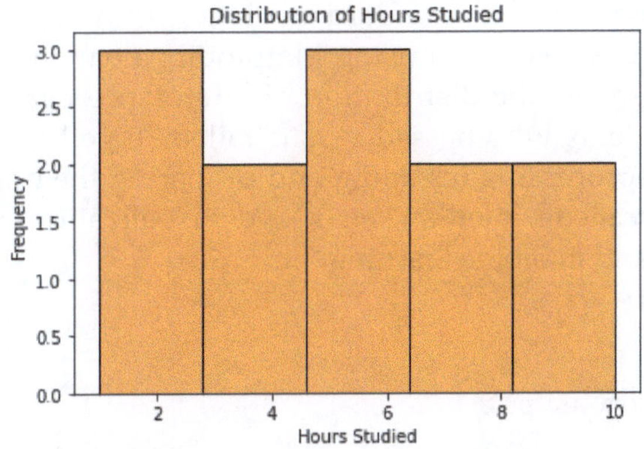

***Figure Appendix B.20**: Histogram of distribution of hours studied*

The previous examples primarily used Matplotlib for basic plotting and customization. While Matplotlib offers fine-grained control over visual elements, it often requires more code to produce statistically informative and aesthetically refined visualizations.

Seaborn is introduced as a higher-level visualization library built on top of Matplotlib, designed specifically for statistical data visualization. It simplifies the creation of complex plots such as distributions, correlations, and categorical comparisons, which are commonly required in real-world data analysis. Seaborn complements Matplotlib by providing built-in support for statistical relationships and cleaner default styles, making it suitable for exploratory data analysis after basic visualization concepts are established.

Note: In practical data science workflows, data cleaning, basic statistical analysis, and visualization are not isolated steps but are performed together in an iterative manner. The example intentionally combines these operations to reflect real-world usage, where raw data must first be cleaned, summarized statistically, and then visualized to extract meaningful insights. This integrated approach helps learners understand how Seaborn fits naturally into an end-to-end data analysis pipeline rather than being used only for standalone plotting.

Example Appendix B.12: Write a program for student exam data analysis with data preprocessing and visualization using Pandas and Matplotlib libraries

This program demonstrates how to analyze and clean a student exam dataset using Pandas and then explore it with visualizations. The dataset contains details such as each student's name, study hours, attendance, and exam score. Since real-world datasets often have errors or missing values, the first step is data preprocessing. Duplicate rows are removed using **drop_duplicates()** to avoid repetition. The program then uses **fillna()** to replace missing study hours or attendance with the mean (average value) or median (middle value) so that missing data does not affect the analysis. In cases where critical information, such as exam scores, is missing, those rows are deleted using **dropna()**. A lambda function is also used to quickly create a rule for marking students as Pass or Fail depending on their exam score (for example, greater than or equal to 60 is a pass). After cleaning, summary statistics are displayed with the **describe()** function, which shows important information like mean (average), median (middle), minimum, maximum, and standard deviation (how spread out the values are). Finally, the cleaned dataset is visualized using Matplotlib: a bar chart compares study hours of students, a histogram shows the distribution of attendance percentages, and a pie chart illustrates the ratio of students who passed versus failed. Together, this example covers the entire pipeline of data preprocessing (cleaning and preparing the data), descriptive statistics (understanding data with mean, median, etc.), and visualization, which are fundamental concepts in data analysis and machine learning:

```
# Import libraries
import pandas as pd
import matplotlib.pyplot as plt
import seaborn as sns
# Create a small dataset with missing values and duplicates
data = {
    "Name": ["Amit", "Riya", "Karan", "Meena", "Sahil", "Pooja", "Arjun",
"Nisha", "Riya"],
    "StudyHours": [8, 6, None, 4, 3, 5, 9, 2, 6],
    "Attendance": [90, 85, 88, None, 60, 75, 95, 55, 85],
    "Marks": [92, 80, 85, 65, None, 70, 96, 45, 80]
}
df = pd.DataFrame(data)
print("Original DataFrame:\n", df)
# Data Cleaning
# Drop duplicates (Riya is repeated)
df = df.drop_duplicates()
print("\nAfter dropping duplicates:\n", df)
# Fill missing StudyHours with mean
```

```
df["StudyHours"] = df["StudyHours"].fillna(df["StudyHours"].mean())
# Fill missing Attendance with median
df["Attendance"] = df["Attendance"].fillna(df["Attendance"].median())
# Drop rows where Marks are missing
df = df.dropna(subset=["Marks"])
print("\nAfter handling missing values:\n", df)
# Data Manipulation
# Create a new column for pass/fail (threshold = 60 marks)
df["Result"] = df["Marks"].apply(lambda x: "Pass" if x >= 60 else "Fail")
print("\nFinal Clean DataFrame:\n", df)
# Visualization
# Bar chart - Students vs Marks
plt.figure(figsize=(8,5))
plt.bar(df["Name"], df["Marks"], color="skyblue")
plt.title("Marks of Students")
plt.xlabel("Students")
plt.ylabel("Marks")
plt.show()
# Histogram - Distribution of Study Hours
plt.hist(df["StudyHours"], bins=5, color="orange", edgecolor="black")
plt.title("Distribution of Study Hours")
plt.xlabel("Study Hours")
plt.ylabel("Frequency")
plt.show()
# Pie Chart - Pass vs Fail
df["Result"].value_counts().plot.pie(autopct='%1.1f%%', colors=["lightgreen",
"salmon"])
plt.title("Pass vs Fail Ratio")
plt.ylabel("")
plt.show()
# Scatter Plot - Study Hours vs Marks
plt.scatter(df["StudyHours"], df["Marks"], color="purple")
plt.title("Study Hours vs Marks")
plt.xlabel("Study Hours")
plt.ylabel("Marks")
plt.grid(True)
plt.show()
```

The output of student exam data analysis with data preprocessing and visualization using Pandas and Matplotlib libraries is shown in *Figures Appendix B.21* to *Appendix B.28*:

```
Original DataFrame:
    Name  StudyHours  Attendance  Marks
0   Amit         8.0        90.0   92.0
1   Riya         6.0        85.0   80.0
2  Karan         NaN        88.0   85.0
3  Meena         4.0         NaN   65.0
4  Sahil         3.0        60.0    NaN
5  Pooja         5.0        75.0   70.0
6  Arjun         9.0        95.0   96.0
7  Nisha         2.0        55.0   45.0
8   Riya         6.0        85.0   80.0
```

***Figure Appendix B.21**: Displaying original DataFrame*

```
After dropping duplicates:
    Name  StudyHours  Attendance  Marks
0   Amit         8.0        90.0   92.0
1   Riya         6.0        85.0   80.0
2  Karan         NaN        88.0   85.0
3  Meena         4.0         NaN   65.0
4  Sahil         3.0        60.0    NaN
5  Pooja         5.0        75.0   70.0
6  Arjun         9.0        95.0   96.0
7  Nisha         2.0        55.0   45.0
```

***Figure Appendix B.22**: Displaying DataFrame after dropping duplicates*

```
After handling missing values:
    Name  StudyHours  Attendance  Marks
0   Amit    8.000000        90.0   92.0
1   Riya    6.000000        85.0   80.0
2  Karan    5.285714        88.0   85.0
3  Meena    4.000000        85.0   65.0
5  Pooja    5.000000        75.0   70.0
6  Arjun    9.000000        95.0   96.0
7  Nisha    2.000000        55.0   45.0
```

***Figure Appendix B.23**: Displaying DataFrame after handling missing values*

```
Final Clean DataFrame:
    Name  StudyHours  Attendance  Marks Result
0   Amit    8.000000        90.0   92.0   Pass
1   Riya    6.000000        85.0   80.0   Pass
2  Karan    5.285714        88.0   85.0   Pass
3  Meena    4.000000        85.0   65.0   Pass
5  Pooja    5.000000        75.0   70.0   Pass
6  Arjun    9.000000        95.0   96.0   Pass
7  Nisha    2.000000        55.0   45.0   Fail
```

***Figure Appendix B.24**: Final clean DataFrame*

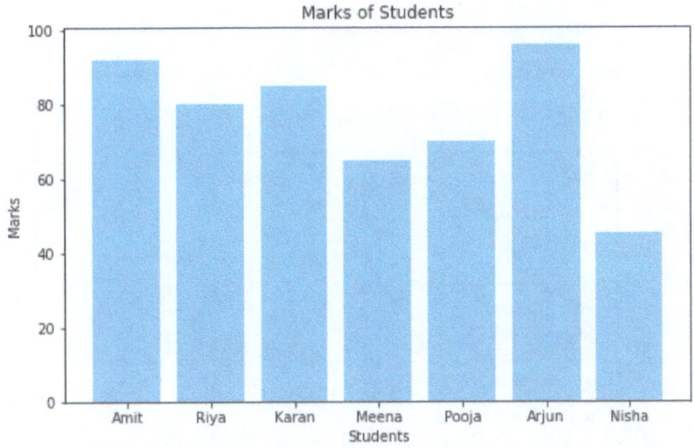

***Figure Appendix B.25**: Displaying a bar chart of students*

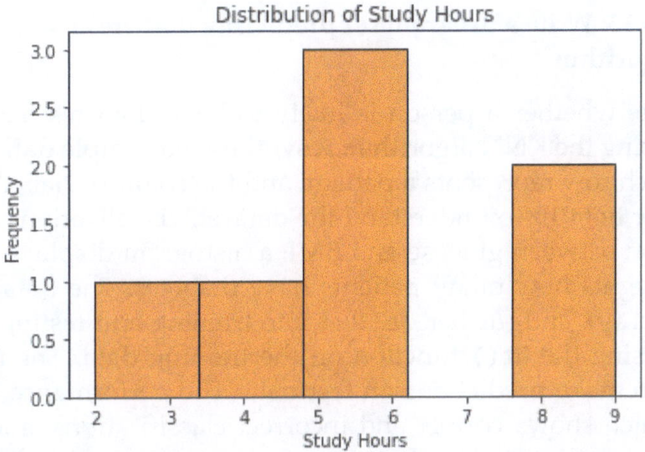

***Figure Appendix B.26**: Displaying a distribution of study hours using histogram*

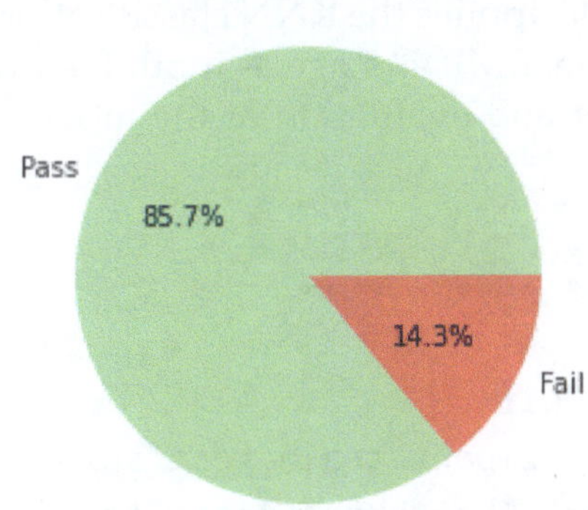

***Figure Appendix B.27**: Displaying students result using a pie chart*

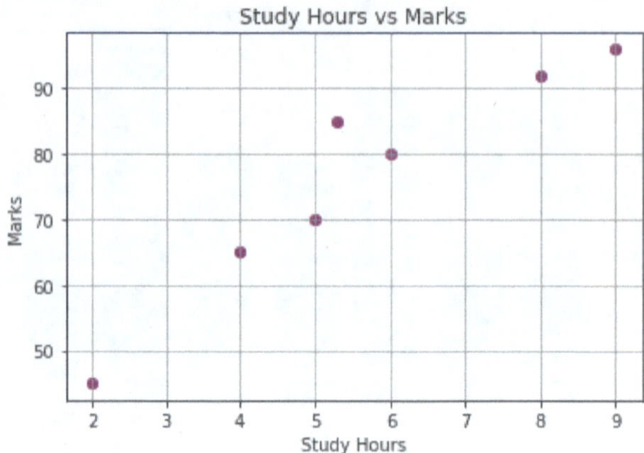

***Figure Appendix B.28:** Displaying study hours and marks using a scatter plot*

Example Appendix B.13: Write a program for predicting diabetes using k-nearest neighbors machine learning algorithm

This program predicts whether a person is likely to have diabetes based on their glucose level, BMI, and age using the KNN algorithm. A synthesized sample dataset is first stored in a DataFrame, where each row represents a patient, and the column Diabetes indicates whether they are diabetic (1) or not (0). To understand the dataset, visualizations are created: a scatter plot shows the relation between glucose and BMI, a histogram displays the age distribution, and a pie chart highlights how many patients have diabetes. The dataset is then split into features (X) and target (y), and further divided into training and testing sets. A KNN model with *k=3* is trained using the **`fit()`** function on the training data. The model then uses the **`predict()`** function to make predictions on test data. The performance is evaluated using a confusion matrix, which shows correct and incorrect classifications, and additional metrics like accuracy, precision, and recall. Finally, the confusion matrix is visualized using a heatmap. A heatmap is a type of visualization that shows data values using colors inside a grid, like a table. Here, instead of just numbers, the grid cells are filled with colors. A darker or brighter color represents higher or lower values, and this makes it easier to see patterns, trends, and correlations in data. This example applies the KNN classification algorithm to predict whether a patient is diabetic using glucose, BMI, and age as input features. The program also includes visual exploration of the dataset and evaluation of the model using a confusion matrix and performance metrics:

```
# Import libraries
# ==========Import Libraries ===========
import pandas as pd
import matplotlib.pyplot as plt
from sklearn.model_selection import train_test_split
from sklearn.neighbors import KNeighborsClassifier
```

```
from sklearn.metrics import confusion_matrix, accuracy_score, classification_
report
import seaborn as sns
# ======Create a small sample dataset=======

# In practice, datasets are uploaded as CSV files,
# typically sourced from public repositories on the internet.
data = {
    "Glucose": [80, 150, 120, 200, 85, 160, 140, 155, 130, 95],
    "BMI": [22, 35, 28, 40, 23, 38, 30, 36, 29, 24], # BMI->Body Mass Index
    "Age": [25, 45, 35, 50, 23, 48, 39, 46, 36, 27],
    "Diabetes": [0, 1, 0, 1, 0, 1, 1, 1, 0, 0]  # 0 = No Diabetes,1 = Diabetes
}
df = pd.DataFrame(data)
# Visualize the dataset
# c=df["Diabetes"] colors the points based on diabetes outcome (0 or 1).
# cmap="coolwarm" gives contrasting colors (blue for no diabetes, red for
# diabetes).
# s=80 makes the points larger
# edgecolor="k" black outline for better visibility.
# plt.colorbar() adds a color legend so students understand what colors mean.
# ======== Data Visualization ==========
plt.figure(figsize=(6,5))
plt.scatter(df["Glucose"], df["BMI"], c=df["Diabetes"], cmap="coolwarm", s=80,
edgecolor="k")
plt.title("Glucose vs BMI (Colored by Diabetes Outcome)")
plt.xlabel("Glucose Level")
plt.ylabel("BMI")
plt.colorbar(label="Diabetes (0 = No, 1 = Yes)")  # legend for colors
plt.show()
# ====Split data for Training into features(X) and target(y)====
X = df[["Glucose", "BMI", "Age"]]  # Features
y = df["Diabetes"]                 # Target
# Split into training and testing data
X_train, X_test, y_train, y_test = train_test_split(X, y, test_size=0.3,
random_state=1)
# ======Train KNN Model========
model = KNeighborsClassifier(n_neighbors=3)  # K=3 neighbors
model.fit(X_train, y_train)
```

```
# ====Predict on test data (Make Predictions)====
y_pred = model.predict(X_test)
# ======Evaluate the model==========
conf_matrix = confusion_matrix(y_test, y_pred)
accuracy = accuracy_score(y_test, y_pred)
print("Confusion Matrix:\n", conf_matrix)
print("Accuracy:", accuracy)
print("\nClassification Report:\n", classification_report(y_test, y_pred))
# =======Visualization of Confusion Matrix========
plt.figure(figsize=(5,4))
sns.heatmap(conf_matrix, annot=True, fmt="d", cmap="Blues", xticklabels=["No
Diabetes", "Diabetes"], yticklabels=["No Diabetes", "Diabetes"])
plt.title("Confusion Matrix")
plt.ylabel("Actual")
plt.xlabel("Predicted")
plt.show()
# ======Histogram of Age Distribution=======
plt.hist(df["Age"], bins=5, color="orange", edgecolor="black")
plt.title("Age Distribution of Patients")
plt.xlabel("Age")
plt.ylabel("Count")
plt.show()
# ========Pie chart of diabetes cases========
plt.pie(df["Diabetes"].value_counts(), labels=["No Diabetes", "Diabetes"],
autopct="%1.1f%%", colors=["lightgreen","red"])
plt.title("Diabetes Distribution")
plt.show()
```

The visualization in the form of a scatter plot is shown in *Figure Appendix B.29*. The x-axis shows the glucose level of patients. The y-axis shows the **body mass index** (**BMI**) of patients. Each point represents a patient, and the color of the point shows whether they have diabetes or not. The blue color (0) denotes no diabetes, and the red (1) color denotes diabetes. The color bar on the right explains this coding. From the plot, we can see that patients with higher glucose levels and higher BMI (red dots) are more likely to have diabetes, while those with lower values (blue dots) tend not to. This helps us visualize the relationship between glucose, BMI, and the chances of diabetes.

The visualization is as follows:

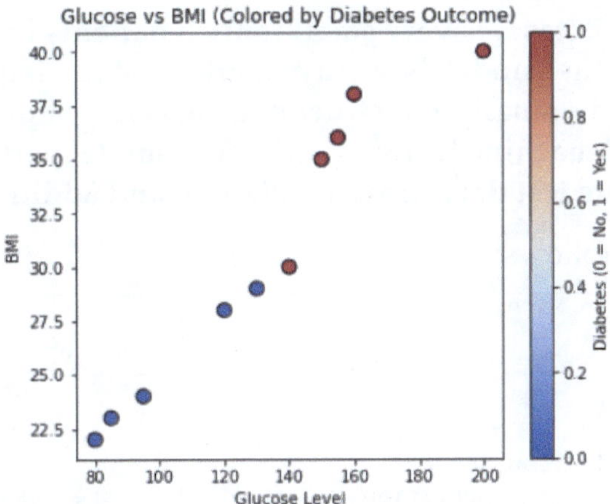

Figure Appendix B.29: Scatter plot visualizing a glucose versus BMI level

A confusion matrix is shown in *Figure Appendix B.30*. The classification report gives detailed evaluation metrics for the KNN model.

- **Precision**: Out of all patients predicted as diabetic, the number of patients actually diabetic.
- **Recall**: Out of all actual diabetic patients, the number of diagnoses correctly predicted by the model.
- **F1-score**: A balance between precision and recall (important when avoiding both false positives and false negatives).
- **Support**: The actual number of samples in each class (two patients with no diabetes, one with diabetes).

From the classification report, it is derived that:

- **Class 0 (No Diabetes)**: Precision = 1.0, Recall = 1.0, F1 = 1.0 denotes perfect prediction.
- **Class 1 (Diabetes)**: The output is 1.0 across all metrics, and the model predicted diabetes patients correctly.
- **Accuracy**: 100% shows that the model correctly classified all patients in this dataset.

  Although the model achieves 100% accuracy in this example, this result should be interpreted with caution. The dataset used is small and simplified, and the model may be evaluated on the same or very similar data it was trained on. Under such conditions, perfect accuracy does not necessarily indicate a robust or generalizable model. In real-world machine learning applications, achieving 100% accuracy is rare and may indicate issues such as overfitting, limited data diversity, or data leakage. Therefore, this example is intended solely to demonstrate the workflow of training, prediction, and evaluation, rather than to represent realistic performance expectations.

Note: However, since the dataset is very small (only 3 patients in test data), getting 100% accuracy may not mean the model is always perfect. With larger data, accuracy may drop. A perfect accuracy in small or instructional datasets should not be considered a benchmark for real-world machine learning tasks. The model performance should always be validated using separate test data, cross-validation, and additional evaluation metrics.

The confusion matrix is as follows:

```
Confusion Matrix:
 [[2 0]
 [0 1]]
Accuracy: 1.0

Classification Report:
              precision    recall  f1-score   support

           0       1.00      1.00      1.00         2
           1       1.00      1.00      1.00         1

    accuracy                           1.00         3
   macro avg       1.00      1.00      1.00         3
weighted avg       1.00      1.00      1.00         3
```

Figure Appendix B.30*: Confusion matrix and classification report*

In the classification report, the macro average means it calculates the metric (like precision, recall, F1-score) for each class separately. Then it takes the average across all classes, without considering how many samples are in each class. This means each class gets equal importance, no matter if it has 100 samples or just 1.

Example: If you have 90 No Diabetes and 10 Diabetes cases, the macro average will still give 50% weight to each class.

However, in the weighted average. It also calculates the metric for each class separately, but here, it takes the average weighted by the number of samples in each class, i.e., support. This means classes with more data points get more importance.

Example: If 90% of the patients are No Diabetes, the weighted average will be influenced more by that class. Since the dataset is tiny (two No Diabetes and one Diabetes), both macro avg and weighted avg come out to 1.0 because everything is predicted correctly.

A confusion matrix heatmap for the diabetes prediction task is shown in *Figure Appendix B.31*. This is a confusion matrix heatmap, which helps us evaluate how well the KNN model predicted diabetes. The rows represent the actual, i.e., true values from the dataset. The columns represent the predicted values from the model. Therefore, it compares actual versus predicted in one grid. The values in the confusion matrix heatmap are discussed as follows:

- **Top-left corner value (2)**: The model correctly predicted two people as No Diabetes, i.e., TN.

- **Top-right corner value (0):** The model did not wrongly predict any No Diabetes person as having Diabetes, i.e., *FP = 0.*
- **Bottom-left corner value (0):** The model did not wrongly predict any Diabetes person as No Diabetes, i.e., *FN = 0.*
- **Bottom-right corner value (1):** The model correctly predicted one person as Diabetes, i.e., TP.

The heatmap colors (*dark = higher, light = lower*) make it visually clear where the model is strong or weak. The dark blue (2) means many correct predictions for No Diabetes. The Light blue (1) color represents fewer predictions for Diabetes, but is still correct, and White (0) color represents that there are no mistakes.

The confusion matrix heatmap is as follows:

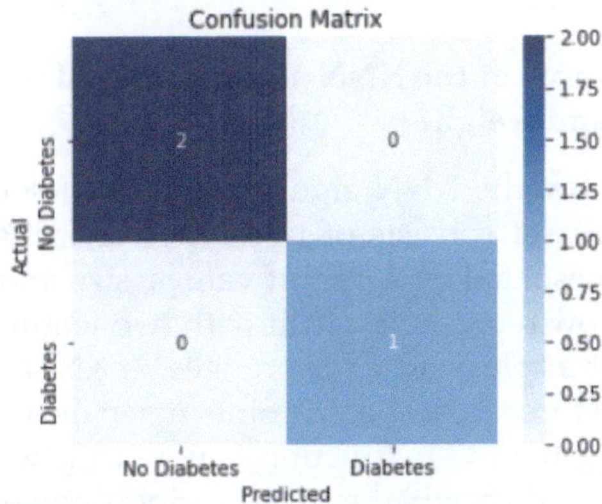

***Figure Appendix B.31**: Confusion matrix heatmap for the diabetes prediction task*

A histogram of the age distribution of patients and their count is shown in *Figure Appendix B.32*:

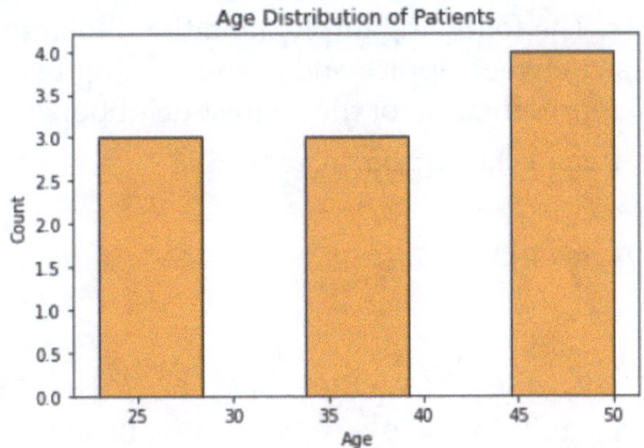

***Figure Appendix B.32**: Histogram of age distribution of patients and their count*

A pie chart of diabetic and non-diabetic patients is shown in *Figure Appendix B.33*:

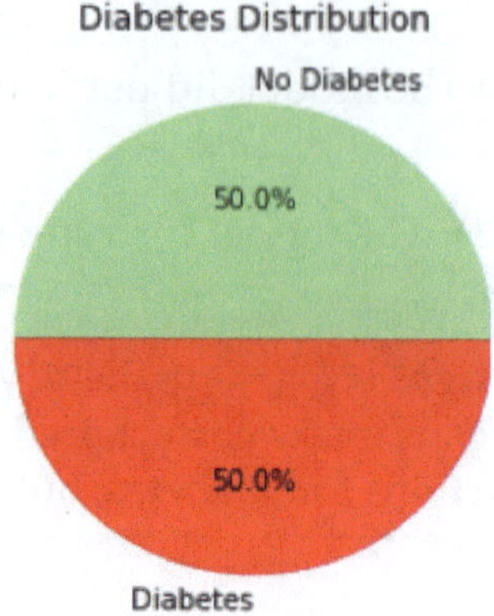

Figure Appendix B.33: Pie chart of diabetic and non-diabetic patients

Example Appendix B.14: Example of the KNN algorithm used to classify fruits (apples and oranges) based on their size and weight

This program demonstrates how the KNN algorithm works for classifying fruits based on their size and weight. The dataset consists of two types of fruits: apples labeled as 0 and oranges labeled as 1, each represented by a pair of values: size and weight. Here, we create a small dataset (X) where each row represents a fruit with two features: its size and weight. The labels (y) are assigned as 0 for apples and 1 for oranges. A KNN model with k=3 is created, which means it will look at the three closest data points when deciding the class of a new fruit. After training the model using the **`fit()`** function, a new fruit with size 2 and weight 90 is given as input, and the model predicts whether it is an apple or an orange using the **`predict()`** function. The **`kneighbors()`** function is then used to find the three nearest neighbors that influenced the classification. For visualization, apples and oranges are plotted with different colors and markers, the new fruit is highlighted with a large star, and its nearest neighbors are emphasized with large circles. This makes it easy to understand how KNN uses distance to decide the class of a new data point, and students can visually see both the dataset and the decision-making process. The following implementation illustrates the application of the KNN classifier to distinguish between apples and oranges using two input features, size and weight, along with a visual representation of the nearest neighbors:

```
from sklearn.neighbors import KNeighborsClassifier
import numpy as np
import matplotlib.pyplot as plt

# Define dataset (Size, Weight)
X = np.array([[8, 140], [7, 150], [5, 120], [4, 60], [3, 50], [3, 55]])
y = np.array([0, 0, 0, 1, 1, 1])  # 0 = Apple, 1 = Orange
```

```
# Create the KNN model with k=3
model = KNeighborsClassifier(n_neighbors=3)

# Train the model
model.fit(X, y)

# Predict for a new fruit
new_fruit = np.array([[2, 90]])
prediction = model.predict(new_fruit)
fruit_type = 'Apple' if prediction[0] == 0 else 'Orange'
print(f"The new fruit is classified as: {fruit_type}")

# Find the k nearest neighbors
distances, indices = model.kneighbors(new_fruit)

# Visualization
# Separate apples and oranges
apples = X[y == 0]
oranges = X[y == 1]

plt.scatter(apples[:, 0], apples[:, 1], color='red', label='Apple',
marker='o')
plt.scatter(oranges[:, 0], oranges[:, 1], color='orange', label='Orange',
marker='s')

# Mark the new fruit
plt.scatter(new_fruit[:, 0], new_fruit[:, 1], color='blue', label='New Fruit',
marker='*', s=200)

# Highlight the 3 nearest neighbors
for idx in indices[0]:
    plt.scatter(X[idx, 0], X[idx, 1], edgecolor='black', facecolor='none',
s=300, linewidth=2)

plt.xlabel("Size")
plt.ylabel("Weight")
plt.title("Fruit Classification using KNN (k=3)")
plt.legend()
plt.show()
```

The output of the example using fruit classification using KNN with K neighbors = 3 is shown in *Figure Appendix B.34*:

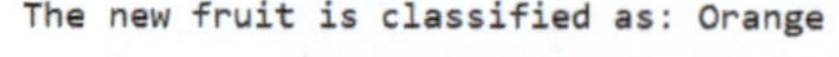

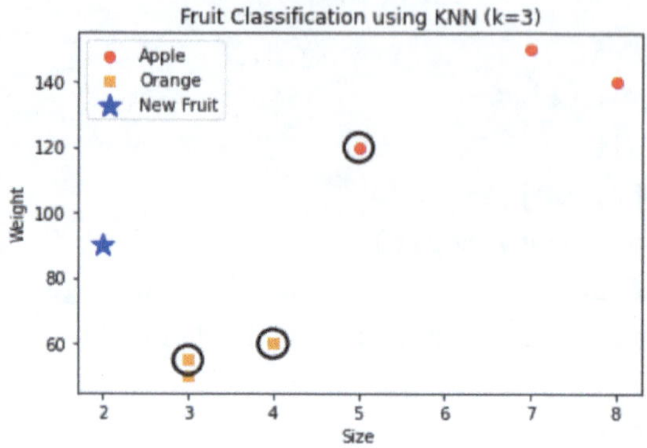

***Figure Appendix B.34:** Fruit classification using KNN (K=3)*

Conclusion

In this appendix, we explored a variety of small yet practical applications to understand how Matplotlib can be used for data visualization. Through examples such as plotting students' marks, analyzing product sales, exploring employee salary distributions, and representing students' interests in subjects, we observed how different types of charts like line, bar, pie, and histogram help convey insights clearly. We also extended these ideas to more detailed projects such as weather data visualization, shopping category analysis, attendance tracking, and library book borrowing trends demonstrating how visualization choices adapt to different data contexts.

The key takeaway is that while raw data provides numerical records, visualization promotes visual thinking by transforming data into interpretable patterns, trends, and comparisons. Matplotlib offers flexible and powerful tools that enable even simple CSV-based datasets to be converted into meaningful visual insights. By practicing these examples, readers gain not only hands-on experience with Matplotlib but also develop the ability to select, interpret, and reason with visual representations, making data analysis more intuitive, insightful, and effective.

Points to remember

The following points are to be kept in mind:

- Line charts are useful to show trends over time, such as students' marks across exams.
- Bar charts help in comparing quantities like product sales or attendance in different subjects.

- Histograms are used to display frequency distribution, such as employee salary ranges.
- Pie charts represent proportions or percentages, e.g., students' interest in subjects.
- Grouped bar charts allow comparison by subcategories, like interest in subjects by gender.
- Pandas functions like dropna(), fillna(), and drop_duplicates() are used for data cleaning and preprocessing.
- Statistical functions such as mean(), median(), and mode() provide useful summary statistics about data.
- A decision tree is a simple ML model that splits data into branches for classification, e.g., predicting student performance.
- KNN is a distance-based algorithm that classifies new data based on the closest examples.
- A confusion matrix compares predicted and actual results, helping to calculate accuracy, precision, recall, and F1-score.
- Accuracy shows the overall correctness of a model, while precision, recall, and F1-score provide deeper evaluation.
- Combining visualization and ML provides a complete workflow: data exploration, cleaning, prediction, and evaluation.

Key terms

- **Matplotlib**: A Python library used for creating visualizations like line charts, bar charts, histograms, and pie charts.
- **Line chart**: A plot used to show changes or trends over time.
- **Bar chart**: A visualization used to compare quantities across different categories.
- **Histogram**: A plot that shows the frequency distribution of data (e.g., salaries, ages).
- **Pie chart**: A circular chart divided into slices to show proportions or percentages.
- **Grouped bar chart**: A bar chart used to compare multiple categories side by side (e.g., male versus female interest).
- **Data cleaning**: The process of handling missing or duplicate values in a dataset using functions like dropna(), fillna(), and drop_duplicates().
- **Mean/median/mode:** Statistical measures used to summarize data: average, middle value, and most frequent value.

- **Decision tree**: A machine learning algorithm that splits data into branches for classification or regression tasks.
- **K-nearest neighbors (KNN)**: A machine learning algorithm that classifies data based on the nearest neighbors in feature space.
- **Confusion matrix**: A table that shows predicted versus actual classifications (TP, TN, FP, FN).
- **Accuracy**: The percentage of correct predictions out of all predictions.
- **Precision**: The fraction of correctly predicted positive cases out of all predicted positives.
- **Recall**: The fraction of correctly predicted positive cases out of all actual positives.
- **F1-score**: A metric that balances precision and recall into a single measure.
- **Features/predictors**: Independent input variables used to train a machine learning model (e.g., study hours, attendance).
- **Target/label**: The dependent variable or outcome to be predicted (e.g., pass/fail, disease status).
- **Comma separated values (CSV)**: A widely used file format for storing tabular data where values are separated by commas.
- **pd.read_csv()**: A Pandas function used to load data from a CSV file into a DataFrame.
- **DataFrame**: A two-dimensional, table-like data structure in Pandas with rows and columns.
- **Series**: A one-dimensional array in pandas representing a single column of data.
- **Index**: The row labels in a Pandas DataFrame
- **plt.plot()**: Function used to create line charts for showing trends or relationships.
- **plt.bar()**: Function used to draw bar charts for comparing quantities across categories.
- **plt.hist()**: Function for creating histograms to display the distribution of data.
- **plt.pie()**: Function used to make pie charts for showing proportions or percentages.
- **plt.xlabel()/plt.ylabel()**: Functions to label the x-axis and y-axis of a plot.
- **plt.title()**: Function used to add a title to the chart.
- **plt.legend()**: Function that displays labels for plotted data (useful for multi-line or grouped bar charts).
- **plt.show()**: Function to display the final visualization on the screen

- **dropna()**: Function used to remove rows/ columns with missing (NaN) values.
- **fillna()**: Function used to fill missing values with a specified value (like 0 or mean).
- **drop_duplicates()**: Function to remove duplicate rows from a DataFrame.
- **mean()/median()/mode()**: Statistical functions to compute the average, middle, and most frequent values.
- **value_counts()**: Function that counts the number of occurrences of each unique value in a column.
- **groupby()**: Function used to group data based on column values for aggregation.
- **fit()**: Function used to train a machine learning model on training data.
- **predict()**: Function used to make predictions on new or test data using a trained model.

Index